Spearhead to VICTORY

In Enemy Hands
Sir Arthur Currie
Legacy of Valour

Spearhead to VICTORY

CANADA AND THE GREAT WAR

DANIEL G. DANCOCKS

Hurtig Publishers
Edmonton

Hurtig Publishers Ltd.
10560–105 St
Edmonton, Alberta
Canada   T5H 2W7

Canadian Cataloguing in Publication Data

Dancocks, Daniel G. (Daniel George), 1950–
  Spearhead to victory

  Bibliography: p.
  Includes index.
  ISBN 0-88830-310-6

  1. Amiens, Battle of, 1918. 2. World War, 1914–1918
— Campaigns — France. 3. Canada. Canadian Army —
History — World War, 1914–1918. 4. World War, 1914–
1918 — Canada. I. Title.
D545.A56D35 1987   940.4'36   C87-091314-x

Editorial / Jean Wilson
Design / First Edition Book Creations / Doug Frank
Jacket Illustration / "Over the Top, Neuville-Vitasse", by Alfred Theodore
Joseph Bastien. Courtesy: Canadian War Museum.
Composition / Attic Typesetting
Manufacture / Friesen Printers

Edited, designed, typeset, printed, and bound in Canada for Hurtig Publishers Ltd.

For my brother Tom
and sisters Carol and Donna

CONTENTS

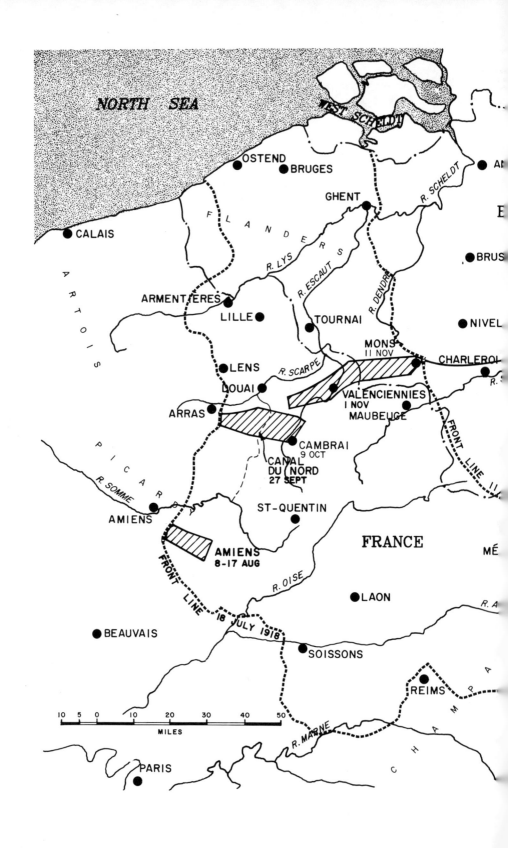

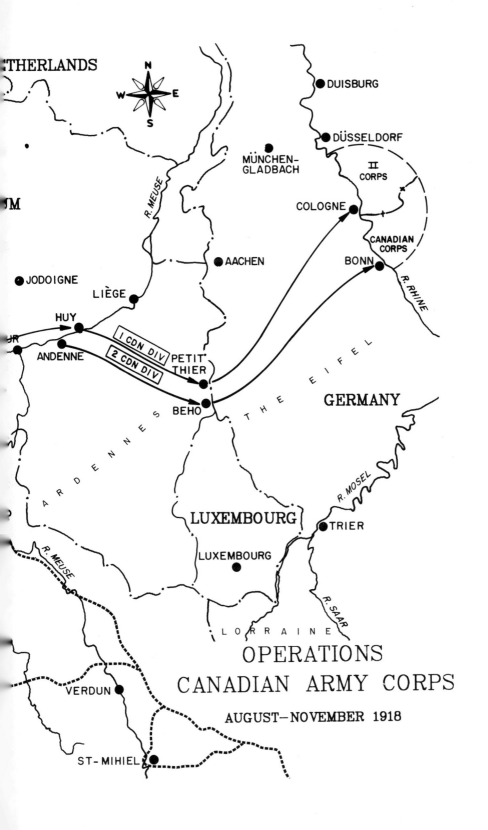

OPERATIONS
CANADIAN ARMY CORPS

AUGUST–NOVEMBER 1918

1 THE TIDE TURNS

The time had come to strike back.

The first few months of 1918 had been grim for the Allied cause. Since 21 March, the Germans had launched one mighty offensive after another, a series of desperate attacks intended to break the stalemate on the Western Front and win the Great War before the full might of the United States could be brought to bear—although, as the Allies would soon discover, American power was more imagined than real. The British Expeditionary Force (BEF), undermanned and overextended—it had 100,000 fewer troops with which to hold a line one-third longer than a year earlier—thanks to the interference of well-meaning but naïve politicians, had suffered fearfully. Its casualties in a month and a half of defensive fighting equalled those of more than three months on the attack in the controversial Third Battle of Ypres, or Passchendaele, in the second half of 1917. The Germans were also aided by incredible good fortune in the form of unusually fine weather, plus thick morning mists which blinded the defenders, as well as an uncanny facility for hitting the British at their weakest points. Only the dogged determination of brave bands of British soldiers, under the steadfast leadership of their commander-in-chief, the stolid Scotsman Sir Douglas Haig, had stopped the enemy drives short of their strategic objectives, the key rail centres of Amiens, on the River Somme, and Hazebrouck, in the north.

Still, the Germans had come dangerously close to success. The French commander-in-chief, General Henri Pétain, had lost his nerve early in the crisis, deciding to withdraw his forces to protect Paris. Field-Marshal Haig was appalled: for the first time since the advent of trench warfare nearly four years earlier, it would no longer be Allied policy to present a unified front to the enemy. Haig realized that catastrophe impended, for if Pétain carried out his plan, the British and French armies would be divided and the war surely lost. In desperation, Haig proposed a solution which he had previously opposed, the appointment of a supreme commander on the Western Front. Haig's choice was a French general, Ferdinand Foch, who enjoyed a reputation as a fighter. Moving with surprising speed, the British and French governments, with American acquiescence, named Foch generalissimo on 26 March.

Foch's role has often been exaggerated. Although he was charged with the strategical direction of the war on the Western Front, he could only co-ordinate the actions of the Allies, relying on "persuasion" to "bring about those concerted actions which result in victory," as he readily admitted. "His method was inspirational," notes historian John Terraine, and nothing more was possible, for Foch had a staff of only twenty officers with which to oversee millions of men. The real power thus lay with the respective commanders-in-chief of the British, French, and American armies—and Field-Marshal Haig, it will be seen, emerged as the key figure because his BEF was the most proficient of the Allied forces. However, Foch's most immediate and important contribution to the cause came with his appointment. He would not permit Pétain to pull back toward Paris, thus ensuring that the Allied front remained intact—and guaranteeing that the Germans would lose the war.[1]

Foch was, indeed, a fighter. A proponent of the attack at all costs, he had been largely responsible for the many futile offensives that bled the French army white during the first two years of the war. Eventually, he fell into disgrace and was relieved of his command. But he was brought back and given an army group in 1917, to help restore the sagging spirit of the French forces, which had finally mutinied in the spring of that year to protest the wasteful attacks that were slaughtering France's finest young men.

Now, as generalissimo, Foch wasted no time looking for a way to retrieve the initiative. On 3 April, just a few days after his appointment, he had suggested to Haig "an offensive by the British Armies, astride the Somme, in an easterly direction, from the Luce and Ancre [rivers], with the object of disengaging Amiens."[2] Plans had been hastily drawn up, and zero day set for 12 April, but these were pre-empted by the Germans, who struck another major blow in Flanders on the ninth.

The fighting in Flanders lasted until the end of April, when the Germans finally halted their offensive, and Foch soon renewed his proposal. On 3 May, he asked Haig to prepare a limited offensive, in order to "give the allied armies the means of re-establishing their moral ascendancy over the enemy." Foch, importantly, added a further suggestion: "The Canadian Corps, for instance, which is well up to strength, might be employed." Foch pursued the point on the sixteenth, when he visited Haig's headquarters and expressed his desire to mount an attack "with the object of disengaging the Paris-Amiens railway line and the Amiens centre of communications." Haig—who, like Foch, recognized that only by attacking could the war be won—was amenable to the idea, as he commented in his diary: "I agreed with his general plan and said I would study my share of the undertaking and let him know. But he must not write his plan nor allow the French commanders to talk about it. Success will depend mainly on secrecy."

2

Next day, Haig assigned the Amiens project to General Sir Henry Rawlinson, whose Fourth Army—one of five field armies in the BEF—held this sector.[3]

A plan of attack materialized quickly. Haig's intention was to employ three Canadian and four Australian divisions in a strictly limited offensive, with objectives no further than five miles distant. In order to ensure the element of surprise, Haig accepted the recommendation of Lieutenant-General Sir William Birdwood, who commanded the Australian Corps at the time, that "a preliminary bombardment should be dispensed with."[4] Zero day was set for 16 June.

But, once again, the Germans upset the Allied timetable. Their third great attack of 1918 fell on the French on 27 May, in Champagne, forcing the Allies to postpone the Amiens operation and rush reserves to the new danger point. However, the enemy offensives were falling into a predictable pattern: opening with spectacular success, the Germans were uniformly unable to exploit their impressive victories and eventually their attacks would peter out in the face of stiffening resistance. The Champagne campaign followed this form, as did another launched on 9 June, just to the north. This one, in fact, ended in disaster when a French counter-attack not only halted the Germans but won back all the ground lost initially.

As always, Foch looked for opportunities to attack. "I did not lose sight," he later explained, "of the offensive task for which the Allied armies must at once get ready and which ought to be undertaken as soon as possible, since it was only by offensive action that they could bring the war to a victorious conclusion." At his direction, Grand Quartier Général, Pétain's headquarters, began drawing up plans for a major assault on the salient created by the German attack in Champagne in late May. While these preparations were being completed, French intelligence scored a coup when it learned of the Germans' intentions to mount their own offensive in the same sector. The French army would have an unpleasant surprise in store for them.[5]

The Germans struck, as predicted, on 15 July. Oblivious to the danger ahead, they enjoyed their usual impressive success at the start. But it was largely illusory. The attack quickly bogged down, and three days later the French, with help from a contingent of American troops, delivered their mighty counter-stroke. By the time the fighting ended on 4 August, the Germans had suffered a defeat of staggering proportions. The French captured, according to Foch, "30,000 prisoners, more than 600 guns, 200 mine throwers, and 3,000 machine guns." But the generalissimo was not content to rest on his laurels. It was the time, he later wrote, to "bring into play all the Allied resources as rapidly as possible, so as to prevent the enemy from recovering before we could effect his definite destruction."[6]

Meantime, the British had been busy, too. On 4 July, the Australian Corps—now commanded by a native Australian, Lieutenant-General Sir John Monash—had carried out a brilliant minor operation at Le Hamel, in the Fourth Army's sector. Executed by troops of the 4th Australian Division, augmented by a small number of Americans, and accompanied by sixty brand-new Mark v heavy tanks, Le Hamel would later be called by one historian "a little masterpiece." General Monash was justifiably proud. "No battle within my experience," he wrote, "passed off so smoothly, so exactly to timetable, or was so free from any kind of hitch." In the process, the Australian bagged 1378 prisoners, an uncommonly large number for such a small attack.[7]

But the importance of Le Hamel transcends its size. Itself based on the remarkable but ill-fated British tank attack at Cambrai in November 1917, Le Hamel displayed the key features that would soon characterize the fighting on the Western Front: with no preliminary bombardment by the artillery, and led by tanks which crushed enemy barbed-wire entanglements and strongpoints, it had been a complete surprise, a rarity in trench warfare. Accordingly, Le Hamel provided the prototype for the victories that would soon follow, "100 days of practically unceasing successful attacks unparalleled in British military history."[8]

The Fourth Army's commander, General Rawlinson, was predictably pleased with Le Hamel, calling it a "quite useful success." The most capable of Haig's five army commanders, the lean and lanky Rawlinson believed that the Australian victory proved the potential for an even bigger and far-reaching success on his front. The Australians had held the Amiens sector for several months, during which time they had acquired intimate knowledge of the terrain, and by their policy of "peaceful penetration"—a euphemism for large-scale raids—had established their moral superiority over the enemy. Rawlinson was not surprised, for he had high regard for these "pretty tough customers," as he described the Australians. "They are certainly original fighters and up to all sorts of dodges, some of which would shock a strict disciplinarian." He also had a good opinion of the Australian leader, General Monash, commenting that "old Monash talks too much but is very good at all the preliminaries," a reference to Sir John's attention to detail and preparation in each operation.[9]

Haig shared Rawlinson's views, both on the Australians and on the possibilities presented by offensive action in the vicinity of Amiens. "The Australian soldier," he had written in May, "is a different individual now to when he first came, both in discipline and smartness." Haig considered Monash to be "a most thorough and capable commander, who thinks out every detail of any operation and leaves nothing to chance." And he was convinced that Amiens was the place to attack, as he outlined in a letter to Foch:

The operation which to my mind is of the greatest importance, and which I suggest to you should be carried out as early as possible, is to advance from the allied front east and south-east of Amiens so as to disentangle that town and railway line. This can be carried out by a combined French and British operation, the French attacking south of Moreuil and the British north of the river Luce.[10]

So it was something of a surprise when Haig rejected Rawlinson's proposal. Sir Henry pressed for Haig's approval at a meeting on 5 July, the day after Le Hamel, but the field-marshal demurred on the grounds that it was premature, "because it would result (if successful) in extending our line at a time when reserves are very small."[11] Of even greater concern to the commander-in-chief was the disposition of German reserves; until it was certain that the enemy would not attack in Flanders, where a British defeat would be disastrous, Haig would be reluctant to commit himself to a major offensive.

Rawlinson returned to his headquarters at Flixécourt, thirteen miles northwest of Amiens, to find himself being badgered by General Monash. The Australian commander paid repeated visits to the Fourth Army, urging his British superiors "to undertake and maintain a long sustained offensive." At one of these meetings, Monash was challenged by Major-General Sir Archibald Montgomery-Massingberd, Rawlinson's chief of staff. "Well, General," said Montgomery, "let us have some specific proposals."

Monash was only too happy to accommodate him. "Reduce my front," he replied, "...and use the Canadians."[12]

Foch, in the meantime, had added his voice to the growing chorus singing the praises of the proposed Amiens offensive. Replying to Haig's letter of 17 July, Foch urged that it should "be carried out at once," suggesting "that the commanding generals of the British Fourth Army [Rawlinson] and of the French First Army [General Eugène Debeney] be asked to at once arrange between them a plan regarding which we would come to a definite understanding later on."[13]

Haig had, in fact, tentatively decided to go ahead. On 16 July, he had authorized Rawlinson and Sir Julian Byng, a former commander of the Canadian Corps who now headed the Third Army, to begin drawing up offensive plans. As Haig explained in his diary, "The preparations for these attacks, I hoped, would distract the attention of the enemy from the *main operation* on my front, which would be carried out by [Rawlinson's] Army." Two days later, he met again with Rawlinson, who recounted in his diary: "I lunched with D.H., and proposed to him an offensive east of Villers-Bretonneux, if he would give me the Canadians. To my surprise and delight, I find he has already decided to do this...."[14]

5

The advantages of an Amiens attack were self-evident. Of no little consequence was the moral ascendancy enjoyed by the Australians here. But there were many other considerations: not only were the enemy defences relatively weak, but there were few reserve formations in the area. The generally flat countryside was also ideal for the large-scale employment of tanks, and the heavily wooded regions behind the British lines would enable attacking units to concentrate undetected.[15]

Planning and preparations proceeded at a hectic pace. However, it was not until 25 July that Haig was finally satisfied that there was no possibility of a German attack in Flanders. Having been assured on that count, he gave the green light to Rawlinson. "I am prepared to take the offensive and have approved of an operation taking place on Rawlinson's front, and steps have been taken to make preparations very secretly in order to be ready...."[16] The tentative date of the attack was 10 August.

Haig and Foch were on the same wavelength. On 24 July, Haig had visited Foch to discuss the situation. Foch heartily approved of the plans for an offensive near Amiens, and the two leaders met again two days later to finalize details of the operation. From this meeting came Foch's instructions for the attack:

1. The object of the operation is to clear Amiens and the Amiens-Paris railway as well as to defeat and throw back the enemy between the Somme and the Avre.
2. For this purpose, the offensive, covered on the north by the Somme, is to be pushed forward as far as possible in the direction of Roye.
3. It will be executed by:
(1) The British Fourth Army, composed at the start of twelve divisions of infantry and three divisions of cavalry supported by
(2) The French First Army reinforced by four divisions. The first will operate north, the second south, of the road to Roye as soon as the possibility of debouching south of the Luce and east of the Avre is assured.

Foch and Haig also agreed that Rawlinson should meet the next day with General Debeney to co-ordinate their preparations. This met with some resistance from Rawlinson who, Haig noted, "was very anxious to carry out his operation alone, without French co-operation, but in view of our limited number of divisions I agreed that Debeney should operate on our right."[17]

One final detail remained to be ironed out, and Foch dealt with it on 28 July. He placed Haig in overall command of the Amiens offensive, putting Debeney's army at his disposal "for the purpose of ensuring perfect coordination." A happy Haig commented in his diary: "I am pleased that Foch should have entrusted me with the direction of these operations."[18]

It took considerable courage for Haig to prepare this offensive because, in doing so, he was flying in the face of British policy. The field-marshal, whose belief in the Western Front as the decisive theatre of operations remained unshaken despite the apparent futility of the fighting to date, stood almost alone among senior British military men and politicians in advocating attacks on the Amiens scale. Indeed, General Sir Henry Wilson, the chief of the Imperial General Staff and the government's primary military adviser, had just drafted a memorandum which outlined future prospects. Entitled "British Military Policy, 1918-19," the 25 July document envisaged minor offensive operations on the Western Front for the balance of 1918, in order to "regain sufficient ground in front of the vital points in France to free us from anxiety." Once that was accomplished, said General Wilson, "we should husband our resources" for the decisive effort in 1919. "For the purpose of calculation the 1st July 1919 should therefore be taken as the date by which all preparations are to be completed for the opening of the main offensive campaign."[19]

Haig was baffled and annoyed by Wilson's memo. "Words! words! words!" he scribbled on his copy. "Lots of words! and little else."[20] Pointedly ignoring Wilson, he went ahead with his own plans.

By 29 July, Rawlinson reported to Haig that "his arrangements were being pushed forward satisfactorily." The same day, Haig held a conference of army commanders, at which he urged a new attitude be adopted. Sensing that the days of static warfare were numbered, Haig stressed that senior officers "must do their utmost to get troops out of the influence of trench methods. We are all agreed on the need for the training of battalion commanders, who in their turn must train their company and platoon commanders. This is really a platoon commanders' war."[21]

As Haig would discover in the days and weeks ahead, the trench mentality was deeply ingrained in the BEF, from top to bottom. His first realization of this came on 5 August, when he reviewed Rawlinson's detailed battle plan. It was, Haig observed, centred on recapturing the line of trenches held by the British prior to the German offensive in March. Haig urged Rawlinson to be bolder:

> I thought that the Fourth Army orders aimed too much at getting a *final* objective on the old Amiens defence line, and stopping counter-attacks on it. This is not far enough, in my opinion, if we succeed at the start in surprising the enemy. So I told Rawlinson (it had already been in my orders) to arrange to *advance as rapidly as*

possible, and capture the old Amiens line of defence . . . and to put it into a state of defence, *but not to delay*; at once reserves must be pushed on to capture the line Chaulnes-Roye.[22]

Rawlinson revised his plans accordingly, issuing the final version on 6 August. The Fourth Army would be led by the Australian and Canadian corps, a concentration of unmatched striking power. The prominence of the dominion formations in the BEF cannot be denied; even British historians admit it. "Most British line divisions," writes John Terraine, the leading expert on the Great War, "were by now neither morally nor materially the equal of the Dominion divisions."[23] The Canadian Corps would occupy the right of the Fourth Army, advancing between the Amiens-Roye road and the Amiens-Chaulnes railway. The Australians, on the Canadian left, would advance the Fourth Army's centre between the railway and the River Somme. North of the Somme would be Lieutenant-General Sir Richard Butler's III Corps; its task was to guard the Fourth Army's left flank. The army's right would be protected by Debeney's French First Army, seven divisions strong.

It was no coincidence that the Canadian Corps had been given the task of taking the line Chaulnes-Roye, which Haig had designated as his ultimate objective in this offensive. Haig had decided, and Rawlinson agreed, that any exploitation of initial success would be made by the Canadians, "reinforced, if necessary, by further divisions." While the Australian official history concedes the possibility "that on Haig's mental list of his shock troops the Canadian Corps was marked before the Australian," it had nothing whatever to do with the respective merits of the two corps. It had everything to do with manpower. In mid-May, Haig had noted with alarm, "The Australian Corps is diminishing owing to lack of drafts," a problem that could only get worse because volunteer recruitment could not match the demand, and Australia had twice, by referendum, rejected conscription. Each of the four Canadian divisions in the field was now bigger than any of the five Australian divisions, and Canada had recently imposed conscription, ensuring a steady supply of manpower which the Australians were in no position to equal. It was clear to Haig that the Australian Corps could not participate in prolonged offensive operations; the Canadians could, and would.[24]

In any event, time was running short. Already the date of the offensive, tentatively set for 10 August, had been changed. On the third, on receipt of reports that the Germans were withdrawing at various points along the Western Front—to shorten their line, in order to build up reserves and take advantage of natural defensive features such as rivers, ridges, and hills—Haig and Foch had agreed to advance the date of the attack. Zero day at Amiens would be 8 August.

It would mark the beginning of the end of the Great War of 1914-18.

2 FORGING A POTENT WEAPON

The Canadians were the key to the Amiens operation. This is hardly a revelation. "The Canadian Army Corps occupied a special position in the B.E.F. in the summer of 1918...," writes John Terraine. "The Canadian divisions were fresh and intact—a powerful accession of strength," and "of very high quality."[1] Only the Australians rivalled them in reputation on the Western Front. And yet, the Canadians had had no major part in the fighting thus far in 1918. Their battles had been primarily political.

The responsibility for fighting these political battles had fallen on the shoulders of the Canadian Corps commander, Lieutenant-General Sir Arthur Currie. A big man, at six-foot-four and 250 pounds, with a booming voice to match, Currie was one of the Great War's remarkable success stories. It was a war that ruined far more reputations than it made, but Currie had risen from the command of a modest militia regiment in Victoria, British Columbia, where he had been a prominent pre-war real estate speculator, to his present position in which he was responsible for the largest armed force Canada had ever fielded. When the war broke out in August 1914, Currie had been sent overseas as a brigadier; a year later, he was a major-general commanding the First Division in the newly formed Canadian Corps. His star had risen steadily, and following the great victory at Vimy Ridge in the spring of 1917, Currie had been promoted again, this time to command the Corps. At age forty-one—compared to fifty-five, the average age of British corps commanders—he was the first non-regular officer to reach the rank of lieutenant-general in the BEF, in which the Canadians served. And his first task in 1918 was to fight a further promotion.

Currie's initial inkling of trouble came on 11 January. On that date, Lieutenant-General Sir Richard Turner, the senior Canadian officer overseas and the man in charge of Canadian forces in the United Kingdom, visited Currie's headquarters "to discuss proposed changes in organization." General Turner explained that the British government had, ostensibly due to a shortage of soldiers, decided to reduce the size of its divisions, from twelve to nine battalions, with the excess battalions being broken up to provide reinforcements for the others. The War Office was anxious to have the dominions, and particularly Canada, follow suit and had come up with a tempting proposal. Noting the presence in England of the Fifth Canadian Division, which had been formed in early 1917, the War Office suggested that if the Canadians accepted the nine-battalion format for its divisions, a new force could be created in France: six divisions in two corps, possibly in a Canadian army. The London-based ministry of the Overseas Military Forces of Canada (OMFC) was receptive to the idea. Certainly Turner liked it, because it meant a corps command for him and service in the field for the first time since late 1916, when he had been given his administrative posting in England. It also posed the happy prospect of ridding the politicians of a major headache, the large number of disgruntled and unemployed Canadian officers accumulating in Britain due to the inefficient recruiting methods being used by Canada.[2]

General Currie, however, was appalled. The Canadian Corps, he believed, had achieved in its present state a very high standard of efficiency, and he pledged that "I shall fight with all the ability I possess any effort that would result in lessening that efficiency."[3]

It was clear to the Canadian commander that the efficiency of the Corps would be the chief victim of the proposed reorganization. To begin with, he could not understand why the Canadians should even consider it: with the implementation of conscription after the federal election in December 1917, the manpower considerations motivating the British "did not in any way apply to us." Even more alarming to Currie was the sheer size of the new organization, as he later wrote:

> The proposed six divisions were to be divided into two Corps of three divisions each. That meant that instead of one Corps staff and four divisional staffs and twelve brigade staffs and 48 battalion staffs, we would have under the new organization 2 Corps staffs, six divisional staffs, 18 brigade staffs and 54 battalion staffs, with probably a Canadian Army staff over all.

This would, in effect, double the number of staff officers serving with the Canadian forces in France and was, according to Currie, "one of the reasons why I most strongly objected to the proposal, because a staff officer is the hardest of all to train and it would have been impossible to double our staff without reducing its efficiency." Currie concluded: "On the ground of common sense and economy such an increase could not be justified in any way whatever."[4]

The whole thing appeared to be a gigantic make-work project. And it was equally obvious to Currie that these many staff positions would be filled by unqualified political appointees. As he caustically commented privately, "Without a very great stretch of imagination you can pretty well know who our officers are who desire the new commands, and can come to as good a conclusion as I as to whether our efficiency would be impaired or not...."[5]

Currie's concerns notwithstanding, it seemed certain that the new organization would be adopted. On 30 January, the Canadian government had approved it in principle, although Prime Minister Sir Robert Borden was less than enthusiastic. On the thirty-first, he authorized his overseas minister, Sir Edward Kemp, to carry out the reorganization "if you are convinced that the necessities of the situation imperatively demand it." The prime minister promised that the government would do its "utmost to provide reinforcements which will keep the six divisions up to strength but the War Office must distinctly and positively be informed that we do not and cannot give any absolute undertaking that this will be possible." He feared that one division might eventually have to be broken up to reinforce the others, which would leave the reorganized force about the same size as the Canadian Corps at present.[6]

In early February, Currie was called to London for consultation. En route, he stopped at General Headquarters (GHQ) to see Sir Douglas Haig on 5 February. The commander-in-chief was familiar with the situation. "Canadian politicians," he had written in his diary in mid-January, "are still trying to put in their own political friends into high commands in Canadian units in France. They also wish for a new organisation." Haig sympathized with Currie, having unsuccessfully resisted the recent reduction of British divisions, which had resulted in the demoralizing destruction of 141 infantry battalions in the BEF. Aware of the pitfalls of dealing with politicians, Haig assumed that Currie would lose this fight and be forced to accept the proposed reorganization. If so, Haig assured Currie that "there is one stipulation I insist upon and it is that you be placed in command of the two Canadian corps with the rank of General and a small army staff."[7]

Haig's well-intentioned assurance complicated matters for Currie because it left the Canadian commander in the position of having to argue against his own promotion! The prospect of leading an army in the field must have been a powerful temptation, and a lesser man might have been swayed. But the high-principled Currie was not the type of individual to put his own interests ahead of those of his men. More than ever convinced that the reorganization was wrong, Currie proceeded to London with renewed determination to oppose it.

The next few days of meetings and memoranda show Currie at his persuasive, and stubborn, best. Carefully marshalling his arguments, and proposing a more attractive alternative, Currie laid his case before Sir Edward Kemp and General Turner. "I have the firmest convictions that there is no good business reason, nor is there any good military reason why the proposed reorganisation should be carried out in the Canadian Corps." Detailing his concerns about the large numbers of unskilled staff officers it entailed, Currie argued that to make such a major change "would be to run a very great risk of reducing the striking value of the Force, with no compensating advantages...."[8]

The clincher was Currie's more desirable and practicable alternative. "The suggested reorganisation into six Divisions of 9 Battalions (total 54 Battalions)," he pointed out, "would [result] in a total addition in round figures of 6,000 men" in the front lines. Instead, Currie recommended the simple expedient of adding "100 surplus men to the establishment of each Canadian Infantry Battalion." He insisted that "the small addition proposed by me will make a far more efficient fighting force, and will produce more actual fighting men, at much smaller cost...."[9]

Logic and common sense won the day. On 9 February, the overseas ministry issued orders to implement Currie's reinforcement plan, by breaking up the Fifth Division—a move which had been under consideration for many months anyway. "The Canadian Corps in the existing formation," Kemp later explained, "had proved itself a smooth-running machine of tremendous striking power, and any radical alteration in its constitution might have resulted in a reduction of such power without any compensating advantages." Prime Minister Borden was relieved, and believed that this reorganization "would have seriously impaired the strength and prestige of the Canadian Corps in France, and perhaps effaced the identity of it."[10]

The ramifications of Currie's victory were considerable. Above all, notes the Canadian official history, "the decisions of February, by maintaining the Canadian Corps intact, preserved the excellent esprit de corps that made it a great fighting team, enabling it to operate with continued high efficiency in the decisive battles of the final year of the war."[11] However, Currie had little time to savour his success because only a few weeks later he found himself embroiled in yet another struggle to preserve the Corps.

The winter of 1917-18 had been a busy one for the Canadians. Attached to the BEF's First Army, they were responsible for the defence of Vimy Ridge, which they had captured the previous April; Sir Douglas Haig considered it to be "the back bone and centre of our defensive system" which "must be held at all costs." The ridge's importance was underlined by several visits made by Haig in late February, on one occasion accompanied by the recently installed prime minister of France, Georges Clemenceau. Vimy was a status symbol, and the Canadian defences were inspected another time by a French general named Roques, a former minister of war and now an adviser to the cabinet in Paris. Roques afterwards declared that he was "satisfied that every effort had been made to secure the Vimy Ridge against any surprise attack." Haig, too, told General Currie that he was "greatly pleased" with the preparations, which were undoubtedly impressive.

The ridge boasted, according to Currie, "250 miles of trench; 300 miles of barbed wire entanglements; 200 tunnelled machine-gun emplacements." The Corps commander, typically, took no credit for these arrangements; it was properly due, he said, to his brilliant chief of engineers, Brigadier-General William Lindsay, of whom Currie would later say, "I never knew a man who knew so much about front-line defences."[12]

Having gone to so much trouble, Currie reasonably expected that the Canadian Corps would remain responsible for Vimy's defence in the German offensives anticipated in the spring of 1918. But GHQ had other ideas. The enemy attacked the BEF on 21 March, and two days later the First and Second Canadian divisions were removed from Currie's command for employment elsewhere. On the twenty-sixth, the other two divisions were taken from him, and Corps headquarters placed in reserve.

A divergence of views lay at the root of these moves. In the British army, the corps was a flexible formation, with headquarters opened and closed and divisions added or deleted—a corps contained at least two divisions and sometimes as many as six—depending on the need. Currie knew this, but he was not prepared to accept it. The Canadian Corps was no ordinary corps; it was Canada's national army. Moreover, Currie later argued, its whole was greater than the sum of its parts, which the British failed to appreciate. Currie believed that

> the Canadians had a distinct advantage, for, while British Divisions were continually being sent from one Army Corps to another, the Canadian Divisions almost invariably fought side by side under the direction of their own Corps Staff and...an intimacy and understanding developed between units and staffs which led to that singleness of thought and unity of action through which the Canadian Corps was considered and later proved itself to be the hardest hitting force on any battle front.[13]

Currie promptly appealed to GHQ. "From the very nature and constitution of the organization it is impossible for the same liaison to exist in a British Corps as exists in the Canadian Corps," he wrote Haig's chief of staff, Lieutenant-General Sir Herbert Lawrence. "My staff and myself cannot do as well with a British Division in this battle as we can do with the Canadian Divisions, nor can any Corps staff do as well with the Canadian Divisions as my own." Added Currie: "I know that necessity knows no law and that the Chief will do what he thinks best, yet for the sake of the victory we must win, get us together as soon as you can."[14]

There was an added consideration, of course. It was rather embarrassing to Currie personally, having his divisions taken away from him, after his eloquent and effective efforts to preserve the integrity of the Corps just a few weeks earlier. His discomfiture was obvious in a letter of explanation to the overseas minister, Sir Edward Kemp. "For a time it may be that the Corps will be divided," he told Kemp. "I have argued verbally and in writing that to get the best out of the Corps it must be kept together....I know that the Commander-in-Chief is most sympathetic with this point of view...."[15]

Kemp came to Currie's rescue. On Good Friday, 29 March, he took the Corps commander's letter to Lord Derby, the British secretary of state for war, together with a covering letter of his own:

> Without in any way presuming to interfere with the conduct of operations in France, permit me to point out that the Canadian Corps has become, as you know, most efficient under its present leadership, and it is believed that the high morale which exists in the Corps is undoubtedly due to the fact that it has been kept together as a unit under Lieut.-General Sir Arthur Currie, in whom the troops have unbounded confidence.[16]

Kemp's intervention brought immediate results. The War Office, at Lord Derby's insistence, directed that the Canadian Corps be reunited as quickly as possible, and on 30 March, Currie was again given responsibility for Vimy Ridge with the Third and Fourth divisions. The First Division returned to him on 8 April, but the Second remained under British jurisdiction until early July.

Certain British corps commanders were glad to be rid of the Canadians, if the experience of Major-General Archie Macdonell is any indication. Macdonell's First Division was transferred to Lieutenant-General Sir Charles Fergusson's XVII Corps, which was charged with the defence of Arras, just south of Vimy. Attending a conference of divisional commanders on 1 April at Fergusson's headquarters, Macdonell was "upset" to learn that the corps commander, having already lost the important high ground at Monchy-le-Preux, was now "willing to abandon Arras." Macdonell would have no part of this defeatist attitude and flatly stated that Arras was at that moment "in Canadian hands" and that he and his troops "had no intention of retiring." If necessary, he said, the First Canadian Division would hold Arras without help from the British. Fergusson later apologized for his remarks, but it was not the last time that the Canadians would have problems with him.[17]

The reunion met with a mixed response. Prime Minister Borden welcomed it, cabling Kemp: "Any proposal to break up the Canadian

Corps would be strongly resented in Canada and would have the most unfortunate effect upon public opinion." Sir Douglas Haig, however, saw it in a much different light. "I could not help feeling," he sniffed, "that some people in Canada regard themselves rather as 'allies' than fellow citizens of the Empire." The seeds of strained relations between the British and Canadians had been sown.[18]

General Currie's troubles were only beginning. Now that the Corps had been reunited, he was handed the daunting task of defending too much line with too few troops. As he noted in his diary on 31 March, the Canadians were "holding 10-mile front with two divisions, altogether too much but owing to lack of men in British Army cannot be helped. I am told we have 430,000 men in Mesopotamia. What a splendid place for a reserve." Several days later, following the return of the First Division, he now had "3 Divisions to hold 28,000 yards of front from south of Hill 70 to the [River] Scarpe." In a meeting with General John J. Pershing, the American commander-in-chief, on 20 April, Currie confessed that it would be almost impossible to hold the Canadian sector "in the face of a determined and powerful offensive using shock tactics." Each of his divisions, he pointed out, was holding a line at least a third longer than those held by British divisions crushed in recent German attacks.[19]

The Canadians worked hard to disguise the inherent weakness of their position. By adopting what Currie called "a very aggressive attitude," the Germans were continually kept off balance by heavy raiding and intensive patrolling; the artillery contributed an elaborate program of harassing fire, including the generous use of poison gas—now utilized by both sides. As well, Currie created a valuable reserve by scraping together a pair of provisional infantry brigades comprised of engineers, tunnellers, and assorted other personnel.[20]

But it was all window-dressing, and Currie knew it. Years later, he claimed that "I often more than half wished that the enemy would attack." This can be dismissed as so much hot air, as his mood at the time revealed. Normally a good-natured man, given to rare outbursts of anger accompanied by prolific swearing, Currie "for the first time in my experience appeared to be perturbed," recalled his chauffeur, Sergeant-Major Lewis Reece. "He was very excited and seemed to lose control of his temper."[21]

Currie vented his angry frustration at the British. He was convinced that the German successes on either side of the elongated Canadian sector were due largely to British shortcomings. "Many British troops are not fighting well," he told his diary. "This is what I expected and what I often claimed during 1917 would be the case. Many of them will not fight and do not fight." He was enraged by an article in *The Times* of London on 17 April, in which the colonial secretary, Arthur Balfour, expressed his "high appreciation of the valour displayed by the Portuguese troops on the Western front." The Portuguese had, in fact, fled at the first hint of trouble, hijacking British bicycles at gunpoint in their haste to escape. "I wonder if Mr. Balfour appreciates the inutterable disgust with which this is read by all who know the truth," Currie complained in his diary. "Hypocrisy. Oh how it has the English people enslaved. We don't want the truth. Camouflage is preferred."[22]

Currie's criticism was, to a certain extent, justified. He knew that in some instances incredibly sloppy preparations had contributed to British defeats; he could cite the case of one corps commander who had his troops building tennis courts at the expense of work on front-line defences. But, on the whole, his comments were unfair. Thanks to political interference, the BEF had been left holding an unusually long line; undermanned, it was still feeling the demoralizing effects of the politically-imposed reorganization of its divisions. And the Germans happened to hit the line at its weakest points, including the sector in Flanders held by the Portuguese Corps. These were far more important factors in the spring crisis than widespread failings on the part of the British military.

Still, Currie was so agitated that he expressed his feelings to his army commander, General Sir Henry Horne. Sir Henry, Currie commented in his diary, "resented any reflection on fighting ability of British Divisions." Horne not only resented it, he reported it to Sir Douglas Haig. The commander-in-chief, who was under no little strain himself, took the opportunity for a diatribe in his diary:

> Currie is suffering from a swollen head, Horne thinks. He lodged a complaint when I ordered a Canadian division to be brought out of the line in order to support the front and take part in the battle elsewhere. He wishes to fight only as a "Canadian Corps" and get his Canadian representative in London to write and urge me to arrange it. As a result, the Canadians are together holding a wide front near Arras, *but they have not yet been in the battle*!

This would remain a sore point with Haig, too. As late as 19 July, in a heated discussion with Major-General Sydney Mewburn, the Canadian minister of militia and defence, Haig would complain "that the British Army alone and unaided by Canadian troops withstood the first terrific blow by 80 German Divisions on March 21st until May 27th....*During* *all this severe fighting, the Canadian Corps had not once been engaged.*"[23]*

It was Haig's turn to be unfair. By minimizing the Canadian contribution to the cause, he overlooked the fact that the Canadian Corps had freed considerable numbers of British troops to shore up the beleaguered battlefront. With less than one-tenth of the strength of the BEF, Currie later commented, "the Canadian Corps was holding one-fifth of the [British] front. Without wishing to draw from this fact any exaggerated conclusion, it is pointed out that although the Canadian Corps did not, during this period, have to repulse any German attacks on its front, it nevertheless played a part worthy of its strength during that period." It was no coincidence, either, that the Canadian sector was the only major part of the BEF's line that was not attacked during the spring of 1918. Currie later suggested, with reason, that the Germans were "afraid to attack," because they had "never yet met the Canadians in battle without suffering defeat."[25]

In any case, Haig soon forgave Currie. In September, at the height of the dazzling Canadian victories that were leading the BEF to unprecedented success, the field-marshal privately confided in Currie: "In all the dark days of this spring, and God knows they were dark enough, one great comforting thought I had was that I still had the Canadian Corps. I knew that I could not be beaten until that Corps was put out of action."[26]

However, Currie was still in a foul mood when, in the first week of May, the Canadians were withdrawn. (Significantly, the three divisions under his command were relieved by two corps, XVII and XVIII, comprising a total of five British divisions.) Placed in reserve, the Canadian Corps was to undergo training in what was, to date, a foreign concept in this war: open warfare. Even now, away from the front lines, Currie was quick to take umbrage at real or imagined slights, as his diary reveals:

> I hear...reports that Canadians are very stout fighters, good on the defensive and also on limited objective offensives though they shake their heads at what we might do in open warfare owing to the absence of regular officers. They forget that our leaders have seen more war in the last three years than the British Army did in its previous 100 years.[27]

* The lack of active Canadian participation did not go unnoticed elsewhere in the BEF. The Canadian Corps was derisively known as "the Salvation Army," while the Canadians were also called "Foch's pets."[24]

As 1918 progressed, the strains between Currie and senior British officers would never be far below the surface.

3 "GOD HELP THE BOCHE!"

The months spent in the vicinity of Vimy Ridge had done much to rejuvenate and revive the men of the Canadian Corps. There is no doubt that, by the end of 1917, Canadian spirits had sagged somewhat. It had been a hard year, highlighted by the battles for Vimy, Hill 70, and Passchendaele, calling for repeated sacrifices that left many veterans war-weary. "I feel 10 years older and look like it too," remarked Sergeant George Gilchrist of the 54th (Central Ontario) Battalion in a letter home. This feeling was reiterated by Lieutenant Arthur Crease of the 29th (Vancouver) Battalion:

> Nearly every one feels at times that scarcely any price would be too great to pay to have this awful business of war stop if only for a few years. It is so disheartening too to find that out of the war area there are so many not only not helping but actively hindering war work—like the strikers and the recklessly and selfishly extravagant.[1]

However, youth is resilient, and the Canadians were, after all, volunteers, and they rebounded quickly. An unusually mild winter made trench life seem much more bearable, according to a medical officer, Major Harold McGill of Calgary:

> On the whole to date the winter has been a much kinder one than was last. We had some heavy snow and severe frost after Christmas. This cold lasted until about the middle of January since when, except for a few raw cold days last week, the weather has been quite mild. We have been favoured with quite a number of bright sunny days, a somewhat unusual feature in the winter climate of this country.

It also helped that the Canadians, for a change, held the high ground and the enemy lived a miserable existence in the mud and water below. It was a reversal of roles that veterans of three long years of trench warfare could well appreciate. "Our patrols could hear Fritz walking in the water and bailing out his trenches," noted one observer, "and their hearts were gladdened by the sound."[2]

The Canadians contributed to the misery with a steady series of what General Currie called "stealth raids." He described a pair of such raids in late February:

> In one case they entered the German trench at daylight, found no garrison there but there was a machine gun in position all ready for firing. They all got back safely, and brought the machine gun with them. In the other case they sneaked in behind a post which consisted of eight men. They killed seven and brought away the other as a sample.[3]

The Canadians, who prided themselves on the manner in which they dominated no man's land—that narrow strip of shell-shocked and bullet-swept territory separating the opposing sides—had long been regarded as trench raiders par excellence. If they had not initiated this form of warfare, they certainly elevated it to an art form.

Indeed, Canadian raids were often cited as models, and operational orders circulated throughout the BEF, as well as the French army, for instructional purposes. These raids never failed to take their toll on German nerves, as evidenced by a letter written by one enemy soldier, a victim of a Canadian raid, to a fellow German: "I hope that the Canadians are not in the trenches opposite you, for they on the darkest night jump suddenly into our trenches, causing great consternation and before cries for help can be answered disappear again into the darkness."[4]

The effect on Canadian morale was marked. Lieutenant Stuart Baird, a subaltern of the 14th (Royal Montreal Regiment) Battalion whose task it was to censor letters written home, marvelled at the mood of the men in the front lines:

> I don't know if this is a problem in psychology or not....In censoring letters I notice that the men in the line who are actually taking the odd chance say "hoping this finds you in the pink as it leaves me at present" and are always merry and bright. They say "*when* I come back." Men on jobs such as I'm on at present aren't nearly so cheerful. They usually rub in the "if I'm spared" stuff. Why?[5]

Here are some samples:

> I suppose you hear & read about a possible Hun attack. He won't come very far on the Canadian Front for our Tommies are too good for him. They are certainly wonderful and have lots of confidence, too, which means a great deal.[6]

We are holding a part of the line which is considered to be of great importance & you can readily read the real meaning of those words. The Boche never knows quite where to find us but he knows very well by now, that if there is some particularly hard work doing we shall probably be in it—& he is rarely mistaken.[7]

And when the Canadian Corps does get into it I think Fritz will know that there has been a fight, because the whole Corps appears to be absolutely fit.[8]

The Canadian Corps had long been regarded, rightly, as an élite corps. General Currie, making no effort to conceal his pride, considered it to be "the most efficient Corps on the whole Western Front." The Canadians were storm troops whose skills were wasted in a defensive role. Nurtured in the complexities of offensive fighting, the Corps was at its best on the attack. And following its withdrawal from the front lines in the first week in May, it was the First Army's intention to take advantage of the aggressive attributes of the Canadians. General Horne's headquarters had drawn up plans for a pre-emptive attack in the hope of disrupting an expected German offensive in Flanders against the neighbouring Second Army. Code-named "Delta," the operation was short-lived. It was soon postponed, then cancelled; such was the manpower shortage in the BEF that Operation Delta would have left the First Army with no reserve formations. But the preparations were not wasted. Currie believed that the work on Delta had exerted "a most vivifying influence on the training of the Canadian Corps."[9]

The two months that followed honed the Corps into a weapon of awesome proportions. It was a period of hard work for everyone, from staff officers down to privates. "Training in open warfare," according to Currie, focused on manoeuvres held during the day and at night. "Much attention is being paid to musketry," the Corps commander observed approvingly, which meant long hours on the rifle ranges. "Platoon manoeuvring will be the keynote of the operations in view," read the training instructions issued by the Eleventh Infantry Brigade. "Section movements under covering fire....Bold patrolling and reconnaissance....Rapid deployment and closing...infiltration....The co-operation of tanks....The co-operation of forward artillery guns and light and medium mortars...use of smoke either by tanks or rifle grenades."[10]

The artillery, not surprisingly, had the biggest adjustment to make in the transition from static to open warfare. "After long months and years of engaging the enemy from static sites, it was strange indeed to get out in the morning and take up three or four positions in succession, practising various methods of attack throughout a long, tiring day before returning to billets." The first manoeuvres were rather chaotic, but the gunners gradually adapted to the new requirements. Awkward at the start, they came to enjoy these rapid movements, as William Ogilvie, a nineteen-year-old signaller in the 21st Battery, Canadian Field Artillery (CFA), recalled:

> It was a wild, thrilling moment to be careening over the country-side....Finally, after what must have been a several mile jaunt, we came to a halt while the gun teams wheeled their guns into battle position along a sunken road and the gun crews prepared to fire and we signallers of the Headquarters Party proceeded further forward to man an "O-pip" [observation post] and flash back firing directions on our Aldis lamps. Although it was just make-believe it felt most realistic.[11]

Less exhilarating, but even more exhausting, were the daily thirty-mile route marches by the "poor bloody infantry." These were gruel-ling affairs, conducted in sweltering summertime heat. The troops carried full packs; in the case of a Lewis light machine-gunner, that meant a load of more than a hundred pounds. General Currie had lately become a devotee of the famous Confederate commander, "Stonewall" Jackson, whose "foot cavalry" had been such terrors during the Ameri-can Civil War. Currie, having recently acquired a copy of Jackson's biography, had apparently decided that his Canadians could equal the exploits of the Confederates: the route marches would ensure it. (Inter-estingly, Currie even affected Jackson's terse instructions, "Press for-ward," in his personal correspondence.)[12]

Despite the hard work, the Canadians went about it with their sense of humour intact. For example, in one training session, the 13th (Royal Highlanders of Canada) and 16th (Canadian Scottish) battalions were designated as German formations for practice purposes, under the command of "General von Quaig"—Lieutenant-Colonel G. Eric McCuaig, the officer commanding the 13th Battalion—and "Colonel der Pecksburg"—the 16th's Lieutenant-Colonel Cy Peck.[13]

The arduous training soon produced the desired effect. Physically, the men were in superb shape, their bodies lean and hard and ready for the rigours that lay ahead. They were prepared mentally, too, thor-oughly familiar with the section and platoon manoeuvres that could, and would, spell the difference between victory and defeat, survival and death. One man who was most impressed was Sir Douglas Haig, who visited the Canadian Corps in late May. "The Canadians," he observed, "are now training and are 50 per cent better than when they first came out of the line."[14]

The Corps was undergoing a subtle transformation at the same time. In many ways, it was a prototype of the army that would fight in World War II, thanks to a series of changes introduced by General Currie, who was willing to make any modifications that would improve the efficiency of the Canadians. In so doing, Currie left his indelible imprint on what was already, in his opinion, "an effective and smoothly working fighting machine."[15] His changes, which served to streamline and fine-tune the Corps, left it a far more powerful formation in the summer of 1918 than the one he took over the previous year.

The biggest and most important change concerned the Canadian Engineers. The Canadians had employed the British formation since the start of the war: each division was assigned three field companies of engineers, plus a pioneer battalion. In theory, the engineers supervised the work—building roads and bridges and headquarters, and so on— and the pioneers carried it out. But there was never enough labour available, and work parties of infantry were often used—too often, in the view of Currie and his chief engineer, General Lindsay, who felt that it was unreasonable "to ask the infantry to fight a battle one day and perform engineering work the next."[16]

It was an arrangement that could be remarkably inefficient at times. In one noteworthy instance, there were troops from fifty-six different units working on a single stretch of road in the Corps area. Lindsay, hoping to remedy the situation, proposed in late 1917 a major reorganization, in which the engineers and pioneers would be lumped together and the whole considerably expanded: Lindsay wanted a brigade of engineers, three battalions, for each Canadian division. Currie readily agreed. "I consider this reorganization to be so necessary," he told the overseas ministry in London, "that I would prefer to go without Infantry rather than without Engineers." Permission was granted on 24 March, but due to the demands of the German offensives, it was well into July before the reorganization was completed.[17]

There was, predictably, some resistance to the plan. The small, professional engineer corps was jealous of its specialized status and fearful of the consequences of dilution. But Currie and Lindsay were convinced that their way was better, and Currie later insisted that events proved them right:

I am of the opinion that much of the success of the Canadian Corps in the final 100 days was due to the fact that they had sufficient engineers to do the engineering work and that in those closing battles we did not employ the infantry in that kind of work. We trained the infantry for fighting and used them only for fighting.[18]

It was such a success that the Canadian engineer organization was adopted by the British army in November 1918.

Another important development saw the expansion of the Canadian Machine-Gun Corps. One senior British officer called the Canadians "pioneers in the higher organisation of machine gun commands," which was due in large part to French-born Brigadier-General Raymond Brutinel, who headed the machine-gunners. Currie believed that Brutinel was "largely responsible for the evolution which has taken place in machine gun tactics. He has been constantly in demand by the French Military Authorities to lecture to them, and the British Army has adopted the Canadian machine gun organization." Previously, each division was allotted four machine-gun companies, which were deployed at the infantry's direction. At Brutinel's urging, the Canadians reorganized these into two-company machine-gun battalions, one per division. For the first time, the machine-guns were treated as a distinctive arm; each battalion was under an officer equal in stature to the divisional artillery commander. Additionally, the motor machine-gun branch was also revamped, with two armoured-car brigades being formed, each of five eight-gun batteries. The Canadians were giving greater credence to the demands of firepower combined with mobility.[19]

Necessity soon forced a further alteration in the machine-gun corps. The British, by reducing their divisions to nine battalions, had retained each division's complement of sixty-four Vickers heavy machine-guns, thus giving them proportionately more firepower than their Canadian counterparts. It was a shortcoming that became alarmingly evident in early April, when the Canadians were assigned an ever-growing share of the front lines. To compensate for his weakness in manpower, General Currie arbitrarily decided to add a third company to each machine-gun battalion, which gave each division ninety-six heavy machine-guns. The need was urgent, and Currie acted accordingly. "Official sanction can come later," he declared in his orders instructing each infantry battalion to "ear-mark fifty of their best and brainiest men" for the new machine-gun units.[20]

The artillery, too, was in the midst of changes. As in other arms, mobility was the key, in the view of Lieutenant-Colonel Andrew McNaughton, the Corps counter-battery officer:

> I wanted to get a much more flexible organization for the conditions we foresaw would come to us when we broke through the line. The transition to open warfare has to be mighty carefully planned.... The deliberate techniques of siege warfare must give way to others even at the cost of some efficiency in the use of weapons...there was no useful purpose to be served in lugging

around a lot of these short-range 9.2-inch howitzers that took thirty-six hours to emplace....I wanted everything on wheels.[21]

Mobility also mattered to the Canadian Army Service Corps. Although horses remained an integral part of the transportation system in all armies, trucks were assuming a larger and more important role as the war went on. In answer to the demands for greater mechanization, General Currie created a mechanical transport company for each division, an innovation that would soon pay dividends.[22]

Intelligence was not neglected either. In a minor adjustment, each infantry battalion was assigned an officer whose sole responsibility was intelligence; it was his duty to ensure that vital information was promptly dispatched to brigade headquarters, which in turn relayed it to division, thence to Corps and army, eventually reaching GHQ. By 1918, intelligence had not only assumed pivotal importance, it had developed into an incredibly complex task, involving, as Currie later noted, "patrols and scouting...and observation posts and all other inter-communication, front line listening apparatus and its protection, the interpretation and wide distribution of aeroplane photographs, the extension of artillery intelligence, the rapid preparation and distribution of tactical sketches, mosaic aeroplane photographs, trench maps, etc." The Canadians were remarkably adept at all phases of the intelligence game and by war's end had evolved, in Currie's words, "a system of collecting and co-ordinating information that could almost be categorized as perfect." Intelligence would be another key element in the success of the Canadian Corps in the coming months.[23]

The cumulative effect of these changes was most impressive. The Corps now had, according to a Currie aide, Lieutenant-Colonel Wilfrid Bovey, "twice as many engineers and three times as many machine gunners as the ordinary [British] corps, a great deal more mechanical transport and more artillery." With each of its infantry battalions one hundred men over establishment—totalling forty-eight officers and 1066 other ranks—a Canadian division now boasted, in round numbers, 21,000 troops, all ranks, compared to the 15,000 or less mustered by a British division at this time. In Currie's opinion, the Canadian Corps now had "the perfect fighting organization," with a total strength of 102,372.[24]*

It did not go unnoticed. Prime Minister Borden, visiting England during June, wrote a proud letter to his cabinet back in Canada:

You would be greatly inspired by the wonderful prestige of the Canadian Army Corps. It is admitted that it is the most effective

* As of 7 August 1918.

and reliable fighting unit of its size in the British forces. In reality, it is almost as strong numerically, and certainly as effective for either offence or defence as any of the British armies, although each army is supposed to comprise two [or more] army corps.

Moreover, Borden considered Currie to be "the ablest Corps Commander in the British Forces; more than that, I believe that he is at least as capable as any Army Commander among them."[25]

Another prominent figure who took an interest in the Canadian Corps at the time was the Allied supreme commander, General Foch. He was so impressed with Currie's organizational changes that he paid a personal visit to Corps headquarters to discover the details firsthand. Afterwards, he declared that the Corps was "an Army second to none, deriving its immense strength from the solid organization of each of its component parts, welded together in battle conditions."[26]

General Currie had every right to be pleased. "I don't think it was ever in better fighting fettle than at the present time," Currie wrote of his Corps in July, "and I look for it to give a wonderfully good account of itself when it next meets the enemy in active operations."[27]

Action would come soon enough, but first came a welcome break from the rigorous training. On 1 July, Dominion Day, the Canadians staged a Corps sports meet near Tinques, a village west of Arras. The engineers constructed a modest stadium which enabled more than 30,000 soldiers to watch the best athletes in the Corps. The guest of honour, the former governor-general of Canada, the Duke of Connaught, headed an impressive visitors' list which included the prime minister, Sir Robert Borden, Canada's leading air ace, Billy Bishop, Generals Foch and Pershing, and Belgium's King Albert. "It was a day that will be long remembered by those present," Currie commented in his diary. "The programme was varied and the event of a high order, not a single hitch occurring from the first event at 10 A.M. to the concluding number, a Concert Party by one of the Divisional Troupes."[28]

The next day, Prime Minister Borden inspected troops of the First and Fourth divisions. In the process, he deftly handled a potentially embarrassing situation. While he was addressing the assembled soldiers, he was interrupted by loud cries, "Leave, leave, what about leave?"—a reference to an election promise of Borden's the previous December, to send veterans of the first contingent, which had gone overseas in 1914, on furlough to Canada. Borden quieted the hecklers: "We all have leave—to do our best until this war shall be won." The prime minister did not allow the incident to spoil his impressions of Canada's fighting forces. He wrote Currie afterwards:

The fine physique, the magnificent spirit and the splendid confidence of the Canadian Army Corps were most impressive. If [only] all our countrymen could have witnessed the gathering on Dominion Day.... The people of Canada are behind you to the end. They understand, as you do, that no indecisive result can repay the nation's sorrow and sacrifice.[29]

One more ceremonial display awaited the Canadians. On Saturday, 6 July, they hosted a military gathering of the clans at Tinques, at which all Highland battalions in the Corps were represented, along with most of those in the BEF: the 15th (Scottish), 51st (Highland), and 52nd (Lowland) divisions participated in the day-long games. They concluded with a march past by massed pipe bands, 284 pipers and 164 drummers, "a soul-stirring spectacle."[30]

Sadly, the time for such pleasant diversions was all too short. Its long period of training and rest came to an end on 15 July, when the Corps moved into the front lines east of Arras, relieving XVII Corps. The Canadians immediately announced their arrival by staging a series of raids on the enemy trenches.

Meanwhile, bigger things were afoot. On 20 July, General Currie received a visit from Major-General John Davidson, the director of military operations at GHQ. While he was not at liberty to divulge details of future plans, Davidson did give Currie and his staff their "first intimation that the Canadian Corps was to be used for offensive operations," and invited Currie to attend a meeting the following day at Fourth Army headquarters at Flixécourt.[31]

Nine officers attended the Sunday conference. Besides Currie and his top staff officer, Brigadier-General N.W. Webber, this select group included the Fourth Army's commander, General Rawlinson, his chief of staff, General Montgomery, his artillery chief, Major-General C.E.D. Budworth, and a senior planner, Lieutenant-Colonel R.M. Luckock. General Monash, along with Brigadier-General Thomas Blamey, represented the Australian Corps, while the Tank Corps' delegate was Lieutenant-Colonel J.F.C. Fuller. Rawlinson outlined plans for the Amiens offensive, which was to be spearheaded by the Canadians and Australians, supported by tanks in unprecedented numbers. Above all, Rawlinson "dwelt upon the importance of secrecy."[32]

If Currie had any qualms, he kept them to himself. But he must have had some, as even the British realized that they were asking a lot of him. General Montgomery later remarked: "The whole Canadian Corps had to be brought down for an attack in less than three weeks—a stupendous task demanding most careful planning and staff work." The problem, of course, was that the Canadians had now to bear the burden of their reputation, which Sir Basil Liddell Hart later noted:

"Regarding them as storm troops, the enemy tended to greet their appearance as an omen of a coming attack." Currie was thus faced with the challenge of moving an élite body of more than 100,000 men, and thousands of horses and wagons, and hundreds of guns and trucks, a distance of over fifty miles, without giving a hint to the Germans![33]*

The answer lay, at least partly, in what John Terraine calls "deception on a grand scale," an admirable forerunner to the more elaborate "preliminaries of Alamein and the D-Day ruses" of World War II. *The Times* of London would later say, generously, "that General Currie used one of the few deliberate ruses in this war that succeeded in deceiving the enemy." Which was true enough, but it must be noted that the Canadians received invaluable assistance from GHQ.[35]

In the interest of security, Currie chose, first of all, to deceive some of his subordinates. Since moving to the Arras sector on the fifteenth, the Corps had been planning an attack on a nearby landmark, Orange Hill, which the Germans had captured during their spring offensive. On his return to Corps headquarters, Currie decided to proceed with these preparations, revealing the Amiens operation to only a select handful of staff officers. This ruffled the feathers of a few senior officers, including Brigadier-General George Tuxford, who complained that anyone who could not be trusted to maintain secrecy was unfit to command.[36] Nevertheless, planning for the Orange Hill attack was soon completed; the plans were shelved for future use, and would one day come in quite handy.

It was not until 29 July that Currie finally disclosed to his divisional and brigade commanders the real operation at Amiens. The same day, the most elaborate part of the deception came into play. Orders were issued for two infantry battalions, the 27th (Winnipeg) and 4th Canadian Mounted Rifles (CMR), to move *north*, to Flanders, along with wireless units and two casualty clearing stations, all of which were temporarily assigned to Major-General Sir Sydney Lawford's 41st Division. Rumours were spread—by GHQ staff officers, no less—that the Canadians were being brought in to make an attack on nearby Mont Kemmel. The presence of the casualty clearing stations was often a signal of impending offensive operations. To reinforce the illusion, the 27th Battalion and 4th CMR carried out a number of raids, "incidentally losing parts of equipment and badges distinctive of Canadians." At the same time, the signallers began transmitting dummy messages "in an

* If the appearance of the Canadians alone could give away the Allied plans, their arrival alongside the Australians would be certain to raise the alarm, because the Germans considered that "the Australians and Canadians are much the best troops that the English have." Field-Marshal Paul von Hindenburg concurred: "The English troops were of varying value. The élite consisted of men from the Colonies...."[34]

easily decipherable code." The latter innovation was a wartime "technological 'first'—the first use of a wireless deception plan...."[37]

There can be no doubt that it was successful. The Germans later admitted that they noticed "the insertion of Canadian troops in the line near Kemmel...but not the shifting of the Corps southwards." Even the Allies were fooled. General Currie afterwards loved to relate how King Albert of Belgium wrote to General Foch, the supreme commander, "and complained that the Canadians were about to launch an assault in Belgium and that he had not been informed."[38]

In the meantime, the rest of the Canadian Corps was headed for Amiens far to the *south*. As before, secrecy was vital. In each man's paybook a prominent warning was pasted: "KEEP YOUR MOUTH SHUT!" It was obvious to everyone that something was up, but aside from a select group of officers no one knew what it was. "There are rumours afloat that the Canadian Corps is getting ready for an attack," Captain K. Weatherbe commented in his diary in late July, "but speculation as to where and when this is to come off is discouraged."[39] When the first units pulled out on the thirtieth, no one below brigade level knew about Amiens; not even battalion commanders were informed.

Currie has been criticized for his apparent preoccupation with secrecy. The official history, for instance, suggests that "the emphasis on secrecy was open to question."[40] But Currie was merely complying with the express wishes of the commander-in-chief, Field-Marshal Haig, and the Fourth Army's General Rawlinson. It also ran counter to everything Currie personally believed in: his view was that preparation *by all ranks* was the key to success. In the Amiens operation, this painstaking preparation was sacrificed, to a certain extent, in favour of the element of surprise. If, however, the end justifies the means, then Currie's stratagem was amply justified and, therefore, beyond criticism.

It was, to be sure, confusing for the troops. Moving by bus, train, and on foot, everyone seemed headed in different directions, as Private Victor Wheeler of the 50th (Calgary) Battalion recalled:

We moved southwest, quickly turned northeast, again due west, straight south and, as if we had lost all sense of direction, we turned due north again, reverted to a southeasterly direction, and continued in this manner *ad infinitum*! The purpose of all this, of course, was to confuse the enemy (*more* than ourselves!) of our probable destination.[41]

Not surprisingly, in these circumstances, the rumour mill worked overtime. Most agreed that the Corps was destined for Flanders, but one battalion that passed through Abbeville, on the French coast, came to believe that "we were going to Russia, we were going to embark."[42] Adding to the general state of confusion was the decision, after 1 August, to restrict all movement to the hours of darkness.

General Currie was seemingly tireless. A man of enormous energy, he was able to put in long hours on the job, sustained only by occasional catnaps. Until recently, he had been plagued by painful bouts of severe indigestion, but this had been corrected by a London specialist, "and thus, I was able to put into these operations every ounce of strength I possessed," Currie remembered, "and I can truthfully say that for three months I averaged at least 17 hours a day." War correspondent Fred Livesay marvelled at the endurance of the Corps commander, "whom one left studying battle reports at two in the morning and heard at breakfast that he had been in the field at six o'clock."[43]

In addition to attending to the apparently endless array of details associated with the Corps move to Amiens, Currie had to find time to take part in conferences with senior British and Australian officers at Fourth Army headquarters. General Rawlinson was delighted with these meetings, and particularly with the contributions of the two dominion corps commanders. "Currie and Monash very pleasant and easy to deal with," Rawlinson wrote in his diary. "No friction or argument of any sort." Not even the decision to advance zero day, from 10 to 8 August, disturbed Currie's calm countenance. Rawlinson's chief of staff, General Montgomery, suspected that the Canadian was uncomfortable. "Methodical, extremely thorough and determined, Currie disliked being rushed over an attack," Montgomery recalled, but he "remained imperturbable and accessible to all. His relations with the Fourth Army were of the most cordial nature and his attitude one of the friendliest."[44]

Privately, the strain was showing. "This operation has been too hurried," he complained in a note to himself. "Divisions marched all night and slept in the day. This sudden departure from the normal ends after a week in many being tired, particularly officers who have plans to prepare." Sloppy marching annoyed him intensely. The Sixth Infantry Brigade angered him on 6 August by taking five hours to cover a distance that should have required only an hour and a half. On another occasion, he considered court-martialling the officers commanding two engineer battalions, the 4th and 5th, whose appearance on the road was chaotic. Although these were, thankfully, isolated incidents, Currie composed another long note to himself, as if to justify his anger:

March discipline is:
1. the ceremonial of war
2. a battalion which is slack in march discipline is slack in war

3. make section commanders feel that when a man falls out in the line of marches his unit is disgraced. A fit man can march 50 minutes [per hour]

4. the more tired the men are, the stricter must be the march discipline

5. inspect feet immediately after every march

6. officers must march in rear of platoons, companies, battalions, etc.

7. once more, the discipline on the march is the discipline of the battle.[45]

Despite Currie's misgivings, things were going remarkably well. The first Canadian units arrived in the Amiens area on 5 and 6 August, and most of the soldiers were somewhat surprised to find that they were not in Flanders, as they had expected. Lieutenant Joe O'Neill of the 19th (Central Ontario) Battalion laughingly recalled the reaction of some of his men: "Oh, if you could have heard their real old soldier stuff about the blankety-blank staff that got us on the wrong train and [sent] us south when we should have been going north!"[46]

In fact, the staff work was superb. The bulk of the Canadian Corps—three divisions, the First, Second, and Third—was concentrated in Boves Wood, a forest outside Amiens. It was the "most fantastic thing," George Bell of the 58th (Central Ontario) Battalion related, "because in the daytime you were in the woods, you weren't allowed to go outside them, and once dark came it just teemed with transport and men...." The noise generated by men, animals, and vehicles was cleverly disguised by low-flying aircraft of the Royal Air Force, which had undertaken this aerial activity several nights earlier in order to allay German suspicions. There were, inevitably, incredible traffic jams, but these were usually sorted out with minimal difficulty and plenty of profanity by military policemen. Indeed, the sight of so many men, guns, horses, wagons, and trucks was awe-inspiring, and according to G.S. Rutherford, a member of the 52nd (New Ontario) Battalion, any feelings of derision towards the Corps staff were soon replaced by a very different attitude: "You had the feeling that everything was well planned, well organized. People knew what they were about, the staff was on the job. Everything seemed to go like clockwork, and for the first time on your march you could hear the troops singing."[47]

The confidence was contagious. After "a heart-breaker" of a march, Corporal Albert West of the 43rd (Cameron Highlanders of Canada) Battalion commented in his diary: "We are in Boves Wood S.E. of Amiens a few miles. The Wood is full of men and all the woods so far as I can see for miles are like this. I am sure there is an ugly surprise in store for Fritz now."[48]

The concentration of the Canadian Corps in such a confined space presented a very real danger. "If the Germans had ever got wise, oh, it would have been a terrible slaughter, because we were packed in there so tight...." Again, the Australians helped out. The sector the Canadians were to occupy had been formerly held by the French XXXI Corps, but in early August the Australians had extended their front and relieved the French. It was done deliberately and openly, with the intention of lulling the Germans into a false sense of security: if the Australians were taking over a longer line, there was little likelihood of an attack in this sector. There was, however, a tense moment or two in the early morning hours of 4 August, when the Germans raided Australian positions on the Amiens-Roye road and made off with five prisoners. If nothing else, the raid indicates the high morale and quality of these Germans, who would not normally go looking for a fight with the Australians. To their eternal credit, the captured Aussies kept their mouths shut about impending operations. Even a hint could have been disastrous for the Canadians, as a grateful Colonel Andy McNaughton recalled many years later: "We lived in dread that one of them would open his mouth, but they did not. I don't know that we've ever paid sufficient tribute to their contribution to the security of the Canadian Corps and I would like to place it on the record now."[49]

One change did arise from the incident. General Currie, who took command of the battlefront held by the 4th Australian Division on 5 August, had originally intended to begin moving Canadian troops into the front lines on the night of 6-7 August. He decided to delay this until 7-8 August, with the last troops getting into position mere hours before the attack took place.

Colonel McNaughton, meantime, was playing an important part in the preparations for the offensive, certainly more notable than his rank would indicate. Officially, he was the Corps counter-battery officer, responsible for the detection and destruction of enemy artillery positions. Actually, he was the de facto commander of the Canadian heavy artillery. Its nominal commander, Brigadier-General R.H. Massie, one of the few British officers still serving with the Canadians, was constantly ill with a recurring tropical malady acquired earlier in his military career. With General Currie's approval, McNaughton worked with the Corps artillery chief, Major-General E.W.B. Morrison, to draw up the gunners' arrangements. Currie had no hesitation in delegating this responsibility to the youthful McNaughton, who he would later describe as "the greatest gunner in the world—not in the British Empire alone, but in the whole world."[50]

The artillery preparations were prodigious. The Canadian Corps had at its disposal 646 guns of all calibres—virtually every Canadian gun in France, plus a number of British batteries. In all, Currie could count on the firepower of seventeen brigades of field artillery and nine heavy brigades. Because of the demands for secrecy, no registration— the selection of targets and calculation of ranges by preliminary shelling—was possible; it all had to be done from maps, and quickly. Assisted by Australian gunners, the Canadians plotted the positions of enemy batteries, ranging on them by carefully calibrating the muzzle velocity of every gun and howitzer and calculating the effects of such factors as temperature, barometric pressure, and wind direction. A complex barrage program was drawn up. According to McNaughton, "the pattern of fire on each enemy battery was made up from guns of separate batteries, which would compensate for any individual errors. The patterns were large but the effect would be sufficient to prevent the firing of more than a few rounds by the enemy."[51]

One man who was not impressed was Major-General C.E.D. Budworth, the Fourth Army's artillery commander. On a visit to Canadian Corps headquarters, General Budworth was plainly baffled by McNaughton's complicated barrage map. McNaughton patiently tried to explain it, but Budworth interrupted him repeatedly. McNaughton, affronted and annoyed, "asked him what he suggested as an alternative but was not enlightened; he turned on his heel and left." McNaughton promptly reported the incident to Currie and Morrison. The Corps commander, he recalled, "asked if I had confidence in my plan and when I replied affirmatively—with emphasis—I was told to carry on with no change."[52]

In other respects, the operation threatened to become an administrative nightmare. Staff officers, both in the Canadian Corps and at the Fourth Army, were hard-pressed to compensate for the strictures of secrecy imposed by Haig and Rawlinson. Canadian quartermasters, for example, were not informed of the offensive until 29 July; the Fourth Army's quartermasters were kept in the dark until, to their surprise, they began receiving requisition orders from the Canadians in the first week of August. In these circumstances, difficulties were unavoidable. "The first request to the Army for 10,000,000 s.a.a. [small-arms ammunition] apparently was not taken seriously," states a Corps quartermaster report, "and s.a.a. came up in small quantities, and could not be supplied to divisions as quickly as they required it." Some formations had to borrow trench munitions—small-arms ammunition, grenades, and flares—from neighbouring French troops to make up the shortfalls.[53]

The physical difficulties were numerous. No corps supply dumps had been established in this area—and, in the interests of secrecy, none could be located here at this late date—and the Canadians were forced to draw on the Fourth Army's main dumps, a day's drive distant. The recently organized mechanical transport companies were forced to meet the demands on their resources. At first, there was a shortage of trucks; that rectified, petrol became the problem. On top of that, there were only two primary roads in the Canadian sector, and one of them was shared with the Australians, which meant considerable congestion and many delays. The Canadian truckers could consider themselves fortunate that it did not rain; utter chaos would have ensued. Nevertheless, minor miracles were performed by the Canadian Army Service Corps on the dark roads in and around Amiens. Priority was given to the artillery ammunition allotted to the Canadians: 291,000 rounds of all calibres, with a total weight of 7065 tons, were trucked from the dumps, six to nine miles away, in three and a half nights. The last delivery was made at 11 P.M. on 7 August, a little over five hours before the attack began.[54]

Despite these amazing achievements, the fact remains that the Canadians came perilously close to giving away the game. Twenty thousand horses had to be hidden in Boves Wood; because of the hurried arrangements, some time passed before water pipes could be laid into the forest. This, General Currie admitted, "caused endless columns of horses to block the roads in the vicinity of the watering points."[55] Only cloudy, misty weather and the fine work of the Royal Air Force prevented German reconnaissance aircraft from detecting this activity.

There were other problems to be faced. One of these was finding suitable billets. While the Australians had taken over the front lines from the French in this sector, the rear areas remained in French hands until the Canadians arrived. Unfortunately, the sanitary conditions were, in the words of one medical source, "far from good; in fact, they could not have been much worse." The experience of the 42nd (Royal Highlanders of Canada) Battalion was regrettably typical:

> Our quarters were in a farm house that had once been nice and clean but was now over-run with millions of flies and spiders. The floors, walls and ceilings were just black with them and the buzz was like a sawmill. I slept on a brick floor that was cold and damp and had not been washed for months. Our cook is very clean, but try as he would he could not cook a single thing without having it befouled with flies. There were flies in our porridge, in our eggs, our meat, our vegetables and even though he would succeed in giving one a cup of coffee without a fly in it one or more of the pests would drop in it before one could drink it. Valiant efforts

were made by our sanitary squad to clean up but the flies defied all attempts to exterminate them.

As a result of these deplorable conditions, large numbers of Canadians contracted diarrhoea, which remained prevalent until they evacuated the area to go into action.[56]

But these discomforts would soon be forgotten. During the night of 7-8 August, the Canadians at last began moving into the front lines. In addition to his gas mask, each soldier was equipped with 220 rounds of small-arms ammunition, two grenades, a pick or shovel, three empty sandbags, an extra water bottle, and forty-eight hours' iron rations (corned beef and biscuits). Watching them move up, war correspondent Roland Hill likened the Canadians to "ghosts of retribution" as they filed through the darkness to form up in the rectangles of white tape laid on the ground to denote their jumping-off points. Each of the three attacking Canadian divisions signalled its arrival by flashing to Corps headquarters the code word "Llandovery Castle."* It was a moonless night, and delays were impossible to avoid. The Third Canadian Division, on the right, did not flash the code word until four o'clock in the morning, only twenty minutes before zero hour.[57]

No one could know it, but the Great War had just entered the period popularly known as "the last hundred days"—though there were, in fact, only ninety-six days left.

An air of quiet confidence permeated the highest echelons of command in the BEF. So tight had been security for this operation that General Rawlinson, the Fourth Army's commander, made no references to it in his personal diary until the evening of the seventh:

> There is nothing to show that the Boche knows what is coming south of the Somme. We shall have eight excellent divisions and three hundred and fifty tanks against him on this part of the battlefront, in a perfect tank country; and three cavalry divisions ready to press through any hole that is made. I have great hopes that we shall win a great success.

Rawlinson's optimism rubbed off on the commander-in-chief, Field-Marshal Haig, who visited Fourth Army headquarters earlier in the day.

---

* The code word referred to the Canadian hospital ship *Llandovery Castle*, which had been torpedoed and sunk by a German submarine on 27 June 1918 en route from Canada to England. Only twenty-four of the 258 Canadians on board survived the sinking. Among the victims were fourteen nursing sisters.

"Everything is going on without a hitch," he wrote in his own diary, "and the enemy seems in ignorance of the impending blow."[58]*

Haig also stopped by Canadian Corps headquarters on 7 August. There, a beleaguered General Currie told him that "it had been a hustle to get ready in time, but everything had been got in except two long-range guns." Haig, still smarting at Currie's unwillingness to split up the Corps during the spring crisis, could not resist a dig at the Canadians, commenting in his diary that they were "very keen to do something."[60]

Keen they were, but the Canadians were more cautiously optimistic. Colonel McNaughton, whose hurried artillery preparations would mean so much to the success or failure of the attack, expressed the sentiments at Corps headquarters in a letter to his wife:

> The last few days have been a terrific strain but at last everything is in order at least so far as one is able to foresee. If things go well it will be a day glorious throughout the ages in the history of our country. If the reverse many a home will be sad. One realizes at a time like this the responsibility of command. Every slip or bit of carelessness costs hundreds of lives.[61]

No one was more conscious of that responsibility than the Corps commander, General Currie. And no one had been under more strain in the execution of a challenge unique in the annals of the Great War, the shift of his élite troops in complete secrecy. The strain told; he was bothered by grave misgivings, as his private writings reveal. But these worries were forgotten on the very eve of the attack when, at dusk, Currie rode out with his staff to watch the last of the Canadians moving up to the front. His sagging spirits were revived by the sight and sound of soldiers singing as they marched past: "Hail, hail, the gang's all here; what the hell do we care now!" At that moment, Currie snapped back to his usual good-natured self. Turning to his staff, he declared in his booming voice, "God help the Boche to-morrow."[62]

He was quite right. Only divine intervention at this point could have saved the Germans from their biggest defeat of the war to date.

---

* Incredible as it may seem, this was perfectly true. There had been, of course, scattered reports of unusual activity behind the British lines about Amiens, but these had been dismissed at the headquarters of General Georg von der Martwitz, whose Second Army would bear the brunt of the Allied attack. "The Army Staff," said one incredulous German officer, "was astonishingly indifferent." The negligence went even higher. Warnings about poor defences and low-quality troops were blissfully ignored by the de facto commander-in-chief, General Erich Ludendorff. So confident was Ludendorff that he issued on 4 August a special order stating that "we should wish for nothing better than to see the enemy launch an offensive, which can but hasten the disintegration of his forces...." Ludendorff would soon be singing a different tune.[59]

4 "THE BLACK DAY OF THE GERMAN ARMY"

A single gun signalled the start of the attack. Some soldiers heard it, but most did not; its sound was swiftly succeeded by the overwhelming roar of 2070 artillery pieces along the Fourth Army's front and hundreds more behind the neighbouring French First Army. It was 4:20 A.M., Thursday, 8 August 1918, "the date of the great turning-point of the War."[1]

The noise was mind-numbing, if not deafening. D.C. McArthur, a gunner working one of the Canadian field batteries, remembered it as "almost solid sound." An infantryman, F.A. Stitt, of the 19th (Central Ontario) Battalion, had a similar recollection: "I never saw anything like it in my life, that barrage on the 8th of August. You couldn't hear yourself think." Moments later, Private Stitt and thousands of men like him, Canadian, Australian, and British, went "over the top," the term the troops used to describe their attacks.[2]

All four Canadian divisions would be in action this memorable day, something that had happened only once before, at Vimy Ridge, in April 1917. Three divisions, each accompanied by forty heavy tanks, led the assault: Major-General Sir Henry Burstall's Second, on the left; Major-General Archie Macdonell's First, in the middle; Major-General Louis Lipsett's Third, on the right. Located to the rear of the Third Division was Major-General Sir David Watson's Fourth, along with Major-General A.E.W. Harman's 3rd Cavalry Division, a British formation which included the Canadian Cavalry Brigade. Watson's division, and the cavalry, would pass through the Third Division later in the day to exploit the initial success.

The battle plan was undeniably ambitious. The Canadian Corps was arrayed on a front of 8500 yards, a little less than five miles, between the Amiens-Chaulnes railway, which denoted the boundary with the Australian Corps on the left, and the Amiens-Roye road, the boundary between the Fourth and French First armies. There were three objective lines, designated Green, Red, and Blue Dotted on headquarters maps. The Green and Red lines marked the points where support elements would leap-frog the leading units of each division and press on to the Blue Dotted Line which, as General Currie pointed out, "was not meant to be a final objective, and the Cavalry was to exploit beyond it should the opportunity occur."[3] Nevertheless, the Blue Dotted Line was some 14,000 yards, roughly eight miles, from the Canadian jumping-off points.

The Canadians had to pay special attention to their right flank. Lacking tanks, the French planned a forty-five-minute preliminary bombardment of the enemy defences. It opened at 4:20 A.M., coinciding with the British barrage to ensure surprise, but the French infantry would not attack until 5:05 A.M. Until they caught up, the Canadian flank would be completely exposed. To protect it, the Canadian Independent Force (CIF) was created. Under the command of Brigadier-General Raymond Brutinel, Currie's brilliant machine-gun expert, the highly mobile CIF contained two brigades of armoured cars, a cyclist battalion, and a section of trench mortars mounted on lorries. The force's assignment was to prevent the Germans from counter-attacking across the Amiens-Roye road. As well, an international platoon was formed, to ensure proper liaison with the French when they did catch up to the Canadians. Under the orders of the 43rd (Cameron Highlanders of Canada) Battalion, this platoon was commanded by an officer of the French 42nd Division, which contributed a small contingent of other ranks, as did the 43rd Battalion. This unique unit acquitted itself admirably on 8 August, capturing thirty prisoners and a dozen machine-guns.[4]

The Canadians attacked in a dense fog. The ground mist had materialized during the night and became so thick that it blotted out the sun later in the morning. Visibility everywhere was "limited to a few dozen feet, or yards." In some places "it was difficult to distinguish the men until they came within a few feet of one." Lieutenant James Pedley, a platoon commander in the 4th (Central Ontario) Battalion, could well attest to the problems posed by the fog. In no time at all, Lieutenant Pedley was lost, and the nervous young officer came "within an ace"— his words—of shooting his battalion commander, Lieutenant-Colonel L.H. Nelles, who suddenly appeared out of the mist and startled Pedley. Pointing his revolver at the gloomy figure before him, the lieutenant was about to squeeze the trigger when he heard a familiar voice. "Keep on, Pedley," said the colonel, oblivious to his brush with death, "you're headed right." Then he faded into the fog, leaving Pedley to breathe a sigh of relief and ponder the possible consequences of his close call with catastrophe.[5]

Of course, the fog worked both ways. While it caused some confusion among the Canadians, it also blinded the defenders, who were unable to find targets for their many machine-guns in the opening minutes. A surprisingly large number of machine-gun nests consequently did not fire and remained undetected until the Canadian support units moved into the battle zone in the late morning, by which time the mist had dissipated. Until then, the Canadians made unusually smooth and rapid progress in the face of light resistance.

The ease of the advance came as a pleasant surprise to infantrymen accustomed to trench warfare, in which gains were measured in mere yards. This day was decidedly different. According to the history of the Royal Canadian Regiment, "the attack progressed with something approaching the clock-like precision of a well rehearsed manoeuvre." Similarly, the 42nd (Royal Highlanders of Canada) Battalion history would describe the battle as "more or less of a route march enlivened by the sight of the panic-stricken enemy running in every direction." In later years, veterans would fondly recall the events of 8 August. Alec Jack of the 54th (Central Ontario) Battalion called it "a picture-book advance," while W.H.S. Macklin of the 19th Battalion remembered that "the shells came over our heads with an appalling shriek in the fog ahead and we simply lit our cigarettes, shouldered our rifles, and walked off after the shells, and this is what we did until we reached the objective...."[6]

The work of the artillery had been superb. The Canadian infantry followed a rolling barrage of shrapnel, high explosive, and smoke shells that moved in hundred-yard lifts at two-to-four-minute intervals. Colonel McNaughton's counter-battery plan had been close to perfect; German guns were not a factor in the early hours of the attack. There had been, McNaughton wrote his wife that day, "little hostile reaction. It appears that we have swamped his batteries." And there was plenty of evidence to support his observation. "I know we saw one German artillery position," said Private George Hancox of Princess Patricia's Canadian Light Infantry. "There were six guns there and all the gun crews were laying dead around them and they hadn't fired a shell." O.J. Thomas of the 54th Battalion recalled a similar episode:

> As we went there were certain German batteries in small woods that we were supposed to look into, and I remember a particular one that I had to take some men into and when we got into this wood where there was a clearing, the German battery was there all right. They hadn't been able to get the muzzle caps off their guns. They had their horses hitched up to their wagons and the drivers were killed on the seats of their wagons, and the rest of them lying around the clearing....

The Canadian gunners knew they had done a good job when wounded infantrymen, en route to the rear on stretchers or in ambulances, called out, "Good work, artillery. Perfect barrage."[7]

None had experienced a day like this before. Most batteries were on the move throughout 8 August, many moving at least four times, others as often as six times, leap-frogging to new forward positions in order to keep up steady shell fire in support of the infantry. "It was the thrill of a lifetime," rejoiced Lieutenant-Colonel F.T. Coghlan, commanding the 9th Brigade, Canadian Field Artillery (CFA). "Never did I think I would have that experience. I shall always remember the atmosphere of excitement and great exultation that came from the gunners, drivers, the horses and the rumble of the guns and wagons...."[8]

There was just one sour note for the artillery. It involved the use of so-called "contact batteries," sections of guns which accompanied the infantry to provide close support. However, the infantry, unaccustomed to such an innovation, made little use of the guns. "For four days we never fired a shot," recalled Bombardier James Logan of the 39th Battery, CFA, "because they moved us all over the front." It was, unfortunately, the rule rather than the exception, and Colonel McNaughton was furious when he found out. He vowed "never again" to give the infantry such control over his guns.[9]

Surprise had been complete. The 19th Battalion, for example, captured a German regimental headquarters* in the village of Marcelcave, near the Amiens-Chaulnes railway. Private F.A. Stitt later related that "after we got the betabbed generals up the stairs from this deep dugout, we investigated the place and found the porridge warm on the table, that's how badly we surprised them." Joe O'Neill, a lieutenant in the same battalion, recalled that "I had my breakfast that morning in a German engineer's dugout with hot coffee still on the stove."[10]

The Germans were surprised not only by the attack, but by the presence of the Canadian Corps, as well. In a convincing tribute to the elaborate security measures that had been implemented, some enemy prisoners flatly refused to believe that they had fallen victim to the Canadians. "We have the most certain information from our Intelligence Department," declared one sceptic, "that the Canadians are in Belgium." General Currie took considerable delight in relating this story after the war:

> A German medical officer who was captured congratulated one of our Senior Medical Officers on the success with which the wounded were being evacuated, and said, "I wish I could congratulate our intelligence service with the same pleasure." On being asked, "What do you mean?" he replied: "Well, we thought you were at Mont Kemmel." They had misplaced the Canadian Corps by seventy miles.

The reaction was routine. "You are of—America?" a German officer inquired of his captor, Lieutenant D.A. Cameron of the 2nd (Eastern

* A German regiment was the equivalent of a British brigade.

Ontario) Battalion. Lieutenant Cameron replied, "Canada," prompting an aghast "Gott in Himmel!" from his enemy.[11]

And there were plenty of prisoners. The Fourth Division's General Watson commented in his diary: "I never saw so many prisoners as taken today. They came trooping down the road by hundreds, & very tame they were too, some without any guards at all." Private Victor Wheeler of the 50th (Calgary) Battalion noted that "they wore mixed expressions of bewilderment, fear, relief and even gladness in their round faces," while Captain Harold Tylor, an engineer, observed in a letter home that many seemed "pleased to be captured." The impression was widespread. Gunner C.M. Wright of the 58th Howitzer Battery remarked that a lot of prisoners wore "smiles that only needed their ears further back to be wider." One jubilant Canadian shouted to a column of captured Germans, "Eh, Fritz, we're off to Berlin," and one responded in broken English: "Ah, you Berlin, me London."[12]

Some Germans were captured with ease that was often startling. In one case, a group of thirteen allowed themselves to be taken by two Canadians who were virtually unarmed! Captain W.W. Murray and Sergeant Alex Sample of the 2nd Battalion set off later in the day to seek a suitable location for the battalion headquarters. Finding a dugout that seemed appropriate, they heard a noise from within. Drawing his revolver, Sergeant Sample leaned inside and fired a shot down the stairs. "Kamerad!" came the cry, and thirteen German soldiers trooped out with their hands in the air. Covering them with his revolver, Captain Murray's delight diminished considerably when it occurred to him that he was holding an empty weapon: he had forgotten to load it that morning.

"Sample," he anxiously whispered, "how many cartridges have you left?"

"None, sir. I just had one in my revolver, and that was the one I shot down the dug-out stairs!"

But the prisoners were passive, and the captain and the sergeant, without a single bullet between them, led their captives to the rear.[13]

Even an Anglican priest bagged some prisoners. Honorary Lieutenant-Colonel F.G. Scott, the First Division's chaplain, was en route to the front when he passed a shell hole from which three dusty and dishevelled Germans emerged, hands held high. Canon Scott patiently tried to explain that, as a noncombatant, he could not accept their surrender. It was to no avail, so Scott reluctantly marched them away, handing them over to the first Canadian troops he encountered.[14]

Thanks to so many prisoners, souvenir hunters had a field day. It was common to see long lines of Germans, their pockets turned inside out, the tunics of their uniforms torn where buttons and badges had been cut off. The Canadians were notorious for such behaviour. Private

42

Frank Baxter of the 116th (Ontario County) Battalion recalled the words of a British officer, who commented that night that "the Canadians appear to have one bad habit. After they capture a prisoner they won't budge a bloody inch until they have taken all his souvenirs." It was a trait the Canadians shared with their Australian cousins, "who were always tourists in spirit," in the delicate words of the Australian official history.[15]

However, all of this leaves a misleading impression. By comparison with other campaigns the Canadians had fought, Amiens was, indeed, "a walk over,"[16] as Sergeant James Van der Water of the 10th (Canadians) Battalion described it in a letter home. But quite a bit of bloody fighting took place, and much heroism was displayed by the Canadians. Ten of them won the Victoria Cross (VC), the British Empire's highest award for bravery in battle, and 3000 others won lesser decorations.

The Canadians were seemingly invincible. On the Corps left, General Burstall's Second Division, with General Macdonell's First Division in the middle, overcame isolated resistance, mostly from machine-gunners, and reached all of their objectives. Both divisions attacked on a one-brigade front, leap-frogging the others to the Blue Dotted Line, across gently rolling ground with "singularly few prominent features," according to Burstall. Fields of grain, interspersed with villages and woods, characterized the countryside here. The defences were generally weak, in Burstall's opinion, "mainly unconnected sections of trench with little local wire entanglement."[17]

Masked by the early morning mist, Macdonell's division got off to a fast start. Brigadier-General George Tuxford's Third Brigade, leading the assault, deployed three battalions: the 13th (Royal Highlanders of Canada) in the centre, flanked by the 14th (Royal Montreal Regiment) on the left and the 16th (Canadian Scottish) on the right. The attackers quickly cut through the German front-line positions—too quickly, perhaps, because when the fog began to lift shortly after six o'clock support troops found themselves under heavy fire from machine-guns that had gone undetected in the original advance. And the resistance stiffened noticeably during the approach to the enemy positions a mile and a half to the rear. The 13th Battalion had an especially tough time and only managed to take its objective, the Green Line, because of the bravery of two men, Private John Croak and Corporal Herman James Good, both of whom won the VC.

Tenacity and initiative brought Private Croak his VC. Croak, a miner from Glace Bay, Nova Scotia, took on a machine-gun nest that had pinned down his company, rushing it and knocking out the gun and crew with a well-aimed grenade. Though severely wounded in the right arm, Croak refused treatment and continued forward. Within minutes, he and his comrades were once again pinned down by heavy fire, this time from a strongpoint defended by several machine-guns. Croak calmly organized and led an attack which overran the position in seconds. Unfortunately, Croak was fatally wounded in the effort.

Corporal Good, however, lived to see his vc. Approaching the Green Line, Good's company encountered three machine-guns. Without waiting for orders, Good single-handedly rushed the nest and killed or captured every German. The advance continued, only to be halted by a battery of 5.9-inch guns, firing over open sights—point-blank range. Good, who in civilian life was a lumberjack from South Bathurst, New Brunswick, calmly collected three privates and led them in a wild bayonet charge. "What the German gunners thought when this assault was launched, no one will ever know," comments the regimental history. "Perhaps in the drill and text books they had studied no instructions were given as to procedure when four Canadian Highlanders engaged a battery with the obvious intent of doing bodily harm."[18] The Germans hastily surrendered, and the 13th Battalion added three field guns to its growing list of trophies.

It was a rarity to have two members of a Canadian battalion win the vc on the same day. In fact, this was the first time it happened during the Great War. Remarkably, it would happen once more during the Amiens operations, and yet again before the end of the war.

The neighbouring 14th Battalion, on the left of the 13th, kept pace, despite treacherous tactics by the enemy. The battalion ran into a heavily defended strongpoint which blocked its path to the Green Line. Using the platoon and section manoeuvres they had practised in recent months, parties of riflemen outflanked the position under the cover of Lewis light machine-guns and rifle grenades which forced the defenders to keep their heads down. Stormed from the flank and rear, the Germans raised a white flag. But when several Canadian soldiers stepped up to accept the surrender, they were shot down in cold blood. A furious fire-fight ensued, but it was rather one-sided and the Germans once more raised their white flag. It was ignored: not a defender left this strongpoint alive.[19]

The 16th Battalion also encountered enemy treachery, in an episode that took on the appearance of a showdown at high noon on the streets of Dodge City. Nearing the village of Aubercourt, which was the battalion's Green Line objective, Lieutenant W.D. Mackie and his platoon were pinned down by heavy fire from a trench defended by four machine-guns. Lieutenant Mackie and a Lewis gunner worked their way around the position and opened a terrible enfilade fire that silenced the enemy guns. Finally, a German officer stood up and seemed to indicate that he wished to surrender. Mackie motioned him to come forward. As the German approached, he suddenly reached for his revolver. Mackie, however, beat him to the draw. After shooting the officer, he and his

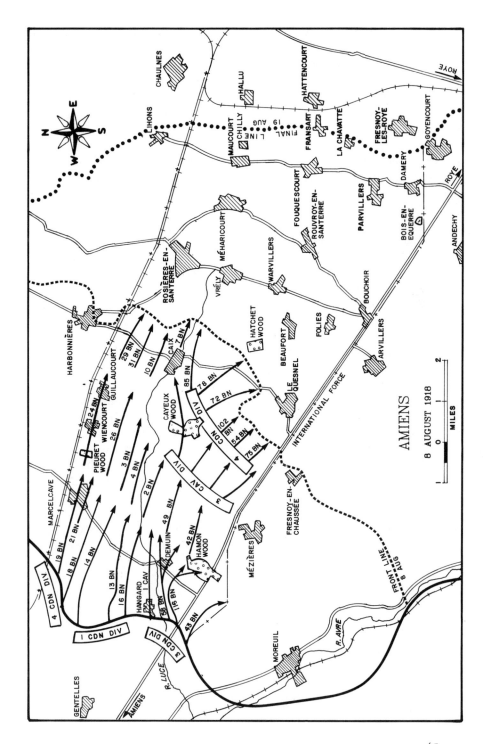

AMIENS

8 AUGUST 1918

MILES

men stormed the trench and captured it. Aubercourt fell soon afterwards.[20]

The Second Division, meanwhile, was having little difficulty taking its Green Line objectives. The village of Marcelcave presented a potential trouble-spot, and special arrangements had been made to deal with it. Because it lay just beyond the range of the field artillery, Marcelcave was subjected to a punishing forty-five-minute bombardment by long-range guns of the Corps heavy artillery. It was most effective. The few surviving defenders were in no condition to muster more than token resistance, and Marcelcave fell to troops of Brigadier-General Robert Rennie's Fourth Brigade following "a little bit of street fighting."[21] The Canadians captured the regimental headquarters mentioned earlier in this chapter, along with a hospital train parked at the village's railway station.

These Canadians owed no thanks to the tanks. Forty Mark v* heavies had been allotted to the Second Division, but they were of little use. The 20th (Central Ontario) Battalion's historian caustically commented that "the heavy fog and smoke minimized the value of the tanks. The infantry had to lead them, and being unable to communicate with them, had to overcome the enemy posts with bombs and rifle grenades."[22] Later, when the fog lifted, the tanks were merely big targets for the German guns; by noon, the Second Division had no more than a handful of its tanks still in action.

Opposition on this division's front stiffened steadily as the day wore on. The Fifth Brigade, passing through the Fourth on the Green Line at 8:20 A.M., encountered what General Burstall later described as "a most stubborn defence...put up by a large number of machine guns scattered throughout the area." Two battalions, the 24th (Victoria Rifles of Canada) and 26th (New Brunswick), had considerable difficulty clearing Pieuret Wood and Guillecourt. That they were able to maintain a slow but steady advance was due, not only to their own skill and determination, but also to the unselfish assistance rendered by the 7th Australian Infantry Brigade on the left. Burstall was generous in his praise of the Australians:

The co-operation...was almost better than could be hoped for. Many instances occurred where our troops were held up along the

---

* There were two types of Mark v, a "male" which carried four machine-guns and two light guns, and a "female" armed with six machine-guns. Weighing more than thirty tons and having a crew of seven, the Mark v had a road speed of 4.6 miles per hour, though it could manage only half that cross-country. The Mark v also had an unfortunate design defect: the radiator was located inside the crew's compartment, with no compensating ventilation, and the heat and fumes were often unbearable.

46

line of the railway, where there was a series of strong machine gun nests, and in such instances the Australians assisted our advance materially by their Lewis gun fire, as well as by sending small parties of Infantry to take part in the assault.[23]

As a result of this resistance beyond the Green Line, the Second Division began to lag behind the First Division, which forged ahead irresistibly. Three battalions of Brigadier-General William Griesbach's First Brigade went into action shortly after eight o'clock in the morning. The 2nd Battalion crossed the River Luce at Aubercourt and pressed along the south bank. North of the river were the 3rd (Toronto Regiment) and 4th (Central Ontario) battalions. All three battalions reached the Red Line, although for a time it looked as though the 3rd would not make it. Scheduled to join the attack at 8:20 A.M., Lieutenant-Colonel J.B. Rogers discovered that a large part of his unit had disappeared in the fog. On his own initiative, he delayed the 3rd Battalion's jump-off in the hope that the wayward companies would show up shortly. Finally, at 8:40 A.M., Colonel Rogers impatiently proceeded without them. The missing men caught up soon, when the attackers were halted by a line of machine-gun posts strung between two clusters of trees. The position lay outside the range of the Canadian field guns, and the 3rd Battalion was pinned down by a storm of fire until "the providential arrival of a tank at 10:55." The Mark v made short work of the defenders, and the last obstacle was removed from the battalion's line of advance. By 11:30, the 3rd was digging in along the Red Line. An "unusual scene" confronted the Canadians, as the regimental historian later wrote:

No guns thundered; the scar of No Man's Land had been left far behind; no trenches or wire entanglements were visible ahead; and the open rolling countryside was broken only by peaceful villages and deep cool woods. Fields of ripening grain waved gently under the August sun. Below the Regiment's position, the River Luce murmured its lazy way among the willows. Nothing could have been more eloquent of the day's success than this quiet and pastoral scene.[24]

The final advance on the First Division's front was made by the Second Brigade of Brigadier-General Frederick Loomis. During the noon hour, the 7th (1st British Columbia Regiment) and 10th (Canadians) battalions crossed the Red Line. The 10th Battalion met virtually no resistance whatever, and became the first Canadian unit to reach the Blue Dotted Line on 8 August. Digging in by 1:30 in the afternoon, the

10th was joined an hour later by the 7th on the right. However, both battalions were left with their flanks in the air because it took several more hours for neighbouring troops to catch up. The Second Division had just reached the Red Line, and it would be early evening—7:15 P.M.—before the 29th (Vancouver) and 31st (Alberta) battalions fought their way to the Blue Dotted Line.

In the meantime, the 10th Battalion missed a golden opportunity to make even more impressive gains. "At this stage," admitted the battalion commander, Lieutenant-Colonel E.W. MacDonald, "the enemy seemed to be entirely disorganized, and were in full retreat...." A short distance away lay the large village of Rosières-en-Santerre, and Colonel MacDonald believed that, had the attack been pressed in the late afternoon, "Rosières could have been captured with very little opposition, and very few casualties." But the village lay in the Second Division's sector, and there was no way MacDonald was going to risk his men—who, it should be noted, had already been subjected to Canadian shell fire that day—in an unsupported assault. Under the circumstances, with the Germans in a disorganized retreat, MacDonald's caution seems to have been unjustified, and it would have unfortunate consequences: Rosières would be taken the following day, but only at the cost of heavy casualties to the 31st Battalion.[25]

By nightfall, the First and Second divisions had secured their objectives along the Blue Dotted Line. It was an impressive achievement: the single-day, eight-mile advance by these two divisions was not only unmatched by any other formations in the Amiens operation, it was unprecedented in Allied experience in the Great War. But there had been nothing fancy about the actions on the left and centre of the Canadian Corps front: they had consisted of a series of frontal assaults executed with, on the whole, admirable precision. Much different was the challenge facing the Canadians on the right, where the Third Division was forced to employ a complex series of manoeuvres.

The lay of the land dictated innovative tactics. Unlike the generally flat ground facing the other two divisions, the Third Division had to effect a crossing of the River Luce and capture a low plateau on the other side. The Luce flowed across and toward the division's front, and it was, in General Currie's words, "an obstacle impassable to troops."[26] In itself an inconsequential stream, there were wide marshes on either side that broadened the river to more than 200 yards; it could be crossed only at existing bridges until the Canadian engineers constructed cork footbridges for the infantry, after the attack had begun. The divisional commander, General Lipsett, did have one advantage, in the form of a narrow bridgehead which would enable him to attack astride the river. And Lipsett was just the man to come up with an ambitious and daring plan. The only British officer commanding a

Canadian division, the Irish-born Lipsett was a career soldier who had been sent to Canada before the war, to help train militia officers. One of his students had been none other than the Corps commander, Currie, who did not hesitate to hand Lipsett the most difficult of assignments.

Lipsett elected to attack with two brigades, one on either side of the Luce. The Eighth Brigade, under Brigadier-General Dennis Draper, would clear the high ground north of the river, seizing the fortified village of Hangard and force, if necessary, a crossing at Demuin. Brigadier-General Daniel Ormond's Ninth Brigade was given the task of breaking out of the bridgehead, where three infantry battalions and a company of fourteen tanks had been covertly assembled "right under the nose of the Boche," as the army commander, General Rawlinson, later put it. Rawlinson, who considered this operation "as essential to success" on the whole front, fully realized the dangers facing the Canadians here. "There was a very serious risk that they might be discovered by the enemy and fired on by artillery; the danger being that if a tank were disabled at the crossing it would block the bridge and causeway, or a tank might break down at the critical time or place, as they had so often done before."[27] Furthermore, Lipsett proposed to divide his forces. One of Ormond's battalions was to strike along the Amiens-Roye road, distracting the defenders with a frontal assault, a diversion which Lipsett hoped would enable the other two battalions to follow the river and outflank the defences at Demuin and Hamon Wood.

The operation went, in Rawlinson's words, "like clock-work."[28] But there were some tense moments. The fog, which was especially thick near the Luce, delayed the Third Division's assembly during the early morning hours of 8 August; some units did not reach their jumping-off points until twenty minutes before zero. And the forty tanks allotted the Third Division got lost in the fog; few managed to get into action before the division took its objectives.

Luckily, the infantry needed little assistance. At zero hour, the right-hand battalion, the 43rd, smartly followed its creeping barrage for a thousand yards, where it occupied dead ground—in other words, a blind spot in the enemy's defences, where the attackers were immune to small-arms fire. The Germans were completely distracted by this threat, as General Lipsett intended, and oblivious to the left hook that would knock them out.

It was delivered by the 58th (Central Ontario) and 116th (Ontario County) battalions. The 58th, on the left, was to hug the river bank and strike toward Demuin, the capture of which would enable troops of the Eighth Brigade to cross the Luce. The battalion did its part to perfection, though isolated pockets of resistance hindered its progress at times. Corporal Harry Miner single-handedly wiped out two machine-gun nests and led an attack on a third, to help clear the way for the 58th. Corporal Miner won the vc for his heroism, but it was a posthumous award: he was fatally wounded taking the last position.

The fighting was intense at times, as Major Henry Rose could attest. The thirty-six-year-old major commanded C Company of the 58th Battalion. When his company was pinned down by machine-gun fire, Major Rose calmly collected a party of thirty men and, after a quick reconnaissance, attempted to outflank the enemy. Rose related subsequent events in a letter home:

> I led my motley platoon across the Hun zone of fire, with only two casualties, I think, and got fairly close in to the flank of the strong point without being discovered. I was not quite certain where the Hun was, so I went on ahead of my men to reconnoitre. I worked along a sunken road about 150 yards to a bit of a bank running at right angles. The patter of the machine gun seemed closer, but I thought I was yet some distance from them, so I stuck my head over this bank, and found the whole thing on the other side. I drew down very quickly of course, but not before a Hun bomber had spotted me, and then over came the cylindrical stick bombs. I dropped into a shell-hole and did some hard thinking. I only had my revolver and there were some three Hun guns and about 30 of the enemy. While I was wondering what to do a Hun bomb dropped on me and lifted me clean out of my cover.

Rose awoke in hospital a couple of days later, with multiple wounds—bullets and grenade fragments—and his only further recollection was of "myself amongst the Huns emptying my revolver as fast as I could." He lived to tell the tale only because his men rushed to his assistance, arriving in the nick of time and capturing the position at bayonet-point.[29]

In the centre of the Ninth Brigade's front, the 116th Battalion—the highest-numbered unit in the Canadian Corps, it was nicknamed the "Umpty-Umps"—was going into action for the first time since arriving in France in the spring of 1917. The Umpty-Umps were led by Lieutenant-Colonel George Pearkes, who had won the vc at Passchendaele the previous October. When one of his leading companies was decimated by German machine-gun fire, losing every officer, Colonel Pearkes took personal charge. He found the attack stalled in front of a trench, named Bade on Canadian maps, atop a hill protecting the battalion's main objective, Hamon Wood. Pearkes's practised eye quickly sized up the situation: looking for a way around, he spotted a slight dip in the ground on the right. Pearkes "took what men I could get...and we went up this hollow where we were more or less immune from enemy fire and we came in on the rest of Bade Trench from the right flank." The Germans were routed, and the 116th Battalion pressed on to Hamon Wood, which fell with surprising ease. The battalion's booty for the day included 450 prisoners, forty machine-guns, and sixteen field guns. "No battalion could have done better," Pearkes proudly remarked, "and few did as well."[30]

Much of the credit must go to Pearkes himself. He was, in the words of Private Frank Baxter, "the bravest man I ever knew." Private Baxter, who was celebrating his twentieth birthday on 8 August, served as Pearkes's runner and went over the top with him that morning.

> Several times...a burst of machine gun bullets or an artillery shell would land very close to us. I would duck my head or fall flat on the ground. I never ever saw Colonel Pearkes even jump. He would often laugh and...said not to worry about the shell that made a loud shriek but the one that landed close and you did not hear, it was the one to worry about.[31]

Pearkes spoke from experience, having been wounded in action several times.

The success of the 58th and 116th battalions broke the back of German resistance. As General Lipsett reported, Demuin and Hamon Wood had fallen "while the enemy's defences in the forward edge of the plateau were still holding out—but when outflanked and taken in reverse, their strong defences, heavily manned with machine guns, quickly ceased to resist."[32] The 43rd Battalion swept through, and by 7:30, Dodo Wood was in Canadian hands.

The second phase of the Third Division's attack began precisely according to timetable, at 8:20 A.M., when three battalions of Brigadier-General Hugh Dyer's Seventh Brigade passed through the Green Line. The 42nd Battalion, in the centre, had a short, stiff fight for Hill 102, which lay across its route to the Red Line. Enemy resistance hinged on batteries of field guns firing over open sights at the advancing Canadian infantry. A Company, under Captain H.B. Trout, came under the point-blank fire of three 8-inch howitzers; the Canadians went to ground, then by sectional rushes worked their way steadily closer to the German guns. "Reaching a point about one hundred and fifty yards short of the battery position, Captain Trout sprang up and led his wildly shouting company down the slope in a headlong charge which completely over-ran the battery, the crew of which scattered in confusion and all were killed or captured." Similarly, Captain J.B. MacLeod's B Company captured a battery of four 4.1-inch guns, by first outflanking it and then charging it from all directions. Most of the gunners surrendered, but "about twenty" were shot as they tried to flee. With Hill 102 in its hands, the 42nd reached the Red Line at 10:20 A.M.[33]

The battalions on either flank came up quickly. On the left, the 49th (Edmonton Regiment) Battalion met "only fractional resistance" en route to the Red Line, as its light casualties—sixty-one—would indicate. The Royal Canadian Regiment, on the right, had an even easier time. In suffering thirty-six casualties, "the men of the Regiment were astounded by the ease with which the advance rolled forward. There had been nothing like it in all their previous experience." Well before noon, the Seventh Brigade had consolidated its Red Line objectives.[34]

Now came the sight that no man who witnessed it would ever forget. Clattering along the roads came "the Cavalry and Royal Horse Artillery trotting and galloping into action—superb horses and beauti- fully turned-out men," as Gunner George Rennison of the 61st Battery, CFA, described in a letter home. It was, he said, "the sight that is the most inspiring in warfare," and few would have disagreed with him. According to Lieutenant Ronald Holmes of the 46th (South Saskatche- wan) Battalion, "it was indeed a sight for the gods, and one that I shan't forget as long as I live. To see such famous regiments as the Scots Greys, the Bengal Lancers, Strathconas, and Fort Garry Horse going into action at the charge, guns coming up at the gallop...was a truly wonderful sight...."[35]

It was just as thrilling for the horsemen. They belonged to the 3rd Cavalry Division, and their task was to carry the attack to the Blue Dotted Line and beyond, if possible, fulfilling an exploitation role for which they had been waiting years. Three brigades of cavalry, the 6th and 7th and Canadian, passed through the Third Division at noon.

The Canadian Cavalry Brigade, commanded by Brigadier-General R.W. Paterson, had begun moving forward at six that morning, after breakfasting on "a snort of Scotch whiskey and a dog biscuit." The Canadian cavalrymen were accompanied by two companies of Whip- pet tanks, thirty-two in all. This was an experiment in mobile warfare: the Whippet, formally known as the Medium Mark A, would, it was hoped, give the cavalry the ability to overcome enemy machine-guns, which had on previous occasions proved more than a match for them. The experiment, however, was a failure. Despite its name, the Whippet was no greyhound. It could manage an impressive road speed of 8.3 miles per hour, but barely half that while travelling cross-country. As Major Roy Nordheimer of the Royal Canadian Dragoons recalled, the cavalry quickly left the tanks far behind. "They...could not keep pace with the horses...."[36]

So the cavalry gamely tried to go it alone. In the process, they demonstrated that soldiers on horseback had become obsolete. Against a machine-gun, infantrymen can go to ground, but a horse cannot;

despite its speed and manoeuvrability, the animal was too big a target to miss. The Royal Canadian Dragoons discovered all of these disadvantages during their attack on Beaucourt-en-Santerre, a heavily defended village. "Even now I cannot listen outside a room full of typists," recalled one dragoon, "without thinking of machine gun barrages." The Dragoons assembled in dead ground a thousand yards from Beaucourt. Sweating under the hot sun, which glinted off lances and sabres, the khaki-clad cavalrymen awaited the signal to charge with nervous excitement. Then came the command, and the men urged their mounts to the gallop. Pennons fluttering, the regiment rode across a rise and into "a regular storm of fire," in the words of Major Nordheimer.

> The squadron was riding hell bent for election for Beaucourt, with swords drawn and yelling like mad. Lieutenant Steve ("Bramwell") Booth, who...was riding alongside of me...gave a grunt and fell dead off his horse.... We were losing heavily on that ride. A horse is a good target and the [machine-]gunners had a field day, for 130 odd men and horses are a great temptation.

Nordheimer estimated that "only about 50 all ranks" of his squadron survived that wild ride—almost every horse was killed. Dismounted, the dragoons engaged Beaucourt's defenders with revolvers and rifles, and waited for the infantry to arrive.[37]

However, the village was captured by another cavalry unit. The Fort Garry Horse mounted a flank attack and seized Beaucourt, also capturing a regimental headquarters, twenty-five prisoners, and a machine-gun. Another squadron of this regiment then helped the Royal Canadian Dragoons repulse a pair of counter-attacks from the north. Late in the afternoon, having fallen far short of the Blue Dotted Line, the Canadian cavalrymen were relieved by infantry from the Fourth Division.

It had been a disappointing day for the Canadian cavalry, but their British counterparts had done slightly better. The 7th Cavalry Brigade took Cayeux Wood, which in turn enabled the 6th Cavalry Brigade on the left to sweep through and assist Canadian infantry in reaching the Blue Dotted Line. In addition, small numbers of British horsemen rode to the final objective on the fronts of both the First and Second Canadian divisions. The 10th Battalion's Colonel MacDonald considered that "they were of very great use" in covering the exposed flanks of his unit.[38]

The Fourth Division went into action in the early afternoon. "What a memorable day this is," exulted the divisional commander, General Watson.[39] Passing through the Third Division at 12:40 P.M. the

Fourth attacked with two brigades, Brigadier-General Victor Odlum's Eleventh on the right and the Twelfth, under Brigadier-General James MacBrien, on the left. Both brigades fought on a two-battalion front, and they quickly caught up to the dismounted Canadian cavalry ahead of them.

General MacBrien's brigade had an easier time. The 38th (Ottawa) and 85th (Nova Scotia Highlanders) battalions reached the Blue Dotted Line shortly after six in the evening, "with little or no opposition," according to General Watson.[40] But MacBrien's remaining two battalions, the 72nd (Seaforth Highlanders of Canada) and 78th (Winnipeg Grenadiers), had problems when they came under heavy fire, first from a wood east of Beaucourt-en-Santerre, where the Eleventh Brigade was engaged in a bitter, bloody battle, and then from the village of Le Quesnel, further east, where the Germans were making a determined stand, rushing reserve troops and machine-guns into the fight. The 72nd Battalion—inspired by its tough commander, Lieutenant-Colonel John Clark, who personally led a platoon that wiped out a pair of enemy machine-gun nests—reached the Blue Dotted Line on a portion of its front before nightfall, but was forced to form a defensive flank on the right, with the 78th Battalion, in order to maintain touch with General Odlum's troops.

The Eleventh Brigade failed to reach the Blue Dotted Line. As soon as it leap-frogged the Third Division, the brigade had been plunged into a furious fight. The 54th (Central Ontario) and 102nd (Central Ontario) battalions attacked the woods east of Beaucourt, where beleaguered cavalrymen were engaged in an unequal shoot-out with the defenders. Three Mark v tanks arrived, but all were knocked out before they could influence the outcome of the battle. Lieutenant-Colonel A.B. Carey, the officer commanding the 54th, took matters into his own hands, rounding up a pair of platoons and leading them in a frontal assault on the wood, without artillery or machine-gun support. Casualties were heavy, but Colonel Carey's party at least gained a toehold in the trees. The diversion also enabled the 102nd Battalion to join the attack. After hard fighting, the Canadians cleared the wood by 4:30 in the afternoon. Besides capturing 159 prisoners, the 102nd included among its trophies "a well-appointed German camp" in which "all sorts of supplies were in evidence, beer, food, including good cake, and a German Field Ambulance full of their wounded and well stocked with hospital supplies."[41]

But the Eleventh Brigade could go no further. Ahead stood Le Quesnel, where machine-guns and field guns had already inflicted such heavy punishment on the neighbouring Twelfth Brigade. The enemy had excellent fields of fire, over ground that was comparatively flat and devoid of cover. The defenders were determined, too. A single German battery firing over open sights knocked out nine tanks that tried to take the village. Moreover, the Eleventh Brigade was under severe fire from the right, where the French were lagging far behind. With the onset of darkness, General Odlum instructed his men to dig in for the night. This was the only place on the Canadian Corps front where the Blue Dotted Line had not been reached, but the Fourth Division would make amends in the morning.[42]

As elsewhere, the tanks had had little impact on the fighting. Nevertheless, the Fourth Division had taken part in an interesting experiment. It was a precursor to modern armoured personnel carriers: specially designed tanks—the Mark v Star, an elongated version of the Mark v—with room for infantry and machine-gun detachments. The theory was that the tanks would be able to transport these troops with impunity through the heaviest fire; they could disembark and engage the enemy at close quarters. Like so much else involving the tanks, the results were less than gratifying. Thirty-four were attached to the Fourth Division on 8 August; only six reached the Blue Dotted Line. "The Infantry detachments in these Tanks suffered severely," commented General Watson afterwards. "Unaccustomed to the heat and fumes, the men became sick; some of them fainting. Detachments of 16 Tanks were obliged to seek the fresh air and follow the Infantry on foot." Watson recommended "that Tanks should not in future be employed this way," suggesting that the extra space in the Mark v Star could be better used "for carrying petrol tins, so that, in the case of a long advance, the Tanks could stop and refill halfway up."[43]

The part played by the tanks at Amiens was not, on the whole, satisfactory. There were, of course, isolated instances where they had performed usefully and spared the infantry some casualties. But the footsloggers did not have much confidence in these mechanical monsters because, as Brigadier-General Dan Ormond later pointed out, "they were so easily stalled, and they were so slow, and they drew fire." The 20th Battalion's historian concluded that "they were of little real assistance" to that unit at Amiens. Initially blinded by the fog, most tanks "didn't catch up until late in the morning," noted Lieutenant-Colonel G. Chalmers Johnston of the 2nd Canadian Mounted Rifles; when they did arrive, they were usually put out of action within minutes.[44]

The tank of this era was too primitive to be decisive on the battlefield. As John Terraine perceptively points out, "it was most effective for breaking *into* the enemy's front. What the technology of 1918 did not permit, however, was the exploitation of a *breakthrough*." In other words, "the tank of 1918 was not a war-winning weapon."[45]

Yet, the myth of Amiens as a great tank victory persists. This is due, in part, to the German desire to explain their crushing defeat.* Many military historians perpetuate the falsehood by describing Amiens as a "massed tank assault." It is true that the British committed an unprecedented number of tanks—414 Mark vs and Whippets, plus 120 older model Mark ivs used as armoured supply vehicles, another experiment that yielded dismal results—but they were spread along a thirteen-mile front. Amiens did reveal the awesome potential of the tank, but its limitations were never more evident. Too slow, hot, and noisy, they were mechanically unreliable and had a very short range: "their tracks lasted only 20 miles." Some statistics tell the stark truth. Out of 414 combat tanks that went into action on 8 August, only 145 were still available for use the following day; by the twelfth the number had dwindled to a mere *six*. As John Terraine observes, "The German empire was not going to be overthrown by six tanks." Many were, of course, salvaged and used again. But losses among the Mark vs were so extensive that the obsolete Mark ivs, which were not bulletproof, had to be pressed into service in later British attacks. Indeed, it can be argued that Amiens was a tragic misuse of tanks, because the gently rolling ground, far from being ideal tank country, merely made these slow-moving vehicles wonderful targets for German gunners. As will become apparent in succeeding chapters, it would have been better to conserve the tanks for use against the established and more elaborate defences of the Hindenburg Line.[47]

By the same token, it has become a popular pastime among historians to ridicule the British high command, and in particular the commander-in-chief, Sir Douglas Haig, for continuing to employ cavalry at this late date, when it had become—or, at the very least, should have been—clear that cavalry was an anachronism on the modern battlefield. Such criticism does not hold up to close scrutiny. Even in the second half of 1918, cavalry remained the only arm with the speed and mobility to exploit success by the infantry. Tanks and armoured cars of this vintage were simply too slow and vulnerable to fulfil the cavalry's role. The horse soldiers filled the technological gap, albeit inadequately, and Haig would have been irresponsible to plan battles without making provision for the exploitation of success.

If the tanks were not responsible for the victory at Amiens, who or what was? The answer is provided by the Canadian official history, which correctly states that "the operation owed its success principally

---

* Field-Marshal Hindenburg, for example, attributed defeat to the weakness of the German defences as well as to the tanks, "which were faster than hitherto." A puzzled Kaiser Wilhelm contributed to the fallacy, commenting, "It's very strange that our men cannot get used to tanks." Numerous regimental histories, such as that of the 119th Infantry Regiment, blamed their rout on "the fire-vomiting iron dragons."[46]

to the work of the infantry and the machine-gunners, valuably supported by the artillery...."[48] These were, significantly, the same services which had carried the burden to this point in the war and which would continue to do so until its completion.

As darkness descended over the Amiens battlefield, the Canadians had cause to be jubilant. It was obvious even to the lowest ranks that the day had been a dazzling success. "Everybody was in the most jovial mood," recalled a gunner, Elmore Philpott. "The troops," recalled Lieutenant R.S. Robertson of the 16th Battalion, "were just like dogs on a leash, as it were. Everybody was keen to go, realizing the magnitude of the advance." Added the 4th Battalion's W.H. Joliffe: "For the first time we felt that we were winning the war."[49]

The Canadian Corps had done a fine day's work. "The surprise had been complete and overwhelming," commented General Currie, with justifiable pride. The Canadians had, in the span of a few hours, driven an unheard-of eight miles into German-held territory; nothing like it had ever been achieved by Allied forces. And the cost had been, happily, light. Total Canadian casualties on 8 August numbered 3868, including 1036 killed. At the same time, they had captured 5033 prisoners* and 161 guns, many of which had been turned on the enemy by specially trained crews known as "Pan-Germanic" batteries.[51]

And they had completedly crushed the forces facing them. According to the German official monograph, only fragments of the front-line formations were left by nightfall on 8 August. Of the 225th Division, which was attacked by the Third Canadian Division, "practically nothing was left of its forward battalions"; its "entire artillery position was lost." The First Canadian Division took on the 117th Division, rated by Allied intelligence as "one of the freshest and most battleworthy divisions of the German Army." The 117th suffered "extraordinarily high losses," including the entire staffs of two of its three infantry regiments; by day's end, it had "nearly quite shrunk to nothing, barely any infantry left." A similar fate befell the 41st Division, which faced both the Second Canadian and 5th Australian divisions on either side of the Amiens-Chaulnes railway. Only "trifling remnants" of the 41st escaped; its artillery component was reduced to a mere three guns.[52]

---

* Large numbers of captives were put to work en route to the rear. "There were hundreds & hundreds of prisoners helping to carry the wounded," remarked one Canadian stretcher-bearer in a letter home. In his opinion, "they surely were a great help to us." Observed a Canadian medical historian: "The German prisoner-of-war is possibly the best stretcher bearer in the world. By his dogged perseverance he will keep going without a whimper for many miles." So efficiently did they clear the Canadian Corps front that, at one point, "the forward area was in danger of running short of stretchers."[50]

Only the Australians were able to keep pace with the Canadians. General Monash, commanding the Australian Corps, had had a good feeling about this operation, predicting just before zero hour that this would be "a very wonderful day for Australia." He was certainly correct. "The advance," states the Australian official history, "was the most bloodless ever made by Australian troops in a great battle...." The Australian Corps plunged seven miles into the German defences in the face of negligible opposition, which was reflected in their modest casualties of approximately 2000—or, about half the number suffered by the Canadians. The Australians captured 7925 prisoners and 175 guns during the day, as well.[53]

However, it was a much different story on either flank. On the Fourth Army's left, Lieutenant-General Sir Richard Butler's III Corps managed only a three-mile advance north of the River Somme. There were, to be sure, extenuating circumstances. The corps had been roughly handled by the Germans in a surprise attack on 6 August and had spent much of the following day trying, unsuccessfully, to regain the lost ground. The troops were not only very tired, they were also young and inexperienced—a problem of some concern throughout the British army, a consequence of the heavy losses incurred during the German offensives in the first half of 1918. Moreover, the ground in III Corps' sector was heavily wooded and, therefore, not suitable for tanks. Regardless of the reasons, the slow British advance had considerable ramifications for the Australians, who were severely enfiladed by German batteries north of the Somme.

The French First Army, on the Canadian right, did somewhat better, gaining five miles on 8 August. But their progress had been made possible primarily by the spectacular success of the Canadian Corps. Indeed, the Canadians had repeatedly helped them overcome obstacles in their path. General Brutinel's Canadian Independent Force materially assisted in the capture of Mézières, a mile southeast of Beaucourt-en-Santerre. Later, Canadian cavalry—a party of Lord Strathcona's Horse—crossed the Amiens-Roye road and took the fortified village of Fresnoy-en-Chausée, holding it until relieved by French troops.

Certainly Sir Douglas Haig was not impressed with the French performance. In the late morning, the British commander-in-chief had urged General Debeney, commanding the French First Army, to commit his cavalry as soon as possible in order to exploit the apparent success. Debeney responded with "many reasons why his cavalry could not get through earlier than to-morrow forenoon at the soonest," wrote a surprised and disgusted Haig. "First, his cavalry was not near enough, and secondly, the French infantry covered all the roads."[54]

But he was understandably happy with his own troops. As he

commented in his diary, "the situation had developed more favourably for us than I, optimist that I am, had dared to hope."[55]

General Rawlinson was equally pleased. Although his Fourth Army had suffered about 8800 casualties on 8 August, the day's bag of prisoners was almost double that figure. Rawlinson attributed victory to "the magnificent work" of the Canadians and Australians, suggesting that "the spirit of the Colonial infantry was probably the decisive factor. I am very proud to have commanded so magnificent an army in this historic battle. The results of this victory should have a far-reaching effect on the Boche morale."[56]

German morale had, indeed, been dealt a blow. Nowhere was this more evident than in the remarks of Germany's quartermaster-general, Erich Ludendorff, who was the de facto commander-in-chief on the Western Front. "August 8 was the black day of the German Army in the history of the war," he declared. "This was the worst experience that I had to go through...." The German official monograph confirms his bleak view:

> As the sun set on August 8th on the battlefield the greatest defeat which the German Army had suffered since the beginning of the war was an accomplished fact. The position divisions between the Avre and the Somme which had been struck by the enemy attack were nearly completely annihilated.... The total loss of the formations employed in the Second Army area is estimated at 650 to 700 officers and 26,000 to 27,000 other ranks. More than 400 guns, besides a large number of machine guns, trench mortars, and other war material had been lost.[57]

Even more telling were the remarks of Kaiser Wilhelm. When informed of the magnitude of the débâcle at Amiens, he was plunged into depression. Later, he privately told General Ludendorff that, in his opinion, "the war could no longer be won."[58]

5 WASTED OPPORTUNITIES

There could be no question about the next step. Field-Marshal Haig visited General Rawlinson at Fourth Army headquarters on the afternoon of 8 August, and reviewed the day's operation. "I told Rawlinson to continue to work on the orders which I had already given," Haig wrote in his diary. The Australian and III corps were to secure the Fourth Army's left flank on the Somme, while the main thrust was to be made by the Canadian Corps "to line Chaulnes-Roye." Rawlinson's orders reflected Haig's wishes.[1]

Surprisingly, the two dominion corps commanders detected no such decisive thinking. General Currie's impression was that his British superiors were actually at a loss:

> The success of the Australians and Canadians was so startling that in my opinion GHQ had no definite ideas what to do.... Senior staff officers hurried up from GHQ to see me and ask what I thought should be done. They indicated quite plainly that the success had gone far beyond expectations and that no one seemed to know just what to do. I replied in the Canadian vernacular: "The going seems good: let's go on!"

General Monash concurred, bluntly believing that Haig "appeared to blunder badly, and be out of touch with the details of the situation, when he came to discuss with me how best to exploit the great victory of August 8th...." The only conclusion that can be drawn from these stories is that they illustrate the degree to which even corps commanders were sometimes left out of the picture.[2]

One thing was certain. Whatever happened on 9 August, it could not be as successful as the eighth. The Germans recovered admirably from their initial shock, and had rushed in substantial numbers of reserves from all over the Western Front. Field-Marshal Hindenburg later suggested that the British blew an unprecedented opportunity to break the German front wide open, contending that he did not have "any troops worth mentioning,"[3] with which to block a further advance. The statement is ludicrous. While the front-line divisions had been wrecked, there were plenty of reserve formations at hand. On 8 August alone, the Germans moved six divisions into the battle zone, and more were on the way. Not only would the Allies have to deal with fresh enemy forces, there could be no possibility of surprise in subsequent attacks here.

The Canadian Corps planned an early start on 9 August. General Currie, at his advanced headquarters at Gentelles, had already scheduled 5 A.M. as zero hour. Unfortunately, the staff at the Fourth Army disrupted his plans—quite possibly contributing to his belief that these British officers did not know what they were doing. Late in the afternoon on the eighth, General Rawlinson arrived at Gentelles to congratulate Currie on the Canadian success; in Currie's absence—he was making the rounds of his divisions—Rawlinson discussed the next day's operations with the senior staff officer, Brigadier-General N.W. "Ox" Webber, a British career soldier with excellent credentials. In the course of their conversation, Webber asked for the British 32nd Division, which had earlier been allotted to the Canadian Corps as a reserve. "Rawly agreed," Webber wrote, "& plans were drafted accordingly." Currie returned soon after Rawlinson's departure, and the Corps plans were finalized: zero hour would be 5 A.M., with the First, Second, and Fourth divisions attacking, and the 32nd Division passing through to continue the offensive in the direction of Roye. Leaving Webber to issue the necessary orders, Currie departed for Corps headquarters at Dury, eight miles away.[4]

Then came the Fourth Army's change of mind. "The necessary orders were on the point of being sent out," recalled Webber, when a message arrived from Rawlinson's chief of staff, General Montgomery, ordering Webber to report to Dury, where the nearest telephones were located, for an urgent discussion. It took Webber two hours to work his way to the rear over roads blocked by interminable lines of troops, trucks, tanks, and prisoners, "& I didn't reach Dury & the telephone till about 8:30 P.M." Montgomery had bad news: the 32nd Division would not be available to the Canadians after all. He explained to Webber that it was far too early in the battle to commit reserves, and he was, in Webber's words, "very irate with Army Cmdr for daring to give away 32nd Div & with myself for aiding and abetting."[5]

This was no minor matter. It was already nearing nine o'clock in the evening, and the next day's orders had to be redrafted and dispatched to the divisional headquarters, which would in turn pass them along to brigades and battalions. Consequently, it was "impossible to keep to [the] 5 A.M. start," said Webber.[6] This was only one of several delays that would plague the Canadians on 9 August.

General Currie's annoyance was clearly reflected in his revised instructions. The Fourth Army had designated objectives up to nine miles away; Currie, realizing that it was an unreasonable demand to make of tired troops, arbitrarily halved the projected advance. Zero hour was set for 10 A.M.—broad daylight—with one exception. The

Fourth Division, which still had to complete the conquest of its previous day's objectives, was to attack at 4:30 A.M. and consolidate the Blue Dotted Line.[7]

The day started auspiciously. The Fourth Division attacked precisely on schedule, led by two battalions of the Eleventh Brigade. The 75th (Mississauga) Battalion had the tough task of taking Le Quesnel and the woods beyond. The resistance was fierce; despite a superb artillery barrage, the Mississauga battalion reeled in the face of furious machine-gun fire, and for several long minutes it appeared that failure was certain. But a brave and desperate bayonet charge turned the tide, and Le Quesnel fell following a short, sharp fight. Among the 75th Battalion's booty was a complete divisional headquarters. But there was no time to relish the victory. After hastily reorganizing, the 75th forged ahead, its flank protected by the 87th (Canadian Grenadier Guards) Battalion. Using bayonets and bombs, the two battalions slowly but surely cleared the German trenches east of Le Quesnel. By eleven that morning, the Fourth Division could report that it was securely on the Blue Dotted Line across its front.

However, it was about the only thing that went according to schedule on the ninth. The Canadian difficulties were, furthermore, symptomatic of those encountered by the rest of the Fourth Army's formations. As the Australian official history wrily remarks, these "operations will probably furnish a classic example of how not to follow up a great attack." The Australians were instructed to co-ordinate their actions with the Canadian Corps, which had now become, as General Currie proudly pointed out, "the spearhead of the attack." But co-ordination in these conditions was extremely difficult, and the reason was primarily technological. Communications were rather primitive—wireless, for example, was still in its infancy—and the rapidity of the Australian-Canadian advance presented major problems in the maintenance of communication links, to the rear as well as on either flank. The transmission of orders was, therefore, a major undertaking.[8]

The Fourth Army's staff complicated things still further by leaving the job of co-ordination to the various corps. One major purpose of an army headquarters is to do precisely that, co-ordinate subordinate units. While an army has the manpower and means to do so, a corps does not. Thus, the Fourth Army committed a grave error by abdicating its responsibility on 9 August. "Our attacks on August 9th were disjointed," admitted General Montgomery, whose interference had had unfortunate consequences for the Canadians. "The real reason was that the Canadian Corps was allowed to fix the zero hour whereas it ought really to have been fixed by Army Headquarters." It was, observes P.A. Pedersen, an unsympathetic Australian historian, "an elementary blunder."[9]

Montgomery's meddling had far-reaching effects on Canadian operations. Besides forcing a later zero, and making the troops attack in broad daylight instead of semi-darkness, the Canadians were forced to juggle their front-line formations to compensate for the absence of the 32nd Division. Since the tired Third Canadian Division had to be employed again, General Currie agreed to narrow its frontage when it passed through the Fourth Division along the Blue Dotted Line; this concession meant, however, that both the First and Second divisions had to side-step units to widen their respective fronts. These movements took time and were, at one point, disrupted by a heavy German bombardment. As a result, zero hour had to be postponed until 11 A.M., but this was still too early for most formations. Only one brigade jumped off at eleven; most of the others did not get started until after one o'clock in the afternoon. The piecemeal attacks were bad enough, but most were made with barely adequate artillery support. The gunners were often not informed of the repeated postponements by the various brigades, and fired their barrages prematurely; when the attacks were eventually launched, the guns were short of ammunition.[10]

The Sixth Brigade—nicknamed the "Iron Sixth"—led off on the left. Brigadier-General Arthur Bell employed two battalions, the 29th (Vancouver) and 31st (Alberta), in his attack on Rosières-en-Santerre. It was a difficult assignment. The village lay a thousand yards from the Canadian lines, ground that was devoid of cover and offered excellent sight lines for enemy machine-gunners. It was clear to at least one young Canadian officer that this attack, in daylight, would result in terrible losses. As he surveyed the scene, Lieutenant G.A. Cunliffe, commanding D Company of the 31st Battalion, asked a scout: "How far is it to the village?"

"One thousand yards, sir."

"One thousand deaths," muttered Lieutenant Cunliffe, who would be one of the first Canadians killed this day, hit in the head by a bullet moments after going over the top.[11]

Rosières fell to the 31st Battalion, but it was a grim fight. The battalion attacked at 11 A.M., behind a barrage that was described by the regimental historian as "comparatively feeble" and "damn poor" by one of the participants, Louis Llewellyn Lent. "Terrible" was the way Private Lent characterized the enemy's machine-gun fire: a platoon of C Company, in the centre of the 31st's attack, was practically wiped out. As the casualties mounted, Lieutenant W.M. Harris collected a handful of C Company soldiers and led them close enough to the village to give them a chance to fight back; with rifle grenades and small-arms fire, they knocked out three machine-guns. Then the tanks arrived. Five had been

63

allocated to the Sixth Brigade, and three were disabled within moments. Following one of the surviving Mark vs, D Company burst into the village, where a bloody door-to-door battle ensued. By four-thirty that afternoon, Rosières was in Canadian hands. "Feeling very tired & hungry, nothing to eat all day," Private Lent wrote in his diary that night, huddled in a shell hole, "but it was the greatest day I ever saw."[12]

At least the Germans were confused, too. Even as the desperate fighting was under way in Rosières, which was an important railhead, a trainload of German reinforcements pulled into the village, right in the midst of the Canadians. Twenty-seven officers and 500 other ranks were taken prisoner as they stepped off the train. Half an hour later, a German ambulance train arrived; it, too, was taken intact.

The confusion spread to the Australians on the other side of the Amiens-Chaulnes railway. On the immediate left of the Iron Sixth was the 15th Australian Brigade, under Brigadier-General H.E. Elliott. The 15th was not scheduled for offensive operations this day; it was merely holding the line, awaiting the arrival of the fresh 1st Australian Division, which was supposed to cover the Canadian flank. But the 1st Division was nowhere in sight when General Elliott was informed by General Bell that the Sixth Brigade intended to attack at 11 A.M. Elliott promptly sought, and received, permission to attack; as the Australian official history notes, "it was unthinkable that the Canadians should be let down." And the Australians paid dearly for their "unselfish spirit," as the Second Canadian Division's General Burstall put it. The two Australian battalions, the 58th and 60th, went over the top ten minutes after the Canadians, with neither tanks nor artillery support, in the face of murderous machine-gun fire. They were soon pinned down, until the Canadians came to their rescue. One of the two remaining tanks of the Sixth Brigade crossed the rail line, and parties of infantry from the 29th Battalion were able to outflank some machine-gun posts and take them from the rear, enabling the Australians to advance.[13]

It was a bad day for the Australians, and even worse confusion existed on *their* left. North of the Somme, General Butler's III Corps was scheduled to attack at 8 A.M. and take its objectives from the previous day. The attack was not launched until 5:30 P.M., and it came nowhere close to success. Once again, the Australians were exposed to gruesome enfilade fire on their left.

The piecemeal attacks continued across the Canadian Corps front. Considering the lack of co-ordination, they were surprisingly successful. On the right of the Iron Sixth, south of the River Luce, the Fifth Brigade opened its attack at 11:45 A.M. Led by the 22nd (French Canadian) Battalion, the assault swept through the village of Vrély, just south of Rosières, all the way into Méharicourt, to the southeast. Major

Georges Vanier, a future governor-general of Canada, related his story in a letter home:

> The Huns were no match for our men who charged M.G.s with perfect coolness as if they were on the parade ground. Their indifference before death was little short of sublime.... I have seen some of my comrades fall beside me and I have had so many narrow escapes myself that I am beginning to think that one should not worry much about possible eventualities.[14]

Major Vanier, whose luck would run out soon enough, ended the day in command of the 22nd Battalion. Its commanding officer, Lieutenant-Colonel T.L. Tremblay, had to assume command of the brigade, after Brigadier-General James Ross was wounded by a German shell that scored a direct hit on his headquarters dugout.

There was no lack of heroism among the French Canadians, and one of them would win the VC. Lieutenant Jean Brillant had already distinguished himself the day before, when he rushed and captured a machine-gun nest. Though wounded, he remained in action, and in the attack on Vrély he led two platoons in an assault that netted fifteen machine-guns and 150 prisoners. Wounded once again, Lieutenant Brillant stubbornly refused to be evacuated. Instead, he led his men in an attack on a German field gun that was firing over open sights. The gun was captured, but Brillant was wounded for a third time, and it was mortal. His VC was, of course, posthumous. Jean Brillant Avenue in Montreal today commemorates this man's bravery.

Farther south still, the First Division attacked with two brigades, the Second on the left and First on the right. These units had had to carry out a complicated side-step during the morning, when they were heavily bombarded by the Germans. Both brigades attacked when they were ready, the Second at 1 P.M., the First fifteen minutes later. Neither had any appreciable artillery support.

The Second Brigade had to cross "flat country with growing crops, which gave the enemy excellent opportunities for destructive machine gun fire over the whole area." That the brigade still succeeded was due in no small part to three VC-winning performances. One was later awarded to a Manitoba farmer, Sergeant Raphael Zengel, a member of the 5th (Western Cavalry) Battalion. Sergeant Zengel single-handedly stormed a series of machine-gun posts whose fire caused heavy casualties. Thanks to Zengel's brave acts, the 5th Battalion reached Warvillers, which fell "without any very great resistance," and pressed as far as the road between Méharicourt and Rouvroy-en-Santerre, in the process taking a trench defended by half a dozen machine-guns which "did a considerable amount of execution," according to the acting battalion commander, Major E. Day. By nightfall, the 5th was digging in along the Méharicourt-Rouvroy road.[15]

The neighbouring 8th (90th Winnipeg Rifles) won a pair of VCs this day. The battalion ran into a German strongpoint at Hatchet Wood, and Frederick Coppins, a twenty-eight-year-old corporal, led four of his men in a wild and impromptu bayonet charge. The four privates were killed and Corporal Coppins was wounded, but he managed to bayonet four enemy machine-gunners and capture four others. The 8th Battalion resumed its advance, but without Coppins, who had to be ordered to the rear for treatment of his serious wounds.

The battalion also lost its commanding officer. Soon after the capture of Hatchet Wood, Lieutenant-Colonel Tom Raddall was fatally wounded by machine-gun fire. His dying words: "Tell Bug I'm hit and take over command."[16] "Bug" was the nickname of Raddall's second-in-command, Major A.L. Saunders.

More difficulties awaited the battalion. Striking north of Warvillers, the troops were pinned down by a series of six machine-gun posts. Movement was nearly impossible in the hail of bullets, and casualties mounted steadily as the Canadians scrambled to find what little cover was available. At that moment, twenty-four-year-old Corporal Alexander Brereton took matters into his own hands. He charged the nearest nest, shooting one German and bayonetting another; the rest of the crew surrendered. Inspired by his actions, Brereton's platoon cheered and charged the other posts, wiping out every one of them. Its last obstacle removed, the 8th soon reached the Méharicourt-Rouvroy road alongside the 5th. Corporals Coppins and Brereton were later awarded VCs for their efforts on 9 August.

But the 8th paid a dear price for success. Its casualties amounted to a staggering fifteen officers and 420 other ranks.[17]

The First Brigade, meanwhile, was having a somewhat easier time of it. Attacking with two battalions, the 1st (Western Ontario) and 2nd (Eastern Ontario), the brigade quickly took its initial objective, the village of Beaufort. Advancing in open formation, these Canadians repeatedly flushed the German defenders from isolated trenches and machine-gun nests, when the Canadians' Lewis guns dealt with them. On the right, the 1st Battalion was forced to detach a party of troops to take Folies, which lay in the Third Division's sector; with the later start by the Eighth Brigade, the village's defenders were able to direct devastating fire onto the First Brigade's exposed flank. The 4th (Central Ontario) Battalion then leap-frogged the 1st and 2nd and carried the attack into the streets of Rouvroy-en-Santerre. Resistance was unexpectedly heavy here, and even with assistance from the 2nd Battalion, the 4th could do no more than get a foothold in the village. Determined to dislodge the Germans, Brigadier-General William Griesbach ordered a final attack in the early evening, to be carried out by his reserve unit, the 3rd (Toronto Regiment) Battalion.

The assault capped what was otherwise a pleasant day for the 3rd Battalion. Passing through the ruins of Beaufort, an enemy canteen was discovered, stocked with cognac and considerable quantities of "rank, evil-smelling German cigars." The cognac was, of course, confiscated immediately, but the cigars were freely distributed as the battalion resumed its march to the front lines. Arriving in the battle zone at seven forty-five that night, the battalion quickly deployed and attacked. Rouvroy fell easily, indicating that the Germans had decided to abandon it anyway. Taking twenty prisoners, a field gun, and four machine-guns, the 3rd Battalion fanned out on the high ground behind Rouvroy and dug in for the night. After dark, the battalion added to its bag of prisoners when several enemy water and ration parties, mostly unarmed, wandered into the Canadian lines.[18]

The day's final action came on the Canadian right. Here, the Eighth Brigade finally jumped off shortly after two o'clock, led by the 4th Canadian Mounted Rifles (CMR). The 4th CMR made swift progress, moving quickly onto the flank of the 4th Battalion on the Rouvroy-Bouchoir road. Its casualties were light, but one death was particularly painful. Captain W.H. Davis, the padre, was killed in action, costing the 4th CMR one of its most popular figures. Captain Davis had won the Military Medal at Passchendaele the previous October, for arranging an informal cease-fire during the battle, in order to sort out the wounded on both sides.

The 5th Canadian Mounted Rifles had more trouble. Going over the top fifty minutes after the 4th CMR, the 5th CMR suffered heavy losses due to machine-gun fire across the Amiens-Roye road. Ignoring its exposed flank, the 5th CMR fought its way into Bouchoir by five in the afternoon. Shortly afterwards, the battalion received a report that the Germans were evacuating Arvillers, in the French zone; a party of the 5th CMR crossed the road and occupied the village, holding it until relieved by French troops that night.

The Canadian Corps could take considerable satisfaction from its performance on 9 August. Despite the many difficulties, the Canadians had prevailed over the enemy, in large part due to their skilful tactics and high standard of training. "Our troops," commented the Third Division's General Lipsett, "had been thoroughly practised in attacking strong points and machine gun nests earlier in the Summer, and the value of their training was exemplified in these operations." Casualties totalled 2574, a smaller figure than the previous day's, when surprise and fog had been such significant factors.* The Corps had advanced another four miles along its front, continuing to set the pace both for the Fourth Army and the French First Army. And it had been done despite the fact that, as General Currie pointed out, "the enemy's resistance stiffened considerably." †[20]

But it had been, as the British official history states, "a day of wasted opportunities." There had been no exploitation of the shattered German front; impressive as a four-mile advance might have been, there was nothing remarkable about this straight-ahead push. Again, only the Australians had been able to keep up with the Canadians. North of the Somme III Corps still struggled, and the French army's performance was still causing concern, not only for Field-Marshal Haig, but for the supreme commander, General Foch, as well. Foch had exhorted the First Army's commander, General Debeney, to "*move fast*, march hard, manoeuvre to the front, *support firmly from the rear* with all the troops you have until the desired *results have been achieved.*"[22] Still the French lagged far behind the Canadians; it was not until the night of 9-10 August that the French XXXI Corps caught up on the Canadian right flank.

It was also disturbingly clear that more spectacular successes would be impossible. The Amiens battle had fallen into a familiar pattern: a successful attack that held promise of open warfare, only to revert to static fighting involving trenches and barbed wire. Certainly there were no illusions at Canadian Corps headquarters as night fell on 9 August. "This advance," General Currie later wrote, "had brought our troops into the area of the trenches and defences occupied prior to

---

* One black mark marred the Canadian record to date. Due to the demands for secrecy, no casualty clearing stations had been located in the immediate rear of the Corps prior to the offensive. This resulted, as General Currie discovered to his discomfiture, in many wounded Canadians suffering fearfully while awaiting treatment at the Fourth Army's overworked medical facilities. Currie visited one casualty clearing station on 8 August, and when he returned on the ninth he recognized many of the faces he had seen earlier, still waiting for attention. It was, he recalled, "a scene of horror that I can never forget," with "ambulance after ambulance full of wounded men, some shrieking, some groaning, some dying, some dead, some just suffering in patience...."[19] Although five Canadian casualty clearing stations were in operation by 12 August, a Fourth Army court of inquiry later ruled that medical measures had been neglected for good cause. However, Currie had learned a lesson: never again did he allow medical needs to be sacrificed to military expediency.

† Since late on the eighth, the Germans had reinforced the front opposite the Canadians with five fresh divisions: the 1st Reserve, 119th, 79th Reserve, 221st, and 82nd Reserve. Four more would arrive subsequently, including the deceptively named Alpine Corps, which was rated by Canadian intelligence as "one of the freshest Divisions of the German Army."[21]

the Somme operations in 1916.* These trenches, while not in a good state of repair, were, nevertheless, protected by a considerable amount of wire, and lent themselves readily to a very stubborn machine gun defence."[23]

Currie lowered his sights accordingly. For 10 August, he proposed a strictly limited attack to clear the maze of trenches ahead. Withdrawing the First and Second divisions into Corps reserve, Currie intended to resume the offensive on Saturday morning with the Fourth Division holding the Corps left and Third Division on the right. The Third's role was restricted to a pre-dawn preliminary attack on the village of Le Quesnoy-en-Santerre. That completed, the long-awaited British 32nd Division would pass through and strike for Parvillers and Damery.

The Third Division carried out its part with stunning efficiency. General Lipsett employed two battalions, the 1st and 2nd Canadian Mounted Rifles, in a surprise attack. Going over the top at 4:30 A.M., the 2nd CMR stormed Le Quesnoy and within two hours had evicted the defenders. The 1st CMR then followed through and, veering to the left, cleared the former British trenches north of the village. Its assignment concluded, the Third Division withdrew for a well-earned rest, as Major-General T.S. Lambert's 32nd Division went into action at nine-thirty and continued the offensive.

The British division was soon in trouble. After making initial progress, taking Bois-en-Equerre, it became apparent that the Germans were determined to stand and fight. The 32nd's main drive on Parvillers and Damery stalled well short of the objectives, and the British were soon subjected to a series of violent counter-attacks. General Lambert ordered his troops to dig in, and advised Canadian Corps headquarters that a further advance on this front would be impossible without appropriate preparation by the heavy artillery.

Much better was the performance of the Fourth Canadian Division, which managed average gains of two miles in the face of often fanatical resistance. General Watson used two brigades in his battle, the Tenth on the right and the Twelfth on the left. Originally, zero hour had been set for 8 A.M., but when the assigned tanks failed to show up, Watson delayed the operation, arguing that "the success of the attack depended almost entirely upon the tanks."[24] Corps headquarters concurred, although the tanks proved to be of minimal use. Finally, nineteen Mark vs appeared, and the Fourth Division went over the top at 10:15 A.M.

Three fortified villages lay in the path of the Twelfth Brigade. The nearest, Maucourt, stood in front of the enemy's maze of trenches, and

---

* The Somme, fought from 1 July to 18 November 1916, was the first major British offensive of the war. The BEF suffered 419,654 casualties—including 57,470 on the first day alone—and gained only eight miles of ground on a twelve-mile front.

fell easily. Directly beyond, in the midst of the old British trench system, was Chilly, which was captured by the 72nd (Seaforth Highlanders of Canada) Battalion following "desperate fighting."[25] During the noon hour, the 78th (Winnipeg Grenadiers) Battalion took over from the 72nd and stormed Hallu, capturing it by two in the afternoon. A subaltern of the 78th, James Tait, distinguished himself in the attack, single-handedly rushing a machine-gun nest and taking twenty prisoners and a dozen machine-guns. Tait, a thirty-year-old Scottish-born surveyor, would make his presence felt again before the day was out.

Taking these objectives was one thing: holding them was quite another. The 72nd and 78th battalions were in exposed positions, especially on their left flank, where neighbouring units had run into trouble. The 38th (Ottawa) and 85th (Nova Scotia Highlanders) battalions had had to make an unusually long advance between Maucourt and the Amiens-Chaulnes railway, and they suffered from enfilade machine-gun fire when the Australians north of the rail line failed to capture Lihons. As was so often the case, the enemy machine-gunners had clear fields of fire, with precious little protection available to the advancing Canadians. The 38th and 85th battalions were finally halted along a line midway between, and north of, Maucourt and Chilly.

This left the 72nd and 78th battalions in a precarious position. And the Germans wasted no time taking advantage of the situation. The first of several counter-attacks was delivered around three-thirty in the afternoon, against both Hallu and Chilly. Things became desperate at seven-thirty that evening, when the final counter-attack of the day was mounted against Hallu; the Germans, in fact, broke into the village and nearly captured the 78th Battalion's headquarters. Under the determined leadership of Lieutenant Tait, who had done so well earlier in the day, a rag-tag collection of staff officers, cooks, clerks, and runners stemmed the enemy advance. Unfortunately, Tait, who was later awarded the VC, was among the Canadians killed in the defence of Hallu.

The Tenth Brigade, meantime, had its hands full. Two battalions, the 44th (New Brunswick) and 46th (South Saskatchewan), led the assault, with the 47th (Western Ontario) and the 50th (Calgary) battalions in close support. According to the 46th Battalion's Lieutenant E.D. "Mac" McDonald, the advance "was reasonably uneventful" for the first two thousand yards or so. Then, as Corporal Curry Spidell recalled, all hell broke loose. "Suddenly Fritz landed a wall of bursting shells in front of us, and I mean a *wall*. The advance stopped. The barrage slackened and we moved again, but not very far. The Germans shortened the range and put another wall down in front of us." Corporal Spidell was wounded by shell splinters in the mouth and shoulder.[26]

The 46th was not to be denied. Braving the heavy shell fire, the battalion burst into the German trench system. It was a bewildering array of fortifications, remembered Sergeant Neil McLeod, "just one trench after another. They were overgrown to some extent. You'd just step out of one trench, and in two or three steps you were down into another one."[27] The fighting was furious, and bloody, but by one-thirty in the afternoon, the 46th Battalion had taken its objectives, the trenches north of Fouquescourt, where a bitter battle was under way in the streets of the village.

Whereas the 46th had been met by murderous artillery fire, the 44th Battalion was greeted by machine-guns en masse. The unit had to cross a wheatfield to reach Fouquescourt, and Private Jack Quelch, writing home a few days later, would never forget "the swish swish" of the bullets ripping through the ripening grain and riddling the ranks of the Canadians. "We were thankfull [sic]," wrote Private Quelch, "to get a little closer into an old trench system in front of the village although it was full of wire, and tough going. It was now a case of rushing from one trench to another and taking what cover you could."[28]

Going to ground in front of Fouquescourt, the battalion summoned help from the artillery. A tremendous barrage was unleashed on the defenders, reducing the village to great piles of rubble. However, the shell fire proved to be a mixed blessing for the infantrymen. It enabled the 44th to take Fouquescourt with relatively little trouble. But there was a mix-up in communications and the bombardment resumed, forcing the battalion to abandon the village. By the time the confusion was cleared up, the Germans had reoccupied Fouquescourt. Grimly, the 44th reorganized and, accompanied by two Mark vs—the only tanks still in action on this front—attacked again. This time, the Germans were driven out of Fouquescourt for good, and by six o'clock in the evening, the 44th Battalion had established a secure outpost line beyond the village.

However, enemy snipers remained active. Private Quelch, patrolling a Fouqescourt side street, was hit in the groin by a sniper's bullet. "I thought a sledge hammer had hit me," he wrote his father. Quelch managed to crawl to the safety of a cellar, where he spent the night. At daybreak, two comrades carried him to a dressing station a mile and a half away. Jack Quelch's war was over.[29]

The 47th and 50th battalions had joined the battle by now. The 47th moved into a gap between the 44th and 46th battalions, while the 50th filled the void between the 46th, on the Tenth Brigade's left, and the right of the Twelfth Brigade. The 50th fought its way through the trenches south of Chilly and reached the railway line south of Hallu. This position was judged to be too vulnerable, and in the early evening the battalion was withdrawn to conform with the 72nd Battalion, holding Chilly.

The withdrawal marked the start of an unforgettable chain of events for Lieutenant Douglas Cunnington. Lieutenant Cunnington had earlier demonstrated his courage by taking out a German machine-gun nest, for which he was later awarded the Military Cross.* Now, as he organized his platoon to pull back, Cunnington took a bullet in the chest. A stretcher-bearer hurried to his aid. Seeing a small hole in the front of the lieutenant's tunic, the bearer turned him over to discover an exit hole the size of a man's fist. Cunnington was left for dead in a pool of blood; his family in Calgary was subsequently informed of his death. But Cunnington was still alive, and a party of Germans later carried him away for treatment. Eventually, he ended up in a military hospital in Düsseldorf, where he spent the remaining months of the war. After the war, Cunnington bumped into his stretcher-bearer on a downtown Calgary street. The man fled, convinced that he had seen a ghost, and Cunnington had to give chase and reassure the fellow of his sanity![31]

The Fourth Division had done remarkably well, but it was hard-pressed to hold its gains. As General Watson remarked in his report, "the situation was by no means satisfactory." Watson was singularly unimpressed by the British 32nd Division. "At no time, during the operation, was the Right Brigade in touch with the 32nd Division on its right, nor were troops of that Division seen." The 78th Battalion was withdrawn from Hallu the next day, since there was no need to retain such an exposed position. The 44th at Fouquescourt was also hard-hit by counter-attacks. Several were driven off during the night, but the Germans resorted to infiltration, sending small groups of soldiers to seek gaps in the Canadian line. The situation became so serious that, just before dawn on 11 August, the 44th Battalion quietly withdrew, clearing the way for a devastating barrage on its forward positions. The infiltrating enemy troops were literally blasted away, and the 44th swiftly secured the line.[32]

Sunday, the eleventh of August, gave proof that the Amiens offensive had just about run its course. The Canadian Corps planned to continue local attacks by the Fourth and 32nd divisions. However, the Fourth did little, aside from consolidating its position and straightening the line. Its attack was scheduled to begin whenever twelve Mark v tanks arrived: they never did show up, and at noon General Currie contacted General Watson to cancel the operation, saying that he "did not intend to push the attack in the face of strong opposition causing many casualties, unless ground could be taken at small cost."[33]

---

* His recollection of this feat of bravery was typically modest. "I charged into a machine-gun nest with this rifle that happened to have a bayonet on it," he commented, "and, as the citation goes, bayoneted all the crew. Actually, the crew, seeing this wild fellow coming at them with a fixed bayonet, put their hands up. I didn't kill anybody."[30]

So the day's only big operation was undertaken by the British division under Currie's command. It was a débâcle. A tragic mix-up between the infantry and the artillery saw the rolling barrage fall far ahead of the advancing British troops, and German machine-gunners in Parvillers and Damery did terrible damage to them. The unfortunate affair left Currie completely disgusted. "This was entirely their own fault," he later wrote. "I visited [General Lambert] the Divisional Commander of the 32nd Division the night before his attack and told him not to make his effort until he was ready, but he was convinced in his own mind that he could with safety kick off in the morning."[34]*

Parvillers cost the 32nd Division nearly 1500 casualties in a matter of minutes. The attack was not renewed. That morning, the army commander, General Rawlinson, telephoned Currie and told him not to press the offensive further "if that would entail heavy losses,"[36] and the Canadian commander readily agreed.

Rawlinson was by now bringing to bear all his influence to draw the battle to a conclusion. As he noted in his diary, "the hostile resistance is stiffening. It is on the 3rd and 4th days of a battle that resistance begins to harden, and then is the time to extend the battle-front, and to put in new attacks by armies on the flanks." As early as 10 August, he had made clear his position in a dramatic confrontation with Field-Marshal Haig at Canadian Corps headquarters.† Hours before, the supreme commander, General Foch, had urged Haig to redouble his efforts on the Amiens front "and try to get to the bridgeheads on the

---

* This did not really surprise Currie. In his opinion, the individual British soldiers lacked initiative "as compared with the Canadians." They were able, he said, to achieve "wonderful results as long as experienced officers were in command," but when such officers were not present the British soldiers seemed unable "to quickly grasp a situation and act with vigor and determination when unforeseen circumstances arise." It was, significantly, an opinion shared by the Australian commander, General Monash, who wrote in September:

> The best troops of the United Kingdom have long ago been used up and we now have a class of man who is without initiative or individuality. They are brave enough, but are simply unskilful. They would be all right if properly led, but their officers, particularly the junior officers, are poor.... Very few English divisions can to-day be classed as first-class fighting troops, relied upon to carry out the tasks set. On the other hand, the Canadians and Australians have never failed to achieve all their objectives strictly according to plan.[35]

† General Currie's advanced headquarters were located in a quarry near Demuin. Currie had moved here on 9 August, after relocating twice the day before in order to keep up with the rapidly advancing Corps. The shift to Demuin caused some grumbling among staff officers who were unhappy with their quarters in the quarry. "Why not the village?" they asked, observing that Demuin had been the comfortable location of an enemy divisional headquarters before its capture by the Canadians. German artillery answered the question later in the day, when Demuin was flattened by a pinpoint barrage. There were no more complaints about the quarry.[37]

Somme." Haig was reluctant to do so without assurances that "the enemy is quite demoralised.... I agree that some German divisions are demoralised, but not all yet!" Haig replied that his own preference was to widen the British front to the north, toward "Bapaume and Monchy le Preux." That afternoon, Haig described his discussion with Foch at a meeting with Rawlinson at Currie's headquarters. Rawlinson, who felt that Haig's strategy was the correct one to pursue at this point, lost his temper. "Are you commanding the British Army," he asked Haig, "or is...Foch?" Rawlinson's sharp words must have stung, but Haig felt that, for the time being, he must defer to Foch's wishes. The Fourth Army would continue its drive on the Amiens front, but Rawlinson warned that "the old Somme battlefield is difficult to get over."[38]

But, first, there was a moment of self-congratulation. On Sunday afternoon, 11 August, the Fourth Army's senior officers gathered near Villers-Bretonneux, in the Australian sector. All corps commanders were present: Currie and Monash, Lieutenant-General Sir Charles Kavanagh of the Cavalry Corps, Lieutenant-General Sir Alexander Godley, who was temporarily in command of III Corps in place of the ill General Butler, and Major-General Sir Hugh Elles of the Tank Corps. They were joined by Haig and Rawlinson and, from London, General Sir Henry Wilson, the chief of the Imperial General Staff. Foch arrived later, accompanied by France's feisty and elderly premier, Georges Clemenceau. Monash vividly recalled the meeting:

Of course there was no thought of serious work or discussion for some twenty minutes, while everybody was being presented to everybody else, and I was personally, naturally—with General Currie—the leading figure in the show, for everybody was highly complimentary and marvelled at the completeness of our success.

Haig had tears in his eyes when he took Monash and Currie aside and told them, "You do not know what the Australians and Canadians have done for the British Army in these days." It was a rare show of emotion for the stolid Scot who commanded the BEF.[39]

Currie and Monash were an unlikely-looking duo. The Canadian was a very big man, yet boyishly shy; at forty-two, he was much the youngest of these high-ranking officers. Monash, of German-Jewish descent, was somewhat older, at fifty-three, balding, with a middle-age paunch. But they had a lot in common. Notably, both were products of the militia in their respective homelands, where both had been highly regarded before the war. And while Monash had only recently been appointed to command the Australian Corps, he was proving himself to be a general of unusual capabilities, just as Currie had done in the year since he had taken over the Canadian Corps. Amiens was the only occasion on which these two corps commanders fought side by side, and they richly deserved the kudos directed their way.

However, the meeting at Villers-Bretonneux had more important overtones. While Foch continued to insist on a renewed offensive on the Fourth Army's front, Haig had concluded that a more imaginative tack must be taken. In view of the enemy reinforcements arriving to oppose the Fourth Army, Haig decided that it was time to widen the battle-front by bringing General Sir Julian Byng's Third Army into action to the immediate north, striking toward Bapaume. In the meantime, the Fourth Army would be given time to "rest and reorganize," as Rawlinson wrote in his diary. "We shall renew the attack on the 15th, deliberately, with as many tanks as we can collect." But he still had serious reservations. "The country over which we shall be working is seamed with old trenches which will be full of machine-gun nests, so I fear we shall have a high casualty list."[40]

Foch was finally coming round to Haig's viewpoint. After thinking about it overnight, he admitted on the twelfth the need for new directions, with "concentrated and powerful attacks" at key points. "These operations," he added, "should be *prepared* promptly and in great strength, by assembling and putting rapidly into their places whatever means are at hand which seem best suited for overcoming the resistance now being encountered, that is tanks, artillery, infantry, in good condition...."[41] That afternoon, he met Haig at Rawlinson's headquarters at Flixécourt, and they agreed that the Fourth Army's offensive would resume on 16 August.

Rawlinson, however, remained reluctant. He wanted the Third Army brought into the battle before the Fourth Army renewed its attacks, instead of doing it the other way around.

He had an ally in General Currie. The Canadian commander shared Rawlinson's reluctance to continue frontal assaults, with no possibility of surprise, against prepared positions stoutly defended by fresh troops. On 13 August, Currie composed a long letter in which he outlined his view of the situation:

> 1. We now find ourselves up against the German trench system as it existed previous to the summer battle of 1916. The trenches are numerous and well constructed, with plenty of dug-out accommodation. They are arranged to meet such an attack as we are contemplating, and further reconnaissance and aeroplane photographs taken today disclose the fact that they are exceedingly well wired.
> 2. It is a system of trenches with which the enemy is familiar and that gives him a great advantage.
> 3. His artillery have doubtless taken up positions from which they

don't need to register because such registrations are already on file.

4. In an attack on these trenches we cannot count on the element of surprise.

5. Four years of experience has taught us that troops attempting to cross uncut wire suffer casualties out of all proportion to any gains they make.

6. We have just carried out an operation which has been a splendid success, with the result that the morale of the troops is exceedingly high. It would be a pity to spoil this valuable morale by going on with an operation which will cost a great many casualties unless the necessity for such an operation is very urgent.

If I may be permitted to make a suggestion I would advise:

1. That if it is absolutely necessary to carry out this attack, that we allow sufficient time to elapse before making it, to give the impression that we are not going to proceed further at present, and in this way we may recover the element of surprise; or better still:

2. That the Canadian Corps be taken out of the line: that the supply of tanks be replenished: then let us go and make an attack somewhere else where I believe we can do equally well if not better than we did here.... I believe if we made an attack on the Third Army front in the direction of Bapaume and in conjunction with an attack by the French from their present line, we could force the Bosche to evacuate the position he holds on this side of the Somme without ever attacking them.[42]

Currie's intervention might well have been the decisive factor. The following day, 14 August, Rawlinson went to see Haig, who commented that the Fourth Army commander "brought photos showing the state of the enemy's defences on the front Roye-Chaulnes. He also showed me a letter he had received from General Currie commanding the Canadian Corps stating that 'to capture the position in question would be a very costly matter.' He (Currie) 'was opposed to attempting it'."[43]

The commander-in-chief quickly made up his mind. In a letter to Foch, Haig explained the difficulties facing the Fourth Army. Noting his agreement to resume the offensive on the sixteenth, "I have directed that the attack be postponed until adequate artillery preparation has been carried out in order to prepare a deliberate attack on the position. This might be carried out in conjunction with the attack from the Third Army front, which is being prepared as rapidly as possible."[44]

Foch, however, proved to be unusually adamant. He insisted that "any postponement would have the most serious consequences," adding: "On the contrary, there is good reason for hastening the action of the British Fourth and French First Armies, and having it speedily followed by an attack of the British Third Army."[45]

The showdown came on Thursday, 15 August. Haig visited Foch at his headquarters at Sarcus, near Paris, and later recorded the outcome of their meeting in his diary:

> I spoke to Foch quite straightly and let him understand that *I was responsible to my Government and fellow citizens for the handling of the British forces.* F.'s attitude at once changed, and he said all he wanted was early information of my intentions so that he might co-ordinate the operations of the other Armies, and that he now thought I was quite correct in my decision not to attack the enemy in his prepared positions.[46]

Foch later admitted that, as a result of this meeting, "I came around definitely to the opinion of Field Marshal Haig." But Haig left Sarcus wondering whether Foch really knew what he was doing, pointing out that, "notwithstanding what he now said, Foch and all his staff had been most insistent for the last five days that I should press on along the south bank and capture the Somme bridges above Peronne, regardless of German opposition and British losses."[47]

One fact emerges with clarity from all of this. Despite Foch's position as supreme commander, it was Sir Douglas Haig who was dictating Allied strategy in the summer of 1918. It was a reality that Foch had to face, and one that Haig was more than willing to accept, because both of them knew that the BEF was the only Allied force capable of defeating the German army. The French army was a mere shadow of its former self, having been bled of its best men in the course of four years of war, while the American army would soon prove to be too inexperienced to be a decisive factor in this campaign.

The new plan was welcomed by Currie and Monash. As we have seen, Currie was convinced that the Amiens operation had run its course, while Monash considered that "the possibility of further cheap exploitation of 8 August had come to an end." Rawlinson noted their reaction to the news: "I think they were relieved." But there was a sad note. While the Australian Corps remained under Rawlinson's command, the Canadians were to be transferred within a few days to General Sir Henry Horne's First Army. The Australians and Canadians had fought alongside each other for the last time in the Great War.[48]

While the main battle at Amiens had ended, minor operations continued for several more days. The Canadian Corps devoted itself to straightening out the front line, making it more defensible while at the same time obtaining suitable jumping-off positions for subsequent offensives. Parvillers, which had caused the British 32nd Division so much grief, remained a primary Canadian objective. It was finally captured on 15 August, but not before a brilliant preliminary operation on the twelfth by the 42nd (Royal Highlanders of Canada) Battalion.

The 42nd Battalion belonged to the Third Division, which relieved the 32nd Division on the night of 11-12 August. The Highlanders wasted no time making amends for the earlier British reverse. Acting on his instructions "to maintain steady pressure" on his front, Lieutenant-Colonel Royal Ewing proposed a daring raid in strength on the maze of enemy trenches between Fouquescourt and Parvillers. The former was held by the 44th Battalion and offered the possibility of turning the German flank. At 12:30 P.M. on Monday, 12 August, a dozen officers and 450 other ranks of the 42nd Battalion went over the top. This would prove to be, in the words of one officer, "the most amazing operation in the history of the Battalion."[49]

The raiders had a field day. Splitting into parties of bombers, riflemen, and Lewis gunners, the men of the 42nd caught the Germans napping. "For the first three hours," reads the battalion report, "progress was rapid and fighting was not severe." By five-thirty that afternoon, the Canadians had killed an estimated seventy Germans with only a handful of casualties themselves. However, a problem became evident on the left, where a platoon of Captain W.A. Graffety's D Company was evidently lost—observers could follow the progress and position of the raiders who periodically fired two white flares in quick succession. Lieutenant-Colonel R.D. Davies, the officer commanding the 44th Battalion, spotted the trouble from Fouquescourt and dispatched his second-in-command, Major D.B. Martin, to redirect the lost platoon. Major Martin did so, but soon afterwards both of the platoon's officers were wounded, and Martin stayed to lead it the rest of the way.[50]

The Canadians did deadly work in the German trenches. For Private Thomas Dinesen, this was to be an unforgettable day, in more ways than one. Years later, the Danish-born Dinesen remembered the ferocious fighting that took place:

> I fire away madly till my magazine is empty; then I fling down the rifle and hurl my bombs at them—the trench is chockfull of dust and smoke. Mac had come up close behind me, his shots thunder right into my ears.... From behind they are throwing bombs by the dozen, without minding in the least who or what they are hitting. They shout and yell: "Give them hell, boys!"... Jack comes up from behind with a fresh supply of Mills bombs.... "Here you are, Fritzie boy, damn you!"... Ah, they have had enough, they are done for, the bastards! A couple of survivors dash off from the post,

and we rush after them, tear our hands and kilts on the wire, jumping across the overturned machine-gun and the dead or dying gunners, running, panting, and perspiring along the dry, hard trench, corner by corner...and then we reach the next machine-gun post and throw ourselves against it, yelling and roaring, with bombs and bayonets, battle-mad—regardless of everything in the world, our whole being intent on one thing alone: to force our way ahead and kill![51]

Private Dinesen dealt with at least five machine-gun posts in this manner. For his courage and leadership, he was awarded the VC.

Major Martin led his party, which included the heroic Dinesen, toward La Chavatte, a village southeast of Fouquescourt. En route, his men rounded up forty prisoners and eight machine-guns. Arriving at La Chavatte, Martin found the defenders manning a long hedge on the outskirts. Despite all the commotion in the area, these Germans were evidently ignorant of impending danger. Taken by surprise, fifty were caught out in the open and the Canadians "mowed them down," in Martin's words. At this point, he continued, "several enemy machine guns tried to get into action behind the hedge but could not maintain fire for any time against our Lewis Guns. I put up a triple green flare here to show our position and we maintained ourselves there for *one* hour." At last, under relentless German pressure from all sides, Martin was forced to conduct a fighting retreat, repelling no fewer than three large counter-attacks during the withdrawal.[52]

Martin's platoon rejoined Captain Graffety's company. D Company was so far forward, in fact, that when the Germans staged an attack on Captain H.B. Trout's nearby A Company, Graffety's men were able to cut down the Germans from the flank as well as the rear. Trout's troops had earlier encountered an unusual strongpoint: a pair of machine-guns mounted in a derelict British tank. The crews fought until they were finally killed by bombers. One German who did not fight to the last was an Alsatian corporal who was so glad to be captured that he happily led the Canadians through the trenches and later helped to repair a German machine-gun which the Highlanders employed in repulsing a counter-attack.

By nightfall, the "fighting was continuous and severe" across the 42nd Battalion's front. With help from reinforcements from the 49th (Edmonton Regiment) Battalion and Princess Patricia's Canadian Light Infantry, the 42nd was able to consolidate much of the captured trench system, and "the situation was well in hand by 11 P.M." The 42nd suffered 148 casualties, while capturing a hundred prisoners and fifty-five machine-guns during its ten-hour running battle; at least a hundred more Germans were killed.[53]

Parvillers was captured by the Canadians three days later. While the 42nd Battalion was going on its rampage through the trenches north of the village, Princess Patricia's Canadian Light Infantry (PPCLI) attempted to outflank Parvillers to the south. However, the PPCLI attack did not get under way until late in the evening of 12 August, by which time the 42nd's operation was winding down. Still, Captain E.M. MacBrayne's attack went well initially: the Princess Pats stormed through 700 yards of trenches, killing at least thirty Germans and taking sixteen machine-guns. Then the attackers ran out of grenades and, as Captain MacBrayne later remarked, "what looked like a very successful fight turned out to be right the other way." In the early morning hours of the thirteenth, the Germans mounted a major counter-attack that caught MacBrayne's outnumbered company on three sides. The captain quickly realized his predicament and faced a choice: retreat or be cut off. The Pats conducted a stubborn withdrawal, during which Sergeant Robert Spall, a seemingly mild-mannered office worker from Winnipeg, won the VC by repulsing, unaided, an enemy assault with his Lewis gun, though his brave stand cost him his life. Spall's VC was the last of ten awarded Canadian soldiers during the Amiens operations.[54]

Following this disappointment, a full frontal assault was arranged for Wednesday, 14 August. The 49th Battalion, on the left, and the PPCLI, on the right, attacked at 6:30 A.M., after a half-hour bombardment that softened the defences. Parvillers was taken following a stiff fight, but the Canadians were robbed of the fruits of victory by one of those inexplicable foul-ups that happen in war. The 49th was withdrawn—on whose orders is not clear—and not only exposed the PPCLI's flank but enabled the Germans to reoccupy Parvillers. However, the Royal Canadian Regiment (RCR) was thrown into action that night, and by dawn on the fifteenth had once again captured the village, this time for good. The cost in casualties to the RCR was "amazingly light": thirty-nine, including two killed.[55]

Damery fell the same day. This, too, entailed a hard fight, although this was not the case at the start. The 52nd (New Ontario) Battalion took the village with such ease that a ruse was suspected. These suspicions were confirmed later in the afternoon, when the Germans launched a two-battalion counter-attack on the 52nd. Advancing in mass formation, the enemy presented wonderful targets to the Canadian riflemen and Lewis gunners. The Germans were routed, leaving 200 prisoners and many dead and wounded behind. Thereafter, they contented themselves with periodic bombardments of the Canadian positions. These were nerve-wracking affairs, as Corporal Albert West, a thirty-eight-year-old member of the 43rd (Cameron Highlanders of Canada) Battalion, would later attest. West, manning a machine-gun post near Damery, vividly remembered the shelling his unit received on the morning of the sixteenth. "It was short but furious," wrote West. "I think he hit every yard but where we lay crouched. Personally I felt it was quite unlikely any of us would be left. Shells exploded in rapid succession in front, right, left, above and behind us, but not a man was hit."[56]

This effectively ended active operations in the Canadian sector. While the artillery carried out "an aggressive programme of harassing fire," intensive patrolling was maintained along the front lines, and small-scale attacks were mounted to further straighten out the line or to secure valuable landmarks. These included the village of La Chavatte, taken by the 13th (Royal Highlanders of Canada) Battalion on 17 August. One of the last Canadians to be killed was a legendary performer. Henry "Ducky" Norwest was a sniper with the 50th (Calgary) battalion. A Cree Indian, Norwest had 115 kills to his credit, and wore the Military Medal and bar. On 18 August, he and his observer, Private Oliver Payne, took up a position near Chilly, in search of a troublesome German sniper. Waiting patiently, Norwest finally spotted his quarry and drew a bead on him. "Suddenly, the instant Ducky fired, [the] German sniper fired," recalled Private Payne. "It missed me but got Ducky right through the head, coming out the other side!"[57]

With the fighting more or less ended, there were plenty of tasks to keep the troops busy. The least pleasant was that of collecting and burying the dead. Due to the size of the battlefield, this chore took a long time to complete; many bodies—all German, who were given the lowest priority by the burial squads—were left decomposing in the hot August sunshine. This was both discomforting and disconcerting to soldiers like Gunner C.M. Wright of the 68th Battery, CFA, who commented in his journal:

> One thing that rather surprises me—that is the way the dead bodies have been left unburied all over this ground. In the week or more since they fell, in this hot weather, decomposition has been rapid and the stench has been rank. We had to bury two ourselves, which being just to windward of our new gun position, and rather ripe, prevented our working. But the whole thing must be very unsanitary as well as very disgusting. What a smell a very dead man does make![58]

A happier task involved salvaging German and Canadian equipment from the battlefield. This could be a fruitful exercise, as Captain H.C. Brewer of the 14th (Royal Montreal Regiment) Battalion reported, after his company spent a single day on salvage duty:

German material:—1 heavy machine gun, 7 medium machine guns, 7 machine gun barrels (spares), 48 loaded machine gun belts in carriers, 6 250-round machine gun belts, 1 medium trench mortar (complete with wheel and spare parts), 2 respirators, 5 mess tins, 5 steel helmets, 10 entrenching tools, 6 water bottles, 15 rifles, 6 bayonets, 20 packs, 10 scabbards, 2 machine gun water tanks, 8 shovels, and 4 picks.

British material salvaged at the same time included:—20 Lee Enfield rifles, 6 entrenching tools, 8 bayonets and scabbards, 6 steel helmets, 2 sets of Webb equipment, 11 sets of Webb pouches, 6 3-inch Stokes gun shells, 30 Lewis gun magazines, 6 haversacks, 2 machine gun pouches, 8 water bottles, 3 shovels, 4 picks, 25 petrol tins, and 1 complete box of s.o.s. grenades.[59]

And all of this material was collected by one company in one small corner of the battlefield! That so much German equipment was salvaged cannot be surprising, considering the magnitude of their defeat, but the large quantities of Canadian and British supplies are surely astonishing.

The Canadians were honoured on the battlefield, for their part in the great Amiens victory. Brigadier-General Hugh Dyer's Seventh Brigade was chosen to represent the BEF on 18 August, when Field-Marshal Haig and General Rawlinson hosted the premier of France, Georges Clemenceau, and the British ambassador to France, Lord Derby—the former secretary of state for war. "The men looked splendid and the officers looked up to their work in every way," wrote an approving Haig. "M. Clemenceau then left for Paris. He said he had thoroughly enjoyed his visit, and congratulated us on all that we had accomplished."[60]

The episode, however, had unhappy consequences. Noticeable by his absence was the Canadian commander, Currie, who was annoyed to find that Rawlinson had arranged the parade without consulting him, even though it involved Canadian troops. This was, in Currie's view, a "discourtesy," and he refused to attend, having scheduled his own inspection tour that day. The dispute did not end there, as Currie commented in his diary:

General Rawlinson came in to see me later and told me how well pleased he was with the appearance on parade of the 7th Brigade. I replied that I was glad he was pleased, but I took occasion to remind him that in my opinion he had no right to order the parade direct. He readily agreed with this contention, and said he was sorry. I also told him that I thought it was discourteous to me for Lord Derby and Premier Clemenceau to see on parade any Units of the Corps without first calling at Corps Headquarters.[61]

82

As trivial as the dispute might seem, it was symptomatic of a larger issue. Currie was distressed to discover that, in the days subsequent to 8 August, the Canadians were not getting their fair share of the credit in the newspapers. "I admit that up to the present," Currie complained on 15 August, "the London press, for some reason best known to themselves, have said very little about the part the Canadians have played in this battle." The press coverage was rarely "fair or just to the Canadians," he contended.

> The operations at Amiens are credited to British troops and the word "Canadian" is not used.... We are British, certainly, and proud to be called such, but a certain section of the English press are evidently determined on a policy to ignore the word "Canadian".... Our own papers in Canada republished the English articles, with the result, that the Canadian people do not even now realize the full extent of the operations in which the Corps has taken part....[62]

It was a concern shared by the Australian commander, General Monash. Sir John was incensed by the British practice "of unduly suppressing references to the deeds of the Australians." He went so far as to warn GHQ "that, unless the performances of the Australians were justly placarded, I would not hold myself responsible for the maintenance of their fighting spirit."[63] In fairness to the British authorities, it was difficult for them to strike a balance between too much or too little coverage of the dominion forces, who were seen by the public as the "glamour boys" of the BEF. While too little credit angered the Australians and Canadians, too much publicity caused considerable resentment among the other troops.

Still, Currie's consternation is understandable. Full Canadian casualty lists were printed in the papers at home, but there was no evident explanation for the losses in the accompanying news reports. For example, the 9 August edition of the Toronto *Globe* carried three front-page articles on Amiens, and the only mention of Canadians was a brief reference in Sir Douglas Haig's official statement: "At the hour of assault, French, Canadian, Australian and English divisions, assisted by a large number of British tanks, stormed the Germans on a front of over twenty miles...." A Canadian Press dispatch completely ignored the Canadian Corps, referring simply to "British and French troops," while an article by a *Globe* special correspondent, Henry W. Nevinson, also made no mention of Canadian troops.

Not content to complain, Currie made a determined effort to publicize the efforts of his Canadians. On 13 August, he issued a special order of the day—perhaps recalling the warm welcome a similar order received in the British papers earlier in 1918*—extolling the deeds of the Canadian Corps:

> The first stage of this Battle of Amiens is over, and one of the most successful operations conducted by the Allied Armies since the War began is now a matter of history.
>
> The Canadian Corps has every right to feel more than proud of the part it played. To move the Corps from the Arras front and in less than a week launch it in battle so many miles distant was in itself a splendid performance. Yet the splendour of that performance pales into insignificance when compared with what has been accomplished since zero hour on August 8th.
>
> On that date the Canadian Corps—to which was attached the 3rd Cavalry Division, the 4th Tank Brigade, the 5th Squadron R.A.F.—attacked on a front of 7500 yards. After a penetration of 22000 yards the line tonight rests on a 10000 yard frontage. 16 German Divisions have been identified, of which 4 have been completely routed. Nearly 200 guns have been captured, while over one thousand machine guns have fallen into our hands. Ten thousand prisoners have passed through our cages and Casualty Clearing Stations, a number greatly in excess of our total casualties. Twenty-five towns and villages have been rescued from the clutch of the invaders, the Paris-Amiens Railway has been freed from interference, and the danger of dividing the French and British Army has been dissipated.
>
> Canada has always placed the most implicit confidence in her Army. How nobly has that confidence been justified: and with what pride has the story been read in the home land! This magnificent victory has been won because your training was good, your discipline was good, your leadership was good. Given these three, success must always come.[65]

It would be uncharitable, even nonsensical, to suggest that Currie had personal motives for seeking publicity for the Canadians. It would

---

* On 27 March 1918, within days of the start of the great German offensive, Currie issued a special order imploring his troops "to fight as you have ever fought with all your strength, with all your determination, with all your tranquil courage." It was widely reprinted in papers across France and Britain; *The Times* of London remarked that it "struck a note that drew a response from the whole Empire." Typically, the Canadian soldiers themselves were unimpressed with it. A battalion commander, Lieutenant-Colonel Alex Ross, refused to read it to his men. "Appeals to the higher ideals," he later explained, "only made them ill." A member of the 50th (Calgary) Battalion was referring to Currie when he sarcastically muttered, "I know one Canadian whose body [the enemy] will never have to walk over."[64]

have been completely out of character for him to do so, because he consistently credited his own success to the fact that he commanded Canadians in combat. Indeed, he had already been honoured: on 12 August, King George v had appointed him a Knight Commander of the Order of the Bath (KCB). And his special order did have some small effect on the British press, although not to the extent that Currie would have liked. On 27 August, *The Times* of London finally admitted to its readers that Amiens had been "chiefly a Canadian battle." But by that time the Canadians were in the midst of more ferocious fighting.

The departure to a new front began on 19 August. On that date, the Second and Third divisions boarded buses and trains for the journey northward to join the First Army about Arras. On the twenty-second, Currie closed his main headquarters at Dury and handed over to the Australian commander, General Monash, temporary responsibility for the other two divisions, which would rejoin the Corps within a few days. Currie and Monash were sincerely saddened by the separation of their forces. "It is a pleasure for me to say, Monash," wrote Currie, "that there are no troops who have given so loyal and effective support as the Australians, and I am sure I speak for all Canadians when I say that we would like to finish the war fighting side by side with you." Monash—who had great personal regard for Currie, later calling him "a giant in stature physically, and he was a giant in mind when he was in France"—replied in kind, crediting the Canadians with "stimulating the Australian troops to their best efforts...and I look forward keenly to future opportunities to fighting shoulder to shoulder with your gallant corps."[66]

It was a much more relaxed Currie who oversaw this movement of the Canadian Corps. Secrecy was not an overriding concern this time, and Currie was free to focus his care and concern on his men, as illustrated by an incident related by Lieutenant-Colonel Bertram Hooper, the officer commanding the 20th (Central Ontario) Battalion:

> The decimated battalion was resting in tired disorder after a march of some kilometres toward our railway embarkation point, when all at once from nowhere loomed the impressive figure of our Chief. I sprang to my feet in consternation at being taken off guard and gave as embarrassed a salute as I am sure the General had ever seen, at the same time barking at my adjutant to call the battalion to attention.... The General with stern reproof in his eye and rebuke in his voice said, "Let 'em rest." He then spent half an hour going from one reclining group to another, smiling down at the men, the warmth and praise in his voice and his human interest reviving them at every step.[67]

En route to Arras, Currie took time to visit General Sir Julian Byng, his predecessor as commander of the Canadian Corps and now commanding the Third Army. "General Byng was good enough to say," a flattered Currie happily recorded, "that he considered the operation of the Canadian Corps in the Battle of Amiens to be the finest operation of the war."[68]

The praise was well merited. The Canadians had, with the Australians, spearheaded the most striking success to attend Allied arms in the Great War. The deepest penetration, fourteen miles, had been made on the Canadian front, including eight on the first day. In the course of the offensive the four Canadian divisions, reinforced by the British 32nd Division, had engaged elements of sixteen enemy divisions. Four had been routed, three of these—the 14th Bavarian, 109th, and 225th—so completely crushed that they were disbanded before the end of August. The cost had not been unduly high. Canadian casualties between 8 and 20 August totalled 11,822, the majority being incurred during the first four days. "It is interesting to note that in this action the ratio of killed to wounded in the Canadian casualty lists was about 1 to 6, as compared with an average ratio of around 1 to 4 in trench warfare." This feature would become even more pronounced in the days and weeks ahead.[69]

Amiens was also the last great battle fought by the Canadian Corps as an all-volunteer force. The Corps departed Amiens slightly stronger than it had been when it arrived, thanks to the 12,200 reinforcements who were assigned its various units between 8 and 24 August. This marked the first major influx of conscripts; by war's end, 24,132 would be taken on strength of units in France, the majority joining infantry battalions, where the casualties were heaviest. Two facts become readily apparent. The first is that the Corps could not have contributed so impressively during the remaining months of the war without the conscripted soldiers who filled its depleted ranks. The second is that the Corps would never again reach the peak of efficiency displayed at Amiens. Henceforth, its performance would slowly but steadily deteriorate because most of the conscripts were not only inexperienced and partly trained, but they also lacked the élan of the volunteers who preceded them.

Certainly, General Currie had acquitted himself well. Victory at Amiens had been made possible, above all else, by the secret shift of the Canadians; this had been Currie's responsibility, and while it had taken its toll on his temper, it had been executed almost flawlessly—and the few flaws, fortunately, had been unnoticed by the enemy. Once the battle had begun, Currie, like the other corps commanders, was given little latitude for personal initiative. It will be recalled, for instance, that the Fourth Army overruled his decision to commit fresh forces on

9 August, which was obviously the time to use them; Rawlinson himself admitted that in all previous battles enemy resistance had invariably stiffened on the third and fourth days of the battle, when it was too late to exploit victory. And Currie, to his credit, was quick to recognize that the offensive had lost its momentum, and became a vocal advocate of a broader battle-front and launching new, punishing assaults elsewhere, to keep the enemy off balance. "Four years of war has taught us that troops cannot cross uncut barbed wire without suffering enormous casualties," he wrote on 15 August, "and I am not going to have a good operation spoiled by over-zealousness."[70] There can be little doubt that Currie's determination to bring the battle to an end influenced both Haig and Rawlinson.

These two much-maligned officers could take considerable satisfaction from the success at Amiens. Often criticized and condemned for being slow, plodding, and unimaginative, Field-Marshal Haig and General Rawlinson had engineered a victory that, seen in retrospect, heralded the beginning of the end of the war. Rawlinson, writing on 31 August, commented: "We have shown that even in trench warfare it is possible to mystify and mislead the enemy."[71]

This is not to say that they were beyond reproach. It is fair to observe that Rawlinson, in particular, was unduly cautious at times, influenced as he was by his chief of staff, General Montgomery, which resulted in the lamentably unco-ordinated attacks on 9, 10, and 11 August. And yet Rawlinson's caution is easily explained. The spectre of Cambrai—the November 1917 tank attack which served as the model for Amiens—unquestionably haunted Rawlinson, as it did other senior British officers, who could never forget how a brilliant early success ended in virtual defeat because too much had been attempted with too few resources.

Haig, too, has been criticized, though with less credibility. David Lloyd George, the British prime minister, relied exclusively on German sources to condemn the field-marshal in his vitriolic post-war memoirs. "Had Haig flung his army into the gap created and pursued the broken and demoralised Germans without respite," Lloyd George charged, "an even greater victory was within his grasp." It must be remembered, though, that Haig could do nothing right, in Lloyd George's view. The prime minister had been trying, since taking office in December 1916, to get rid of Haig, "a second-rate Commander," in Lloyd George's opinion, "intellectually and temperamentally unequal to the command of an Army of millions." These remarks denied Haig the recognition as the architect of the biggest Allied victory of the war, and they must be dismissed as an amateur's verbose exercise in character assassination.[72]

By any reckoning, Amiens had been an impressive victory for the Allies. The Fourth Army's losses amounted to 22,202 for the period

8-11 August, while the French had lost 24,232 men killed, wounded, and missing. The Germans, on the other hand, suffered an estimated 75,000 casualties: the British alone had captured 22,000 prisoners and more than 400 guns.[73]

The defeat had a devastating impact on the Germans. Particularly distressed and disillusioned was Chief Quartermaster Erich Ludendorff, the de facto commander-in-chief on the Western Front. Ludendorff later lamented that "our losses in prisoners had been so heavy that General Headquarters was again faced with the necessity of breaking up more divisions to form reserves." Worse than that, in his view, was the psychological state of the German army, which he discovered in interviews with divisional commanders on the Amiens front:

> I was told of deeds of glorious valor, but also of behavior which, I openly confess, I should not have thought possible in the German Army; whole bodies of our men had surrendered to single troopers or isolated squadrons. Retiring troops, meeting a fresh division going bravely into battle, had shouted out things like "Black-legs" and "You're prolonging the war".... Everything I had feared, of which I had often given warning, had here, in one place, become a reality. Our war machine was no longer efficient.

Concluded Ludendorff: "The war must be ended."[74]

Some German generals tried to make excuses. One was Oskar von Hutier, who commanded the Eighteenth Army—and who was, coincidentally, Ludendorff's brother-in-law. "We were up against the élite of the French Army," Hutier explained, "and the celebrated Canadian Corps."[75]

But Kaiser Wilhelm agreed with Ludendorff. The Kaiser attended a conference on 14 August at Spa, where Ludendorff and his ostensible chief, Paul von Hindenburg, had their headquarters in, of all places, the Hôtel Britannique. After listening to Ludendorff's dismal description of the defeat at Amiens, Wilhelm concluded that Germany's situation was impossible. He instructed his foreign minister to initiate peace negotiations through neutral intermediaries.

6 BREAKING THE HINDENBURG LINE

"Tout le monde à la bataille"! With those stirring words, Ferdinand Foch—recently promoted to marshal—urged the Allied armies into action in the wake of Amiens. There was, as Field-Marshal Haig noted at the time, nothing sophisticated about Foch's strategy, which was merely "a simple straightforward advance by all troops on the western front [in order] to keep the enemy on the move." Foch and Haig were in complete agreement on the need to keep pounding the battered Germans. However, Haig was finding this easier said than done.[1]

There were few believers on the home front. Four heartbreaking years of war had produced a plethora of pessimists. While Haig discerned unprecedented and unmistakable evidence of cracks in German discipline, with enlisted men refusing to obey orders and officers unable to enforce their authority, most of Britain's civilian leaders were preparing for a 1919 campaign. The field-marshal discovered this alarming fact on 21 August, when he hosted a visit by the minister of munitions, Winston Churchill. Haig was pleased to hear that Churchill was "most anxious to help us in any way," but worried that his arms production program was geared to peak in the middle of 1919, when the War Office forecast the beginning of the decisive offensive on the Western Front. "We ought to do our utmost to get a decision this autumn," Haig lectured Churchill. "We are engaged in a 'wearing out battle,' and are outlasting and beating the enemy. If we allow the enemy a period of quiet, he will recover, and the 'wearing out' process must be recommenced.'[2]

Haig was having a hard time convincing some of his own generals. His intention was to gradually widen the battle-front, first by bringing into action the Third Army, on the immediate left of the Fourth Army, then by committing the First Army, on the left of the Third. The latter army, under General Sir Julian Byng, was to strike at Bapaume, an important communications centre, but Haig was unhappy with Byng's battle plan, which he considered to be "too limited in scope." Byng was apparently concerned about his flanks during the proposed operations, but Haig argued that this was no time for such worries, "that his objective was to break the enemy's front, and gain Bapaume as soon as possible." He also urged Byng to "use the cavalry to the fullest possible extent" to exploit success. Added Haig: "Now is the time to act with boldness, if we only hit the enemy hard enough, and combine the action of all arms in pressing him, his troops will give way on a very wide front and acknowledge that he is beaten."[3]

The Third Army attacked on 21 August. That night, after making modest gains along his front, General Byng decided to halt the offensive, in order to reorganize for the next push. Haig was astounded. "I expressed *the wish* that the attack should be resumed at the earliest possible moment," he complained in his diary. "The enemy's troops must be suffering more than ours, because we are elated by success, while the enemy is feeling that this is the beginning of the end for him, viz., DEFEAT." When the Third Army failed to resume the attack on the twenty-second, Haig was irate. "I cannot think this is necessary. I accordingly issued *an Order* directing *the offensive to be resumed at the earliest moment possible*."[4]

Frustrated by Byng's over-caution, Haig issued a note to all his army commanders the same day. In it he stressed "the changed conditions" that now existed on the Western Front. "It is no longer necessary to advance step by step in regular lines as in the 1916–1917 battles. All units must go straight for their objectives, while reserves should be pushed in where we are gaining ground."[5]

Byng's army resumed its offensive on 23 August. It was quite successful, with 5000 prisoners being captured during a two-mile advance toward Bapaume. The following day, the Fourth Army joined the attack astride the River Somme. However, progress on the fronts of both armies slowed noticeably on subsequent days.

German strategy at this point was obvious to all. Despite calls by some senior generals to retreat, Ludendorff determined to conduct a fighting withdrawal to the Hindenburg Line, with the intention of buying time—delaying the Allies until the onset of winter precluded further operations—while inflicting maximum losses. The Hindenburg Line was an imposing barrier, but it was not really a line. It was a series of in-depth defensive positions, each linked to the others, centred on Siegfried-Stellung (*Stellung* is the German word for "position"), which covered Cambrai and Saint-Quention. Three other, newer and weaker, positions lay to the south, stretching as far as Metz. To the north stood Wotan-Stellung, known to the British as the Drocourt-Quéant, or D-Q, Line. These defences were old, having been built after the battle of the Somme in 1916, as a last line of resistance.

Despite Foch's wish to commit "tout le monde" to the fight, only the BEF was prepared for major offensive operations in the latter part of August 1918. The French and American armies would not be ready until well into September. It was ironic, therefore, that the British faced the enemy's most elaborate defences. "Strategically the main offensive was made at the wrong place," observes the British official history, "because the Army that was most fighting-fit happened to be holding that front." However, there was no way to avoid the situation. Everything, Sir Douglas Haig realized, "depended in a peculiarly large degree upon the British attack.... It was here that the enemy's defences were most highly organised. If these were broken, the threat directed at his system of lateral communications would of necessity react upon his defence elsewhere." And he was under no illusions about the strength of the Hindenburg Line, especially Siegfried-Stellung and Wotan-Stelling. "The whole series of defences," he later wrote, "with the numerous defended villages contained in it, formed a belt of country varying from 7,000 to 10,000 yards in depth, organised by the employment of every available means into a most powerful system, well meriting the great reputation attached to it."[6]

A frontal assault, Haig knew, would be costly and time-consuming. If the BEF had to fight its way to the Hindenburg Line, it might well be exhausted before staging its decisive drive. Herein lies the importance of the Drocourt-Quéant Line. Haig believed that "a sudden and successful blow, of weight sufficient to break through the northern hinge of the defences to which it was [the enemy's] design to fall back, might produce results of great importance." If the D-Q Line could be penetrated, it "would turn the whole of the enemy's organised positions on a wide front southwards."[7]

To carry out this vital task, Haig selected his storm troops, the Canadians. Marshal Foch concurred completely in this decision. In a private conversation with Brigadier-General Raymond Brutinel, commander of the Canadian Machine-Gun Corps, Foch said, "I think the Canadians are the force on which I can rely to clean up between Arras and the Hindenburg Line. That's going to be a long task, a hard one, but the Canadians know that ground so perfectly and they are so determined that I think I can trust them to do so." Foch called the Canadian Corps "the ram with which we will break up the last line of resistance of the German army."[8]

The challenge facing the Canadians was formidable indeed. Striking in a southeasterly direction along the Arras-Cambrai road, they would encounter a bewildering array of defences. The nearest was the former British defensive zone, 5500 yards deep, captured by the Germans earlier in the year, with the old enemy front line beyond it, all overlooked by three heights that dominated the gently rolling countryside: Orange Hill, Chapel Hill, and Monchy-le-Preux. Two miles east of Monchy stood the Fresnes-Rouvroy Line, while a mile further on was the D-Q Line itself. And there was much more: the unfinished Canal du Nord ran across the rear of the D-Q Line, and on the other side of the canal were several partially completed defensive systems which protected Cambrai. Throughout the whole area were innumerable trenches and switch lines linking the main positions, along with natural obstacles such as sunken roads and rivers with steep banks that could be easily defended. The total depth of these defences was more than twenty miles—well over twice the extent of any other point on the Hindenburg Line.

With justification, General Currie later called this series of positions "without doubt one of the strongest defensively on the Western Front." Moreover, there could be little chance of surprise, "other than that afforded by the selection of the actual hour of the assaults." The importance was self-evident, too, since these defences "formed the pivot of the movements of the German Army to the south, and the security of the Armies to the north depended also on these positions being retained. There was consequently little doubt that the enemy was alert, and had made every disposition to repulse the expected attacks."[9]

Time was a key consideration. When, on the evening of 22 August, Currie met with his divisional commanders, the offensive was tentatively scheduled to begin on Sunday, the twenty-fifth. Currie, who never liked to be hurried in his battle preparations, was unhappy about the date selected by the First Army, and said so. He pointed out "that this gave barely 48 hours to concentrate the necessary Artillery, part of which was still in the Fourth Army area, and that, furthermore, the Canadian Corps had sentimental objections to attacking on the Sabbath Day."[10] As a result, zero day was postponed until Monday, 26 August.

Still, it would be a hustle to get ready. And it would have been impossible had the Canadians not been familiar with the lay of the land. It will be recalled that just before departing for Amiens, the Corps had been planning an attack in this area. The Canadians, Currie noted, "particularly benefited by all the reconnaissance and plans made for the capture of Orange Hill during the period of simulated activity at the end of July." This factor, along with the excellent administrative arrangements in the First Army's sector, "enabled the Canadian Corps to undertake to begin, with only three days' notice, the hardest battle in its history."[11]

Currie, characteristically, contemplated the future with complete confidence. A lesser commander might have allowed himself to be overwhelmed by the potential difficulties, but Currie had great faith in the efficacy of the Corps. All units, he noted, were "in fighting condition. The efficiency of the organisation peculiar to the Canadian Corps, and the soundness of the tactical doctrine practised, had been proved and confirmed. Flushed with the great victory [at Amiens] they had just won, and fortified by the experience acquired, all ranks were ready for the coming task."[12]

Not everyone shared his confidence. A visibly anxious Sir Douglas Haig, underlining the importance of these operations, took the unusual step of visiting Canadian Corps headquarters at Noyelle-Vion on four consecutive days, 24 through 27 August. The commander-in-chief knew that the D-Q Line would be a tough nut to crack. "Do you think it can be done, Currie?" he repeatedly asked. "Do you think it can be done?"

"Yes," Currie calmly assured the field-marshal, "we will break it."[13]

Once again, as at Amiens, the high standard of Canadian staff work was evident. This remarkable point cannot be stressed enough, because Canada had begun the war with only a handful of staff officers. Of necessity, British officers in large numbers had to be employed in the Canadian Corps, but by the summer of 1918 nearly all had been replaced by Canadians—a tribute to the generally understated and underrated Canadian proficiency in the art of war. That said, it must be noted that the top two staff officers in the Corps were British. At this time, these men were Brigadier-General N.W. Webber and Brigadier-General George Farmar. Webber was later replaced by another Britisher, Brigadier-General Ross Hayter.

It was staff work that made possible the rapid preparations for the offensive. General Currie took command of his battle sector on 23 August. By the following day, two divisions—Burstall's Second and Lipsett's Third—had moved into the front lines. The other two divisions were en route from Amiens and would not arrive for a few days. This suited Currie, who had "decided to do the fighting with two Divisions in the line, each on a one-Brigade front, thus enabling both Divisions to carry on the battle for three successive days; the other two Divisions were to be kept in Corps Reserve, resting and refitting after each relief." Anticipating severe and prolonged action, Currie directed his divisional commanders "to keep their support and reserve Brigades close up, ready to push on as soon as the leading troops were expended."[14]

The objectives for 26 August reflected Currie's optimism. On the right half of the Corps front, the Second Division would attack south of the Arras-Cambrai road, taking Chapel Hill and pressing beyond to storm the southern heights about Monchy-le-Preux. On the left, the Third Division would strike between the road and the River Scarpe; its objectives were Orange Hill and Monchy-le-Preux. To cover the Canadian flank north of the Scarpe, the British 51st (Highland) Division was temporarily placed under Currie's command; the Canadian right would be protected by Lieutenant-General Sir Charles Fergusson's XVII Corps, which belonged to the Third Army.

The artillery, as always, was expected to pave the way for the infantry. An impressive array of guns had been assembled to support the Canadian Corps: seventeen brigades of field artillery and nine brigades of heavy artillery. The gunners were the chief beneficiaries of the earlier battle preparations. With most of their targets already registered, they could concentrate on the job of moving the guns into place and stockpiling ammunition, which they did "with a minimum of confusion."[15]

The paucity of tanks was marked. The 3rd Tank Brigade was assigned to the Canadian Corps, and Currie asked that it "supply, if possible, nine Tanks to each attacking Division each day." Currie also prescribed tactics designed to preserve these precious machines, declaring, "as a general principle, that Tanks should follow rather than precede the Infantry." Despite these measures, the tanks would contribute little; their shortcomings were never more apparent. Just five tanks went into action with the Third Division on 26 August, and all were knocked out. The Second Division was accompanied by eight, and only three survived the day.[16]

To give the Canadians a further edge, Currie opted for a night attack. This was something he normally did not favour, believing from personal experience that the drawbacks outweighed the advantages. But Currie knew that the Germans would be expecting a dawn attack, which was common practice in the BEF, because the British were usually attacking from west to east and could take advantage of the sunrise silhouetting the enemy while the twilight protected the attackers. Currie, however, chose to be unpredictable. "I decided to attack at three o'clock [in the morning] instead of the usual dawn hour, hoping in this way to surprise the enemy. The previous nights had been very bright moonlight, and as the forecast was good it was considered justifiable to advance the hour."[17] It is one more example of Currie's flexibility, a trait that contributed so much to his success.

The decision brought him into conflict with GHQ. A staff officer who had previously served with the Canadians, Lieutenant-Colonel John Dill—one of three such British officers who later rose to the rank of field-marshal—arrived at Corps headquarters to protest. GHQ, he said, preferred that the Canadians attack at dawn, in order to co-ordinate with the Third Army on the right. Currie flatly refused to alter his plans, and his top staff officer, General "Ox" Webber, bluntly told Dill: "All we want from General Headquarters is a headline in the *Daily Mail* the morning after the attack reading, 'The Canadians in Monchy Before Breakfast'." Zero hour remained 3 A.M.[18]

Since Haig made no mention of this concern during his many visits to Currie's headquarters, it seems likely that it originated with his chief of staff, Lieutenant-General Sir Herbert Lawrence. Lawrence would have known that Haig, in any event, would not be able to convince the Canadians to revise zero hour, because the field-marshal almost always acquiesced to Currie's point of view whenever a difference of opinion arose with his British counterparts. So, to argue the matter, Lawrence selected a staff officer who was familiar with the Canadians.

The Canadians did have one thing going for them: the enemy's great respect. Consequently, they were able to score a victory even before their offensive was launched. It happened on the Second Division's front, at Neuville-Vitasse, a famous pre-war health resort that had been fought over so many times that it was now nothing more than a pile of rubble. After relieving British troops in the line during the night, the 31st (Alberta) Battalion sent out strong patrols on the morning of 23 August. These were pinned down by heavy machine-gun fire, but after dark the patrolling resumed. To their surprise, the Canadians found that the Germans were abandoning Neuville-Vitasse; by dawn on the twenty-fourth, the remains of the village were securely in Canadian hands. Costing ten casualties, the 31st Battalion skirmish was the first of many bloody battles awaiting the Corps.[19]

The defenders, who belonged to the German 39th Division, explained the decision to abandon Neuville-Vitasse simply and succinctly: "the commitment of the Canadians, the best British troops, had been recognized."[20]

There can be no question of Canadian moral superiority. A German officer who was later captured "declared that when his men knew that the Canadians were in front of them they would not fight, and he shot five of them *pour encourager les autres.*"[21]

In spite of all the difficulties, the Canadians took the Germans by surprise on Monday, 26 August. "The night was overcast with clouds," General Currie sourly noted, "and it was none too bright at zero hour." However, the darkness caused more problems for the defenders than for the attackers, even though the last of the Third Division's assault battalions got into position a mere five minutes before zero hour. Accompanied by a barrage that was described as "excellent," the Canadians quickly overran the enemy positions along the entire line.[22]

Both Canadian divisions relied on manoeuvre and innovation. The Second Division found that it did not have sufficient artillery to cover its whole front effectively, so General Burstall—an amiable but colourless man, he was a rarity among Canadian soldiers, a professional who had attended the British army's Staff College at Camberley, Surrey, before the war—deliberately left untouched a pocket of enemy defences in the centre. Burstall planned a pincer movement, outflanking the position on either side, and then mopping it up—"an entirely new departure for an attack against a more than less organized hostile position of defence," certainly in the Canadian Corps and probably in the entire BEF. And it worked perfectly. Attacking on a two-brigade front, the Second Division encountered generally light resistance. According to the Sixth Brigade's General Bell, "the enemy had no

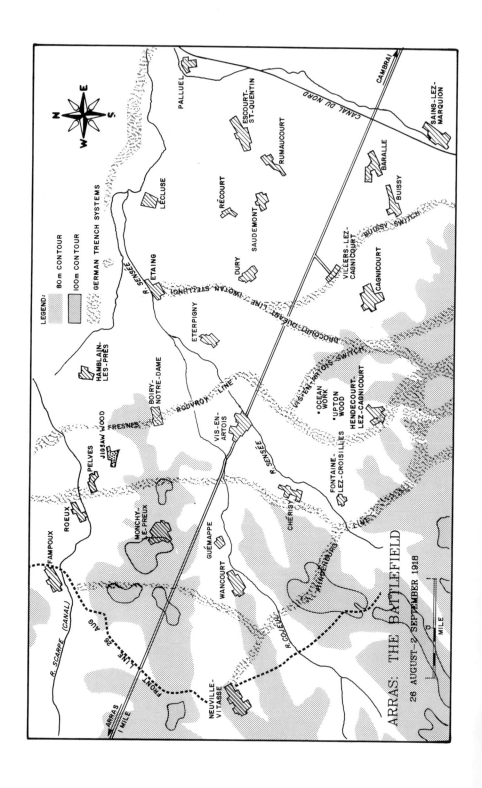

ARRAS: THE BATTLEFIELD
26 AUGUST–2 SEPTEMBER 1918

stomach for a fight." As planned, the 27th (Winnipeg) and 28th (Northwest) battalions outflanked the enemy pocket opposite Neuville-Vitasse and rounded up the surprised defenders with ease. General Rennie's Fourth Brigade enjoyed similar success, striking along the Arras-Cambrai road and surging across Chapel Hill. By nine in the morning, both brigades had taken all their objectives.[23]

Meantime, Orange Hill and Monchy-le-Preux were falling to the Third Division. General Lipsett, the divisional commander, had rejected a frontal assault on Orange Hill as being "a very hazardous and costly operation" and decided to turn the position to the north, "which did not appear to be so well organized for defence." Once through the front line, the valley of the Scarpe would protect the attackers and enable them to swing south and roll up the defences on the hill. Lipsett's plan was executed brilliantly. Three battalions of Brigadier-General Dennis Draper's Eighth Brigade led the assault: while the 5th Canadian Mounted Rifles (CMR) launched a diversionary attack, the 4th CMR, followed by the 2nd CMR, struck north along the Scarpe. Breaking through the flimsy defences here, the 2nd CMR swung south and, as Lipsett envisaged, overran the positions on the hill. The 1st and 5th CMR then carried the assault to Monchy-le-Preux. Here, too, the enemy appeared unable to offer more than token resistance. By seven-thirty, Monchy and its heights were held by the Third Division.[24]

A member of the 5th CMR won the Victoria Cross in the battle for Monchy-le-Preux. Twenty-six-year-old Lieutenant Charles Rutherford left his company on the approach to Monchy in order to check on the progress of another company. When Lieutenant Rutherford returned, he could find no sign of his men, and, assuming they had gone ahead, hurried to catch up. "I'm a hell of an officer," he thought. "I should be ahead of my men, not behind them." As he neared the outskirts of the village, he stumbled upon a heavily defended pillbox. Standing in the open, armed only with a pistol, his quick wits saved him. "You fellows are my prisoners!" he shouted, waving his Colt revolver. Rutherford waited nervously as he watched two officers confer; the next thing he knew, they had surrendered to him. Rutherford had single-handedly captured forty-five Germans and three machine-guns. He later added thirty more from a machine-gun post in the vicinity and so earned the VC for his quick-witted performance.[25]

The Canadian attack continued through the morning and into the early afternoon. The Second Division turned its attention to the high ground beyond the River Cojeul which, with its dry bed, was actually a natural trench. The main effort was made by troops of the Sixth Brigade, supported by the Fourth near the Arras-Cambrai road. Taking the villages of Wancourt and Guémappe—the latter fell around four in the afternoon—the Canadians crossed the Cojeul's steep banks and struck for the high ground to the east. This attack was launched under a powerful artillery barrage at 4:30 P.M. by the 27th (Winnipeg) and 28th (Northwest) battalions. Despite enormous fields of barbed wire, they took the rise, only to come under murderous enfilade fire from the right, where British troops had not yet silenced a German strongpoint. It was knocked out in short order by a company of the 28th which crossed into the British sector. The 27th Battalion, meanwhile, was trying to break into a trench code-named "Egret": one company managed to get a toehold in the trench but could not hold on in the face of furious fire on both flanks. However, General Bell, the Sixth Brigade's commander, was determined to end the day in control of Egret Trench, to secure a sound jumping-off line for the following day. The 27th and 28th battalions carried out his wishes, waiting until after dark, then attacking separately and without artillery support. The Germans, taken by surprise, were driven out of Egret Trench. "The operation was brilliantly carried out," wrote an approving Bell.[26]

Equally fierce fighting took place north of the road. To continue the Third Division's advance, General Lipsett chose to commit fresh troops, instructing General Dyer's Seventh Brigade to leap-frog the weary Eighth. Two battalions, the Royal Canadian Regiment (RCR) and Princess Patricia's Canadian Light Infantry (PPCLI), stormed the woods east of Monchy and south of Pelves. Fighting their way through a seemingly interminable series of trenches and barbed-wire entanglements, neither battalion made much progress. And, for the first time this day, the Germans were able to muster a series of violent counterattacks. Most were broken up by the Canadian artillery, but they forced the Canadians onto the defensive and ended their advance on 26 August. So severe were these attacks that General Dyer was forced to rush both his reserve battalions to the aid of the beleaguered RCR and PPCLI. The 49th (Edmonton Regiment) covered the brigade's exposed flank on the Scarpe, while the 42nd (Royal Highlanders of Canada) covered the road on the right.

Thus ended a good day for the Canadian Corps. Although the 51st (Highland) Division, north of the Scarpe, had had trouble keeping pace, the two Canadian divisions had done very well. They had penetrated the maze of German defences some 6000 yards, or more than three miles, taking "more than 2,000 prisoners" and "a few guns," according to General Currie. "To-day has been a most successful one," wrote a delighted Douglas Haig. "The capture of Monchy-le-Preux at the cost of 1,500 casualties was quite extraordinary. The enemy knew the value of this position in his system of defences and so devoted much labour to strengthening it...."[27]

The Canadian Corps continued its attack early Tuesday morning, 27 August. It was not, unfortunately, very well co-ordinated. The

Second Division, plagued by the first of a series of problems, was unable to go over the top until 10 A.M., owing to the difficulty in getting forward its reserve brigade as well as the late arrival of the eight tanks assigned to this operation. As a result, the Third Division, attacking on schedule at 4:30 A.M., went into action with its flank exposed. To make matters worse for everyone, it rained heavily during the night, turning the pockmarked ground into a sodden and slippery mess.

The day's objectives were ambitious. General Currie proposed to develop the attack in two phases: in the first, the Fresnes-Rouvroy Line would be pierced; in the second, he hoped to breach the Drocourt-Quéant Line. The ultimate goals for the two Canadian divisions— Etaing and Dury for the Third, Cagnicourt for the Second—would have entailed an advance of about five miles, the whole distance heavily defended by machine-gun posts, interconnected trench systems, sunken roads, and vast quantities of barbed wire. In setting such distant objectives, Currie clearly anticipated a reduction in the enemy's resistance, when reality would be quite the contrary.*

Fresh troops spearheaded the Third Division's drive to the Fresnes-Rouvroy Line. General Ormond's Ninth Brigade, supported by a battalion from each of the Seventh and Eighth brigades, jumped off in a steady rain. The 52nd (New Ontario) Battalion, along with the 58th (Central Ontario), took two small woods by nine-thirty that morning. But few other gains were possible. Boiry-Notre-Dame remained in enemy hands, despite a determined effort by the 116th (Ontario County) Battalion: machine-gun fire from Pelves and nearby Jigsaw Wood foiled every Canadian attack. Complicating the Third Division's task was the fact that its front had effectively doubled since the previous day. Having to extend its flank along the Scarpe while driving deeper into the German defensive system, Lipsett's formation now held nearly 7000 yards of the Corps front, compared to the 3500 yards at zero hour on the twenty-sixth.[29]

Only one other noteworthy advance was made this day. Near the Arras-Cambrai road, the 43rd (Cameron Highlanders of Canada) Battalion, with help from the 2nd Canadian Mounted Rifles and 18th (Western Ontario) Battalion, fought its way into Vis-en-Artois. The experience of one member of the 43rd typified the hard fighting encountered by these units. Corporal Albert West, of B Company, took up a position in a shallow sunken road across the Cojeul. Corporal West recounted his brush with death late that night:

---

* On 26 August, four German divisions faced the Canadian Corps: the 48th Reserve, north of the Scarpe, with the 35th, 39th, and 214th on the south side. These were reinforced the following day by two more divisions, the 21st Reserve and 26th Reserve.[28]

Over came the shells. The [sunken] road was only a trap as the sides were so worn it gave us little or no protection. Every hit on the road meant losses. Men were falling fast. Mr. Williams and Major Charlton were seriously wounded and a number of men.... It was a hot spot alright. In fact a short time there and none would be safe.... We all moved down to the end of the cut and halted when someone cried out, "For God's sake, let us get out of here," [and] we all ran around a bank to our left and flopped. Just then a high explosive shell landed just where we had been bunched. A lucky move for us.[30]

The Second Division attacked at 10 A.M. Fresh troops of Brigadier-General T.L. Tremblay's Fifth Brigade led the assault, supported by elements of the Fourth Brigade. General Tremblay employed three battalions: the 26th (New Brunswick), 24th (Victoria Rifles of Canada), and 22nd (French Canadian), from right to left. Tremblay was not concerned at the late start, later noting that there were advantages to having a few hours of daylight before zero. It gave his men a chance to familiarize themselves with the ground, and it might have made the enemy relax a bit when dawn passed without an attack.[31]

And, for a while, it did appear that the delay might pay dividends. Debouching from Wancourt Ridge, the Fifth Brigade enjoyed considerable success during the late morning. While the 22nd and 24th battalions took Chérisy, the 26th stormed across the River Sensée. By noon, Lieutenant-Colonel A.E.G. MacKenzie, the thirty-eight-year-old officer commanding the New Brunswick battalion, reported to brigade headquarters: "Battalion crossing Sensée River. Battalion H.Q. with reserve Company. Enormous number of prisoners passing through. Hun Artillery very heavy. Our casualties light. We are in touch with Royal Scots on the right and 24th Battalion on the left."[32]

However, the attack quickly ran out of steam on the other side of the Sensée. Scrambling up the steep bank, the Canadians were soon pinned down by machine-gun fire, and shell fire from German guns in the vicinity of Upton Wood was severe, too. Even the Royal Air Force compounded the Canadians' problems, when British Sopwith Camels strafed them "for over a quarter of an hour,"[33] according to an irate Tremblay. Worse, their artillery support was negligible. The Sensée marked the extreme range of the Canadian field guns, and while these batteries were moved forward, the infantrymen were left to their own resources. Unable to work their way through the massive barbed-wire entanglements, they were stopped 200 yards beyond the river. Casualties mounted rapidly. Among the injured was the officer commanding the 22nd Battalion, Major Arthur Dubuc, who lost an eye; Lieutenant-

Colonel William Clark-Kennedy of the 24th took temporary command of both battalions.

By late afternoon, it was apparent that the Second Division had been stopped in its tracks. General Currie, acknowledging the "very heavy opposition,"[34] ordered General Burstall to consolidate the day's gains and prepare for tomorrow's operation.

Tuesday, 27 August, had been rather disappointing. While Currie had hoped to get beyond the D-Q Line, the Canadians had been stalled short of the Fresnes-Rouvroy Line. There can be no question that the Corps commander was surprised by both the quantity and quality of German resistance. "The enemy throughout the day pushed a large number of reinforcements forward," he later wrote, "bringing up Machine Gun Units in motor lorries.... Hostile Field Batteries in the open, firing over open sights, showed remarkable tenacity, several remaining in action until the personnel had been destroyed by our machine gun fire." In view of the furious fighting that had taken place, Currie considered relieving the Second and Third divisions on the night of the twenty-seventh, with the First and British 4th divisions, respectively. But the British division was delayed en route to the battle zone, and Currie decided against a partial relief, believing that "it was undesirable at this stage to employ a fresh Division alongside a Division which had already been engaged." This was regrettable, because the Second Division desperately needed to be taken out of the line, as its performance on 28 August would attest. It was a rare mistake by Currie, and one that he cannot really be faulted for making, since it would become apparent only through hindsight. In any case, Currie, to his credit, lowered his sights for the next day's effort. "The objective for the day was the capture of the Fresnes-Rouvroy Line, the possession of which was vital to the success of our further operations."[35]

Even so, Wednesday, 28 August, brought mixed results. Despite overnight rain, it turned out to be a "warm and bright"[36] day. But there were no tanks available to support the weary infantry, and, as on the previous day, the two Canadian divisions attacked independently. The Third Division, as before, went first, attacking at 11 A.M.; the Second did not go over the top till 12:30 P.M.

The Third Division's attack was outstandingly innovative. General Lipsett noticed that the enemy's artillery fire "had been heavy but scattered" in this sector, and that "the hostile machine guns were our real difficulty." Therefore he concluded "that an attack on a small front covered by a concentration of all our possible Artillery to smother the machine gun nests would be justifiable as the Germans did not seem sufficiently well organized to concentrate their Artillery against it effectively." Lipsett employed all three of his brigades: the Ninth, in the centre, would attack first, supported by every available gun; the Seventh and Eighth would attack an hour and a half later. However, the Eighth and Ninth Brigades had to be slightly reorganized due to a certain intermingling of their units. The 4th Canadian Mounted Rifles of the Eighth Brigade was attached to the Ninth, in exchange for the 43rd Battalion.[37]

The operation was a great success. The Ninth Brigade went into action at 11 A.M. with its four battalions deployed along a 1000-yard front. With superlative and overwhelming artillery support, the Ninth Brigade breached the Fresnes-Rouvroy Line "without much difficulty"—Lipsett's words—and secured Boiry-Notre-Dame with its adjacent heights. The second phase went equally smoothly, beginning at 12:30 P.M., when the brigades on either side of the Ninth joined the attack. On the right, the Eighth Brigade, led by the 5th Canadian Mounted Rifles and the 43rd Battalion, crossed the Sensée and took the high ground beyond. On the left, the Seventh Brigade was similarly successful. The 49th Battalion stormed the fortified village of Pelves, which the regimental history later described as "a veritable nest of machine guns." At the same time, the PPCLI, with help from the Royal Canadian Regiment and the 42nd Battalion, finally captured nearby Jigsaw Wood. "There was hand-to-hand fighting in the wood," recalled Sergeant T.T. Shields of the PPCLI. But the Canadians prevailed, capturing 175 prisoners and over thirty machine-guns. The Third Division had smashed the Fresnes-Rouvroy Line across its entire front.[38]

The Second Division's story was, sadly, much different. As he had done the day before, General Burstall committed two brigades to the attack, the Fourth along the Arras-Cambrai road and the Fifth on its right. But, due to its heavy casualties, the Fourth Brigade was, in Burstall's opinion, "practically a composite battalion," its reserve composed of collected cooks, clerks, and other headquarters personnel. The Fifth Brigade was in little better condition. In retrospect, Burstall saw that these units had little chance of succeeding on 28 August: "our men had started the day tired, with the wire opposing them practically uncut...the enemy's trenches were extremely strongly held by both machine guns and infantry."[39]

The defences were, indeed, imposing. A.L. Barry, a subaltern of the 26th Battalion, later stated that "I never saw such a naturally good defensive position...the ground sloped down to the German front line which had been taken, then upward to a rise held by heavy machine guns." Beyond, the "enemy light artillery was firing at us over open sights about three-quarters of a mile away—a real Balaclava."[40]

Many officers had misgivings. One such was Major Georges Vanier, the acting commander of the 22nd Battalion, who shared a headquarters dugout with the 24th's Colonel Clark-Kennedy. When they received the order to renew the attack, the two officers exchanged glances. "Oh, it'll be all right," Clark-Kennedy assured Vanier, who realized that this was merely bravado. Vanier then set off to make his preparations.

I called a meeting in a large shell hole of the few officers who were left. I told them about the new attack and, in the circumstances, there was only one thing to do. When the barrage fell the officers were to rise and call on the men to follow, and that is what happened. But we didn't get very far. The barrage was not a heavy one, and there were many enemy machine-guns.[41]

The 22nd, attacking at 12:30 P.M., lost every officer. Major Vanier was among the wounded, hit by a bullet in the side, "and I should have been very fortunate indeed to come off with it only. But this was to be one of my bad days. As I was being dressed by the [stretcher-]bearer a shell exploded at my side causing rather unpleasant shrapnel wounds to my...legs." Vanier subsequently had his right leg amputated above the knee. In fact, all three battalion commanders in the Fifth Brigade's attack became casualties. Colonel Clark-Kennedy of the 24th was severely wounded, but stubbornly refused to be evacuated; he was later awarded the VC for his inspirational leadership. Less fortunate was the 26th Battalion's Colonel MacKenzie, who was killed by a burst of machine-gun fire during the assault. His scout officer, Lieutenant Barry, called MacKenzie "the best soldier from whom I ever took an order."[42]

The Second Division's attack was a failure. There were too few troops taking part, too many of them were killed or wounded, and they received too little help from their artillery. "At nightfall," related a disappointed General Currie, "the general line of the 2nd Canadian Division was little in advance of the line held the night before, although a few parties of stubborn men were still as far forward as the wire of the Fresnes-Rouvroy Line." Currie ordered the Second and Third divisions withdrawn that very night, replaced by the First and British 4th divisions. The Corps commander fully realized the implications of the Second Division's unsuccessful attack. "This will interfere seriously with the future events," he told his diary, "as the 1st Division must take the Fresnes-Rouvroy line before getting a jumping off line" for the subsequent assault on the Drocourt-Quéant Line. Currie duly informed First Army headquarters that the Corps would be unable to mount an attack on the D-Q Line before 31 August.[43]

The cost of operations to date had been high. In three days of stiff fighting, the Corps had incurred 5801 casualties, the majority in the Second and Third divisions. As always, some units had lost more heavily than others. Two battalions of the Second Division had been especially hard-hit: the 22nd lost 501 men, including every officer; the 20th counted 442 casualties. The only saving grace was that, as General Currie pointed out at the time, "the wounds so far are not nearly as severe as those on the Somme, the most of them being clean bullet wounds which ought to heal rapidly. From the reports I have seen, I think the proportion of killed is very small indeed."[44]

Nevertheless, the Corps had done well so far. As the Third Division's General Lipsett proudly noted, the Canadians had advanced five and a half miles "over very difficult and broken country, through a maze of trenches," in just three days. Added Lipsett:

> I know no finer example of what can be done by courageous and determined men than this attack; all the battalions had been heavily engaged and done a great deal of marching, some had been engaged with very little sleep since 3 A.M. on the 26th, and still all responded to the call for a final effort....

Currie publicly congratulated the men of both divisions, assuring them that their efforts had "paved the way for greater success to-morrow. Keep constantly in mind Stonewall Jackson's motto 'Press Forward'."[45]

Nevertheless, Currie was uncomfortable with the situation. While the Fresnes-Rouvroy Line had been broken between the Scarpe and the Arras-Cambrai road, it remained intact south of the road. And Currie was far from pleased with the progress of the British 51st Division north of the Scarpe, complaining that "they have not got along as far as is necessary. I believe fresh troops should be put in there in order to force the Germans back completely to the Fresnes-Rouvroy line north of the Scarpe."* Because of the heavy concentration of German artillery there, Currie was concerned about enfilade fire: "our only road, the Arras-Cambrai road, is practically under Field Gun fire." He also knew that things would not get easier:

> We are now trying to break the hinge of the German position, and if we are successful great and important results might reasonably follow.... For this reason the Boche will fight us very hard. Further south I believe he is fighting simply a rearguard action having his mind fully made up to retire to the Hindenburg line.[46]

Currie was in no hurry. While he was fully aware that time was of the essence, he refused to be rushed into a hasty, ill-conceived attack. As he commented in the privacy of his diary: "Believing the Quéant-Drocourt line to be the backbone of [German] resistance, we have decided to put all our strength against it, not to attack it until we are ready, then go all out."[47] The Canadian Corps would storm the D-Q Line on 2 September.

---

* This occurred on the night of 29-30 August, when the British 11th Division, under command of xxii Corps, took over the line astride the Scarpe.

The enemy would be ready, too. The importance of the position is indicated by the inordinately large numbers of German troops that had been moved in. Three divisions—4th Ersatz, 16th, and 58th—held the remaining fortifications in front of the D-Q Line, which in turn was held by four divisions: 1st and 2nd Guard Reserve, 3rd Reserve, and 22nd. In addition, the 7th Cavalry and 11th divisions were in close support, making a total of nine enemy divisions facing the Canadian Corps.

The Canadians had plenty of preparing to do. Vital was the artillery's work, softening up the defences. Wire-cutting was the chief task, and the gunners spent the three days prior to the attack blasting wide swaths through the fields of barbed wire which protected the D-Q Line. By zero hour, the Corps heavy artillery had cleared fourteen passable lanes for the infantry.

No less important was the need for proper jumping-off lines. This meant capturing the Fresnes-Rouvroy Line south of the Arras-Cambrai road, along with a number of strongpoints and fortified areas, including the Vis-en-Artois switch line, Ocean Work, and Upton Wood. North of the road, several fortified villages—the most important being Eterpigny—blocked the path to the D-Q Line. The job of clearing this ground fell to the two newest divisions in the Canadian Corps front, the First Canadian and the 4th British.

The First Division's General Macdonell took up the challenge with characteristic enthusiasm. At fifty-four, Macdonell was the elder states-man among the Canadian divisional commanders. A professional sol-dier who wore his hat at a jaunty angle to show off his silver hair, and who sprinkled his personal correspondence with Gaelic phrases, Mac-donell had complete confidence in the capabilities of his men. Within hours of moving into the front lines, the First Division had prepared a series of attacks designed to clear the defences in front of the D-Q Line. The key, of course, was the Fresnes-Rouvroy Line, which would be assaulted on Friday, 30 August, by General Griesbach's First Brigade. Griesbach, a former mayor of Edmonton and a pre-war militia officer of some repute, devised an ingenious scheme; years later, Macdonell would compliment him on "your daring plan & its good courageous execution."* Observing that the neighbouring British had captured Hendecourt-lez-Cagnicourt, Griesbach proposed to outflank the

---

* It was a plan that Griesbach jealously guarded from the prying eyes of his Third Brigade counterpart, Brigadier-General George Tuxford, who had an unfortunate habit of claiming undue credit for himself, a trait that did not endear him to his colleagues. As Griesbach wrily remarked years after the war, "I remember seeing Tuxford on the day of our attack on the Fresnes-Rouvroy line, but he was not particularly welcome, as I was adverse [sic] to giving him any opportunity of taking a hand in my show, for fear that I might subsequently find that it had become his show."[48]

Fresnes-Rouvroy Line and roll it up with an attack from two directions. To carry it out, a complex artillery barrage was required; it was expertly designed by the First Division's artillery chief, Brigadier-General Herbert Thacker. Griesbach called Thacker's bombardment "a master-piece," pointing out "that he only had a few hours to do this job."[49]

Macdonell eagerly accepted the proposal. "I saw at once," he later remarked, "that Griesbach's conception was a winner."[50]

Zero hour was 4:40 A.M. on 30 August. There was no preliminary bombardment. Three battalions took part: the 1st (Western Ontario) and 2nd (Eastern Ontario), which formed up in the British zone near Hendecourt and attacked in a northerly direction, and the 3rd (Toronto Regiment), which launched a frontal assault southeastward. Accompanied by Thacker's complex barrage, which moved from right to left across the First Division's front, the Canadians swept through the German defences in the darkness. Although surprised, the enemy put up stout resistance in places; the 2nd Battalion reported that "in many instances German machine guns remained in action until the infantry had entirely surrounded them and killed their crews." The attackers converged, as planned, on Upton Wood, where "German prisoners complained bitterly that the Canadians seemed to have been coming at them from all directions." By mid-morning, Griesbach's brigade had cleared most of the Fresnes-Rouvroy Line on its front.[51]

However, the Canadians came dangerously close to losing it all. Having captured Upton Wood, the 1st and 2nd battalions dug in facing the wrong way, despite a specific warning from Griesbach. "I had cautioned them on this point before the attack and had pointed out that when they had gained their objective their line was to run North and South facing East." In the confusion, they looked north, inadvertently presenting the enemy with an exposed flank. The Germans were quick to take advantage of the weakness: a savage counter-attack hit the Canadians late in the morning. The two battalions "broke under the German attack," Griesbach recalled unhappily, but the day was saved by the imperturbable commander of the 2nd, Lieutenant-Colonel L.T. MacLaughlin. Recounted Griesbach: " 'Little Mac' happened around at this moment, as good men have a habit of doing, and pistol in hand drove the bolters back in a counter attack which restored the line. 'Mac' got shot in the leg for his pains...." The close call at Upton Wood notwithstanding, the First Brigade could take considerable satisfaction in its day's work. At the cost of 652 casualties, the brigade took more than 1000 prisoners and ninety-nine machine-guns.[52]

Heavy but localized fighting continued for the next two days. On 31 August, the Second Brigade cleared the strongpoint named Ocean Work; General Tuxford's Third Brigade captured what was left of the

Vis-en-Artois switch line on 1 September, although subjected to repeated counter-attacks from the D-Q Line. With only hours to spare, the First Division had secured its jumping-off points.

North of the Arras-Cambrai road, the British 4th Division was engaged in bitter fighting as well. This division was considered by Sir Douglas Haig to be "one of the best in the Army," and General Currie credited its troops with great tenacity. They had, according to Currie, "doggedly pushed ahead, crossing the valley of the Sensée River and capturing the villages of Haucourt, Remy, and Eterpigny," in spite of "very difficult, thickly wooded country." But the 4th Division's losses in these preliminary operations were heavy, and the commander, Major-General T.G. Matheson, informed Currie "that it was doubtful whether the assault on the D.Q. line on the frontage allotted to the Division (2,500 yards) could be undertaken with a fair chance of success."[53]

This forced a last-minute change in Currie's plans. On the night of 31 August-1 September, a brigade of General Watson's Fourth Division had moved into the front line between the First Division, on its right, and the 4th Division. Currie now ordered Watson to bring forward a second brigade, which reduced the British division's frontage by 1000 yards. This move was completed just "a few hours before zero," Currie noted. Even as this alteration was being made, the Germans continued to make repeated and violent counter-attacks on the Canadians throughout the afternoon and evening of 1 September. "The hand to hand fighting," said Currie, "really continued until zero hour the next day, the troops attacking the Drocourt-Quéant line as they moved forward taking over the fight from the troops then holding the line." The enemy, knowing what was coming, spared no effort to forestall the renewed Canadian Corps offensive. It would all be to no avail.[54]

At first glance, there was nothing exceptional about Currie's plan to break the D-Q Line. It would involve three divisions—from right to left, the First and Fourth Canadian and British 4th—mounting a frontal assault on the enemy's powerful fortifications. Supported by 741 guns and howitzers of all calibres, and scheduled for dawn, the proposed operation was, apparently, no more than another siege-style attack that was typical of the Western Front. But Currie had added a wrinkle. Once the D-Q Line had been breached, Currie intended to push through Brutinel's Brigade—formally known as the Canadian Independent Force—of armoured cars and cavalry astride the Arras-Cambrai road. The Corps commander wanted to do more than merely smash the D-Q Line: he wanted to seize the crossings of the Canal du Nord, as well as the high ground beyond. If it worked, it was conceivable that Cambrai, the hub of German communications in all northern France, might fall. It was ambitious and daring, displaying not only Currie's grasp of mobile warfare, but also his gambler's instinct—a quality that marks great commanders and separates them from the mundane.

There were, to be sure, some subordinates who had reservations. General Watson commented in the privacy of his diary: "It is a very ambitious programme, & I doubt if it can be carried through to the extent they have laid down." Lieutenant-Colonel Andy McNaughton, the Corps counter-battery officer, later called it "a plan fantastic in conception and, from the start, improbable of success." Although Currie would have welcomed their input, for he always encouraged his officers to speak freely and propose alternatives, it seems that neither Watson nor McNaughton expressed any concerns to the Corps commander.[55]

As zero day approached, another problem arose that required Currie's attention. It involved a disagreement with a British corps commander, Lieutenant-General Sir Charles Fergusson, whose XVII Corps operated on the Canadian right. The arrogant, overbearing Fergusson was one of the few British officers with whom Currie did not get along, and this episode merely reinforced their enmity toward each other. Currie was upset to learn that XVII Corps had delayed its zero hour on 2 September; the British planned to attack two hours after the Canadians, in broad daylight. Currie considered that the delay would expose "our flank to such an extent as to prejudice the success of our operation," and visited Fergusson's headquarters on Sunday, 1 September. Forcefully stating his case, Currie "induced them to change their plans somewhat." While Fergusson refused to reschedule his attack, he did agree to place a British brigade behind the First Canadian Division, to protect the Canadian flank until XVII Corps went over the top. Satisfied with the compromise, Currie returned to his own headquarters in an optimistic mood: "Everything looks promising for the success of tomorrow's operation providing we can get a good start at zero hour."[56]

Currie's confidence was well founded. He knew, better than anyone, the enormous capabilities of the Canadian Corps. There was, in his view, no German position that could withstand a Canadian attack. The Corps was never stronger; on the eve of the D-Q Line operation, it numbered 148,090, all ranks. Two-thirds—101,599—were Canadians, the balance British. Despite the impressive array, Currie spared no effort to minimize the inevitable sacrifices these men would have to make. "I do not ask them to do anything where I think they haven't a chance," he explained. "They know that fact, I believe. We try to pave the way for them, and when we ask them to deliver the goods they never fail."[57]

Canadian morale was sky-high. Typifying the mood of the men was the 14th (Royal Montreal Regiment) Battalion, which had taken part in the severe fighting in front of the D-Q Line on 1 September. The 14th was scheduled for a support role on the second; "at least 40 [soldiers], suffering from flesh wounds, refused evacuation and declared themselves able and willing to take part in operations planned for the morrow."[58]

The D-Q Line was not to be underestimated. "It consisted of a front and support line, both abundantly provided with concrete shelters and machine-gun posts and protected by dense masses of barbed wire." In short, it was a superb example of German military engineering, with every strongpoint mutually supporting and sited to offer the best fields of fire for the machine-gunners who formed the core of the defence. To the rear, angling southeastward in front of Villers-lez-Cagnicourt, stood the Buissy switch line, which linked the D-Q Line to the main Hindenburg position. And behind all these defences lay the Canal du Nord. The whole sector, moreover, was manned by "eight fresh Divisions." As one historian has perceptively observed, "months might well have gone into preparation for an attack such as that contemplated, but months were not available."[59]

The Canadian Corps attacked at 5 A.M. on Monday, 2 September. With faint light along the eastern horizon, it would prove to be "a beautiful day, with just a hint of autumn in the air." The air was also full of Canadian shells. The 741 guns and howitzers marshalled for this assault was the biggest number to back a Canadian attack during the war's last hundred days. The bombardment that exploded over the heads of the advancing British and Canadian infantry, who followed the rolling barrage as closely as they could, was nearly deafening. "Mere words," commented one participant, "cannot describe the overpowering noise of the roaring torrent of shells, nor the grandeur of the scene as from a mile away we watched the sparkle of shell-bursts all along the glacis slopes, and the red German rockets rising above the smoke to call for help."[60]

The bombardment was as effective as it looked and sounded. Coming as it did in the wake of three days of systematic shelling by the Corps heavy artillery, the Canadian shell fire pounded the enemy defences to rubble. One officer's experience exemplifies the fine work of the artillery. Later in the day, Lieutenant-Colonel Harold Matthews, of the First Division's staff, mounted his horse to survey the scene; "in one place I rode my horse right through the wire as it had been left by the shell fire without difficulty."[61]

Where the artillery failed to cut the wire, the tanks did the job. Six companies of Mark vs, totalling fifty tanks, were assigned to the Corps, two companies to each of the attacking divisions, and although few survived the day, they often won rave reviews from the infantrymen.

H.A. Love, a subaltern in the 85th (Nova Scotia Highlanders) Battalion, remembered that day vividly:

> The tanks were...five or six minutes late, and we finally fell in behind them and went along, and our barrage was wonderful. And the tanks, you see, the tanks cut a lot of the wire for us. We were following along in single file behind the tanks and, strange as it may seem, I had great difficulty in keeping my men in single file. They wanted to get in there, they wanted to get at them.[62]

The daunting defences of the D-Q Line were smashed with surprising, almost ridiculous, ease. Across the Corps front, the forward German line was captured by eight o'clock that morning; in many places, large chunks of the support line had been taken, too. For the first few hours, prisoners were easy to come by. "I never saw the enemy so cowardly," commented Lieutenant-Colonel Cy Peck, who commanded the 16th (Canadian Scottish) Battalion and who would win the VC this day. "Prisoners surrendered in shoals. They outnumbered us vastly, but they were in a demoralized condition." Consider the case of B Company of the 8th (90th Winnipeg Rifles) Battalion. The company cornered a German platoon whose officer refused to surrender. The stand-off lasted but a few minutes: the officer was shot by one of his own men, and forty-six enemy soldiers swelled the battalion's bag of prisoners.[63]

Not all Germans in the front lines were so quick to give up, as the 47th (Western Ontario) Battalion found. One of its platoons, under Lieutenant H.A. Black, came upon a trench defended by two officers and forty other ranks, with four machine-guns. Lieutenant Black calmly split up his platoon. While Lewis gunners and rifle grenadiers pinned down the defenders, Black led a bayonet charge. The Germans fought to the last man, literally: not one of them surrendered.[64]

However, the opposition stiffened steadily as the morning went along. By the time the Canadians had completed the conquest of the D-Q Line support positions, they had outrun the maximum range of most of the field guns.* As a result, the infantry had to press the attack with minimal artillery support after mid-morning, in the face of galling

---

* Mobile batteries of 18-pounders—the standard field gun in use by the BEF by this point in the war—were used effectively throughout the day. There were two such batteries per division, and the gunners reported that they enjoyed "some of the best shooting of the war," particularly against "enemy batteries in the open and movement in large bodies." The Canadians also employed captured guns, although the Germans had by now learned to spike these weapons before abandoning them. Still, using cannibalized parts, specially trained teams put fifteen German 77-millimetre guns and three 5.9-inch howitzers into action on 2 September, firing over 600 rounds at their former owners.[65]

machine-gun fire. Veterans of long years of fighting on the Western Front had never seen anything like it. Among the wounded was Sergeant Arthur Shelford of the 54th (Central Ontario) Battalion, who later wrote of his experience:

> Personally, I could never quite understand how anyone survived at all in an attack of this kind, for it was over dead-level country with the enemy in trenches firing all the machine-gun bullets they could at us, not forgetting the numerous shells dropping around us. The ground resembled a hail-storm, as the bullets hit all around us, and, I suppose, it really was a hail-storm, only the hail was bullets.[66]

The attack soon lost its momentum. Most of the tanks had been knocked out by the middle of the morning, and, having little help from their artillery, the Canadian infantrymen were on their own. Left to their own devices, they responded brilliantly and bravely, as they had on so many Great War battlefields previously. Individual initiative and incredible heroism enabled the Canadians to prevail in the face of adversity: seven would win the Victoria Cross, the most won by Canadians in a single day in the entire war.

General Currie's concerns about his right flank were soon realized. Thanks to the British refusal to co-ordinate their attack with the Canadians, the Corps was engulfed in a storm of enfilade fire. It was the 16th (Canadian Scottish) Battalion, on the extreme right, that paid the price. Everything seemed to go wrong for this battalion. No tanks arrived in time for zero hour, and it ran into several broad belts of barbed wire that had been missed by the barrage. The two leading companies of the 16th lost every officer killed or wounded, but the surviving men cut their way through the wire by hand, then took on the enemy's machine-guns. Sergeant F.E. Earwaker later wrote of the battle in the barbed wire:

> I was in a shell-hole with Lance-Corporal Bob Currie of my platoon, two or three privates whose names I have forgotten, and Sergeant Sandy Reid of another company. You couldn't see very clearly. Daylight hadn't quite come.
>
> We had been there but a short time when Lieut. [A.C.] Campbell-Johnston passed word along to try once more. We all got up together and didn't get more than five yards before we met with the heaviest fire from the trench in front of us that I have ever faced. Down I went into a shell-hole, Lieut. Campbell-Johnston flopped on his stomach right in the wire about twelve feet to my right. Sergeant Reid was about the same distance ahead of me in the wire. Lieut. Campbell-Johnston raised himself on his hands, look-

111

ing to the front, evidently trying to see how much chance he would have to go forward, when they got him in the head. I then threw out a smoke bomb and Sergeant Reid came back into the shell-hole.

There we were. Every time we exposed ourselves they opened fire on us from the trench in front, and enfilade fire from the high ground on our right. We decided before making another move to wait for a tank, and soon we heard one to the left about a hundred yards behind us. We signalled to it with our helmets, but the tank did not see us so we sat down to wait, shooting rifle grenades over at the German trench.[67]

A tank eventually arrived, but it was Lance-Corporal William Metcalf who saved the day. Private J.H. Reill remembered Metcalf's heroic display:

When the tank came to within three hundred feet of the German wire, a heavy machine-gun fire was opened on it from the front trench. Corporal Metcalf jumped up from the shell-hole where he was and with his flags pointing towards the enemy's trench, led the tank towards it and then along it. The enemy kept heavy machine-gun fire on the tank and as it got close to the trench commenced to throw at it clusters of bombs tied together.

When we afterwards got into the trench, we found seventeen German machine-guns at the same place, and all of them had been well used. How Metcalf escaped being shot to pieces has always been a wonder to me.[68]

For his bravery, Metcalf was awarded the vc, the first of two won by the 16th Battalion on 2 September.

The other vc went to its doughty commander, Colonel Peck. The portly Peck revelled in front-line combat, never missing an opportunity to personally lead his battalion into action. At Vimy Ridge, the previous year, Peck had been so ill that he could hardly walk, but he accompanied his battalion over the top, finally collapsing after all its objectives had been taken. Now he was at it again, leading his men in an attack on a strongpoint that netted thirty prisoners. When the battalion was pinned down in barbed wire in front of the D-Q support line, Peck personally fetched a tank and directed it toward the wire. "I do not know how the Colonel escaped being riddled by bullets," recalled Sergeant W.J.F. Reith.[69] But, to Peck's disgust, the tank rumbled off the wrong way.

At great cost, the battalion cut its way through the barbed wire. It was time-consuming work, and losses mounted steadily. Peck realized that he would not have enough men to attack the Germans once the wire was cut, so he again braved the heavy fire to collect his reserves from the rear, then personally led them in the attack on the D-Q support line. By one in the afternoon, the 16th Battalion was on its final objectives, thanks in large part to the colonel, who was later awarded the vc.

The enfilade fire remained a problem all day long. The 16th Battalion was leap-frogged by the 15th (48th Highlanders of Canada) Battalion, which carried the attack on the Buissy switch line. But the 15th was stopped well short of its goal, suffering crippling casualties from the right. It was not until six o'clock that evening that the British troops on the right were able to catch up to the Canadians and seal off the open flank.

The Buissy switch line fell to other units of the First Division. One notable achievement was the capture of Cagnicourt by the 14th (Royal Montreal Regiment). The fighting was fierce. The 14th Battation attacked Cagnicourt at 8 A.M. On the approach to the village, Lieutenant A.L. McLean led an attack on a German machine-gun post. A furious fire-fight ensued, and after some considerable time two enemy gunners stood with their hands in the air. Lieutenant McLean went over to accept their surrender, but he was treacherously shot dead at point-blank range. McLean's enraged platoon stormed the machine-gun nest in a furious bayonet charge to avenge their officer's death. Every defender was killed, but the Canadians were far from satisfied. Minutes later, a group of Germans emerged from Cagnicourt, possibly intent on surrendering, but no one in the 14th Battalion was interested enough to find out: the Germans were slaughtered in a hail of bullets.

The battle for Cagnicourt ended soon after. The 14th fought its way into the village and, after clearing the streets, prepared to mop up the cellars, where German troops inevitably hid. An enemy medical officer approached Lieutenant G.B. McKean, vc, and pleaded for his own life and those of the wounded in his care. Lieutenant McKean gave that assurance and was about to set off with a mopping-up party when the German intervened. "Wait!" he cried. "I will get them up." As the Canadians watched in amazement, the officer went from cellar to cellar, summoning the occupants. By the time he was done, the 14th found itself in charge of nearly 1000 prisoners, far more men than this Canadian battalion could muster.[70]

Troops of the Second Brigade cleared the Buissy switch line to the north. The 7th (1st British Columbia Regiment) Battalion led the assault at zero hour, sweeping through the D-Q front and support lines with relative ease. Corporal William Rayfield, a Vancouver realtor in peace-time, went on a one-man rampage. Rushing a trench, he killed two Germans with his bayonet and captured ten others. Then he stalked an enemy sniper who was causing many casualties; the sniper escaped, but Corporal Rayfield rounded up thirty more prisoners in a nearby trench. He won the VC for his efforts.

The 10th (Canadians) Battalion passed through at 8 A.M. Four tanks accompanied the 10th, but within forty-five minutes, all had been disabled. The battalion commander, Lieutenant-Colonel E.W. MacDonald, was not impressed with the tanks, commenting that "their organization did not seem to be as good as might have been wished for." Once the tanks were put out of action, the 10th Battalion's attack faded in the face of devastating machine-gun fire, "which made a normal frontal advance impossible." Colonel MacDonald threw out his timetable and ordered his three attacking companies to infiltrate the enemy positions, making use of cover wherever possible, and outflank the defenders, under the protection of Canadian massed machine-gun fire. "In this manner," MacDonald later reported, "a slow and steady, although perhaps not brilliant attack was made, and the advance continued." Sergeant Arthur Knight, an English-born carpenter from Regina, played a large part, repeatedly rushing the enemy by himself, killing several Germans and capturing twenty-three others. Sergeant Knight won the VC, but the award was posthumous; he was fatally wounded later in the day.* The climax of the attack came at Villers-lez-Cagnicourt, which Colonel MacDonald described as "a fortress." It fell to the 10th "after hard fighting" in the late afternoon. By six o'clock in the evening, the battalion had cleared the Buissy switch on its front in what can only be considered a remarkable feat of arms: at the cost of 233 casualties, the 10th Battalion had taken all its objectives and captured 700 prisoners and 150 machine-guns.[71]

The First Division's operation had been a considerable success, but such was not the case in the centre of the Canadian Corps, where the Fourth Division was struggling along the Arras-Cambrai road. It will be recalled that this division had originally planned a single-brigade assault, but this was increased to two brigades because of the British 4th Division's heavy losses in the preliminaries. The last-minute and hasty arrangement was unfortunate, because this was arguably the most important part of the entire Corps front. It was here that General Currie hoped to exploit victory by the bold use of a mixed force of cavalry and armoured cars under Brigadier-General Raymond Brutinel. As it turned out, Brutinel's Brigade had little to exploit.

It did not help that the Fourth Division's front was overcrowded. On the left, Brigadier-General Ross Hayter's Tenth Brigade, with three battalions, was to attack the village of Dury, while on the right, Brigadier-General James MacBrien's Twelfth Brigade would employ

* Knight Crescent in Regina commemorates the sergeant.

114

three battalions to take Mont Dury, a long, low rise astride the Arras-Cambrai road. In close support was Brigadier-General Victor Odlum's Eleventh Brigade, with Brutinel's Brigade immediately behind, ready to rush along the road toward the Canal du Nord after Mont Dury had fallen. The divisional commander, General Watson, was clearly at fault for using too many troops in such a small area; General Currie must share the responsibility.

The Tenth Brigade had to overcome a number of difficulties in executing its part in the plan of attack. It had been selected at the last minute to relieve part of the British 4th Division; having to make a ten-mile forced march, the brigade barely made it to the front in time for the assault. On arrival, the two leading battalions discovered that their jumping-off lines were actually held by the Germans. Nevertheless, the 47th (Western Ontario) and 50th (Calgary) battalions broke through the D-Q line front and support lines, the defenders being, in General Hayter's words, "easily captured or killed." Leap-frogging, the 46th (South Saskatchewan) Battalion swept into Dury, securing it by seven forty-five that morning. A sergeant, George Kentner, was "surprised at the slight resistance offered" at Dury. "Entering the town and chalk pits we found large numbers of troops who quickly obeyed our order to come out. Never had I seen so many prisoners taken in such a manner." The 46th Battalion counted 120 prisoners, along with nine machine-guns.[72]

Things changed quickly, however. The 46th had a harrowing fight ahead of it when, at noon, the Germans launched a major counter-attack that caught the Canadians by surprise. Rallying, the battalion quickly recovered the lost ground in a wild charge that Sergeant Kentner would never forget:

> In an instant we were all over, racing forward, yelling and screeching and cursing as wildly as men ever did. One element in our favour was surprise. The sight of us charging across the open ground, with fixed bayonets, and our weird, wild, almost insane cries disheartened Fritz.... They began to run but our bullets were cutting them down. We were bent on their destruction and had no thought of mercy. Some threw down their rifles and rushed towards us stumbling. In all, we took perhaps a dozen prisoners. Only a few escaped to their lines.

The Canadian line having been restored, Kentner was treated to the sobering sight of ground "strewn with khaki and grey-clad bodies," mute evidence of the ferocious fight for Dury.[73]

On the right, there was serious trouble. The Twelfth Brigade's attack got off to a promising start, but was fast reduced to a bloody shambles. Despite "exceptionally good" artillery support, the 38th (Ottawa) Battalion was soon stopped by heavy small-arms fire. "Tanks were slow in getting into action," complained the officer commanding the 38th, Lieutenant-Colonel C.M. Edwards, "and their value was lost."[74] The battalion's assault might have been an utter disaster had it not been for the admirable conduct of Private Claude Nunney, who displayed great initiative rallying his comrades and urging his companions toward their objectives on Mont Dury. Private Nunney, a burly Irishman who had earlier won the Distinguished Conduct Medal and the Military Medal, added the vc to his collection for this performance. It was, however, posthumous; severely wounded, Nunney died two weeks later.

The 72nd (Seaforth Highlanders of Canada) Battalion had better luck. Its initial advance through the D-Q front line "was made without great difficulty," according to Lieutenant-Colonel John Clark. The tanks assigned the 72nd arrived in time to assist in the capture of the support position and enabled the battalion to carry the crest of Mont Dury. Its final objective was marked by a sunken road, which was captured by a handful of Canadians. Sergeant K.A. Campbell, accompanied by a pair of privates, outflanked the road, then attacked in the face of overwhelming odds. The defenders promptly surrendered—the trio of Canadians took more than fifty prisoners.[75]

Having taken Mont Dury, the troops of the Twelfth could go no further. Descending the reverse slope, they were subjected to remarkably accurate and heavy long-range machine-gun fire. "Our men here went down like nine-pins," recalled Arthur Foster, a stretcher-bearer in the 38th Battalion.* Horatio Cromwell of the neighbouring 85th (Nova Scotia Highlanders) escaped unscathed, a state of affairs he could "ascribe only to the Divine Protection," as he remarked in a letter home. "I look back on our advance through machine gun and shell fire over open country and I feel that nothing but the power of prayer ever saved me...."[77]

The reason for the intense enemy fire in this sector was simple. After eight o'clock, the Canadian artillery stopped firing on a 1000-yard front astride the Arras-Cambrai road, to enable Brutinel's Brigade of cavalry and armoured cars to exploit the capture of Mont Dury.

---

* Private Foster would win the Military Medal this day, for tirelessly assisting wounded men, despite the heavy fire. "I did not feel much like a hero," he later wrote, "for I was under the impression that a hero was never frightened, but they told me it didn't matter how I felt for it was what I did that counted. I was so tired after the battle I slept 3 days in a deep dugout."[76]

Unfortunately, this force failed miserably. It made little headway, finding "that wire, trenches and sunken roads practically confined the movements of this mobile outfit to the Arras-Cambrai Road itself and this was rendered well nigh impassable within our lines by traffic and, further forward, by fire from machine guns and batteries firing over open sights...." The few armoured cars that got through were quickly knocked out. However, General Brutinel blamed his cavalry for the fiasco, charging a lack of initiative on the part of a British regiment, the 10th Royal Hussars, which he had placed at the head of his column.

> In my opinion the resistance was not properly tested at that time: the cavalry was reluctant to test it and did not do it, and patrols were withdrawn early and their reports were of negative value. I ascribe the original failure to break a resistance which was considerably shaken at the attitude of the leading Group, which showed a desire to spare casualties in Men and Horses.

And, Brutinel bitterly pointed out, the 10th Hussars had almost no casualties.[78]

This was not the worst of it. An erroneous report indicated that one or more armoured cars had reached the canal; to avoid shelling their own men, the Canadian artillery continued to withhold the fire that might have smothered the enemy's guns. "It was six or seven hours," fumed Colonel McNaughton, at Corps headquarters, "before I could get the guns back on those German batteries that came to life as we lifted off."[79] In the meantime, the Fourth Division's infantry remained at the mercy of the machine-guns raking the reverse slope of Mont Dury.

In the midst of this chaos, another flaw in Canadian plans became evident. Part of the problem of course, was the result of General Watson deploying too many troops in such a small area. This error was compounded by committing his reserves on that bullet-swept reverse slope, where they came under intense fire on ground that had already been captured and where, mixed with the assault units, they presented the enemy with outstanding targets. The fresh troops were, in effect, wasted, because they could accomplish nothing. The 78th (Winnipeg Grenadiers) Battalion, the Twelfth Brigade's reserve unit, was pinned down within minutes of going into action. It did little more than add to the growing casualty list.

The Eleventh Brigade exemplified the confusion. The brigade commander, General Odlum, appears to have lost control of the situation. Personally going forward to find out what was happening, Odlum was chagrined to discover that his two leading battalions, the 75th

(Mississauga) and 87th (Canadian Grenadier Guards),* had got involved in the battle prematurely. Their patrols had moved forward "too rapidly," in Odlum's opinion, "so drawing on their battalions and causing them to be involved too soon." Both battalions suffered more than 300 casualties crossing the crest of Mont Dury, which seemed to exert a magnetic effect on other units. All they did was provide target practice for German machine-gunners. Perhaps the saddest story was that of the 102nd (Central Ontario) Battalion, which committed only a single company to the one-sided fight—and lost an unbelievable 186 casualties.[80]

By early afternoon, it was clear that the Fourth Division was getting nowhere. With the artillery having difficulty re-establishing its neutralizing fire, the infantry could make no headway. If the Canadian Corps was going to reach the Canal du Nord under these circumstances, another set-piece assault with proper artillery support would have to be arranged. General Currie issued his instructions accordingly, intending to resume the advance at first light on 3 September.

However, it proved to be impossible to organize such a major undertaking on short notice. Having shattered the D-Q Line, the Canadian infantry battalions were simply too disorganized, and there were unforeseen snags in co-ordinating the necessary artillery backing. When Tuesday's dawn came and went, with no apparent progress in preparations for the new set-piece operation, Currie issued new orders to his divisions, "giving them instructions to patrol energetically, following up such patrols with sufficient strength to gain the high ground overlooking the crossings of the Canal."[81]

In any event, there was no need to attack. During the night, the Germans admitted defeat and withdrew across the Canal du Nord. By Tuesday night, the Canadian Corps had cleared the west side of the canal. But there was no possibility, at this time, of forcing a crossing. The enemy had destroyed all the bridges, and the reinforcements being rushed into the sector indicated the determination of the Germans to hold the canal at all costs.

General Currie was later criticized by a senior British officer for supposedly failing to follow up the victory at the D-Q Line. Major-General W. Hastings Anderson, the First Army's chief of staff, argued that the Canadian Corps should have made a more vigorous effort to

---

* Two members of these units won VCs on 2 September, and both men were non-combatants. One was the medical officer of the 75th, Captain Bellenden Hutcheson. An American, Captain Hutcheson braved enemy fire all day to treat wounded troops and organize their evacuation. Similarly, a baby-faced twenty-five-year-old stretcher-bearer of the 87th, Private John Young, dressed wounds under fire and helped carry out several injured soldiers. Remarkably, both Hutcheson and Young escaped unscathed.

To be pasted in A.B. 439 and A.B. 64.

KEEP YOUR MOUTH SHUT!

The success of any operation we carry out depends chiefly on surprise.

DO NOT TALK.—When you know that your Unit is making preparations for an attack, don't talk about them to men in other Units or to strangers, and keep your mouth shut, especially in public places.

Do not be inquisitive about what other Units are doing ; if you hear or see anything, keep it to yourself.

If you hear anyone else talking about operations, stop him at once.

The success of the operations and the lives of your comrades depend upon your SILENCE.

If you ever should have the misfortune to be taken prisoner, don't give the enemy any information beyond your rank and name. In answer to all other questions you need only say, "I cannot answer."

He cannot compel you to give any other information. He may use threats. He will respect you if your courage, patriotism, and self-control do not fail. Every word you say may cause the death of one of your comrades.

Either after or before you are openly examined, Germans, disguised as British Officers or men, will be sent among you or will await you in the cages or quarters or hospital to which you are taken.

Germans will be placed where they can overhear what you say without being seen by you.

DO NOT BE TAKEN IN BY ANY OF THESE TRICKS.

Ptd. in France by A.P. & S.S.   Press C. X477. 500000. 7/18.

To ensure secrecy prior to the attack at Amiens, this warning was pasted in the paybooks of all Canadian, Australian, and British troops.
Glenbow Archives, Calgary

Field-Marshal
Sir Douglas Haig (*right*)
with Lieutenant-General
Sir Arthur Currie.
Public Archives Canada/PA-2497

General Sir Henry Rawlinson.
Imperial War Museum/Q-4032

General Sir Henry Horne.
Imperial War Museum/Q-2425

Lieutenant-General Sir John Monash.
Australian War Memorial/A-2697

Major-General
Sir Archibald Macdonell.
Public Archives Canada/PA-42974

Major-General Louis J. Lipsett.
Public Archives Canada/PA-7442

Major-General Sir Henry Burstall.
Public Archives Canada/PA-2277

Major-General Sir Frederick Loomis.
Public Archives Canada/PA-2192

Major-General Sir David Watson.
Public Archives Canada/PA-2116

Brigadier-General Andy McNaughton.
Public Archives Canada/PA-34150

Amiens. 8 August 1918: Canadian troops advancing past French soldiers in foreground.
Public Archives Canada/PA-2925

An Australian lieutenant (*right*) addresses his platoon before leading it into action
at Amiens, 8 August 1918.
Australian War Memorial/E-2790

Canadian infantry supported by tanks attacking at Amiens, 9 August 1918, with German prisoners en route to the rear.
Public Archives Canada/PA-3668

Wounded Canadians arrive at an advanced dressing station near Amiens.
Public Archives Canada/PA-2930

German regimental officers captured by the Canadians at Amiens.
Public Archives Canada/PA-2985

General Currie inspects enemy guns captured at Amiens.
Public Archives Canada/PA-3046

The Drocourt-Quéant, or D-Q, Line: fields of German barbed wire.
Public Archives Canada/PA-3280

The D-Q Line: the Canadians attack, 2 September 1918.
Public Archives Canada/PA-3145

Canadian heavy guns in action, 2 September 1918.
Public Archives Canada/PA-3133

German prisoners captured at the D-Q Line.
Public Archives Canada/PA-3035

Two of the seven Canadians who won the Victoria Cross on 2 September 1918:
Lieutenant-Colonel Cy Peck (*right*) and Lance-Corporal William Metcalf, both of
the 16th (Canadian Scottish) Battalion.
Public Archives Canada/PA-6792

Canadian engineers bridging the dry bed of the Canal du Nord.
Public Archives Canada/PA-3287

Dead German machine-gunner, Canal du Nord.
Public Archives Canada/PA-3202

Canadian troops advancing toward Cambrai: the flat ground devoid of cover is typical of the area.
Public Archives Canada/PA-3256

The price of victory: headstones in the military cemetery at Haynecourt, near Cambrai.
author photograph

Canadian troops enter Cambrai unopposed, 9 October 1918.
Public Archives Canada/PA-3270

Sergeant Hugh Cairns of the 46th
(South Saskatchewan) Battalion.
The Victoria Cross he won at
Valenciennes on 1 November 1918
was the last Canadian vc of
the Great War.
Public Archives Canada/PA-6735

The first Canadians to enter Valenciennes, 1 November 1918.
Public Archives Canada/PA-3377

General Currie enters Mons on the afternoon of 11 November 1918.
Public Archives Canada/PA-3524

The Second Canadian Division crosses the Rhine at Bonn, 13 December 1918.
Public Archives Canada/PA-3774

Going home: troops of the First Canadian Division board the liner *Olympic* at
Southampton, 16 April 1919.
Public Archives Canada/PA-6048

Prime Minister Sir Robert Borden (*centre*), with his overseas minister, Sir Edward Kemp (*right*), and Major-General S.C. Mewburn (*left*), the minister of militia and defence.
Public Archives Canada/PA-5725

The headstone of Private George Lawrence Price, the last Canadian killed in the
Great War. Saint-Symphorien Military Cemetery, Belgium.
Author photograph

cross the canal on the third. "Possibly a visit from a higher commander"—a clear reference to Currie—"or his senior staff officer...a short conference, a direct order, and the thing might have been done." Anderson suggested that a great opportunity had been lost, including "the saving of nearly a month, and of the heavy casualties of the Canal du Nord battle" later in September. But Anderson's criticisms are hard to take seriously. Comfortably sequestered far to the rear, he was obviously out of touch with reality and overestimated Canadian capabilities in the wake of a hard battle.[82]

Currie had no intention of mounting an immediate assault on the Canal du Nord. Such a frontal attack, without proper preparation, would have been "unwise," in Currie's judgement, for several reasons, which he outlined in his diary:

(1) The Canal itself is a serious obstacle, (2) The marshes on the eastern side make difficult going, (3) It is strongly defended by machine guns from the trench system running parallel to the Canal, (4) The high ground on the east gives a perfect command of the approaches, (5) The more we advance to the eastward the more violent becomes the enfilade fire.

It was clear to Currie that an attack "could not...be undertaken singly by the Canadian Corps, but had to be part of a larger scheme."[83]

There was a further consideration. The Corps had suffered 5622 casualties in the course of crushing the D-Q Line, bringing its losses since 26 August to 11,423. It was, Currie could see, "slightly in need of repairs." To launch another major operation so soon, without allowing for rest, reorganization, and reinforcement, would have been rash and irresponsible; Currie was neither.[84]

The Corps could take pride in its performance to date. Since beginning the offensive southeast of Arras on 26 August, the Canadians had fought their way through twelve miles of German defences, capturing 10,492 prisoners, 123 guns, and 927 machine-guns.* The D-Q Line had been the crowning achievement. Currie called the results "gratify-

---

* Due to German book-keeping practices, it is impossible to estimate enemy losses at the D-Q Line. But there can be no doubt that they were enormous. Prisoners taken early in the fight admitted that the Germans had been preparing their own attack that morning at 6:30. Thus, they had an unusually large number of troops in the forward trenches, and these men suffered severely in the Canadian barrage. S. Sprostin, a member of the 10th (Canadians) Battalion, later commented that "I never saw so many German dead as there was around that place. Thousands of them." General Currie wrote: "In one part of the battle field an officer counted forty-six Canadian dead and over four hundred German dead."[85]

ing," noting that the Corps had captured more than 5000 unwounded prisoners from eight divisions, while penetrating "the enemy's defences to a depth exceeding 6,000 yards." His only disappointment was with the British, including those under his command and those in XXII Corps north of the River Scarpe. Currie, recognizing the weakness of the British 4th Division, had not only reduced its front but deliberately limited its objectives; these were not taken until after the German withdrawal on the night of 2-3 September. Currie was also disappointed in the slow advance north of the Scarpe, where the Germans had concentrated much of their artillery. "I looked to take a great many guns," he remarked, "but the slow progress of the attack on the north has given the enemy a chance to get many of his guns away."[86]

As usual, Currie would take no credit for success.* This was, he insisted, due solely to "the unparalleled striking power of our Battalions and the individual bravery of our men." After studying the many commendations for medals, he was even more impressed. "One is simply struck speechless with the record of gallantry therein set forth." The seven Victoria Crosses won on 2 September were a record for the Canadians, prompting Currie to comment: "It is truly impossible for me...to find words to adequately express the truly wonderful fighting qualities our men have displayed. I cannot say any more; a lump comes in one's throat whenever you think about it."[88]

Since early August, the Canadian Corps had compiled a remarkable record. The period of less than a month, Currie proudly pointed out, had seen "the secret move from the Arras front of a force the size of the Canadian Corps, the launching of it into battle within a week, fighting it hard for a fortnight and, before the last Division had left the line down there, to have begun a fight back again at Arras. It needs organization of the most perfect description to carry out moves of this magnitude."[89]

Comparisons were inevitable. "It is a question," Currie wrote in his diary on 3 September, "whether our victory of yesterday or of August 8th is the greatest, but I am inclined to think yesterday's was." He offered a number of valid reasons:

> [At Amiens] we went up against an enemy who was prepared for the offensive; here he was prepared for the defensive. There his trenches were not particularly good ones; he had no concrete emplacements; he had little wire; his guns were all well forward in order to help him in the advance he proposed to make.... Here we went up against his old system, that which he has never had

---

* In a letter to an acquaintance shortly after the D-Q Line, Currie commented: "I am afraid some of my old friends are attaching to me more credit for the victories of the Canadian Corps than I deserve."[87]

anything stronger anywhere. His guns were echeloned in great depth, and so we were constantly under artillery fire.... It is practically his last, and certainly his strongest system west of Cambrai.... Today on our front we identified elements of nine German Divisions, making fourteen German Divisions that we have met and defeated since a week ago.[90]

It was of no little consequence to Currie "that the first troops to break the Hindenburg system were the Canadian troops, and they broke that system at its most vital point."[91]

No one was more pleased with the Canadian victory than the commander-in-chief, Field-Marshal Haig. "To-day's battle," he wrote on 2 September, after a visit to the Drocourt-Quéant battlefield, "has truly been a great and glorious success." He was immensely relieved by it because he was under a lot of political pressure at this time. Well aware of Prime Minister Lloyd George's animosity, Haig knew that the failure of any operations against the Hindenburg Line would cost him his job. A reminder of this arrived on 29 August, just four days before the Canadian Corps attacked the D-Q Line, in the form of a telegram from General Sir Henry Wilson, chief of the Imperial General Staff in London:

Just a word of caution in regard to incurring heavy losses in attacks on Hindenburg Line as opposed to losses when driving the enemy back to that line. I do not mean to say that you have incurred such losses, but I know the War Cabinet would become anxious if we received heavy punishment in attacking the Hindenburg Line, without success.

Haig immediately divined the meaning behind this wire. "If my attack is successful, I will remain on as C. in C. If we fail, or our losses are excessive, I can hope for no mercy!... What a wretched lot of weaklings we have in high places at the present time!"[92]

That Haig, in these trying circumstances, proceeded with the attack on the D-Q Line reflects not only his confidence in the Canadian Corps, but also his firm faith in the BEF as a whole. The field-marshal's trust was well founded, as events would soon prove. Following his visit to the D-Q Line on 2 September, he optimistically commented in his diary that "the end cannot now be far off, I think."[93]

The effects of the Canadian victory were far-reaching. On 2-3 September, while the remnants of the D-Q Line defenders were withdrawn behind the Canal du Nord, the German high command authorized widespread withdrawals along the entire Western Front.

Field-Marshal Hindenburg admitted the significance of the Canadian attack when he wrote in his memoirs:

> On September 2 a fresh hostile attack overran our lines once and for all on the great Arras-Cambrai road and compelled us to bring the whole front back to the Siegfried Line. For the sake of economizing men we simultaneously evacuated the salient north of the Lys which bulged out between Mont Kemmel and Merville.

Added Hindenburg's chief subordinate, General Ludendorff: "It was no easy decision to withdraw the entire front line from the Scarpe to the Vesle, but it shortened our line and economized men, which, considering our huge wastage, was an advantage worth some sacrifice...."[94]

At a single stroke, the Canadian Corps had achieved two things: it had forced the enemy to abandon all the ground won at such enormous cost during the first half of 1918, and it wrecked Ludendorff's plan to conduct a gradual, fighting withdrawal to the Hindenburg Line.

The Canadians also gave Kaiser Wilhelm a nervous breakdown. "Now we have lost the war!" Wilhelm wailed when he received the bad news from the D-Q Line. "Poor Fatherland!" The distraught Kaiser thereupon went to bed and refused to get up for twenty-four hours.[95]

7 CRUCIBLE AT CAMBRAI

The Canadians had earned a rest. It was Field-Marshal Haig's intention, in the wake of the battle of the D-Q Line, to give it to them. "After these two successful battles, namely, Amiens and Arras," recalled General Currie, "the Chief of the General Staff [Lieutenant-General Sir Herbert Lawrence] came to me and intimated that the Commander-in-Chief was particularly well pleased with the conduct of the Canadians, and that he hoped it would not be necessary to employ us in any further big operations during the year."[1] But this proved to be impossible. Haig soon realized that if the war was to be won in 1918, the Canadian Corps would have to lead the way.

Haig's high hopes were shared by Marshal Foch, the supreme commander. As the field-marshal discovered on 4 September, Foch was "particularly pleased" as a result of the breaking of the D-Q Line, referring to it as "la grande bataille" and predicting "that it would produce a great effect on the enemy's plans.... He is most hopeful," Haig noted, "and thinks the German is nearing the end."[2]

On the other hand, Haig was still having trouble convincing the home authorities. Both military and civilian leaders in London remained firm in the belief that 1919 would be the decisive year. The minister of munitions, Winston Churchill, had gone even farther, preparing a memorandum urging that the British "should be content to play a very subordinate role in France, and generally in the Allied Councils, during 1919" and gear "for the decisive struggles of 1920." Haig scribbled on the margin of his copy of the Churchill memo: "What rubbish! Who will last till 1920—only America??"[3]

Haig wasted no opportunity to exhort the London authorities to greater efforts. In a 7 September letter to General Wilson, the chief of the Imperial General Staff, he begged for all available "men, aeroplanes, tanks, etc." to be sent to France. "The situation as regards the enemy is most favourable to us at the present moment," he argued, "so it ought to be exploited as soon as possible and to the utmost of our power." Similarly, he lectured Churchill when the latter visited GHQ:

> I told him that I considered that *the Allies should aim at getting a decision as soon as possible*. This month or next, not spring or summer as the Cabinet proposed. And that our greatest effort should be made at once, so as to take advantage of the present disorganised state both of the German Army and of the German

plans. Our reserves of ammunition, and programmes of future construction should also be reviewed in this light ....[4]

But Haig had a credibility problem. He had been making the same claims and appeals, more or less, since 1916 and they were wearing thin. No one was more pessimistic than Lord Milner, the secretary of state for war. On 10 September, Haig met Milner at the War Office in London, where the field-marshal outlined the results of the recent fighting. The BEF, said Haig, had in four weeks captured 77,000 prisoners and 600 guns. "There has never been such a victory in the annals of Britain," he maintained, recounting the meeting in his diary:

> *It seems to me to be the beginning of the end* ... in my opinion, the character of the war changed. What is wanted now at once is to provide the means to exploit our recent great successes to the full. Reserves in England should be regarded as Reserves for the French front, and all yeomanry, cyclists and other troops now kept for civil defence should be sent to France *at once.*
>
> If we act with energy now, a decision can be obtained in *the very near future.*

Haig seems to have thought that he had won over the secretary for war. "Lord Milner fully agreed," he remarked in his diary, "and said he would do his best to help."[5]

Actually, Milner was far from convinced. This became apparent to Haig later in September, when the secretary paid a visit to GHQ. Haig recorded the thrust of their conversation:

> I had another talk with Milner. He states that recruiting is very bad, and that if the British Army is used up now there will be no men for next year. He was quite satisfied that I should do what I deemed best in the matter of attacking or not. I pointed out that the situation was very satisfactory and that in order to take advantage of it every available man should be put into the battle at once. In my opinion, it is possible to get a decision this year; but if we do not, every blow that we deliver now will make the task next year much easier.[6]

Haig could not have helped his case by hedging his bets; "but if not" was an important qualification, particularly to politicians who feared that Haig would ruin the Empire by winning a war of attrition.

In any case, Milner remained unconvinced. Returning to London, he met with General Wilson, who noted afterward in his diary: "He thinks Haig ridiculously optimistic and is afraid that he may embark on another Passchendaele.''[7] In fact, Milner had made up his mind to sack Haig if the war did not end soon. And the man selected to succeed Haig was the commander of the Canadian Army Corps, Sir Arthur Currie.

Haig's job had been on the line for a long time. Since December 1916, to be precise, when David Lloyd George had become prime minister. Lloyd George held Haig personally responsible for what he viewed as the senseless slaughter on the Western Front. The two men were in total disagreement: whereas Haig correctly looked on the Western Front as the main theatre of operations, where the war would be won or lost, Lloyd George preferred to squander British resources in Italy and the Middle East—"side-shows," the soldiers contemptuously called them. Knowing that he lacked the political clout to get rid of Haig, Lloyd George had spent the better part of two years trying to undermine Haig's authority and force his resignation. But the commander-in-chief dourly accepted the abuse heaped on him by the cunning Lloyd George, who continually sought possible successors. So great was his contempt for British professional soldiers, Lloyd George could find no credible candidates. Then, in June 1918, he met General Currie.

The meeting came about as a result of a conference of the Imperial War Cabinet. The Canadian prime minister, Sir Robert Borden, had been so deeply distressed by Lloyd George's description of events on the Western Front in the spring of 1918, when the British had come so close to defeat, that he solicited Currie's views. The Canadian Corps commander happily complied, believing that the BEF had too many senior British officers—divisional and corps commanders—who were unfit. Borden later passed along to the war cabinet Currie's impressions, which Lloyd George mistakenly interpreted as criticism of Haig and the high command. Lloyd George asked to meet Currie; Borden arranged it the same day, 13 June. "I was greatly impressed with Currie's views," Lloyd George recollected. "They were, I felt, sane and common-sense. His great ability, his strength of purpose, and his lack of the fetishes common to the British officers were most noticeable." Lloyd George liked Currie, and began to pay closer attention to him and to his fellow dominion corps commander, Sir John Monash. Had the war been prolonged, these two men would have been given the key positions in the BEF in 1919, according to Lloyd George: "I had not met Monash at that time and my later idea, after I had got to know Monash, was to make him Chief of Staff and Currie Commander-in-Chief.''[8]

This was not idle chatter on the prime minister's part. On 14 September, the secretary of state for war stopped at Canadian Corps headquarters. As Currie recalled, "I was told by Lord Milner...that if the war went into 1919 I would be placed in command of the British Army.''[9] Of course, this did not happen, because the war ended in 1918, due in large part—ironically enough—to the efforts of Currie and his Corps.

Important things were happening on the Western Front in September 1918. A most significant event occurred on the twelfth: the American First Army, half a million strong, attacked at Saint-Mihiel in the first large-scale American action since the United States had declared war seventeen months earlier. The Americans did well, taking 15,000 prisoners and an impressive 460 guns, at the cost of 7000 casualties. The same day, the BEF mounted the first of two operations that enabled it to close on the Hindenburg Line. General Byng's Third Army cleared an enemy outpost line around Havrincourt, followed on 18 September by an even greater success by General Rawlinson's Fourth Army, spearheaded by the Australian Corps. Field-Marshal Haig described Rawlinson's victory:

> We met and defeated 13 enemy divisions in front line together with 3 more divisions brought up from reserve—a total of 16 divisions. . . . The enemy only fought well in a few places, but opposite the Australians he surrendered easily. Over 3000 prisoners were taken by the two Australian divisions engaged, and our losses were very small.[10]

The stage was now set for a series of operations that would prove to be decisive. The American, French, Belgian, and British armies were poised to mount major attacks in rapid succession on a wide front. The purpose, explained Marshal Foch, was to "prevent [the enemy] from bringing up units in proper form, capable of waging a well ordered battle, and from assembling artillery and infantry in defensive position of any considerable extent and prepared in advance—in short, prevent him from conducting any battle on a large scale, even a defensive one."[11]

However, such defences did exist, in the form of Siegfried-Stellung, the heart of the Hindenburg Line, opposite the BEF, between Cambrai and Saint-Quentin. In making his preparations, Haig weighed his options carefully, knowing what was at stake:

> Throughout our attacks from the 8th August onwards, our losses in proportion to the results achieved and the numbers of prisoners taken had been consistently and remarkably small. In the aggregate, however, they were considerable [180,000], and in the face of them an attack upon so formidably organised a position as that which now confronted us could not be lightly undertaken. Moreover, the political effects of an unsuccessful attack upon a position so well known as the Hindenburg Line would be large, and would

go far to revive the declining morale not only of the German Army but of the German people.

But Haig, "convinced that the British attack was the essential part of the general scheme," chose to storm the Hindenburg Line with as much vigour and determination as possible.[12]

At the same time, Haig had no intention of beating his head against a brick wall. Contrary to his popular image as a blundering butcher, the field-marshal was determined to give his beloved BEF every possible chance of success, as he outlined to his army commanders at a conference on 21 September:

> We are confronted by a strong, well sited series of defences, and the enemy appears to have collected a certain number of reserves behind the Cambrai-St. Quentin front. I therefore do not propose to attack until the American-French attack has gone in. This latter attack *might* draw off some of the enemy's reserves from our front. I therefore would like to attack two or three days *after* the main American-French attack.[13]

It is at this point that Haig's unmistakable influence over these operations emerges with clarity. Haig insisted that the Franco-American offensive in the south be co-ordinated with the BEF's, arguing that the Allied attacks must be made "*concentrically*, viz., against Cambrai, against St. Quentin, and against Mézières from the South." Marshal Foch, after listening to Haig's advice, adopted the British commander-in-chief's plan virtually word for word, filling in only the dates:

> *September 26th*—A Franco-American attack between the Suippe and the Meuse [toward Mézières].
> *September 27th*—An attack by the British First and Third Armies in the general direction of Cambrai.
> *September 28th*—An attack by the Flanders Group of Armies between the sea and the Lys, under the command of the King of the Belgians.
> *September 29th*—An attack by the British Fourth Army, supported by the French First Army, in the direction of Busigny.[14]

The Canadian Corps was given a task of paramount importance. As General Currie was informed on 15 September, the Corps, leading the First Army, was to force a crossing of the Canal du Nord and strike at Cambrai, a vital centre of communications. There was no doubt that the Germans would defend Cambrai with ruthless, even fanatical, determination; its loss would be disastrous for the enemy cause because it would render the rest of the Hindenburg Line untenable.

The Corps recovered quickly from its heavy fighting in late August and early September, although conditions were far from ideal. To begin with, the weather was terrible. One veteran, writing home on 14 September, complained that "it's been raining heavily, very slippery indeed, & it is [an] awful job to scrape off the mud & chalk from the puttees, etc. Even the big trucks find it very difficult to go along the roads, the mud is so bad." One memorable storm savaged the encampment of the 11th Canadian Field Ambulance, prompting the unit historian to remark that "the orderly room, canteen and medical tents foundered with all hands in the wee damp hours."[15]

The Germans added to the Canadians' misery, subjecting them to steady sniping and shelling from the high ground east of the canal. On 5 September, a sniper's bullet wounded Brigadier-General Victor Odlum as he reconnoitred the canal line. Two days later, the 31st (Alberta) Battalion endured a prolonged bombardment of high explosives and poison gas, losing 107 casualties, "the heaviest it had ever experienced in a single day from hostile artillery action while simply holding the line." From their vantage point north of the River Scarpe, the Germans also commanded the Arras-Cambrai road and routinely shelled it. This was merely an "annoyance" rather than serious interference with Canadian transport, but it did cost the Corps one of its best battalion commanders. Lieutenant-Colonel George Pearkes, VC, the officer commanding the 116th (Ontario County) Battalion, was wounded by shell fire along with twenty-five of his men while resting near Guémappe. Colonel Pearkes survived his terrible injuries—"part of his intestines were exposed and had to be held in"—and he spent the rest of the war convalescing in England. Resuming his distinguished career, Pearkes eventually became lieutenant-governor of British Columbia.[16]

Despite the drawbacks, the Corps took advantage of the relative lull to "reorganize, refit and rest."[17] A steady stream of reinforcements, most of them conscripts,* filled the depleted ranks of the Canadian infantry battalions, which had suffered the great majority of the casualties. Morale among the men remained generally high, as their writings reveal:

Our men are superb. They are marvellous and all their victories, this change of trench warfare to open fighting, has raised the

---

* There was little resentment or ill feeling shown the newcomers. As William Ogilvie of the 21st Battery, CFA, observed, the conscripts "seemed a nice bunch of fellows"[18] and were accepted by the veterans.

morale a thousand percent, greater than all the instruments of warfare is the spirit of our men—invincible—indestructible.[19]

Our casualties were very heavy and some of the best have gone, but fortunately a large percentage were only wounded. It was very comforting in walking over the battlefield afterwards to notice that there were ten times as many German dead as ours, besides the thousands of prisoners we took. We absolutely fought him to a finish and beat him at every turn. It was grand to be in it.[20]

Not so bad for four divisions. We have captured over a hundred square miles of territory, over three hundred guns, 21,000 prisoners, hope we killed twice as many, as General Currie said in his speech, and met and defeated thirty German divisions.[21]

There was also a mood of growing resentment among some Canadian soldiers. It was widely rumoured, and often believed, that General Currie was volunteering the Corps for the toughest tasks and the heaviest fighting. "The majority of men in the corps consider Currie to be the biggest human butcher in the British Army because the Canadians have been mercilessly cut up in the front part of all the recent advances," noted Trooper George Hambley of the Canadian Light Horse. "Certain it is that he cares nothing for the amount of life wasted so long as the object is attained."[22] As unfair as this remark may be, it would, in the days and weeks ahead, become an increasingly common complaint among the Canadians.*

No one could accuse the Canadians of resting on their laurels. Senior officers spent much time analyzing the battle of the D-Q Line in the hope of applying the lessons to future fighting. There was considerable disappointment in the Fourth Division's failure to achieve a clear-cut breakthrough at Mont Dury. Brigadier-General James McBrien of the Twelfth Brigade cited four reasons:

(a) Absence of simultaneous effort by all attacking Brigades and Independent Force [Brutinel's Brigade] at the appointed hour, viz., 8 A.M. Only the leading Bns. of the 11th Bde. and the 78th Bn. went forward on time.
(b) Exceedingly strong M[achine-]Gun opposition from North, South and East.

---

* It was a feeling shared by their Australian cousins, who believed that they, too, were shouldering an unduly large share of the fighting. Commented one angry Australian: "Drunk with success, the Australian leaders continued to hurl their decimated battalions into the thick of the bloody conflict . . . in order that a group of mad militants might appease their inhuman appetite for blood and glory."[23]

(c) Strong Artillery fire.

(d) Lack of a covering Artillery Barrage with smoke, and the assistance of tanks.[24]

Criticism of Brutinel's Brigade was commonplace. General MacBrien was, like most others, far from impressed by the armoured cars. MacBrien noted that "they are unable to deal with or withstand the fire of hostile Machine Guns," and suggested that they would likely "be of more use from a defensive point of view than in the offensive. In their present form they appear to be very vulnerable and unable to force a passage where there is opposition."[25]*

The tanks continued to be a mixed blessing. Where they were available, their value was beyond dispute. "There is no question that German Infantry will not fight tanks," reads the battle report of the 3rd Tank Brigade, which fought under the Canadian Corps at the D-Q Line. "It appears to be even fast becoming a fact that their machine gunners will not do so either. There has been abundant proof that all M.G. fire has stopped on the approach of a tank...." Sadly, there were few tanks available, and even these did not last long in action. Of seventeen tanks that accompanied the First Canadian Division on 2 September, only seven survived the day.[27]

Even at this late date, artillery remained an indispensable feature of fighting on the Western Front. There had been problems, but the Canadian gunners had done yeoman work in the offensive east of Arras. They had fired 847,990 rounds of all calibres, weighing 20,424 tons, twice the quantity expended at Amiens. "The gunners may be truthfully said to have spent almost the entire eight days August 26th to September 2nd, firing with one hand and hauling ammunition with the other." Where problems had occurred, these were attributable to communications, which were often "too slow" even for this type of warfare.[28]

The infantry, too, had some retrospective thinking to do. There were alarming signs of flaws in the training of many infantrymen. General Odlum, the Eleventh Brigade's commander, was puzzled by "the failure of our men (riflemen, Lewis gunners and Vickers gunners alike) to take on targets at over 700 yards," when the Germans were employing the fire of "distant machine guns" with considerable effect.[29] Given the growing proportion of conscripts, these failings can-

---

* General Brutinel angrily rejected the criticism. "The task given the force," he insisted, "was consistent with its strength and within its scope." Brutinel argued that it was the passive attitude of the British cavalry under his command, rather than the limitations of the armoured cars, that led to the disappointing performance of his brigade.[26]

not be entirely surprising. They could have been corrected if there had been time for proper training—but there was none.

Unreasonable expectations might have been a factor as well. As Lieutenant-Colonel John Clark of the 72nd (Seaforth Highlanders of Canada) Battalion pointed out, it was unrealistic to expect a grand breakthrough when confronted by the quantity and quality of the German defences. "It is difficult," Colonel Clark commented, "for a unit which has carried out an attack against a highly organized trench system to undertake an open warfare scheme immediately afterwards, owing to the fact that casualties among leaders are unavoidable before the change." And more than a little credit must be given the enemy. Lieutenant-Colonel E.W. MacDonald of the 10th (Canadians) Battalion noted that the Germans were using "exceptionally good troops" to man the D-Q Line. "They fought bitterly until the end in almost every instance, and in many cases were killed rather than captured. Moreover, they were in considerable force and greatly out-numbered our attacking companies." Colonel MacDonald's words contained a chilling warning of future events for the Corps.[30]

An important command change took place at this time. Major-General Louis Lipsett, arguably the best of the four divisional commanders in the Canadian Corps, was transferred to command a British division. It is a measure of Lipsett's reputation that Sir Douglas Haig himself made the decision to give General Lipsett new responsibilities. "Lipsett expressed a preference to remain with the Canadians," General Currie observed in his diary. Although their association dated back to the militia staff course taught by Lipsett before the war, Currie made no effort to retain him, undoubtedly out of a desire to have all his divisions commanded by Canadian officers. Lipsett, indeed, felt "great disappointment...on being forced to leave the Third Canadian Division which I have commanded for two years and three months." Unable to enlist Currie's aid, Lipsett had no choice but to acquiesce, and on 13 September he departed to take over the British 4th Division. He was succeeded by Brigadier-General Frederick Loomis, another civilian soldier who made a name for himself in France. The change meant that there were now no British officers attached to the Canadian Corps above the rank of brigadier.[31]

The entire Corps was, in any case, soon preoccupied with preparations for its next great battle. "This attack," Currie readily admitted, "was fraught with difficulties."[32] The Canadians were to strike on 27 September, leading the First Army and protecting the flank of the Third Army in its drive on the Hindenburg defences in front of Cambrai. Their assignment was doubly difficult: not only did they have to force a crossing of the Canal du Nord, but they had to take the heights of Bourlon Wood on the other side. Bourlon was the key to success, as experience had shown. The British had attacked near here in November 1917 but failed to capture Bourlon, which the Germans promptly used as a springboard to counter-attack and turn a great victory into a disappointing defeat for the BEF.

The canal itself was, Currie realized, "a serious obstacle." The Corps commander knew that it would not be easy to get across it:

> The Canal du Nord...was under construction at the outbreak of the war and had not been completed. Generally speaking, it followed the valley of the River Agache, but not the actual bed of the river. The average width was about 100 feet and it was flooded as far south as the lock, 800 yards south-west of Sains-lez-Marquoin, just north of the Corps southern boundary. South of this and to the right of the Corps front the Canal was dry, and its bottom was at the natural ground level, the sides of the Canal consisting of high earth and brick banks.[33]

Currie devised a daring plan. Ruling out a frontal assault on the flooded canal facing the Canadian Corps, Currie quickly appreciated the possibilities presented by the 2600-yard dry stretch to the south. Currie proposed to side-step the Corps, punch across the canal with two divisions, and then, with two more divisions, "expand later fan-wise in a north-easterly direction to a front exceeding 15,000 yards." It would be an "intricate manoeuvre," he realized, which would demand the "most skilful leadership on the part of the commanders, and the highest state of discipline on the part of the troops." The dangers, too, were apparent:

> The assembly of the attacking troops in an extremely congested area known by the enemy to be the only one available was very dangerous, especially in view of the alertness of the enemy. A concentrated bombardment of this area prior to zero, particularly if gas was employed, was a dreaded possibility which could seriously affect the whole of the operation and possibly cause its total failure.[34]

His divisional commanders stood behind him. At a conference on 24 September, Currie was pleased to see that, after approving the final details of the plan, "everyone appeared confident." The First Division's General Macdonell enthusiastically endorsed it. "The very boldness of the plan intrigued me," he recalled, "and I was all for it."[35]

However, the plan landed Currie in hot water. The First Army's commander, General Sir Henry Horne, was deeply disturbed when he saw what Currie had in mind. "I don't believe I ought to let them do it," Horne remarked to his chief of staff, Major-General Hastings Anderson, who tried unsuccessfully to reassure him: "If Currie says they can do it, they will."[36]

Horne remained adamantly opposed. Not that he lacked confidence in the Canadians; quite the contrary. "No one," he later remarked of them, "could wish to command better troops." But Currie's battle plan was, in Horne's professional judgement, too complicated to be practicable. "It is an axion that a military operation should be as simple as possible, and the larger the operation the greater the need for simplicity. No one can claim that the operation under consideration was simple . . . ." Horne frankly shuddered at "the possibilities of failure with heavy loss."[37]

The First Army commander did his best to convince Currie to revise his plan. But the big Canadian could be stubborn, particularly when he believed he was right. Unable to make any headway, Horne referred the matter to the very top. Even that failed to produce the desired results. When Field-Marshal Haig visited Canadian Corps headquarters on the twenty-first, he backed Currie—as he usually did in such situations. Horne, however, was not easily discouraged, and attempted one more ploy. He turned to General Sir Julian Byng, who had been Currie's predecessor with the Canadian Corps. Horne knew that they had a special relationship based on mutual respect and confidence. If anyone could talk sense into Currie, it was Byng.

Sir Julian dropped by Currie's headquarters on 24 September. Characteristically, he came straight to the point. "Currie, I have read over your plans and I know they are as good as they can be made, but can you do it?"

"Yes," Currie replied, his conviction firm.

"Do you realize," resumed the genial Byng, "that you are attempting the most difficult operation of the war? If anybody can do it, the Canadians can do it, but if you fail, it means home for you."[38]

Byng had summed up the situation in a nutshell: Currie was placing his reputation on the line. But the Canadian commander stubbornly clung to the belief that his plan could, and would, work. And so it stood, with one change to mollify General Horne. "If," as Horne pointed out, "the advance of the supporting divisions was delayed until plenty of time had been allowed to make sure that the leading divisions were firmly established [across the canal], then the danger of confusion was much reduced." Accordingly, Currie rescheduled the second phase of the attack until mid-afternoon.[39]

Now it was up to Currie to "deliver the goods," as he liked to say.

Preparations for the attack were carried out with typical skill and efficiency. Currie later described this immense undertaking:

The line [along the Canal du Nord] was held very thinly, but active patrolling at nights and sniping were kept up. A complete programme of harassing fire by Artillery and Machine Guns was also put in force nightly. The Corps Heavy Artillery (Brigadier-General R.H. Massie) carried out wire-cutting, counter-battery shoots and gas concentrations daily, in preparation for the eventual operations.

Light railways, roads, brigades and waterpoints were constructed right up to the forward area, and the bridging material which would be required for the Canal du Nord was accumulated well forward. Ammunition dumps were established at suitable places.

Detailed reconnaissances of the Canal and trenches were carried out by aeroplane, and also by daring patrols, and all available documents regarding the Canal construction were gathered with a view to preparing the plans for the future attack.[40]

Corps intelligence officers compiled an amazingly accurate picture of the enemy defences. According to an intelligence report dated 18 September, the Canal du Nord Line was given a low rating. Despite "exceptionally strong" barbed-wire entanglements, the enemy trenches were "not sufficiently good to afford adequate cover or protection in a heavy bombardment. Troops in the line would appear to be very vulnerable to shrapnel fire." Beyond, the Marquion Line was described as being "in very poor condition," while the defences around Bourlon Wood were little better: "the few trenches visible... would appear to be in very poor condition" although it was possible that wire and machine-guns were hidden in "the foliage and undergrowth." The report added, significantly, that "the area between these systems is dotted with old excavations, dugouts, and shelters, any of which might be utilized for M.G. defences." It also warned of numerous sunken roads which would serve as improvised trench lines and cause the Canadians considerable trouble in the days ahead.[41]

Surprise would be virtually impossible to achieve. Despite Currie's strict orders that all movements in the Corps sector be carried out after dark, it was difficult to conceal the preparations for the attack. Not only did the enemy have excellent observation from the heights at Bourlon, but the landscape occupied by the Canadians was flat and almost treeless. There was nowhere to hide the camps, horselines, and vehicle parks which, according to a Second Division report, made the vicinity appear "as populous as Coney Island on July 4th."[42]

Currie's complex battle plan set out three objective lines, designated by colours: Red, Green, and Blue. The first phase of the attack would carry the Canadians to the Red Line, which included most of the defences of the Canal du Nord and Marquion lines. The Green Line lay 1500 yards to the east; its capture would include the villages of Marquion and Bourlon. Another advance of 2000 yards would leave the Corps on the Blue Line, the final objective for 27 September, and in possession of Fontaine-Notre-Dame and Sauchy-Lestrée, Pilgrim's Rest on the Arras-Cambrai road, plus the balance of Bourlon Wood and its commanding high ground, which was essential to the overall success of the operation. To execute his plan, Currie would lead with two divisions, the First on the left and the Fourth on the right. In the second phase, the Corps front would be dramatically widened with the commitment of two more divisions: the Third would move onto the right of the Fourth, while the British 11th—temporarily under Currie's command—would advance on the left of the First. All four divisions would then press the attack to the Blue Line.*

The artillery, as always, had a crucial role to play. Because of the confined area of the Canadian attack, it was impossible to assemble all of the necessary guns before zero hour. As at Amiens, batteries of field guns would be moved forward in close support of the infantry; this movement would begin at zero plus four hours, by which time it was expected that the engineers, in a major test of their recent reorganization, would have several bridges constructed across the canal. The leap-frogging of batteries was difficult, but the gunners had "proved that barrages can be successfully carried through to a considerable depth, involving as many as three 'relays,' without sacrificing anything in the way of effectiveness."[43] It speaks volumes for the skill of the Corps artillery commander, Major-General Edward "Dinky" Morrison, and his staff.

Even more important, the artillery would have to protect the Corps before the attack began. As Currie realized, the Canadians would be most vulnerable to a German bombardment. If that happened, Lieutenant-Colonel Andy McNaughton, the Corps counter-battery officer, was authorized to retaliate with every gun at his disposal. "These arrangements," Currie noted, "were to be put into effect, in any case, at zero hour, to neutralise the hostile defensive barrage on the front of attack."[44]

Despite the precautions, the hours prior to zero were nerve-wracking. It was, said Currie, "a night full of anxiety." To his immense

---

* The remaining Canadian division, Burstall's Second, was assigned to the Corps reserve. This formation had been in action more or less steadily since the spring, and Currie, sensing that it was exhausted—this was, possibly, a factor in its disappointing performance in the attack on the Fresnes-Rouvroy Line—chose to give it a good, long rest. The way things turned out, the Second Division took part in no more major operations before the war ended.

relief, "apart from the usual harassing fire and night bombing nothing untoward happened."[45]*

At 5:20 A.M. on Friday, 27 September, the Canadian Corps stormed the Canal du Nord. An eardrum-shattering barrage opened at that moment, dazzling the waiting infantry. "I had never seen such a sight before or since being at Vimy," recalled Private William Green of the 4th (Central Ontario) Battalion. Even the gunners themselves were impressed. Private Lawrence Eyres of the 2nd Canadian Siege Battery commented, in a letter home after the battle, that "all you could see for miles and miles along the front was the flashing of guns, and Fritzie's line was a mass of smoke and bursting shells."[47]

By contrast, the German reply was almost non-existent. This was due to the brilliance of the Canadian counter-battery fire, which was never more effective than in this operation. The enemy had prepared for the attack by quietly assembling in the vicinity of Bourlon Wood 230 guns, "double that of what might be expected on a normal front." And these guns had deliberately withheld their fire in the hope of escaping detection. It was a futile hope. Canadian counter-battery officers pinpointed 113 German gun positions before the attack; within minutes of zero hour, 80 per cent of these had been knocked out.[48]

Lost amid the pandemonium was the sound of Vickers heavy machine-guns. These had long been a standard feature of Canadian attacks on the Western Front, and twenty-four batteries of these guns were employed at the Canal du Nord in "one of the most complicated barrage fire programs ever devised." The machine-gunners' job was "to keep down snipers from among the trees and to disorganize the defence." Their actual contribution was of dubious value, but there can be no questioning their psychological impact, both on the Canadian troops and the Germans. During this day, the Vickers gunners would fire the astounding total of 320,000 rounds of ammunition.[49]

Within moments, the Canadian infantrymen were on their way. The ground was somewhat slippery, thanks to an overnight rainfall, and, due to the overcast sky, "I am afraid it was a little dark," observed General Currie. But these factors were of no consequence. "Prisoners stated that our attack was excellently supported by Artillery fire," commented a Corps intelligence report, "and that the attacking troops

---

* Not until after the battle had begun did the Canadians realize what a close call they had had. They captured an order which detailed plans for an attack by the German 187th Division at 9 A.M. on 27 September—less than four hours after the Canadians attacked—in a bid to recapture the Buissy switch line and possibly pre-empt the impending Allied offensive on this front.[46]

followed the barrage so closely that they were upon them before they could man their trenches...."[50]

In places, the defenders were all but annihilated. The 188th Infantry Regiment, which belonged to the German 187th Division, was completely crushed by the Canadians. The regimental history, describing 27 September as "the blackest day of the Regiment," reported that "at the end of the day only a little band of men was left."[51]

The canal itself proved to be no more than a minor inconvenience to the determined Canadians. Hugging the barrage, the infantry crossed within minutes: jumping to the dry bed of the canal, most used scaling ladders to get up the far bank. One attacking battalion, the 14th (Royal Montreal Regiment), failed to receive its allotment of ladders but that did not slow it down in the slightest. As Major C.B. Price recalled, his men simply "climbed on each others' shoulders and got up." Due to the speed of the crossing, losses were light. Apart from costly encounters with isolated machine-gun nests, "the leading troops advanced across the Canal with little or no casualties."[52]

The Fourth Division had the day's most important assignment. Unless the heights at Bourlon could be captured, and quickly, the Canadians across the canal would be courting disaster: they would not only be exposed to a counter-attack, they would have no easy line of retreat either. To carry the high ground, General Watson decided to utilize troops from all three of his brigades. General Hayter's Tenth Brigade would force the canal and drive to the Red Line, where the other two brigades would be committed, General Odlum's Eleventh on the right and General MacBrien's Twelfth on the left. The Eleventh would take Bourlon, but without attempting a costly frontal assault. Instead, a double envelopment was envisaged, with the various battalions swinging to the right and left and attacking the heights from the flanks and rear. In the meantime, the Twelfth Brigade would take Pilgrim's Rest, a key hill to the north of Bourlon.

The attack started smartly. Two battalions led the Fourth Division's assault on the canal. On the right, the 44th (New Brunswick) Battalion encountered little resistance, reaching the Red Line by seven-thirty. Its losses were low—forty killed, 157 wounded—and were far exceeded by the number of prisoners, over 300 in all, half of them routed from a single dugout. The battalion commander, Lieutenant-Colonel R.D. Davies, met a captured cavalry officer who admitted that the Germans had "expected to hold the Canal Line for many days." The Canadians, he grudgingly conceded, had been "magnificent, but had not our artillery failed to support us we should have given you more trouble."[53]

To the left, the 46th (South Saskatchewan) Battalion had more difficulty. Having crossed the canal, this unit was held up at a sunken road tenaciously defended by four machine-guns. The 46th eventually

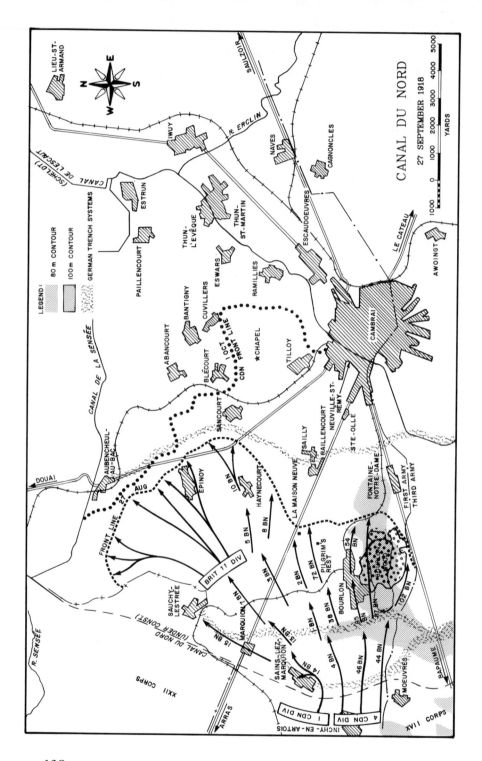

CANAL DU NORD
27 SEPTEMBER 1918

prevailed, but the casualties were rather heavy; one platoon lost all of its officers and non-commissioned officers, and came out of the battle commanded by a senior private. Among the wounded was Sergeant Don McKerchar, who was struck by shell fragments soon after going over the top. "Seven pieces in my right arm and a bad bruise across the back of my head," he ruefully recalled. "I don't remember hitting the ground."[54]

The 50th (Calgary) Battalion—nicknamed "Page's Pets," after the commanding officer, Lieutenant-Colonel Lionel Page—then drove home the attack to the Red Line. By seven-fifteen, the 50th was digging in along the objective, after several serious fights with German machine-gun posts. "Our fear of the machine-gunners," wrote Private Victor Wheeler, "was only matched by our respect for them." Many of these posts had been overrun earlier by the 46th Battalion, but not mopped up, and the 50th paid dearly for this neglect. The loss of one officer was particularly painful: when Captain D. Fraser was killed by a shell burst, the 50th lost the last of the four company commanders who had gone into action at Amiens seven weeks before. An act of remarkable bravery carried the 50th to its objective. The battalion was pinned down by machine-gun fire, when Private Richard Bloor leapt to his feet and charged the enemy. So ferocious was his one-man attack that the Germans fled to a nearby dugout, where 146 of them later surrendered. Private Bloor was fatally wounded in the process, and there was much bitterness in the battalion when he was not awarded a posthumous VC.[55]

On schedule, the Eleventh and Twelfth brigades passed through the Tenth. The Eleventh, charged with the crucial task of taking Bourlon Wood, had plenty of problems to overcome. To begin with, it had no tank support. Three Mark IVs—obsolete machines that were not even bullet-proof—had been allotted to the Eleventh, but the tank commander approached General Odlum just before zero hour, complaining about the old, unreliable 1917-vintage vehicles and his tired crews. Angrily, Odlum dismissed the officer. "I informed him that, as it was apparent he would not be of any assistance to the Brigade, I had no further time to waste with him."[56]

To make matters worse, the projected pincer movement on either side of Bourlon Wood soon became impracticable. This was no fault of the Canadians. The British 52nd (Lowland) Division on the right was unable to keep pace and exposed the Canadian flank to deadly enfilade fire. Odlum's right-hand battalion, the 102nd (Central Ontario), was forced to form a defensive flank along the Bapaume-Cambrai road, where enemy fire precluded any possibility of a turning movement south of Bourlon Wood. The situation was not helped either when the 102nd's commanding officer, Lieutenant-Colonel Fred Lister, was wounded during the afternoon. It was, however, a memorable day for another member of this battalion, Lieutenant Graham Lyall, who personally stormed a strongpoint and captured thirteen prisoners, four machine-guns, and a field gun. He later added ninety-two more prisoners and five machine-guns to his bag for the day.

Fortunately for the Canadians, the manoeuvre on the other side of the heights was a complete success. The 87th (Canadian Grenadier Guards) Battalion, supported by the 78th (Winnipeg Grenadiers), fought their way into the village of Bourlon. This battle was highlighted by the heroism of Lieutenant Samuel Honey of the 78th. When all the company's officers and non-commissioned officers were killed or wounded, Lieutenant Honey calmly reorganized his men, then led them to their objective. En route, he single-handedly knocked out a machine-gun post, capturing ten Germans. Later in the day, he tirelessly helped to repel four counter-attacks. Honey's performance was rewarded with the vc; sadly, he was killed in action two days later.

The heights at Bourlon fell with astonishing ease. The 54th (Central Ontario) Battalion passed through the village, skirted Bourlon Wood to the north, then took the high ground from the rear. That this vantage point had been left virtually undefended is indicative of the enemy's confusion. With darkness falling, the 54th, reinforced by two companies of the 75th (Mississauga) Battalion, pressed on toward Fontaine-Notre-Dame. In a nearby dugout, the Canadians captured a German regimental commander and his whole staff. "He was," in General Odlum's words, "tremendously surprised to be captured," having earlier arranged a three-battalion counter-attack on Bourlon Wood and believed that it had been retaken. The 54th was stopped short of Fontaine-Notre-Dame by darkness and by heavy fire from the right. This was, therefore, the only place on the Canadian Corps front where the Blue Line was not reached on 27 September. But the most important objective, Bourlon Wood—described by one regimental historian as "seven hundred acres of oak trees, shattered, sombre and accursed"—was firmly in Canadian hands.[57]

North of Bourlon, the Twelfth Brigade was fashioning a fine success. While elements of the 85th (Nova Scotia Highlanders) Battalion helped to clear the village, the 38th (Ottawa) Battalion struck for the rail line which ran toward Sauchy-Lestrée. However, the 38th was held up at a sunken road heavily defended by machine-guns. Two members of the support battalion, the 72nd (Seaforth Highlanders of Canada), saw what was happening and quickly took the initiative. Lieutenant J.M. Knight and Private C.C. Graham, with a Lewis light machine-gun, outflanked the position, then poured devastating enfilade fire into it. Fifty Germans surrendered, and the 38th resumed its advance to the rail line. But the confusion on the battlefield, compounded by the blinding smoke and deafening noise, was taking a toll on the battalion's cohesiveness. One of the first to reach the objective was a stretcher-bearer, Private Arthur Foster, who had been separated from his company. He was joined here by the battalion commander, Lieutenant-Colonel S.D. Gardner, who asked the whereabouts of the rest of the men; Foster could only shrug his shoulders. "Well, we're lost," the colonel admitted to the private, "so we'll keep together." Eventually, the others began to filter forward, and the 38th was able to consolidate its hold along the railway. This cleared the way for the supporting 72nd Battalion to pass through.[58]

Crossing the rail line, the 72nd soon found itself under "terrific" machine-gun and shell fire. Particularly galling fire came from the left, where a nest of enemy field guns fired at the Canadians at point-blank range. Led by Captain W.C. Ross, C Company crept to within fifty yards of the battery, then charged. It was all over within moments; Captain Ross and his men captured 119 Germans and eight 77-millimetre guns.[59]

Its flank secure, the 72nd now turned its attention to the main objective, the hill known as Pilgrim's Rest. This feature lay half a mile to the east, a gentle slope devoid of cover, and there must have been more than a few men wondering whether they had any real chance of getting there. But Canadian determination again paid dividends. At 2:45 P.M., C and D companies launched a wild "bayonet charge, accompanied by loud cheering, which appeared to have a demoralizing effect on the enemy," reported a proud Lieutenant-Colonel Guy Kirkpatrick, "as their surrender was immediate."[60] More than 200 Germans were led away into captivity. Later, in the evening, the 72nd Battalion sent out battle patrols to establish outposts beyond the Blue Line. Three more 77-millimetre guns were captured by these patrols, bringing the battalion's bag of field guns for the day to eleven.

Meanwhile, the First Division was executing with near-flawless precision a complicated series of manoeuvres. At one point, this formation was fighting in four directions simultaneously: east, northeast, north, and west. The divisional commander, General Macdonell, chose to commit two brigades to the canal crossing; elements of these, plus his reserve brigade, would exploit toward the Blue Line. General Currie, mindful of the Mont Dury débâcle, told Macdonell that it was "a good plan, but that too many men were involved" in the initial assault. But Macdonell was able to assure Currie that all these troops were needed, as, indeed, they were.[61]

Both of Macdonell's attacking brigades were led by a single battalion. The First Brigade, on the right, was preceded by the 4th (Central Ontario) Battalion, which crossed near Inchy-en-Artois. The infantrymen were materially aided by the work of two field guns from the 1st

Battery, CFA, which had been moved to the edge of the canal at the express request of the brigade commander, General Griesbach. Under the direction of Lieutenant H.H. Pinney, the two 18-pounders fired fifty rounds at point-blank range into German positions on the other side of the canal, enabling the 4th Battalion to reach the Red Line on schedule and with light losses—142, all ranks, killed, wounded, and missing.[62]

At First Brigade headquarters, General Griesbach waited anxiously for three-quarters of an hour for news of the attack. Plagued by slow communications, his view obscured by smoke and semi-darkness, Griesbach remained in ignorance until shortly after six o'clock, when the first prisoner arrived. "He was very excited," recalled Griesbach, "and...spoke English sufficiently well to say that the 'English' were over the Canal and all his comrades were killed."[63]

With the First Brigade well on the way to the Green Line, the neighbouring Third Brigade was matching its success. The 14th (Royal Montreal Regiment) Battalion, undeterred by the lack of scaling ladders, quickly crossed the canal and mopped up the machine-gun posts along the far bank. Lieutenant A.T. Howell went ahead of his platoon and personally wiped out one nest, and a second post nearby surrendered to him. Later in the morning, he captured thirty-eight Germans hiding in a dugout. His performance won Lieutenant Howell the Military Cross and enabled the 14th Battalion to outflank the village of Sains-lez-Marquion, setting the stage for one of the most innovative small-unit attacks of the entire Great War.

The 14th Battalion assaulted Sains-lez-Marquion from the rear, assisted by a special bombardment. Prepared by First Division headquarters, General Macdonell gave the credit for this so-called "monkey puzzle barrage" to his brilliant artillery chief, General Thacker, who seemed to specialize in unusual arrangements, as he demonstrated in the attack on Upton Wood prior to the D-Q Line. The barrage actually rolled toward the Canadian lines, with the men of the 14th Battalion following close behind the wall of shrapnel and high explosive. Lieutenant C.E. Tuttle, who commanded 1 Company, led the attack sitting on top of a tank. The defenders, stunned by the savagery of the barrage and seemingly under attack from all directions, had little stomach for a fight. By eight-thirty, the 14th was in firm possession of the village, along with "between 300 and 350 unwounded prisoners."[64]

Fresh troops continued the offensive at mid-morning, when the 13th (Royal Highlanders of Canada) Battalion passed through the 14th on the Red Line. Led by a bagpiper, the 13th struck toward the village of Marquion, but was soon stopped by a belt of barbed wire which the artillery had missed. One company was fortunate enough to find a narrow gap that enabled it to get through, in single file and under heavy fire. The other two attacking companies, however, were pinned down in the wire.

At this critical moment, four tanks arrived. The infantrymen cheered, but their joy was short-lived. Two subalterns braved the enemy machine-gun fire to reach the tanks and direct them toward the barbed wire. The Mark ivs lurched forward, then abruptly halted. Their commander, a young second-lieutenant, explained to a disbelieving Lieutenant R.A.C. Young that he was running low on fuel and would have to leave. Over Young's protests, the tank commander slammed his door and led his squadron away, leaving the Canadian infantry to cut their way through the barbed wire by hand. They did it, but the cost was high; as Major Ian Sinclair, the acting battalion commander, later wrote, "the help of one tank at this critical moment would have cut our casualties to a quarter." Once through the wire, Major Sinclair reorganized his weary, depleted force for the attack on its final objective, Marquion.[65]

British troops came to the rescue. Around mid-day, units of the 32nd Brigade of the 11th Division were able to cross the canal at four points between Sains-lez-Marquion and the Arras-Cambrai road, and a company of the Manchester Regiment moved smartly onto the left of the beleaguered 13th Battalion. Together, the British and Canadians assaulted Marquion. A relieved Major Sinclair later remarked on "the magnificent way in which the Manchesters' attack went forward. In spite of heavy fire, the whole battalion behaved as if carrying out a field day practice." After the fall of Marquion, the 15th (48th Highlanders of Canada) Battalion completed the Third Brigade's conquest of the Blue Line.* The 15th, luckily, encountered only slight opposition because it, too, received no help from the Tank Corps. "I saw no tanks, nor signs of any," noted the battalion commander, Lieutenant-Colonel J.P. Girvan, "during the operations of Sept. 27th."[66]

The First Brigade had, meantime, reached the Green Line and was preparing to continue its advance to the final objective, the Red Line. This assignment fell to two battalions, the 2nd (Eastern Ontario) on the right and the 3rd (Toronto Regiment) on the left, which were soon halted by furious machine-gun fire along the railway embankment that crossed the brigade's front. Casualties mounted; one company of the 2nd Battalion lost all of its officers in the hail of bullets. They were not pinned down for long, because the neighbouring 72nd Battalion, en route to Pilgrim's Rest, broke through the defenders and routed them. This enabled the 2nd and 3rd battalions to resume their advance. They

---

* Crossing the canal at mid-morning, the 15th was accompanied by the Third Brigade's doughty commander, Brigadier-General George Tuxford, who personally captured twenty-two Germans, flushing them from the cellar of a château at pistol-point.

encountered minimal resistance, aside from isolated machine-gun nests. The enemy machine-gunners were, in General Griesbach's words, "inclined to continue firing until the assaulting infantry is on top of them and then to surrender after having inflicted a maximum of casualties. Our men are disinclined to admit that the enemy can have it both ways."[67] Lieutenant George Kerr of the 3rd Battalion won the VC when he single-handedly charged four machine-guns defending the Arras-Cambrai road, taking thirty-one prisoners in the process and clearing the way for the battalion's capture of the Blue Line.

By early afternoon, both battalions were well established on the final objective. The 2nd, holding a farm named La Maison Neuve, just north of Pilgrim's Rest, was greeted by the sight of a colossal traffic jam on the road to Cambrai, as German infantry, wagons, and artillery caissons made good a chaotic escape. Few guns got away. It transpired that the First Brigade alone had captured fifty-six field guns, the approximate artillery allotment for a whole division; the 3rd Battalion accounted for twenty-six. General Griesbach speculated afterward that the lay of the land was responsible for so many guns being on his brigade's front. "The area of the attack of the First Brigade was a trough through which and in which the gun retirement lay and in which were to be found the only gun positions."[68]

The exploitation phase of operations was ready to get under way by the middle of the afternoon. However, it would not be as extensive as General Currie had foreseen. The slow progress of XVII Corps to the south made it impossible to commit the Third Division on the right of the Fourth as planned; there was no room for the Third at this time, and the heavy enfilade fire would have inflicted considerable casualties without compensating results. It was, nevertheless, a great disappointment, because it precluded any possibility that the Canadians might have captured the crossings of the Canal de l'Escaut at Cambrai. The situation on the left was more promising, and units of the First Canadian and British 4th divisions enjoyed some success. By nightfall, the latter had reached the village of Epinoy, stopping just shy of the Canal de la Sensée. This advance enabled Canadian troops to reach the Douai-Cambrai road, in fighting which grimly foreshadowed events to come.

The Second Brigade led the First Division's attack. Two battalions of this brigade had already seen hard fighting in the battle to reach the Blue Line. The 7th (1st British Columbia Regiment) Battalion, its flank exposed by the 13th Battalion's difficulties at Marquion, was slowed by heavy fire, and the men watched in dismay as their carefully orchestrated barrage moved ahead irrevocably, leaving them behind. By late morning, reported Major David Philpot, "it [had] developed into a straight fight with Lewis Guns and rifle fire against large numbers of the enemy... who was putting up a stubborn fight with machine guns and

144

rifles and also firing over open sights from 2 Field Guns dug in along the ridge...." Communications with brigade headquarters were cut, and Major Philpot was unable to arrange artillery support for his battalion. But the men of the 7th were determined: singly and in pairs, they cut their way through the enemy's barbed-wire entanglements and attacked the machine-gunners. With assistance from the 8th (90th Winnipeg Rifles) Battalion, the 7th secured the Blue Line by two in the afternoon.[69]

Twenty minutes later, the offensive resumed, led this time by the 5th (Western Cavalry) Battalion. Striking towards Haynecourt, this unit had a relatively easy time; there was little organized opposition, and the 5th captured the village with forty-six casualties. A much tougher time awaited the 10th (Canadians) Battalion which leap-frogged and attacked the high ground east of Haynecourt. Losses were heavy, for there was little cover on the long, gentle slope; the Germans took full advantage of their excellent fields of fire and turned it into a killing-ground. Worse still, the 10th ran into several broad belts of uncut barbed wire. Cutting their way through by hand, the Canadians finally reached the Douai-Cambrai road, only to be halted once again by another vast field of barbed wire covered by machine-guns. Seeing the attack stalled here, Lieutenant-Colonel E.W. MacDonald, the officer commanding the 10th, reconnoitred his front and decided that it "was not practicable" to press the assault; darkness was descending, and he was uncertain about the situation on either flank. Ordering his men to dig in along a sunken road just west of the highway, MacDonald sent out battle patrols throughout the night to harass the enemy.[70]

The status of this sector remained unstable at nightfall. All evening long, the enemy repeatedly counter-attacked in the direction of Haynecourt, at the rear of the 10th Battalion, and the 5th Battalion was hard-pressed to hold it. Reinforcements from the 8th Battalion arrived in time to keep the Germans out of Haynecourt.

No one worked harder for victory on 27 September than the Canadian engineers. Indeed, their performance was particularly gratifying for General Currie, who had ignored warnings of dire consequences earlier in the year when he authorized their reorganization. The Canal du Nord operations more than vindicated his decision. Prior to the attack, the engineers had repaired eighteen miles of road and built seven miles of tramway lines, "a rate hitherto unknown in this war." On the twenty-seventh, the engineers built seven foot-bridges for the infantry, as well as ten larger bridges for the use of the artillery: the first batteries had rolled across the canal by eight o'clock in the morning. In addition, specially trained teams constructed two 110-foot steel bridges which were operational the following day. All of this was done under fire; on more than one occasion, the engineers had to take up rifles, cross the canal, and subdue snipers and machine-gunners that had been overlooked by the infantry.[71]

By day's end, the Canadians could be pleased with their efforts. Exulted Colonel McNaughton, in a letter to his wife, it had been "a wonderful day for Canada and a terrible blow to the Germans. The end of the war is appreciably closer." General Currie was happy to hear that "nearly one hundred officers and three thousand prisoners were reported captured...nearly one hundred guns had been taken as well." During 27 September, the Canadian Corps had tangled with five German divisions, reinforced by two others later in the day.[72]*

All ranks were buoyed by the victory. "The spirit of our Canadian boys is surely wonderful," wrote one young artilleryman. "They come down the line wounded, some seriously, but they all have a cheery word or a smile if possible, and as long as they can get a cigarette they are happy." Trooper George Hambley, a cavalryman serving as a signaller at Twelfth Brigade headquarters, wrote in his diary that night:

> The advance this morning was a sight never to be forgotten.... In both directions the horizon was obscured by the white fog of bursting shells which marked the retreat of the enemy—the line slowly receded—leaving the scattered remnants of the fight.... As the barrage was lifting back like the rolling away of a mist I could see Germans coming on the run toward our lines and lifting their hands to each man they met....[74]

According to a Corps intelligence survey, German prisoners confirmed "that our attack was a complete surprise"; they were also "unanimous in their admiration for our barrage and general artillery fire.... Our harassing fire on roads in rear areas during the attack greatly impeded movement—many roads being quite impassable."[75]

The prisoners, predictably, were thoroughly demoralized and discouraged. "You don't know it," one shouted to a Canadian gunner in perfect English, "but the war's over." Private Lawrence Eyres, a thirty-year-old member of the 2nd Canadian Siege Battery, wrote home:

> The general opinion of prisoners when questioned on their way to the cages is that the war is nearly over, and they all say that we are going to win. Whether they are so frightened that they say this, or whether it is their candid opinion, is hard to say, but surely to goodness they must have begun to realize by this time that Germany and her allies are out of luck so far as winning this war goes.[76]

---

* These included the 7th Cavalry, 49th Reserve, 1st Guards Reserve, 12th, 22nd, 58th, and 187th divisions.[73]

146

A prisoner made General Currie's day. A count who commanded a cavalry regiment was brought to Corps headquarters, where Currie graciously served him lunch. In return, the German "paid a great tribute to the attack as carried out this morning, and stated further that in the German Army everyone agreed that the Canadian troops were most to be feared in all the Allied Armies." Other visitors during the day included the commander-in-chief, Field-Marshal Haig, and the First Army's General Horne, both of whom praised the Canadian achievement.[77]*

The date, 27 September, was more significant than anyone could realize. It marked the half-way point in the war's last hundred days.

It may be argued that at the Canal du Nord, General Currie had won his greatest victory of the war. Considering his many impressive achievements since taking command of the Canadian Corps—Hill 70 and Passchendaele in 1917, and Amiens and Arras in the last few weeks—this is a statement of substance. Despite daunting difficulties, Currie had come up with a daring plan which had been carried out in almost all phases and with relatively light losses. Marshal Foch remarked in his memoirs that the Canadians displayed "magnificent dash" in crossing the canal, while General Sir Henry Rawlinson later told Currie that it had been, quite simply, "a marvellous feat." Yet, the dazzling success of 27 September would be almost forgotten in the furious fighting of the following four days.[78]

There would be no rest for the enemy. As Currie commented in his diary, "all divisions were to continue the attack tomorrow morning."[79] During the night, the Third Division would be moved into the front lines on the Bapaume-Cambrai road, with instructions to capture Fontaine-Notre-Dame as quickly as possible. The Fourth Division, reduced to a single-brigade frontage, would resume the offensive in the centre, while the First Canadian and British 4th divisions advanced on the Corps left. But, in spite of the prevailing mood of optimism at all levels, it was clear to anyone with a map that things would not get any easier. The gently rolling countryside north of Cambrai was barren of cover, and German machine-gunners had already given ample evidence of their ability to make effective use of these outstanding fields of fire.

---

* Currie would have been gladdened, too, to see the newspaper headlines at home. In sharp contrast to the Amiens operations, the Canadians were given their full share of the credit, as exemplified by the front page of the Toronto *Globe* on 28 September:

  BRITISH TRIUMPH IN CAMBRAI AREA

  MOST IMPORTANT DEFENSES ARE CARRIED BY CANADIAN TROOPS

  CANADIAN DIVISIONS TAKE BOURLON WOOD

  GEN. HAIG'S ARMY BREAKS ALL OPPOSITION

  Quick Progress Made in Dashing Attacks in the Cambrai Area—Canadians Use Scaling Ladders to Cross Canal du Nord—Germans are Utterly Broken

Moreover, the Corps was running out of room to manoeuvre. With its northern flank restricted by the Canal de la Sensée, and the southern flank soon to reach the Canal de l'Escaut, the Canadians were moving into an increasingly constricted battle zone, in the face of an unusually large number of enemy troops. The stage was set for a slugging match of unrivalled ferocity.

The next day's operations followed a familiar pattern. In the wake of a spectacular success, the Canadian Corps fell victim to confusion caused by inconsistent communications and unavoidable delays which resulted in a series of piecemeal attacks. While the Third and Fourth divisions struck at 6 A.M. on the twenty-eighth, the First Division deliberately delayed its assault for three hours, in the hope of improving the protection for its flanks. Time was another factor. "On account of short notice given to battalions to carry out operations," complained Lieutenant-Colonel Donald Sutherland, the acting commander of the Ninth Brigade, "junior officers and N.C.OS. had only a vague idea of what was required of them, consequently when senior officers became casualties there was no officer with sufficient knowledge of the plan to direct operations."[80] Equally serious was the lack of opportunity to conduct a proper reconnaissance, a dangerous deficiency given the fact that the Corps now faced the Marcoing Line, the last organized defences before Cambrai. It was a failing for which the Canadians would pay dearly.

It might have been expected, in any case, that the Third Division would have problems. The three senior officers directing its operations on 28 September were all rookies. The divisional commander, Major-General Frederick Loomis, had been promoted barely two weeks earlier. And both brigades employed by General Loomis were led by men unfamiliar with their commands: the Seventh's Brigadier-General John Clark had been in charge for less than three weeks, while the Ninth was under the temporary command of the above-mentioned Colonel Sutherland.

Still, the Third Division began the day well enough. Both brigades attacked on a one-battalion front. On the right, the 43rd (Cameron Highlanders of Canada) Battalion led the way for the Ninth Brigade, storming Fontaine-Notre-Dame on the road to Cambrai. The village fell swiftly. The 43rd's commanding officer, Lieutenant-Colonel W.K. Chandler, reported that "the entire garrison of the town surrendered with very little resistance." In fact, commented Colonel Chandler, the advance through Fontaine was "almost in the nature of a chase, the Germans were bent on getting away and our men could not keep up with them."[81]

The neighbouring Royal Canadian Regiment (RCR) got off to a good start, but its attack bogged down rather quickly. Accompanied by four tanks—which the RCR's commander, Lieutenant-Colonel C.R.E. Willets, bluntly labelled as "useless"—the battalion followed a devastating barrage that carried the Canadians into the Marcoing Line. By nine o'clock that morning, these defences had been cleared, and the RCR pressed the attack on the support positions. This is where the regiment ran into trouble, in the form of a vast field of barbed wire which had escaped detection in aerial photographs due to the vegetation that had grown through, over, and around it. The RCR was stopped cold, and casualties mounted alarmingly. Colonel Willets was wounded. Among the dead was Company Sergeant-Major C.H. Pope, who had been ordered on leave just before the battalion went into action; the stubborn sergeant-major accompanied his unit, took part in the attack, and was killed by a shell burst.[82]

The RCR did manage to get a toehold on the German defences, thanks largely to the efforts of one man. Lieutenant Milton Gregg, the New Brunswick schoolteacher who commanded D Company, went forward by himself to seek a way through the wire. Eventually, he found what he was looking for: a narrow gap that would afford single-file passage. Collecting a small party, Lieutenant Gregg led them through the entanglements by "a series of short sprints and quick tumbles." Then the Canadians went to work on the defenders. A nearby strongpoint was stormed; it surrendered, and Gregg suddenly had forty-eight prisoners on his hands. As usual, the Germans were quick to counter-attack, and Gregg's brave little band repeatedly repulsed the enemy, making good use of hand grenades. When the supply of bombs ran low, Gregg, though wounded, ignored the German fire and ran the barbed-wire gauntlet to fetch a case of grenades; on his return trip he was wounded a second time. Gregg was later credited with killing eleven Germans and capturing twenty-five others, plus a dozen machine-guns. For his heroism and leadership, he was awarded the VC.[83]

This was, however, strictly a local success. Elsewhere, the RCR could make no headway in the wire. Determined to break the enemy defences, the brigade commander, General Clark, organized a new attack and sent in a fresh battalion, the PPCLI. Displaying the élan for which it was rightly famed, and aided by an effective barrage, it made short work of the Marcoing Line support positions. By early afternoon, the PPCLI and the remnants of the RCR were in full command of the enemy defences on their front. But no further progress was possible, due to problems on their right flank, where the Ninth Brigade's attack had stalled.

Following the capture of Fontaine-Notre-Dame by the 43rd Battalion, the 52nd (New Ontario) Battalion was committed to the battle for the Marcoing Line on this front. "The attack came to a standstill" within minutes, in the face of devastating machine-gun fire. According to the officer commanding the 52nd, Lieutenant-Colonel W.W. Foster, "the enemy had, if anything, reinforced his machine guns." The abortive attack had cost the battalion 259 casualties, without gaining any appreciable amount of ground.[84]

With plenty of daylight still available, the Third Division prepared a renewed effort to reach the Douai-Cambrai road, the Seventh Brigade's objective, and Sainte-Olle, the Ninth Brigade's objective. Reinforcements moved up in the early afternoon, in preparation for a 3 P.M. assault by both brigades between the Arras-Cambrai and Bapaume-Cambrai roads. But the attack had to be postponed until 7 P.M. when it was learned that the artillery was having difficulty procuring the necessary ammunition for a suitable barrage.

When it was finally launched, the renewed offensive made little headway. This was no fault of the artillery's; the accompanying bombardment was described as "most effective." On the Seventh Brigade's front, the PPCLI went over the top with the 49th (Edmonton Regiment) Battalion on its right. The Princess Pats had, by this time, lost their commanding officer, Lieutenant-Colonel Charlie Stewart, who was killed by a shell burst while preparing the attack. More serious was a wide belt of barbed wire blocking the way to the Douai-Cambrai road; overgrown with vegetation, it could not be detected on aerial photographs. The PPCLI ran into it after advancing more than a mile. Despite the darkness that was descending over the battlefield, the Pats made a determined effort to overcome this obstacle. After some searching, a narrow gap was discovered, but it proved to be a death-trap. The men who rushed it were caught in a murderous cross-fire; more than forty bodies were later recovered here, within the space of twenty yards. Under the cover of darkness, the PPCLI withdrew a couple of hundred yards to a more secure position.[85]

This withdrawal led to a heated exchange between the brigade commander, General Clark, and the acting commander of the PPCLI, Captain George Little. Clark was upset when informed that the Pats had pulled back and asked, "Little, do you know the first principles of war?"

"I'm not sure," replied the captain. "What are they?"

"Well, one of them is to keep whatever you've got."

"We never had it," growled Little, "don't worry."[86]

No one else on the Third Division's front fared much better. The 49th Battalion went nowhere, not only because of the PPCLI's problems, but because Sainte-Olle remained in enemy hands. Deadly machine-gun fire swept the open fields, making movement impossible for the men of the 49th. Two battalions of the Ninth Brigade attacked the village, without success. The 58th (Central Ontario) went in first, clearing the remaining Marcoing Line defences in its path. Then the 116th (Ontario County) Battalion tried to take Sainte-Olle. But Major A.W. Pratt, the acting battalion commander, soon called off the attack. "The village appeared to be strongly held by machine guns," explained Major Pratt, "and as no reconnaissance of the ground could be made, it was decided that we would not attack until the following morning."[87]

It had proved to be a long day for the Fourth Division, too. General Hayter's Tenth Brigade had shouldered the burden on its front, committing all four battalions. Two went over the top at zero hour at 6 A.M.: the 50th (Calgary) on the left and the 47th (Western Ontario) on the right. Both battalions broke into the Marcoing Line, but not before bitter and bloody fighting. Attacking north of Raillencourt, the 50th was soon pinned down by machine-gun fire in front of yet another previously undetected belt of barbed wire. Lieutenant H.A. Sharpe seized a pair of wire-cutters and, braving the bullets buzzing about him, cut a passage through the rusty wire. His platoon followed him, and together they charged a nearby trench: enfiladed by Canadian Lewis guns, more than eighty dead defenders were counted in this abattoir. In clearing this section of the Marcoing Line, the 50th captured an impressive total of 450 prisoners. The Calgarians were inspired by the unusual sight of an officer on horseback leading them into action. "We have the Boche on the run, men!" shouted Major J.L.R. Parry. "We have the Boche on the run!" It was something of a miracle that both Major Parry and his horse were uninjured. Not so fortunate was the battalion commander, Colonel Page, who was wounded by a shell burst.[88]

The 47th Battalion had been given a difficult task. Before reaching the Marcoing Line, it would have to fight its way through the fortified village of Raillencourt. Immediately beyond the Marcoing Line lay another village, Sailly, which was also heavily defended. The machine-gun fire that greeted the battalion was staggering, according to a survivor, Fred Bass. The men were "just mowed...down," recalled Bass, "just like grass. It was terrible."[89] Somehow, the 47th reached Raillencourt, and took it. Then, with excellent support from the artillery, the battalion broke the Marcoing Line. But it could go no further.

General Hayter now committed his two remaining battalions. The 46th (South Saskatchewan) Battalion leap-frogged the 50th, while the 44th (New Brunswick) passed through the 47th. The 44th took Sailly, but neither of the fresh units made much progress toward the Douai-Cambrai road. By mid-morning, the Tenth Brigade's attack had broken down completely. The 46th's acting commander, Major Jack Rankin, blamed the artillery, contending that the barrage that accompanied his assault was "pretty thin." The 44th, too, complained about the work of the artillery. The battalion was counter-attacked repeatedly during the late-morning—at least four times after 10 A.M.—and each attack was repulsed by small-arms fire alone; the artillery, for some unexplained reason, did not respond to sos signals "for some hours," according to the battalion commander, Colonel Davies.[90]

The gunners vindicated themselves that night, when the two battalions renewed their attack. General Hayter was determined to reach his objective, the Douai-Cambrai road, and promised the 44th and 46th battalions "plenty of artillery" when they jumped off. He lived up to his promise. The 46th, under a powerful barrage, reached the road and dug in by dark; the 44th, delayed by counter-attacks which continued during the afternoon and weakened by heavy losses, also made it to the road, but not until three the following morning. By that time, the 44th had only a hundred men still in action, with just a pair of unwounded officers.[91]

Only one other Canadian attack took place on 28 September, and it should not have been attempted. The previous day's operations had seen the First Division drive a deep salient into enemy territory, and the 10th (Canadians) Battalion had ended the day hung up in a vast field of uncut barbed wire just beyond the Douai-Cambrai road. Colonel Mac-Donald, the officer commanding the 10th, had recommended that no further offensive action should be undertaken here until proper preparations, which included cutting the wire, had been made. As the colonel later wrote, "it was with some surprise that we received the order of attack...." Not the least of the 10th Battalion's difficulties was the terrain. Looking down a shallow valley, the high ground on either side was outside its jurisdiction, meaning that the 10th would have to rely on advances made by neighbouring formations before it could hope to make any progress. Zero hour was postponed from 6 A.M. until 9 A.M. to give the troops on either flank an opportunity to catch up to the 10th's exposed position. This was clearly inadequate; as we have seen, units of the Fourth Division did not reach the road until late on the twenty-eighth.[92]

The 10th Battalion seemed to be jinxed. Shortly before zero, Colonel MacDonald discovered, to his horror, that the artillery's barrage line coincided with his own front line. To avoid being bombarded by their own guns, he ordered his men to make a hasty withdrawal. Carried out in broad daylight, under enemy fire, this move cost the battalion "at least 50 unnecessary casualties," in the colonel's opinion. Then, when the barrage finally opened, he said, it "was of such a feeble nature that for our purpose it was practically useless." Attacking with both flanks exposed, the 10th tried for two hours to cut its way by hand through the barbed wire, but it was all in vain. The battalion's determination and the futility of its situation were exemplified by the efforts of Captain Jack Mitchell, a company commander. Captain Mitchell was wounded twice in his search for a gap in the wire. Refusing to be evacuated, refusing even to have his wounds dressed, he persisted in his hunt for a way through the wire. Before he could find one, he was wounded again, this time fatally. Colonel MacDonald could not conceal his anger when he later wrote: "This attack was worse than useless and resulted in approximately 100 casualties which could have been avoided...."[93]

After two days of hard fighting on 27 and 28 September, it was evident that things were not going to get easier for the Canadian Corps. Hopeful progress had been made, especially on the Corps right front. The last major defensive position before Cambrai, the Marcoing Line, had been breached between the Bapaume-Cambrai and Douai-Cambrai roads, and Canadian troops were closing in on the suburbs east of the Canal de l'Escaut. But the Germans had given every indication of their willingness to contest this ground, foot by bloody foot. South of the Canadians, XVII Corps was making painfully slow progress in its drive on Cambrai, enabling the enemy to shift disproportionately large reserves to face the Canadian Corps. In addition to the seven divisions already opposing the Canadians, the Germans rushed in one more on 28 September, with elements of five more arriving during the twenty-ninth and thirtieth.* This brought the total number of enemy divisions, in whole or in part, identified by Corps intelligence to thirteen, plus— and, it could be argued, even more importantly—thirteen independent machine-gun companies, élite marksmen units sent in at the express wish of the German high command.[95]

Even more disturbing than the mere numbers involved, it was clear that the Canadians were not facing the demoralized and dispirited troops that were in action elsewhere on the Western Front. While there were instances of enemy soldiers surrendering to the Canadians with relative ease, "some units fought bitterly and skilfully until reduced to little bands of exhausted men."[96]

Lack of co-ordination again plagued the Canadians when they resumed the attack on 29 September. Of the five brigades in the battle, two attacked at 6 A.M., two others at 8 A.M., and the fifth another half-hour later. The reasons for this arrangement are obscure, but it seems likely that the artillery was at least partly responsible. One battalion commander, Lieutenant-Colonel Royal Ewing of the 42nd (Royal Highlanders of Canada), was warned to expect only a light barrage, due to an insufficient number of guns.[97] It is possible that the zero hours were deliberately staggered in a bid to give the artillery a better chance of supporting each attack. If so, it did not work; this proved to be a dismal day for the Canadian gunners.

---

* The 207th Division moved in on 28 September, and the 18th Reserve, 26th Reserve, 35th, 220th, and 234th divisions were added on the next two days.[94]

All three brigades of the Third Division saw action on Sunday, the twenty-ninth. Its two right-hand brigades, the Eighth and Ninth, attacked at 6 A.M., while the Seventh waited until 8 A.M. The Ninth Brigade, on the extreme right, dispatched a battalion to aid the British troops struggling south of the Bapaume-Cambrai road. The 58th (Central Ontario) Battalion crossed the army boundary and swiftly cleared the Marcoing Line which had been blocking the advance of the British 57th Division, as far as the Canal de l'Escaut. Meanwhile, the 116th (Ontario County) Battalion renewed the battle for Sainte-Olle. The Umpty-Umps found the enemy machine-gun fire unabated from the night before. Arthur Bonner, who took part in the attack, never forgot the experience:

> I think we had about two companies pretty well wiped out there. They met us with machine-gun fire and just wiped out platoon after platoon as it went over. I remember one platoon of B Company. They were right in extended order, in line, their officer, a Lieutenant Norton, just in behind them, and they were all lying there dead, the whole platoon just wiped out to a man.

Bonner's recollection was not far off the mark: A Company of the 116th Battalion was left with only five men unwounded, while B Company was reduced to three officers and twenty-five other ranks.[98]

The defence of Sainte-Olle centred around a trench on the outskirts of the village. As soon as this became apparent, Major Pratt, the officer commanding the 116th, called on the artillery for assistance. A nearby field battery responded promptly, its 18-pounders focusing their fire on the trench with admirable accuracy and pinning down the defenders. Pratt then committed his remaining two companies, which outflanked and took the trench, along with a hundred prisoners and fifteen machine-guns. By noon, the 116th had secured Sainte-Olle. But the cost had been high: 250 casualties.

While the Umpty-Umps waged their bloody battle for Sainte-Olle, two battalions of General Draper's Eighth Brigade swung north of the village and struck for Neuville-Saint-Rémy, a suburb of Cambrai. The 1st and 2nd Canadian Mounted Rifles (CMR) suffered severely from machine-gun fire in the vicinity of Sainte-Olle even as they deployed in the open fields. With no cover, their flank exposed, the CMR battalions made little progress until Sainte-Olle finally fell. The deadly fire removed, the two battalions surged into Neuville-Saint-Rémy, but not before another outstanding act of bravery. The 2nd CMR was briefly halted by a machine-gun post on the Douai-Cambrai road. A company commander, Captain John MacGregor—one of Canada's most decorated soldiers, with the Distinguished Conduct Medal, the Military

Cross and bar, and, soon, the Victoria Cross—grabbed a rifle and attacked the position. Captain MacGregor killed four of the gunners and captured eight others, and was later awarded the vc. By nightfall, these two Canadian battalions were at the edge of the Canal de L'Escaut. Across this waterway, scants yards away, lay their ultimate objective, Cambrai—so close, and yet so far.

Two more brigades went over the top at 8 A.M. on 29 September. General Clark's Seventh Brigade attacked with the Fourth Division's Twelfth Brigade on its left. The latter formation was under the command of Lieutenant-Colonel James Kirkaldy, since Brigadier-General James MacBrien had been wounded the previous afternoon.* Neither brigade received much help from the artillery, and neither got much further than the Douai-Cambrai road. The Seventh Brigade's objective was the village of Tilloy, on the edge of the low plateau that overlooks Cambrai from the north, while the Twelfth aimed at Sancourt and Blécourt, villages directly north of Tilloy. The Twelfth came tantalizingly close to success, but the Seventh was stopped well short of its goal.

Two battalions led the Seventh Brigade's assault. The 49th (Edmonton Regiment) and 42nd (Royal Highlanders of Canada) followed a barrage that was described as "thin and ineffective." As was so often the case, the Canadians had to cross ground that offered no cover, and casualties from enemy machine-guns mounted rapidly. The 49th Battalion, on the right, reached the road but could not get across it. Despite taking 150 prisoners, the 49th's losses were so heavy that it had to be reinforced by the 2nd CMR in order to hold its modest gains.[100]

The 42nd Battalion had an even worse time, coming to grief in the same belt of barbed wire that had decimated the PPCLI the previous night. The weak barrage failed to gap the wire, and the Highlanders had to cut their way through by hand. The Germans, sitting silently behind their massed machine-guns, watched and waited until the men of the 42nd were deep in the vast entanglement. Then, all hell broke loose as the Germans opened a devastating fire. "The leading ranks went down like ninepins," reads the regimental history, "many, their clothing caught in the wire, hung there helpless under the stream of bullets." Within minutes, most of the officers had fallen, including the man leading the attack, Major C. Beresford Topp, who was severely wounded. Not a single soldier retreated. Instead, singly and in pairs, the

---

* General MacBrien, whose brigade was not involved in the fighting on the twenty-eighth, was wounded because he recklessly exposed himself to enemy fire. He was hit in the leg by a stray bullet while riding his horse near the front. Private Arthur Foster of the 38th Battalion remembered seeing MacBrien galloping about "as if there was no danger whatever."[99]

Highlanders worked their way through the wire, suffering casualties at every step. Once through, they exacted revenge, rushing the machine-gunners and putting them to the bayonet. Some fled, but most were killed at their guns.[101]

Having reached the road, the 42nd and 49th battalions were pinned down by machine-gun fire from a railway embankment three hundred yards beyond. The hail of bullets was so heavy that it was tantamount to suicide for a man to stand up. The Corps heavy artillery tried to assist by deluging the embankment with high explosives during the noon hour, but the bombardment failed to dislodge the determined enemy machine-gunners. Indeed, the Germans even mounted a counter-attack, but it was repulsed.

In these trying circumstances, the work of the Canadian stretcher-bearers was marvellous. Two in particular, both belonging to the 42nd Battalion, won high praise for their courage under fire. Private M.T. Jackson spent all afternoon in the open, often within a hundred yards of the enemy, treating the wounded and dragging them to safety. His performance was later called "little short of miraculous." Private Albert Gibson remained on duty continuously for seventy-two hours, rescuing at least twenty-five seriously injured comrades. Three were hit and killed by German bullets as Gibson dressed their wounds.[102]

The Twelfth Brigade had, by day's end, fared no better. Jumping off from positions along the Douai-Cambrai road, this brigade ended up with very little to show for its efforts, but it actually came close to an incredible victory. Two battalions headed the Twelfth's operation, the 38th (Ottawa) on the right and the 72nd (Seaforth Highlanders of Canada) on the left. The 38th was stopped in its tracks. This was largely due to unbearable fire from the right, where the 42nd and 49th battalions were having so much trouble. But at least part of the problem was inexperience, according to the acting commander of the 38th, Major F.A. Rowlandson,* who observed that this assault "would seem to prove that the troops [are] not fully trained in the use of fire and movements."[103] It was a complaint that would be echoed by Major Rowlandson's peers.

The 38th Battalion's attack stalled in a matter of minutes. The few survivors took refuge in a sunken road, and there endured machine-gun fire which Private Arthur Foster later described as "the heaviest" he had ever seen. Private Foster, a stretcher-bearer, vividly remembered the terrible scene:

* The battalion commander, Lieutenant-Colonel S.D. Gardner, was wounded on 28 September.

After finding an old gun pit, I began to trail the [wounded] fellows into it from all directions. The bullets would pass so close to my ear that the snap of them would make me dizzy, and there were actually [expended] bullets lying on top of the wounded men; I could kick loose bullets in the grass.

Foster did not escape unharmed. Later in the day, he was wounded by a bullet through the body and shrapnel in the neck, but he lived to tell the tale to his grandchildren.[104]

It was the 72nd Battalion that came so close to success on this front. In fact, the 72nd took its objectives, Sancourt and Blécourt, but could not hold them, having both flanks exposed and being unable to rush up reinforcements. This battalion went into action somewhat under strength, with sixteen officers and 373 other ranks; the survivors would be greatly outnumbered by the prisoners brought back after the battle.[105]

The 72nd started smartly, thanks to a barrage that, on this day, was unusually potent. The battalion crossed the Douai-Cambrai road with relatively light losses and stormed Sancourt. The village fell after a short, sharp fight, yielding 250 prisoners. In a nearby sunken road, another 120 Germans were captured, along with twenty machine-guns. The battalion pressed on, reaching the railway embankment half-way between Sancourt and Blécourt. But casualties were adding up quickly, as the formations on either flank had been left far behind. Caught in a deadly cross-fire, the 72nd dug in.[106]

A truly amazing episode ensued. Lieutenant J.M. Knight and five other ranks, belonging to B Company, crossed the rail line and cautiously worked their way towards Blécourt. This little party then launched a surprise attack and, incredibly, captured the village. In the process, they rounded up "at least 150 prisoners," although many of these later escaped when they realized how few Canadians were holding them captive. It soon became apparent they would not hold Blécourt for long, either, as the Germans were making obvious preparations for a counter-attack. With no reinforcements able to reach him, and his entire party wounded, Lieutenant Knight reluctantly decided to retire. The group returned to the rail line, with eighty prisoners in tow.[107]

This position proved untenable, too. Although reinforced by the 85th (Nova Scotia Highlanders) Battalion, the Canadians were being ravaged by machine-gun fire from three directions. The 72nd withdrew to Sancourt, but even this had to be relinquished, when the Germans brought down a tremendous bombardment. The battalion ended the day dug in along the Douai-Cambrai road, in almost the same place it had started.

The last of the Canadian attacks to be launched on 29 September proved to be a near disaster. The 8th (90th Winnipeg Rifles) Battalion was to lead the Second Brigade's drive on Abancourt, due north of Blécourt. The officer commanding the 8th, Lieutenant-Colonel A.L. Saunders, had been opposed to this operation, having witnessed the "real sorry jackpot" in which the 10th Battalion had found itself the previous day. Facing the prospect of advancing down a shallow valley, Colonel Saunders realized that success "was wholly contingent... upon the advance of flanking units, on the lip of a saucer. If flanking units did not advance on either side of this draw, then whatever unit assaulted up the draw would be exposed to enfilade fire from machine guns...." Saunders registered his complaints, but he was overruled. As a result, he later wrote, "we were to reap the fruits of such a hurried affair, engineered by Higher Commands, regardless of Battalions."[108]

Every effort was made to give the 8th Battalion a reasonable chance of success. General Macdonell, the First Division's commander, delayed the attack, originally scheduled for 6 A.M., until 8 A.M., to allow the British 11th Division time to take the high ground overlooking the Canadian sector. The British failed. They were halted well short of the Douai-Cambrai road, but they gamely agreed to try again at 8 A.M., whereupon Macdonell delayed the 8th Battalion's assault for another half-hour. The British failed again, but there was no reprieve for the 8th.[109]

The battalion attacked at 8:36 A.M., following a brief bombardment. Four tanks were supposed to accompany the assault, but they failed to arrive, and the operation proceeded without them. The barbed wire that had caused so much trouble for the 10th Battalion a day earlier was found to be well cut, but only a handful of attackers got beyond it. Devastating machine-gun fire—first from the left, where the British had been defeated, then on the right, where the 72nd Battalion had been halted—raked the 8th Battalion mercilessly. C Company lost all its officers, ending the day commanded by a corporal. Aside from a toehold in the Marcoing Line, the 8th Battalion had precious little to show for its sacrifice. Colonel Saunder's anger and frustration were excusable and understandable.

The twenty-ninth of September had been a costly day for the Canadian Corps. Casualties totalled 2089. With the exception of the slight gains made by the Third Division, the Corps had made little progress in the face of fanatical opposition. "It was a day of very bitter fighting," remarked the Third Division's General Loomis, "and the enemy fought very well, and very noticeable was the lavish use of his M.G.s of which he had an abnormal quantity." Nevertheless, General Currie decided to continue offensive operations. Well aware of the large German forces arrayed against the Corps, Currie clearly felt that he had to retain the initiative in order to preclude the possibility of a major counter-attack, a fear that had more than a little basis in reality, as subsequent events would demonstrate. It cannot be doubted that Currie would have welcomed a day or two to properly prepare further attacks, but there was no time. A delay, he knew, would enable the enemy to shift the high-calibre machine-gunners from the Canadian front to oppose the Third and Fourth armies to the south. The bottom line was that the Canadian Corps *had* to continue its attacks.

Currie planned his operations on 30 September in two phases. In the first, the Third and Fourth divisions were to push across the plateau north of Cambrai, reaching the line Tilloy-Bantigny, after which Brutinel's Brigade of armoured cars was to rush through and capture the canal crossings at Eswars and Ramillies. "The second phase, to take place on the success of the first, provided for the seizing of the high ground overlooking the Sensée River by the 1st Canadian Division and 11th (British) Division."[110]

Monday, 30 September, was a near-calamity. This is a tribute to the courage and determination of the multitudes of German machine-gunners, rather than a condemnation of the Canadian Corps. In fact, these attacks were better co-ordinated than the previous day's, with both divisions in the first phase jumping off precisely at 6 A.M., as dawn broke along the eastern horizon. And the artillery support was superb, save for one aspect which, while no fault of the gunners', adversely affected the entire operation.

Two battalions of the Seventh Brigade led the way on the Third Division's front. The choice of this brigade was questionable; it was tired and depleted, seeing action for the third consecutive day. The PPCLI and RCR stormed the railway embankment east of the Douai-Cambrai road, taking it with surprising ease in the wake of a brief but effective barrage that fell "with ghastly accuracy," in the words of the PPCLI's history. In a single hundred-yard stretch, the Canadians captured thirty-six machine-guns, a measure of the enemy's determination to stop them.[111]

Crossing the embankment, however, brought mixed results. The PPCLI, attacking Tilloy, "really had a picnic," according to the acting commander, Captain Little. By seven-thirty in the morning, Tilloy had been taken, along with a battery of 77-millimetre guns and fifty machine-guns. Reinforced by a party from the 49th Battalion, the PPCLI had consolidated its hold on the village by mid-morning. The brigade commander, General Clark, was justified in calling the capture of Tilloy "a very brilliant feat of arms." But it was the sole highlight of the action this day.[112]

There was trouble on the left of the PPCLI. The RCR, debouching from the rail line, was soon stopped by a storm of machine-gun fire, much of it coming from the direction of Blécourt, where the Fourth Division was bogged down. As a consequence, the RCR was effectively pinned down, although one adventuresome group—twenty men, led by Lieutenant W.G. Wurtele—reached the chapel midway between Tilloy and Blécourt. But they were isolated, a thousand yards ahead of the main body of the battalion, and were soon forced to withdraw.

A key feature of the Fourth Division's attack was supposed to be a smokescreen laid down by the artillery. This would, it was hoped, blind the enemy machine-gunners until the Canadian infantrymen could overrun them. The artillery did its best, but that was not good enough. "It was impossible to procure sufficient smoke shells to form an adequate smoke screen, in advancing against M.G. nests." The little smoke quickly drifted away, leaving the men of the Eleventh Brigade at the mercy of the machine-guns.[113]

The 75th (Mississauga) Battalion, supported by the 54th (Central Ontario), led the attack. Both battalions barely made it to the jumping-off lines in time, both being heavily shelled en route from the rear; the 75th was assembled with a mere three minutes to spare. Following an effective rolling barrage, the 75th quickly captured Sancourt and pressed on to the railway embankment in the face of machine-gun fire from Blécourt and Abancourt. By the time the battalion reached the rail line, it had been decimated. By day's end, the 75th could muster only three officers and seventy-five other ranks; the survivors were temporarily amalgamated with the 54th Battalion.

The 54th had plenty of problems of its own. The battalion commander, Lieutenant-Colonel A.B. Carey, was wounded during the shelling on the way to the front line. The barrage was, in the words of Claude Craig, "a peach and the worst I ever went through." Continued Craig:

> We lost an awful lot of men going through and after we were through we had the machine-gun fire to put up with. We crossed a sunken road and a level road and came to the railway lines...and we had got about fifty yards past this when I was hit in the wrist. The bullet went through my wrist and into a diary and flattened a steel mirror that I carried just over the heart. Got bandaged up and started to get out of it.[114]

As the 54th Battalion valiantly attacked Blécourt, the Germans delivered the coup de grâce. A counter-attack met the Canadians head-on, and the situation suddenly changed dramatically: it was no longer a question of capturing Blécourt, but of holding the marginal gains already made. The remnants of the 54th and 75th battalions were forced back to the railway embankment, where they were reinforced by the 87th (Canadian Grenadier Guards) Battalion, which had been standing by to exploit the Eleventh Brigade's expected success. Instead, the 87th found itself engaged in a desperate defensive battle that lasted most of the morning. "The situation was very obscure," wrote the 87th's commanding officer, Lieutenant-Colonel Kenneth Perry, who soon discovered that his unit "had been very badly cut up."[115] The battalion had actually been reduced to the approximate strength of a company in the space of a few hours. But the Canadians prevailed: the German counter-attack was repulsed and the railway embankment was secured.

The calibre of German resistance had come as an unpleasant surprise to the Canadians. "It was not expected that the enemy would employ such large numbers of troops in this operations," wrote the Fourth Division's commander, General Watson. "The result showed clearly that the enemy had no intention of withdrawing." Similar, but much more heated, was the comment of the Eleventh Brigade's General Odlum:

> From the start the operation did not go well. It was based on false assumptions, namely that the enemy was beaten and would with-draw, and that a smoke screen would be an ample protection for the left of the attack against the fire that would naturally be expected from Blécourt Valley and the high ground south of Abancourt. The result showed that the enemy had no intention of withdrawing. As for the smoke screen, the less said the better. It was a total failure.[116]

There was no further fighting on 30 September. A disappointed General Currie cancelled the second phase of operations, then summoned his senior subordinates to a mid-day conference at Fourth Division headquarters at Quarry Wood, near Bourlon. There, Currie carefully weighed his options and concluded that the best course was to keep attacking. He later explained his difficult decision:

> The tremendous exertions and considerable casualties consequent upon the four days' almost continuous fighting had made heavy inroads on the freshness and efficiency of all arms, and it was questionable whether an immediate decision could be forced in the face of the heavy concentration of troops which our successful and, from the enemy's standpoint, dangerous advance, had drawn against us. On the other hand, it was known that the enemy had suffered severely, and it was quite possible that matters had reached the stage where he no longer considered the retention of this position worth the severe losses in men and moral[e] consequent upon a continuance of the defence.[117]

161

Zero hour on Tuesday, 1 October, was set for 5 A.M.,* an hour before dawn. Currie proposed to attack simultaneously with all four of his divisions in the line—from north to south, the British 11th, and First, Fourth, and Third Canadian—while his reserve formations, the Second Division and Brutinel's Brigade, were alerted to be ready to exploit any breakthrough that might occur. The objectives were roughly the same as those of the previous day's operations, but the key was quite clearly the British division on the Corps left. Unless and until the high ground between Aubancheul-au-Bac and Abancourt was taken, the formations further south would be exposed to the deadly enfilade fire that had already caused so many problems. Currie must have been tempted to employ Canadians in this important mission, but successfully resisted the urge. That he did so makes a mockery of the claims of some Canadian veterans who bitterly accused him of giving them the toughest tasks in the waning weeks of the war.

Much to Currie's disgust, the British 11th Division failed miserably. Its attack was "halted by heavy uncut wire almost before it began to advance." Currie contended, in later years, that the defeat stemmed from a half-hearted effort by the British, who, he said, "used only three companies when they promised to use three battalions. It was a direct betrayal on their part, for had three battalions attacked with vigour the enemy's resistance would have been easily overcome." That is doubtful, but the fact that Currie could use a word like "betrayal" thirteen years afterward reveals the extent of his anger. In any event, he was correct in arguing that the British fiasco on the left made difficulties elsewhere "inevitable."[118]

The failure produced a domino effect. The first to feel it was the neighbouring First Canadian Division. Here, General Griesbach's First Brigade went over the top with two battalions, the 1st (Western Ontario) and 4th (Central Ontario), attacking toward Abancourt. Under an excellent barrage and the cover of pre-dawn darkness, these battalions made good progress in the early going. But neither got much farther than the railway line that blocked the approach to Abancourt. With the arrival of daylight, the troops were subjected to machine-gun fire raking their left flank and rear. One man won the VC near Abancourt: Sergeant William Merrifield of the 4th Battalion single-handedly wiped out a pair of machine-gun nests. But bravery alone was not enough, and the 1st and 4th battalions spent the rest of the day pinned down along the embankment, suffering 388 casualties to no obvious purpose.

---

* At one minute after midnight—0001 hours—on 1 October, the British army adopted the twenty-four-hour clock. However, for the sake of consistency, the balance of this narrative will be based on the twelve-hour clock.

Next to be affected was the Third Brigade. Even under ideal conditions, this brigade had been given a tall order, the taking of three fortified villages that had already caused a lot of grief: Blécourt, Bantigny, and Cuvillers. Again, the attackers enjoyed initial success, thanks to the combination of darkness and fine artillery work. The 13th (Royal Highlanders of Canada) Battalion stormed and captured Blécourt, at the cost of ninety-one casualties. Among the dead, however, was a company commander, Captain A.G.C. Macdermot, who was killed by a treacherous German who came forward to surrender; the German, in turn, forfeited his life to Macdermot's angry men.[119]

It was still dark; the Third Brigade's attack was going like clockwork. By six, the 13th Battalion had been relieved by two others, the 14th (Royal Montreal Regiment), which struck for Bantigny, and the 16th (Canadian Scottish), which attacked Cuvillers. Both battalions had had difficulty assembling prior to zero hour. In dark, unfamiliar country, "in pouring rain," the 14th was ready with only ten minutes to spare; the 16th did slightly better, getting into position twenty minutes before zero. Both reached their objectives swiftly. By seven-thirty, the 14th Battalion had taken Bantigny, along with a hundred prisoners. The 16th completed the capture of Cuvillers by eight o'clock, en route overrunning a sunken road where a dozen machine-guns—"I never saw so many machine-guns in any place in my life," recalled Lieutenant John Dunlop—and nearly a hundred Germans were captured. It was strangely silent in this sector; the 16th Battalion cooks in Cuvillers brewed tea for the troops.[120]

The quiet was too good to last. Suspicious, Captain R.C. McIntyre of the 16th Battalion investigated:

It seemed altogether too quiet for me and together with Lieutenant [James] Rodgers and a party of men I decided to make a thorough reconnaissance of our left flank and endeavour to gain touch with our flanking battalion [the 14th]. We worked over to the left and rear of Cuvillers but failed to discover any Canadians, and were returning when we saw parties of the enemy coming down from the north with the evident intention of cutting off our retreat. We hastened back to the company. By this time heavy flanking fire was pouring in on us, and I realized that the front of the attack had suddenly swung round from east to north.[121]

The two battalions were soon subjected to repeated and violent counter-attacks. By nine that morning, the 14th had repulsed three, all the while enduring increasingly heavy machine-gun fire from the left and rear, where the First Brigade had been halted before Abancourt.

Losses were mounting rapidly as the 16th Battalion fought to hold Cuvillers. Three of the four company commanders were killed; only the above-mentioned Captain McIntyre survived. The acting battalion commander, Major Roderick Bell-Irving, disappeared during a reconnaissance patrol; his body was discovered a few days later.

Practically surrounded, cut off from reinforcements, and running low on ammunition, the 14th and 16th battalions reluctantly retreated. But the withdrawal was conducted coolly and calmly. The 16th pulled back first, while the 14th provided covering fire. Then, slowly and stubbornly, the 14th evacuated Bantigny and retired down the shallow valley toward Blécourt. At one point, the Canadians ran out of ammunition, but kept up the fight by retrieving the rifles of dead Germans. Under relentless pressure, the two battalions reached Blécourt, where they dug in. But the devastating fire from the left made it impossible to hold even this, and in the late morning they retired to a more secure position that left them about 600 yards from their original jumping-off line. By this point, there were only seventy-eight unwounded survivors of the 16th Battalion; the 14th was little better off, with just ninety-two.

The domino effect ended south of here. The Eleventh Brigade, enjoying "perfect" artillery support, reached the road linking Cuvillers and Ramillies by mid-morning, but the brigade commander, General Odlum, was under no illusions about the relative ease of the operation so far. "Prisoners poured in from the start," he later wrote, "and so many battalions and regiments were identified that it was evident at once that the fight would be a hard one." Led by the 102nd (Central Ontario) Battalion, these Canadians enjoyed remarkable success. Despite dreadful enfilade fire, thanks to the Third Brigade's retirement from Bantigny, Cuvillers, and Blécourt, the 102nd escaped with relatively light casualties, 177, while capturing 443 prisoners and thirty-two machine-guns. Lieutenant Graham Lyall personally accounted for eighty of the prisoners and seventeen of the machine-guns, bringing his individual captures since the Canal du Nord to an amazing 185 prisoners and twenty-six machine-guns, along with a field gun! His excellent efforts brought him a well deserved VC.[122]

Among the 102nd's casualties was Lionel Greenslade. The twenty-three-year-old private would long remember the hail of machine-gun bullets he faced that day:

> I can remember getting shot-at several times—the bullets whizzing around your head, you know, like bees.... I ran down to this sunken road, and just as I got down there I saw this machine-gunner down the road, and he let off a burst and got me in the arm. I just felt like somebody hit me in the arm with a hammer, and my

arm was useless, of course . . . . It went right through—it was a clean wound.[123]

The 87th (Canadian Grenadier Guards) Battalion now joined the attack, passing through the 102nd in a bid to exploit success. The 87th was really only a company; its heavy losses the previous day had reduced it to only four officers and 124 other ranks. It is odd that this unit was asked to undertake an attack in such a weakened condition, but it did so, according to Lieutenant-Colonel Kenneth Perry, "cheerfully and steadily." Patrols from the 87th actually reached the outskirts of Eswars, in the face of galling machine-gun fire. Major A.W.W. Kyle recalled his narrow escape from injury:

I had five bullet holes in my equipment and uniform. I had bullet holes in my water bottle. I had them through the arm of my coat. I had a bullet in the sole of my shoes from these machine-guns, but I never got a scratch. Unbelievable. It was just a miracle I never got a scratch. But they were being knocked down around me like flies.[124]

Led by Colonel Perry, who was later awarded the Distinguished Service Order, the survivors of the 87th retired to the relative safety of the salient created by their comrades of the 102nd Battalion. There was no let-up in the enfilade fire from the north, but the battered brigade held on to the salient. General Odlum had no doubt that his tired troops would prevail in this situation. "It was apparent," he commented afterward, "that both [sides] had been fought to a standstill and that the enemy, while he still could put up a defensive fight, had had almost enough."[125]

The remaining attack that took place on 1 October was also the most ambitious. The Ninth Brigade was to strike due east of Tilloy and take the high ground a thousand yards away, then swing sharply to the right and capture the crossings of the Canal de l'Escaut at Pont d'Aire and Ramillies. To carry out this far-reaching scheme, Colonel Sutherland, the brigade commander, chose to employ all four of his battalions.

Once more, the Canadian assault started promisingly. The 52nd (New Ontario) Battalion, with the 43rd (Cameron Highlanders of Canada) on its right, had little trouble taking the gently rising ridge east of Tilloy. But, crossing the crest, the attackers encountered machine-gun fire described as "overwhelming" by the 43rd's commander, Lieutenant-Colonel W.K. Chandler. In this storm of fire, said the 52nd's Lieutenant-Colonel W.W. Foster, "it was impossible to get forward." Although the 52nd lost every officer and most of its non-commissioned officers, it still managed to capture 250 prisoners and thirty machine-guns.[126]

The lay of the land was most unfavourable. In the opinion of Lieutenant-Colonel Alex Ross, there was little likelihood of success here:

It was quite impossible to carry out the attack from the ridge overlooking Cambrai from the north. The ground slopes right down to the canal. Absolutely flat. Not a vestige of cover of any kind at all on it. Well, to advance in daylight down that against entrenched troops concealed in the canal bank was absolutely impossible.[127]

In a bid to revive his stalled attack, Colonel Sutherland committed his remaining units, the 58th (Central Ontario) and 116th (Ontario County) battalions. They gave it a good try; the 116th captured a hundred prisoners and several machine-guns and three field guns. But, in the process, the battalion lost half its strength; the survivors withdrew to the ridge "by two's and three's." Major Pratt, the officer commanding the 116th, considered that the battalion's valiant effort had been wasted, later complaining that the already considerable difficulties were "increased owing to the fact that there had been no opportunity for anyone to reconnoitre the assembly positions or view the ground over which we attacked, also the time which could be devoted to explaining to the men even the merest outline of the plan to attack was almost negligible."[128]

It had been a disappointing day. As the Fourth Division's General Watson observed, "The day's fighting again showed that the enemy had no intention whatever of withdrawing." There were, nevertheless, positive points about the operations on 1 October. The Corps had managed an average gain "of about a mile" along its front, including the valuable ground around Tilloy, which gave the Canadians command not only of Cambrai but also of the valley of the Escaut. Equally heartening was the performance of the Canadian artillery, which had in a single day redeemed itself after inconsistent contributions since the Canal du Nord. The Canadian gunners fired more than 7000 tons of ammunition of 1 October, twice the daily average of these operations. "The guns were seldom without a target," first as they laid down the rolling barrages that accompanied the infantry, and then as they helped to repel the repeated German counter-attacks. Consider the comment of one rueful prisoner, who told his Canadian captors: "You think our artillery barrage is bad. You want to be in one of your own over there. You fellows are even killing the sparrows on our side. Nothing could live through it...."[129]

General Currie had no intention of continuing the attacks. Appalled by the violence of the counter-attacks, Currie refused to risk the gains already made at such heavy cost. "To continue to throw tired troops against such opposition, without giving them an opportunity to refit and recuperate, was obviously inviting a serious failure, and I accordingly decided to break off the engagement."[130] It is the mark of a superior commander to know when to attack and when *not* to attack. Currie knew that, while the Canadian Corps had fallen short of its main objective, Cambrai, the capture of the high ground overlooking the city had rendered the enemy's position untenable. The fall of Cambrai was now just a matter of time.

In the five days of fighting, the Corps had acquitted itself well. In breaking the last organized defences on this front, the Canadian and British troops under Currie's command had captured 7059 prisoners and 205 guns. At the same time, they had drawn an inordinate number of German forces to this sector. Currie later pointed out that "on our front of 5½ miles, the enemy used 13 divisions and 13 independent machine gun units. In the same operation, on a front of 10 miles to the South of us [opposite the Third Army] he used six divisions. That shows you the importance he attaches in stopping the Canadian Corps. He acts as if he thought that if he succeeded in stopping us, he stopped everything."[131]

The results were even more impressive when considered in the context of the campaign launched southeast of Arras on 26 August. Since that date, the Canadians had battled through twenty-three miles of enemy defences, including the imposing Drocourt-Quéant Line and the formidable Canal du Nord, while liberating 116 square miles of occupied French territory. They had "engaged and decisively defeated 31 German Divisions . . . in strongly fortified positions and under conditions most favourable to the defence," capturing 18,585 prisoners, 371 guns, and 1923 machine-guns.[132]

The cost had been undeniably high. Casualties for the period 22 August–11 October totalled 30,806, and two-thirds of these were incurred in the battles for the Canal du Nord and Cambrai. "I regret the number of casualties," Currie explained to a cabinet minister, Sir Edward Kemp, "but I do not consider that anyone can regard them as excessive when the extent and severity of the operations are considered." In a letter to a personal friend, Currie outlined his position this way:

A flank attack is always a hard attack, in this case our flank was exposed for twenty-five miles. The Germans fought us exceedingly hard all the way, for whenever the Canadian Corps goes into a battle he seems to throw a far higher proportion of men and ammunition at us than he does at any other part of the front. He assumes that if he stops the Canadian Corps, everything else stops.

167

This is a point that should be remembered by the people of Canada when they think of the casualties....[133]*

There is one further important consideration concerning the casualties: most of the men survived. "A noticeable feature of the casualties is the small proportion of killed," noted the 50th (Calgary) Battalion's Colonel Page, who was himself wounded. "A large proportion of the wounded are slight bullet wounds."[135] Over the course of the war, it was typical that fatalities would account for one-quarter to one-third of the losses in any given engagement, and these were largely due to the terrible injuries inflicted by artillery shells. But in the battles of Arras and Cambrai, German guns had not been a major factor; machine-guns did most of the damage. Bullet wounds were at least clean, compared to the grotesque mutilations caused by shrapnel. Consequently, only *one-seventh* of the Canadian casualties in this period proved to be fatal.†

Another unusual facet of the casualties was the heavy loss among senior officers. In the five days of fighting near Cambrai, the Canadian Corps lost two brigadiers and seven battalion commanders, which served to impair the efficiency of the affected units.‡

Currie had mixed feelings about the fighting just concluded. On the one hand, there was his intense pride in the enormous contributions the Canadian Corps was making to the Allied cause. "The 47 Divisions fought by the Canadian Corps since August 8th," he commented in his diary, "is 25% of the German Army, so that we have more than pulled

---

* Clearly, Currie expected to be criticized for the casualties incurred by the Corps. A formidable opponent had, in fact, already raised the issue with the prime minister. In a 1 October letter to Sir Robert Borden, Sir Sam Hughes—a backbencher and disgraced former minister of militia and defence—condemned what he called "the useless massacre of our Canadian boys, as has needlessly occurred at Cambrai.... I have on other occasions drawn your attention to the massacres at Lens [Hill 70], Passchendaele, etc., where the only apparent object was to glorify the General in command." He demanded "the removal of incompetents.... Bull-head and incompetence are traceable by the horrible casualties.... Any ass can sit back and simply order battalions to go forward to certain death." Borden did not respond, but Hughes later launched a series of slanderous attacks on Currie while enjoying parliamentary immunity.[134]

† An interesting example is the 75th (Mississauga) Battalion. Its casualties on 30 September were considered to be so serious by General Odlum, commanding the Eleventh Brigade, that the battalion "ceased to be a factor during the remainder of the operations." The 75th lost 389 men, but only twenty-five were killed, or one in almost sixteen.[136]

‡ The brigadiers were Arthur Bell (Sixth) and James MacBrien (Twelfth); the battalion commanders were Lieutenant-Colonels S.D. Gardner (38th), Lionel Page (50th), A.B. Carey (54th), Fred Lister (102nd), Charlie Stewart (PPCLI), and C.R.E. Willets (RCR), plus Major Roderick Bell-Irving (16th). Stewart and Bell-Irving were the only fatalities among these officers.

168

our weight." As he later told Prime Minister Sir Robert Borden: "It was as if we said to the American Army, to the French Army, to the Belgian Army and to the rest of the British Army, 'You look after three-quarters of the German Army and we will take care of the rest'." The statistics also enabled him to further justify the heavy losses. "You cannot meet and defeat in battle one-quarter of the German Army without suffering casualties," he pointed out. If nothing else, the numbers amount to a tribute to the enemy's high regard for the Canadian Corps. Indeed, the Germans were so impressed with the Canadians that they seriously misjudged the strength of the Corps, which may be another reason for the vast forces they threw at the Canadians. According to a captured intelligence document, the Germans believed that they were facing "at least twelve Canadian divisions."[137]

At the same time, Currie was not entirely satisfied with the Canadian performance. This was apparent during a visit to the headquarters of the 42nd (Royal Highlanders of Canada) Battalion later in October, when he addressed the assembled officers with typical frankness:

> Gentlemen, I want you to forget that I am the Corps Commander and to tell me quite frankly just what you think went wrong with the last show. I want to know exactly what you are thinking, whether you believe mistakes have been made by higher commanders or not. I want you to feel quite free to speak to me man to man and nothing you say will be held against you.[138]

Currie was also deeply disillusioned, if only for the moment. "We have never known the Boche to fight harder," he wrote on 4 October. "He is like a cornered rat, and I believe will fight most desperately until beaten absolutely and totally. I do not think that he can be finished this year...."[139]

Many others in the Corps felt the same way. Interviewed forty-five years later, Brigadier-General John Clark remembered looking at the casualty lists and feeling, "somehow, that I had failed in the leadership that the troops were entitled to." Continued Clark:

> Never have I felt so depressed as I felt after that battle. It seemed impossible to break the morale and fighting spirit of the German troops. We felt that this Boche could not be beaten, certainly not in 1918. He fought magnificently and in a most determined fashion. He discouraged a great many soldiers in the Canadian Corps.

Another brigadier, John Stewart, commented in his diary "that the Boche is still full of fight and the war will last for some months yet. We are having a tough fight with the Boche."[140]

In fact, the Canadians had cause to celebrate. Unknown to them, the situation in the enemy camp was fast reaching the breaking point. The Germans had been staggered by the punishing, co-ordinated blows delivered by the Allies at wide points along the Western Front. Moreover, they lacked the reserves required to respond to these offensives—in no small part thanks to the high-quality and numerous forces which had been committed to the Cambrai front to combat the Canadian Corps. The first blow had fallen on 26 September, when the American First and French Fourth armies struck between Reims and Verdun. On the twenty-seventh, two British armies joined the orchestrated offensive, the First breaching the Canal du Nord and the Third driving to the Canal de Saint-Quentin. On 28 September, the Second Army and the tiny Belgian army attacked in Flanders, quickly capturing Passchendaele Ridge, which had been won at such great cost in 1917 and then, tragically, lost in the spring of 1918. The final British attack was mounted on the twenty-ninth, when the Fourth Army, led by the Australian Corps, cracked the main Hindenburg Line defences at Saint-Quentin.

The effect was electrifying. It will be recalled that in the wake of Amiens, the German high command had urged the Kaiser to put out armistice feelers through neutral nations. Wilhelm had ordered this done, but in late September, General Ludendorff was mortified to discover that the government "had done nothing whatever to secure peace." On 28 September—the day after the Canadian Corps crossed the Canal du Nord—Ludendorff met privately with Field-Marshal Hindenburg, arguing that armistice proceedings must be initiated immediately. "Our one task now was to act clearly and firmly," Ludendorff later wrote. Hindenburg agreed, and on 3 October he urged Berlin to make "an immediate offer of peace to the enemy." It was no longer possible to win "by force of arms," Hindenburg said in a strong message to the cabinet, adding that "the only right course is to give up the fight, in order to spare useless sacrifices for the German people and their allies. Every day wasted costs the lives of thousands of brave German soldiers."[141]

The German government acted on Hindenburg's grim words. On 5 October, an armistice proposal was drawn up and submitted to American President Woodrow Wilson, via Switzerland. The Germans, perceiving President Wilson to be the weak link among the Allies, based their offer on the American's controversial Fourteen Points, a list of the conditions Wilson considered essential before the war could be concluded. Neither the British nor the French embraced all the president's points, making no secret of their desire for an unconditional surrender. The German peace proposal was soon rejected, and the fighting on the Western Front continued.

170

Ludendorff was irate. He considered that the civilian leaders in Berlin were being frivolous in their pursuit of peace because they refused to accept the reality of the crisis facing the German army. Ludendorff frankly feared the collapse of the army as "first one and then another division failed. The number of shirkers behind the front increased alarmingly.... The men who fought in the front lines were heroes, but there were not enough of them.... Our losses...were heavy. Our best men lay on the bloody battle-field. Many of our battalions could muster only two companies."[142]

On the other hand, the Allies were exuberant at this turn of events. On 6 October, Sir Douglas Haig visited Marshal Foch, who pointed to a newspaper and said: "Here you have the immediate result of the British piercing the Hindenburg Line. The enemy has asked for an armistice."[143]

Haig had good reason to be pleased with the BEF. In smashing Siegfried-Stellung, the centre-piece of the Hindenburg Line, the British had captured 36,000 prisoners and 380 guns. While Haig never doubted that it could be done, he noted in his diary that "an Army Commander (gather it was Byng) stated in August...that we would never get beyond the Hindenburg Line! Now we are through that line!"[144]

Still, there were high-level doubters in the BEF. One of them was the Fourth Army's commander, General Rawlinson, who wrote of Haig in his diary: "He thinks we shall finish the war this year, and I hope he may be right, but it is no certainty."[145]

8 PURSUIT

The Canadian Corps captured Cambrai on Wednesday, 9 October.

The preceding week had been relatively quiet. "Many patrol encounters took place, in which some prisoners were captured, and our Artillery and Machine Guns kept the enemy under continual harassing fire day and night."[1] General Currie was informed by First Army headquarters that a change in direction was planned, that the Canadians would soon be trading places with xxii Corps, which had been operating on their left—and lagging so far behind that the Drocourt-Quéant Line was still intact on the British front north of the River Sensée. The first step in the switch took place on 7 October, when the First Canadian Division was temporarily attached to xxii Corps. Meanwhile, the remainder of the Canadian Corps completed the conquest of Cambrai.

This was to be carried out in two stages. According to orders received by Currie on the sixth, the Canadians were to co-operate with the Third Army's xvii Corps, which was slowly advancing on Cambrai south of the Canal de l'Escaut. In the first stage of the proposed envelopment, xvii Corps would take Awoingt and the high ground south of the city; that done, the Canadian Corps would force a crossing of the canal. The main thrust was to be made by the well rested Second Division, striking east of Cambrai, seizing the bridges—which were, for the most part, intact because of the enemy's stubborn refusal to abandon the west side of the canal—and cutting off the defenders' line of retreat. The Third Division was to make a simultaneous secondary assault directly into the city.

General Currie quickly ruled out a daylight operation. This was due to his concern for the Second Division, which would have to cover the same exposed slopes which had cost the Canadians heavy casualties on 1 October. "In spite of the difficulties of a night operation," Currie later explained, "it was decided that the 2nd Canadian Division would attack by night, and attempt to seize the bridges before they were blown up by the enemy."[2]

The first phase got under way at 4:30 A.M. on 8 October. While the Canadian Corps contributed an artillery demonstration along its front to distract the defenders, Lieutenant-General Sir Charles Fergusson's xvii Corps launched its final drive on Cambrai. But progress was unexpectedly slow, and as the day wore on it became apparent that the British would not reach Awoingt before the Canadians' planned zero hour, 1:30 A.M. on the ninth. On his own initiative, Currie went ahead with the Canadian attack, although, as his diary reveals, he was more than a little concerned:

> I am somewhat anxious about this attack, because the first orders received stated that we were not to try to cross the Canal until the Third Army had secured Awoingt. This they have not yet succeeded in doing and unless we go tonight before they reach Awoingt we shall not be able to go until tomorrow night.[3]

He need not have worried. Dubbed "Peace Proposal," the operation was "a brilliant success," in Currie's words. "The unusual hour of one-thirty was evidently a great surprise and an effective one as well."[4] The Canadians caught the Germans in the midst of preparations for a withdrawal, part of a planned large-scale retreat between the Oise and the Scarpe later that day. Consequently, the Canadians—who went into battle wearing white armbands to distinguish themselves from the enemy in the darkness—had little difficulty taking their objectives. West of the Canal de l'Escaut, the Sixth Brigade occupied Blécourt, Bantigny, and Cuvillers, which had been abandoned, while the 27th (Winnipeg) Battalion entered Ramillies and, later, Eswars.

The Fifth Brigade, assisted by Canadian engineers, seized the bridges at Pont d'Aire. There were three: two smaller spans, side by side, leading to the main crossing into Escadoeuvres. Of the minor bridges, one had earlier been dynamited, but the other was found to be intact, with no explosive charges attached. A party of engineers under Captain C. Norman Mitchell proceeded to the main bridge, reaching it around 2:30 in the morning. Although wired for demolition, it was apparently unguarded, and Captain Mitchell set about defusing the charges. Before he could finish, the Germans attacked. Mitchell interrupted his work to help the sappers drive off a pair of attackers, during which the captain personally killed three of the enemy and captured a dozen, then calmly continued his job of securing the bridge. This was completed by four o'clock, and troops of the Fifth Brigade, led by the 25th (Nova Scotia Rifles) Battalion, slipped into Escadoeuvres. Mitchell was later awarded the Victoria Cross, the only Canadian engineer to win it during the Great War.

The Third Division crossed the canal with equal ease. Two battalions of the Eighth Brigade, the 4th and 5th Canadian Mounted Rifles, entered Cambrai unopposed, crossing on partially demolished bridges. Much of the city was in ruins, but the Canadians found that the enemy intended to utterly destroy it. "This beautiful city," wrote an indignant Currie, "had been wilfully set on fire by the Boche. We are doing our best to confine the damage but much destruction has already been wrought."[5] Fortunately, the speed and surprise of the Canadian crossing prevented the Germans from executing their planned vandalism with characteristic efficiency.

Within hours, the city had been secured. To enter Cambrai that morning was an eerie experience, as Private J. Corry of the 25th Battalion recalled. "The fires were still burning, but there was hardly anybody around, not even the enemy.... It was very, very quiet. All you could hear was the crack and banging of the artillery, do you see, and the fires burning."[6] The Canadian engineers again proved their worth, fighting fires and disarming mines and booby traps all over Cambrai, a job performed so well that the city was deemed safe enough for a visit the following day by Field-Marshal Haig, accompanied by General Currie.*

Currie's chief concern, now that Cambrai had been taken, was to ensure that the Canadians received the credit. He privately suspected that the British were conspiring to deprive the Canadians of this distinction:

> A day or so ago received instructions from the [First] Army that our parties nominated to look for booby traps were to report to Third Army officials who evidently were determined to get all the credit for the capture of Cambrai. In that they were forestalled and it is a fitting climax to all the hard fighting of the Corps in this action that to us has fallen the honour of being the first troops to enter and pass through the city. Of this there is no doubt and in future [there] should never be any question.[8]

It may seem to be a minor point, but it was a sign of Currie's worsening relations with certain British commanders in the waning weeks of the war, a relationship that would hit its nadir within a month.

Although the fall of Cambrai was no more than anticlimactic, Currie was exuberant. In a letter to the Third Division's General Loomis, Currie congratulated this formation for having "brought to a highly successful conclusion twelve days of victorious fighting," and

---

* Currie was later the target of a vicious personal attack in Canada's Parliament. On 4 March 1919, Sir Sam Hughes stood in the House of Commons and denounced Cambrai as "a dirty, little, one-horse town, with narrow streets, an ideal spot for machine gun positions and booby traps. Why any man of common sense would send soldiers in there, unless it were for his own glorification, I cannot comprehend...." Hughes maintained that "our boys [were] blown up in hundreds" defusing booby traps, which he said should have been done by German prisoners. He added that "any General who would undertake to attack Cambrai by suburb or street fighting, should be tried by court-martial." Obviously, Hughes was not a man to let facts stand in his way, particularly when performing under parliamentary immunity.[7]

rewarded the division by moving it into Corps reserve on the evening of the ninth. Currie also had a fresh view of the war situation. Only a few days earlier, he had resigned himself to another year of war. Now, with Cambrai in Canadian hands, he "felt that we would defeat Germany" before the end of the year.[9]

The Canadian operation had, if nothing else, hastened the enemy's departure on this front. Air reconnaissance at dawn on 9 October revealed that the Germans had abandoned the angle between the Sensée and Escaut canals, a fact confirmed by the destruction of all remaining bridges over those waterways. The British 11th and Canadian Second divisions quickly consolidated the area. The latter formation, encountering no more than token opposition, directed its Fifth Brigade to advance on Naves, a village due east of Cambrai. For a while, it seemed that long-awaited open warfare had truly arrived and, on Currie's orders, Brutinel's Brigade of armoured cars, with the Canadian Light Horse, crossed the canal to lead the pursuit.

The cavalrymen enthusiastically and energetically took the lead. The Canadian Light Horse had never before seen action as a unit—although some of its members had served, at various times, as signallers and machine-gunners attached to the infantry—and so was blissfully unaware that cavalry had become obsolete, though reality would rudely intrude within a matter of a few hours. Soon stopped by machine-gun fire, the regiment responded with its first, and only, charge, which a breathless Trooper George Hambley recounted in his diary:

The glorious charge over the top which the Canadian Light Horse was to have made has materialized—in all except the glory. And this morning we of the Fourth Troop have one horse left on the line to show for the troop's mad charge.... Mr. Sharpe and the rest of the 4th Troop, A Squadron, were ordered to follow C Squadron over as a patrolling outpost. Our orders were to proceed to an old farm on a sunken road halfway up a long gentle incline. There is a small bit of a river course running between the fields of plowed land—from it on the northeast the fields slope gently to the crest of the rise about a kilometre away. Our orders took us out around the village of Naves, across the railroad tracks to the east end of the village and out toward the little river. We spread out into sections—Dan Reaves, Joe Scanlon, Corp. Marlowe and myself on the right, Mr. Sharpe, Braggins, Tim Sheppard and Larry Bell in the centre, and the machine gun section on the left.

While skirting the village we had been galloping along through plowed fields, turnip patches, over spur railroads, steep embankments—our horses were quite tired before we came to the

175

little narrow river. At the time we would have considered it quite impossible to jump the stream—but our objective being in sight we charged it and with a heroic struggle every horse got down, jumped and up the other steep side.

Then a mad gallop began. Dan and Joe got tangled up in a telephone line—Joe's old mare went down. Dan had to cut off the saddle to free him—the rest of us galloped on across the field and up the slope. The crest of the hill was lined with three or four enemy machine guns and as we galloped along they all opened up. Bullets began to plow up the dust and sizzle through the air. Every horse was doing his best. Every rider urging them on toward the farm, our objective.

A bullet hit old Nix near the right temple—he went down like a stone. I came down on my head—Nix turned over right on top of me, quivered all over and never moved again. My helmet had rolled away somewhere. I attempted to get out from under my horse but had a hard struggle to free my feet—at last I raised his legs and got out. I lost no time in getting around behind the horse's body out of the hail of bullets. As I looked around I found that I had no broken bones—only a battered head and a sprained wrist.

Only a few minutes had elapsed but the rest were just mounting the objective to the road. Joe had cut off his saddle—pulled out his sword—mounted the old mare bareback and dashed to the field past me. He made the objective too. I saw the boys get to the road— then horse after horse fell down and men rolled off...it was a miracle indeed that anyone of us came out at all as such a mad adventure was never seen before.[10]

The cost to the Canadian Light Horse had been a dozen men and forty-seven horses. The tattered regiment withdrew later in the day, after infantry of the Fifth Brigade caught up and dug in for the night west of Naves.*

---

* This was not the last Canadian cavalry charge of the war. That honour went to the Canadian Cavalry Brigade, which staged a stunning success later the same day while leading the advance of the Fourth Army. The brigade commander, Brigadier-General R.W. Paterson, unleashed his three regiments—Lord Strathcona's Horse, Royal Canadian Dragoons, and Fort Garry Horse—at mid-morning, and the horse soldiers carried out a succession of spirited attacks on the German rearguards. The day's highlight belonged to the Fort Garries, who made what Sir Douglas Haig later called "a dashing charge" at Gattigny Wood, capturing 200 prisoners. By nightfall on 9 October, the Canadian Cavalry Brigade had galloped eight miles and captured 400 Germans, at a cost of 168 men and 171 horses killed, wounded, and missing. It was, in the words of one historian, "a gratifying final success for horsed troops in a war that had afforded all too little opportunity for the kind of open action for which they had specifically trained."[11]

Thursday, 10 October, was a relatively quiet day. While the British 11th Division completed clearing the angle between the Sensée and Escaut canals, the Second Canadian Division occupied Thun-l'Evêque and Thun-Saint-Martin, on either side of the Canal de l'Escaut, and continued a cautious advance eastward on a two-brigade front. On the right, the Fourth Brigade easily took Naves, while on the left, the Sixth Brigade moved on the village of Iwuy. However, resistance stiffened steadily during the day, and it became evident that the Germans were going to fight a major rearguard action on the Canadian front. The enemy had no way of knowing, of course, that the Canadians were getting ready to shift to a new sector. On the evening of the tenth, two British divisions came under Currie's command, the 49th, which moved onto the right of the Second Canadian Division, and the 51st (Highland) Division, which was kept in reserve near Escadoeuvres. This would facilitate the trade of fronts the following day between the Canadian and XXII corps.

Before departing, the Canadians delivered one final set-piece assault. Iwuy, the sprawling village on the heights east of the dry bed of the River Erclin, was the key to the German rearguard, and General Currie instructed the Second Canadian Division to take it, while the British 49th Division covered its right flank. Zero hour was set for 9 A.M. on 11 October.

General Burstall, the Second Division's commander, devised a complex and ambitious battle plan. His intention was to attack on a two-brigade front: one battalion of the Sixth Brigade, on the left, was to capture the village, while two battalions of the neighbouring Fourth Brigade took the high ground which overlooked Iwuy to the east. Brustall would then commit his reserve units to the north and east as far as three miles. It would not be easy, because the German defenders were a determined group. Lieutenant Doug Oliver of the 18th (Western Ontario) Battalion could attest to this, after seizing a toehold across the Erclin the previous day. Oliver remembered that "the machine-gun fire [was] so violent you could lie on your back and watch the berry bushes being clipped off above your head.... We couldn't move at all."[12] A similar reception awaited the troops of the Fourth and Sixth brigades.

The attack went in on schedule. The 28th (Northwest) Battalion had the tough task of taking Iwuy, and a desperate battle ensued, street by street, house by house. The fighting lasted most of the day, and the 28th only succeeded with help from the 31st (Alberta) Battalion. The exploitation phase was duly cancelled by General Burstall, not only because it took so long to take Iwuy, but because of a serious situation on the right. Here, the 20th (Central Ontario) and 21st (Eastern Ontario) battalions had to carry out a complicated manoeuvre, due to the constricted lay of the land. The 20th Battalion was to lead the attack,

177

swinging in front of the 21st, then fanning out across the high ground to the east; the 21st would then move up and fill the gap between the 20th and Iwuy. With the village still in enemy hands, the 20th Battalion had a terrible time, suffering grievously from enfilade machine-gun fire: its losses in this operation would total 330. Finally, Lieutenant Wallace Algie, a mild-mannered bank employee from Toronto, asked for volunteers and led them to attack the village and clear away the offending fire. They succeeded, but not before Lieutenant Algie was fatally wounded; he was awarded a posthumous Victoria Cross.[13]

Then the Germans counter-attacked. "My God," said one watching Canadian, "look at them houses moving." These words signalled the start of an action unique in the Canadian experience in the Great War. For these were not houses but tanks—the only time Canadian troops faced them. Seven of these lumbering giants—both German-made and captured British ones—led the attack at ten-thirty that morning. The Germans forced back the 20th and 21st battalions, as well as units of the neighbouring British 49th Division. However, the crisis was quickly averted when a battery of Canadian field guns rushed up to deal with the tanks, knocking out six of them,* while the guns of the 2nd Canadian Motor Machine-Gun Brigade stopped the supporting infantry, raking them "with a stream of bullets at ranges of less than 400 yards." Before the day ended, the Canadians and British recaptured much of the ground lost in the counter-attack, but General Burstall wisely ruled out a resumption of the offensive on 12 October. According to Burstall, his brigadiers "informed me that, taking into consideration the exhaustion of their troops and the large proportion of inexperienced officers and men, they would not be fit to continue the operations on the following day without suffering excessive casualties."[15]

This small battle marked, for the Canadians, the end of the fighting on the Cambrai sector. At 5 P.M. on 11 October, the Canadian and XXII corps formally traded places, with General Currie handing over his front to Lieutenant-General Sir Alexander Godley and taking charge of the latter's line to the north. The Canadian Corps front was held by four divisions, two British—the 56th (London) and 11th—flanked by the First Canadian, on the left, and on the right by the Second Canadian. However, the 11th would soon be squeezed out by the northward advance of the Second Division; the 56th would be relieved by the Fourth on 16 October, giving the Corps an all-Canadian front.

---

* These statistics come from General Currie's interim report on 1918 operations. However, there are conflicting figures. The Canadian official history puts the number of enemy tanks in action at "some half dozen"; the history of the 20th Battalion says there were only four, one of which was captured, while the other three fled the scene.[14]

The First Division had, in the meantime, been busy. Since joining XXII Corps on 7 October, General Macdonell's troops had manoeuvred the enemy out of the intact stretch of the Drocourt-Quéant Line between the Scarpe and Sensée rivers. Keeping up steady pressure on the Germans, through a combination of aggressive patrolling and raiding, the division had closed on the Canal de la Sensée by dawn on the twelfth. Currie was most pleased with its performance, as he wrote Macdonell: "The reports indicate that you are not having a period of rest in your present sector. I see that on each successive night you manage to get an Officer and some twenty odd men prisoner. I congratulate very much all concerned on the result."[16]

The Canadian Corps was now facing in a generally northward direction, ranged along the Canal de la Sensée. General Currie had no intention of forcing a crossing. The Corps was "tired and depleted in numbers," and he considered that the canal "in its flooded condition was a serious obstacle, the few crossings possible being narrow and easily defended." In any case, there was growing evidence that the Germans were getting ready to retreat again. "Prisoners reported the evacuation of civilians and the removal or destruction of all stores, also that roads and railways had been prepared for demolition." These indications were confirmed by Canadian observers who filed reports of "numerous and frequent explosions and fires behind the enemy's lines." The Canadians gave the enemy no rest, as General Currie instructed his troops to raid and patrol across the canal, while the artillery fired barrages every day.[17]

An interlude of several days passed, while the Corps patiently played its waiting game. During this period, one happy event, and one of great sadness, visited Currie's headquarters. On Monday, 14 October, Edward, Prince of Wales—the future King Edward VIII—joined Currie's staff. A junior officer who visited the front-line troops under the nom de plume "Captain Windsor," the prince was universally liked. Brigadier-General George Farmar remarked that Edward was "most anxious to get a job and equally anxious to do it well." Currie was delighted to have royalty on his staff. Farmar, a British officer, recalled that the Corps commander once said of the prince: "Isn't it a strange thing that that little fellow is the bond which holds us together?"[18]

The same day also brought grief. Currie was saddened to learn of the death of Major-General Louis Lipsett, who had recently been transferred from command of the Third Canadian Division to the British 4th. Lipsett was shot and killed by a sniper while making a personal reconnaissance to the outpost line. It was typical of Lipsett to risk his life in that manner, but Currie considered it a waste: "This seems such an unnecessary proceeding and has cost the country the life of a very valuable and experienced officer." Lipsett's funeral was held the following day, at the military cemetery at Quéant. It was attended by a large Canadian contingent, led by Currie; the firing party and band were supplied, appropriately, by the 8th (90th Winnipeg Rifles) Battalion, which Lipsett had taken overseas in 1914.[19]

Dramatic developments soon overshadowed these events. As the Canadians had discovered in the attack on Cambrai on 9 October, the Germans had begun a general retirement along almost the entire front facing the BEF, between the Oise and Scarpe rivers. The Hindenburg Line, on which the German high command had placed such high hopes, had been broken with decisive finality, the main Siegfried position being pierced by the Third and Fourth armies, a victory made possible by the enormous sacrifices of the Canadian Corps. On 8 October, General Ludendorff reluctantly authorized a wide withdrawal the next day. This was, he admitted, "a great disappointment to us. I had hoped that the Siegfried line would have held much longer." The Germans, behind a series of strong rearguards, were to pull back to a new defensive position, the Hermann Line, which ran from Flanders in north, through Valenciennes, to the Oise in the south. But the Hermann Line, "whose construction was but little advanced," was merely a series of thin and loosely connected defences. Ludendorff was under no illusions that it could be held for long.[20]

Ludendorff also knew, as did most of his commanders, that the German army was on the ropes. In October, twenty-two divisions would have to be disbanded for lack of reinforcements. Crown Prince Rupprecht, who was responsible for the Germans' northern group of armies, wrote on 18 October of the alarming state of affairs:

> Our troops are exhausted and their numbers have dwindled terribly. The number of infantry in an Active Service Division is seldom as much as 3,000. In general the infantry of a division can be treated as equivalent to one or two battalions, and in certain cases as only equivalent to two or three companies. Quantities of machine-guns have been lost, and there is a lack of trained machine-gun teams. The artillery has also lost a great number of guns and suffers from a lack of trained gun-layers.... There is also a lack of ammunition.... I do not believe that there is any possibility of holding out over December....[21]

Things on the home front were equally grim. Germany was on the verge of anarchy, gripped by widespread food riots and by an epidemic of influenza that was as deadly as it was demoralizing.

The enemy would get no respite, if Field-Marshal Haig had his way. The British commander-in-chief sensed that, at last, the war had entered its final phase. "We have got the enemy down, in fact, he is a beaten Army," he wrote on 10 October, "and my plan is to go on hitting him as hard as we possibly can, until he begs for mercy."[22]

Meanwhile, the Germans resumed their retirement. The experience of the Canadian Corps was typical, as General Currie related:

> Test barrages were carried out on the Corps' front each morning to ascertain the enemy's strength and attitude, and on October 17th the enemy was found extremely quiet and did not retaliate to our Artillery fire on the front of the 1st Canadian Division. Patrols were, therefore, sent out on that front and succeeded in crossing the Canal in several places, meeting only slight opposition. Stronger patrols followed and made good progress.[23]

The main formations followed hard on the heels of the patrols, as the Canadian engineers threw cork footbridges across the canal. The Second and Fourth divisions were slowed by isolated machine-gunners, but the First Division on the left moved rapidly, and by nightfall had liberated the large city of Douai. The Canadians found the inhabitants delirious with joy; less happily, they found that "every factory, warehouse, and private dwelling had been sacked" by the Germans.[24]

The chase was on. But this would not be a pursuit like bloodhounds tracking a rabbit. As always, General Currie's main concern was to minimize casualties and, anticipating the potential for chaos in these operations, issued orders on the seventeenth designed to rein in his Corps. "The G[eneral] O[fficer] C[ommanding] desires that special care be taken to see that ground in front is well reconnoitred before advancing, to ensure that the troops do not become engaged against the enemy holding strong positions."[25]

In any event, it was not easy to catch the Germans. Lieutenant Ronald Holmes of the 46th (South Saskatchewan) Battalion related his experiences in a letter home:

> We kept going that night and until the afternoon of the following day, when, just as we were appearing over a rise, his rearguard let us have it from strongly fortified positions, so we could do nothing but await darkness when it was decided to attack. This we did, and seized certain high ground that would give us the advantage the following day, but our foxy friend didn't wait for us but moved again in the night. This sort of business lasted for six days, and we drove him back eighteen miles in what I call the most miserable kind of fighting. The weather was wet, and sleeping out in cabbage patches is a much overrated pastime.[26]

The difficulties in mounting an effective pursuit were immense.

181

Thanks to the wet weather, it was impossible to make use of aerial reconnaissance. Every day, the Germans enjoyed the protection of a "heavy mist that settled in the mornings and lasted generally until dusk."[27] The enemy contributed by leaving an extraordinary trail of destruction. Anything they could not take with them was destroyed. More serious, from the pursuers' point of view, was the systematic sabotaging of communications: railway tracks torn up, bridges blown up, roads cratered. Some of the craters were so big that the Canadian engineers often found it faster and easier to build bridges across them rather than trying to effect repairs.

General Currie personally experienced the effectiveness of the enemy's vandalism. For two days, 19 and 20 October, he tried to visit the headquarters of the First Brigade, "but after trying half a dozen roads could not reach it owing to craters having been blown in all the roads." There were, to be sure, more serious implications than the mere disruption of a general's travel plans. The evacuation of the wounded was slowed considerably and, according to Colonel A.E. Snell, the Canadian Corps medical chief, "had casualties not been comparatively light the task would have been impossible." There was also a shortage of supplies of every description. Motor transport faced a sixty-mile round trip from the nearest railheads; not only were the roads in terrible condition, but the trucks themselves "were showing signs of the hard usage they had received since the 1st of August, prior to the battle of Amiens."[28]

Currie's concern soon showed. He fumed in his diary:

[T]he fact remains that the enemy is making a very orderly and practically unmolested retirement. Our trouble is that the troops are very tired and that the getting forward of supplies is becoming very difficult owing to the distance away of rail heads. Our Higher Authorities do not seem well enough organized to push their rail heads forward fast enough.[29]

It was of little consolation to Currie that these problems were not unique to the Canadian Corps. Indeed, the Canadians were making much better progress than the British corps on either flank. And the supply difficulties facing the BEF were being repeated everywhere along the Western Front—and were considerably worse in the relatively untried American and Belgian armies. Herein lies the ultimate irony of the Great War. The long-awaited phase of open warfare had finally arrived, and the Allies were unable to take advantage of it. They were discovering something that the Germans had learned on two previous occasions, during the opening weeks of the war and in the spring of 1918: that defeated defenders could retire faster and in better order than victorious attackers could pursue them; the attackers, leaving behind their artillery and supplies, could advance only as fast as the tired legs of the infantry could carry them. Given the limited technology available, it was extremely difficult—and, at times, impossible—to properly provision armies of millions of men on the move. It is a point often overlooked by historians, blinded by hindsight, who condemn the generals—and British generals, in particular—for pursuing a policy of attrition, which was really the only practicable method of bringing the Great War to a conclusion.

Nevertheless, a mood of optimism prevailed among the Canadians. Lieutenant John Gaetz of the 19th (Central Ontario) Battalion remarked in a letter home that "there seems to be a brighter day ahead of us now than ever before. The fighting is of a much different type now, as we are quite in the open and moving practically all the time." Similarly, Lieutenant Frank Leathers of the 19th Battery, CFA, told his father:

> I am having a great time. It isn't at all like it used to be. Things happen quickly nowadays. Orders are only issued an hour or two before their execution. Everyone is so busy they have no time to start the rumours that used to be the bane of our existence.[30]

The chase at times assumed a sporting air. On 19 October, two battalion commanders, Lieutenant-Colonel Dick Worrall of the 14th (Royal Montreal Regiment) Battalion and Lieutenant-Colonel Cy Peck of the 16th (Canadian Scottish), were riding near the front when they spotted a party of German horsemen. The colonels gave chase, but "the enemy horses were fast and easily left the Canadians behind."[31]

The Canadians revelled in the role of liberators. General Currie considered it "a most inspiring sight to go through these towns and witness the joy of the inhabitants. All the houses are decorated with French flags and the people seem overjoyed to greet the British soldiers." Added the Corps commander: "Many of the men had a bed to sleep on again but whether alone or not I cannot say." The civilians "cannot do enough for us," agreed Brookes Gossage, a twenty-one-year-old subaltern with the 66th Battery, CFA:

> Every house you go near, you are hauled in and made to drink black coffee till you can hardly see. For the last three nights I have slept in a feather bed.... The troops coming out of the line are absolutely bedecked with flowers, and the horses carry so many that the poor beasts don't know what to make of it.

In one village, related Private George Key of the 49th (Edmonton

Regiment) Battalion, "we could have bathed in coffee and vegetable soup," while a veteran gunner recalled: "We were fairly drowned with coffee and felt like stuffed birds as we flitted on."[32]

The warm welcome seemed to make it all worthwhile. "The soldier felt that, after all, they've been telling us that we're fighting for freedom," remembered W.H.S. Macklin, a veteran of the 19th Battalion, "and here are the people that we are liberating and the very reception that the soldier got was enough to convince him that this was, in fact, true."[33]

But the liberation of so many towns and villages posed a problem. On 19 October alone, when the Canadian Corps advanced more than six miles, nearly forty communities were freed, including the large industrial town of Denain. By the twentieth, the Corps had liberated an estimated 40,000 people, a figure that soon swelled to 70,000. Despite their generous greetings, these French people had very little to eat, and the Canadians had to feed them, taxing an already strained transportation system. The troops themselves provided part of the answer, as Currie proudly pointed out: "Many of the units have voluntarily given up 15% of their rations to the inhabitants...." As a result, no one went hungry.[34]

Valenciennes was soon within reach of the Canadians. By the evening of 23 October, the Third and Fourth divisions had cleared the enemy from the west side of the Canal de l'Escaut, which blocked the Canadian approach to the city, and Currie halted the advance. "The XXII Corps on our right had been held up along the Ecaillon River," he explained, "and the VIII Corps on our left had not been able to make any considerable advance, chiefly owing to supply difficulties, and were some distance behind us." Uncomfortable with the situation, Currie opposed any attempt to take Valenciennes at this time, deciding instead "that we should make good the west bank of the Canal and stand fast until the flanking Corps had made progress."[35]

The city of Valenciennes and environs were the keystone to the Hermann Line, and both sides knew it. The BEF was now moving, albeit slowly, in position to storm this last line of defence, and Field-Marshal Haig intended to mount his main attack on the Hermann Line following the fall of Valenciennes, "which I regarded as a necessary preliminary."[36] But it would be a tough nut to crack. The Germans had sited their defences in the vicinity of Valenciennes with characteristic cunning. The Canal de l'Escaut, which bordered the city's west side, was already a significant obstacle; German engineers had managed, by blasting dykes and opening sluice gates, to flood vast stretches of the surrounding countryside on either bank of the canal. The only practicable approach to the city, therefore, was from the south, where 150-foot

Mont Houy stood, two miles from Valenciennes. As clear evidence of the importance attached to this area, the Germans had posted five divisions*—all of them, it should noted, under strength—here, two along the canal and three on Mont Houy.

A joint British-Canadian operation was proposed by the First Army. The army commander, General Horne, outlined his intentions at a 27 October conference at Auberchicourt, his advanced headquarters, eleven miles west of Valenciennes. In the first phase, on 28 October, General Godley's xxii Corps would capture Mont Houy; on the thirtieth, the Canadian Corps would assist Godley's troops in securing the eastern and southern approaches to Valenciennes, followed by a complete envelopment of the city on 1 November. The Third Army's xvii Corps was to co-operate in all phases of the operation. The most important objective was, obviously, Mont Houy, but xxii Corps staff officers "anticipated no undue difficulty in its capture,"[37] despite the fact that the 51st (Highland) Division had already tried and failed twice to take it.

General Currie did not share the confidence of xxii Corps and its staff. After the conference at Auberchicourt, Currie met with Andy McNaughton, now an acting brigadier-general who commanded the Canadian Corps heavy artillery,† and bluntly told him that if the British failed to "take that damned hill we will have to. The war must be nearly over now and I do not want any more fighting or casualties than can be helped." Currie then told McNaughton: "I want you to go to your opposite number and offer him all possible assistance; get up all the guns you can and all the ammunition you can find."[38]

The Canadians, Currie and McNaughton knew, had much to offer. With their position west of Mont Houy, they were able to enfilade the defences, as well as fire on the enemy's rear areas with impunity. McNaughton promptly went to see Brigadier-General A.S. Jenour, who commanded the heavy artillery in xxii Corps, and offered to use Canadian guns and expertise to cut the thick belts of barbed wire on the southwest slopes of the hill. General Jenour was "either incredulous or offended," recalled McNaughton, and he refused to consider the pro-

---

* From north to south: 234th, 220th, 6th, 35th, and 214th.

† His predecessor, Brigadier-General R.H. Massie, had been invalided home to England soon after the battle for Cambrai.

posal, arguing that the Canadians might endanger the advancing British troops.[39]*

The British attack on Mont Houy was a failure. Launched at 5:15 A.M. on Monday, 28 October, there was no possibility of surprise, since the Germans had captured two cyclist-orderlies carrying plans of the operation.[41] The Highlanders of the 51st Division almost succeeded anyway. They actually took Mont Houy, but were driven off by a mid-afternoon counter-attack.

The defeat at Mont Houy produced a clash between General Currie and First Army's headquarters. The Fourth Canadian Division was to relieve the 51st on Mont Houy at 4 P.M. on the twenty-eighth, but Currie cancelled it, pointing out that it had been agreed that the British were supposed to be in possession of the hill "before we relieved." The situation as it existed, he believed, was too confused and chaotic to permit a smooth changeover, and the relief of the 51st Division was not carried out until the evening of the twenty-ninth. General Horne's chief of staff, Major-General Hastings Anderson, later criticized Currie's decision, arguing that it was based on an inflexible interpretation of the First Army's instructions. "Certainly 24 hours would have been saved," said General Anderson, not to mention the considerable work and embarrassment of making a wholesale change in plans:

> It meant changes in the orders of the Third Army for its XVII Corps and in the orders of formations within that Corps, and in the orders of the XXII Corps and Canadian Corps, and of all their subordinate formations.... Doubtless the Third Army said that the First Army never knew their own mind: and lower formations wondered why those above them could not settle what they wanted to do, and stick to it.[42]

Of course, Currie had more in mind than the sensitivities of certain high-ranking officers. His heavy artillery chief, General McNaughton, answered Anderson's criticism by declaring that to proceed with the

---

* Returning to Canadian Corps headquarters, McNaughton witnessed an amazing aerial dogfight. The sky seemed to be filled with German aircraft, attacking a single British Sopwith Snipe, which shot down four of the enemy before crash-landing safely within Allied lines. The pilot proved to be a hell-for-leather Canadian major, Billy Barker, from Dauphin, Manitoba. Major Barker won the Victoria Cross for this impressive perform-ance, which brought his total kills to fifty. Despite being wounded in the hip, thigh, and elbow, the twenty-four-year-old Barker was unchastened by the experience. "By Jove," he wrote a colleague from his hospital bed, "I was a foolish boy but I taught them a lesson. The only thing that bucks me up is to look back & see them going down in flames. I wish some of you had be[en] with me & we would have got more." An admiring McNaughton called the episode "the most magnificent encounter of any sort which I have ever witnessed."[40]

existing plans "would have involved us in continuing an operation already badly deranged, without any chance of organizing for the effective use of our artillery in support of our infantry; would have invited a fourth failure, and, even if success had attended our troops, inevitably a bloody price would have been paid. No one was more relieved than the Canadian Heavy Artillery when General Currie firmly declined to accept these unfortunate conditions." There was a further advantage, insisted McNaughton, because the Canadian gunners "would have a full and proper opportunity to do our work free from the hysteria of a suddenly improvised attack."[43]

The Canadians spent two full days preparing their assault on Mont Houy. General Horne had drastically revised his plans for the capture of Valenciennes: all phases were rolled into one, scheduled for 1 November, with the burden falling almost entirely on the Canadian Corps. General Currie accepted the challenge with complete confidence in the capabilities of the Corps.

No battle would better demonstrate the incredible power and skill of the Canadian artillery. The Corps, holding ground south and west of Mont Houy, was in a position which General McNaughton realized "gave rather unique opportunities for the use of artillery." General Currie appreciated the possibilities, too. "I told Andy McNaughton that I thought this would be the last barrage I would ask him to make in the war." The thirty-one-year-old McNaughton replied: "Well, by Jove, it will be a good one." It would, indeed, be good. Very good.[44]

The preparations perfectly reflected the quiet confidence of these Canadians. The assault force would be small—"only one infantry brigade," noted General Anderson at First Army headquarters. This would be the Tenth Brigade, under its new commander, Brigadier-General James Ross,* who planned to employ three battalions in his attack, with one to mop up. By Currie's estimate, there would be "not more than fourteen hundred bayonets." The artillery, however, would be the difference. A total of 303 guns of all calibres were arrayed to support the assault, and they would deliver "the heaviest weight of fire ever to support a single infantry brigade in the whole war." In McNaughton's opinion, the Mont Houy operations was the classic example of Currie's determination "to pay the price of victory in shells and not in the lives of men."[45]

---

* General Ross, who formerly led the Fifth Brigade until he was wounded at Amiens, had assumed command on 28 October, replacing Brigadier-General Ross Hayter, who moved to Corps headquarters as Currie's chief of staff. Hayter succeeded Brigadier-General N.W. "Ox" Webber, who departed for England to oversee the British army's demobilization preparations. This arrangement meant that, for the first time, every general officer in a combat command in the Corps was Canadian. However, the two top staff officers remained British—Hayter, and the reliable George Farmar.

There were problems, to be sure. Not the least of these was an order from GHQ expressly forbidding any bombardment of Valenciennes and its suburbs. According to the Fourth Division's General Watson, "We were badly handicapped in the knowledge that Valenciennes itself must not be destroyed and still far more so, by the thousands of civilians who had evidently been purposely left in the many villages with a view to the enemy's own protection against our artillery fire." If that was the purpose, it failed, thanks to what Watson called the "considerable daring and initiative" of the Canadians.[46]

Potentially more serious was a dispute over ammunition. The First Army's headquarters sent instructions to McNaughton stating that, in the latter's words, "I had to be moderate in the use of ammunition" in the forthcoming operation. The First Army was preaching the conservation of shells for continued fighting in 1919, but McNaughton had no intention of obeying these orders. "I had a Corps Commander who wanted the maximum shooting that could usefully be done," he explained, "and I thought that he could do the wrestling on that level." Not surprisingly, no one at the First Army was interested in tangling with Currie, and the Canadians went ahead with an unprecedented expenditure of shells.[47]

The results were dramatic. Precisely at 5:15 A.M. on Friday, 1 November, the Canadian barrage exploded overhead. The waiting infantrymen were most impressed. "I never saw anything like it," remarked one subaltern. There had been no preliminary registration; the gunners fired strictly from maps compiled from aerial photographs. From their vantage points south and west of Mont Houy, the Canadian artillery raked the defences back and forth and side to side. The Germans retaliated with a barrage which was, at first, "very heavy," in Currie's opinion, "but shortly afterwards slackened down under the influence of our efficient counter-battery fire."[48]

The infantry went over the top, and within forty-five minutes, large batches of dazed and demoralized prisoners were appearing in the Canadian lines. By eight o'clock, it was, according to the brigade commander, General Ross, "perfectly clear from all sources of information that the advance had been a remarkable success." However, it was not until later in the day that anyone truly realized just how remarkable it had been. Currie reported that "we captured 1,800 prisoners, buried over 800 Boshes [sic] afterwards on the field, and sustained less than 400 casualties ourselves, of whom only 80 were killed; thus causing over 2,600 permanent casualties to the enemy with only 80 permanent casualties to ourselves."[49]

Four Canadian battalions crossed Mont Houy this day. The 44th (New Brunswick) Battalion on the right and the 47th (Western Ontario) led the attack, with the 46th (South Saskatchewan) leap-frogging the

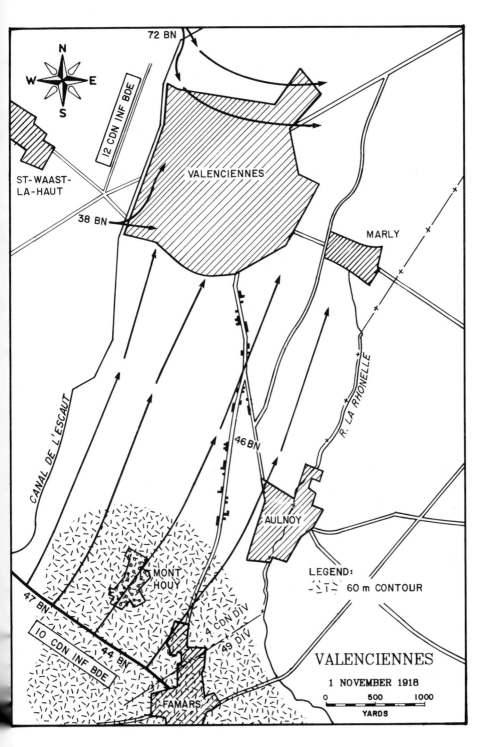

72 BN

12 CDN INF BDE

ST-WAAST-
LA-HAUT

38 BN

VALENCIENNES

MARLY

CANAL DE L'ESCAUT

R. LA RHONELLE

46 BN

AULNOY

MONT
HOUY

LEGEND:

60 m CONTOUR

4 CDN DIV

49 DIV

47 BN

10 CDN INF BDE

44 BN

FAMARS

VALENCIENNES

1 NOVEMBER 1918

0   500   1000

YARDS

189

44th, and the 50th (Calgary) Battalion mopping up in their wake. Aside from isolated machine-gun resistance, the 47th had little trouble reaching its final objective, the southern outskirts of Valenciennes, "on time." The 44th, with only half the distance to travel, was equally successful, overrunning the pinnacle of Mont Houy and then capturing the village of Aulnoy, which had been spared by the Canadian artillery and where a stiff fight was expected. But Aulnoy fell quickly and easily, despite its strong garrison. The 44th rounded up eighty-three machine-guns in Aulnoy, along with three 77-millimetre field guns and an estimated 800 prisoners, at the cost of eighty-nine casualties. One German company commander told his captors "that it was impossible to see or even form an opinion as to which direction his attackers were coming from, so he could do nothing but surrender with his whole company."[50]

The 46th Battalion, passing through the 44th, had somewhat more difficulty. "Machine gun bullets were like hailstones, coming four or five feet in front of us," recalled Private Charlie Skeates. "You couldn't believe it unless you had experienced it." The battalion commander, Lieutenant-Colonel Herbert Dawson—nicknamed "Dismal" by his men—later described the action:

> The fighting...along the Famars-Valenciennes and Aulnoy-Marly roads was deadly work. Many enemy were killed by the parties of the 46th Battalion working with bayonet, bombs and Lewis Guns. The area was packed full of Germans. Every cellar contained numbers.[51]

At one point, the Saskatchewan battalion was pinned down by a field gun firing over open sights. Under the covering fire of Lewis light machine-guns, Private W.J. Wood single-handedly rushed and captured the gun and its crew. Later, Major Richard Gyles and thirteen other ranks took on a hundred Germans in a brickfield near Marly that had been missed in the barrage. While their comrades distracted the defenders, six of these Canadians—including Sergeant Hugh Cairns, whose name will reappear shortly—outflanked the position and enfiladed the enemy. Fifty survivors surrendered, along with three field guns, a trench mortar, and seven machine-guns.

Hundreds more prisoners were taken by the 50th Battalion, mopping up behind the attackers. "It was impossible to avoid taking so many," reported the battalion's acting commander, Major J.L.R. Parry, "as they surrendered in batches of from 20 to 50, but some very useful killing was also achieved"—chilling words, indeed. The battalion suffered forty-three casualties during this part of the operation, but lost eighty-four more later in the day, when the Germans used an unidenti-

190

fied poison gas against the Canadians. "The gas," said Major Parry, "was scarcely perceptible to the senses, and, in many cases, the effect seemed to take some hours to develop, then coming on quite suddenly."[52]

While the Tenth Brigade gained the southern suburbs of Valenciennes, the Twelfth Brigade seized footholds in the city itself. Two battalions, the 38th (Ottawa) and 72nd (Seaforth Highlanders of Canada), took advantage of the distraction created by the battle for Mont Houy and made daring crossings of the sixty-foot-wide Canal de l'Escaut at mid-day. The 38th had no particular difficulty, but the 72nd had to display determination and initiative to get across the canal. Its crossing was covered by a field gun which moved right up to the bank, as well as by riflemen and machine-gunners in upper-storey windows of nearby houses. Two companies crossed into northern Valenciennes via collapsible boats, rafts, and a cork-float bridge hidden by Canadian engineers along the western edge of the canal. Machine-guns in an enemy outpost briefly endangered the crossing, but the field gun went to work and the Germans, in the words of one officer, "scurried to get out of the place like rats." By early afternoon, the 72nd Battalion had secured the city's railway station and yards, while the engineers were already building bridges over the canal.[53]

The balance of the day was spent in patrolling and consolidating the Canadian gains against counter-attack. It was far from uneventful. In mid-afternoon, the Germans were detected massing near Marly for an apparent attack against the Tenth Brigade and the neighbouring 146th Brigade of the British 49th Division. The artillery prepared a rude reception; waiting until 4:35 P.M., when the enemy concentration was judged to be nearly complete, a rolling barrage by nine batteries of 6-inch howitzers was laid across the assembly area, smashing the attack before it could begin. However, the Germans were able to mount one late in the afternoon against the 49th Division, driving it back some distance, "thereby occasioning us some anxiety for a time," according to General McNaughton.[54]

One series of patrols was most memorable. Carried out by the 46th Battalion, the patrolling resulted in the last Victoria Cross to be won by a Canadian in the Great War. It went to Sergeant Hugh Cairns, a twenty-one-year-old apprentice plumber from Saskatoon. Cairns had already had an outstanding day; in addition to helping to capture the strong-point in the Marly-area brickfield, he had personally accounted for three machine-guns and eighteen prisoners, besides killing seventeen others. The athletic Cairns, it seems, had a death wish. His brother, Albert, had been killed at the Drocourt-Quéant Line, and "Hughie said he'd get fifty Germans for that," recalled one of his comrades. "I don't think he ever planned to come back [to Canada] after Abbie got killed."[55]

Now, in the late afternoon, Sergeant Cairns ventured into Valenciennes on a one-man reconnaissance mission. In the course of this, he discovered a courtyard full of German soldiers who were evidently getting ready to make some sort of an attack, possibly a raid. Cairns hastily retreated, then met Lieutenant John MacLeod and three other ranks on patrol in Marly. After listening to Cairns's report, Lieutenant MacLeod and his party followed the sergeant to the courtyard. The Canadians, with guns blazing, burst through a door and the enemy, completely stunned, swiftly surrendered. There were at least sixty Germans facing the five Canadians.

The ensuing scene might have come from a Sam Peckinpah movie. But there were no slow-motion special effects, and the splashing blood would be horrifyingly real. A German officer approached the Canadians, apparently with something to say. Instead, he pulled out a pistol and shot Cairns through the body. Cairns fell to his knees; he riddled the officer with his Lewis gun, then turned his fire on the enemy soldiers scrambling to retrieve their weapons. Cairns was wounded again, this time in the wrist, but he kept up a steady stream of deadly fire until finally collapsing in a pool of blood. Dragged to safety, he was wounded once more before he could be evacuated. Cairns died the next day, without knowing that only a handful of Germans survived the bloodbath in the courtyard.*

The Canadians occupied Valenciennes the next morning. The city was abandoned during the night by the defeated enemy, and 2 November was spent in pursuit of the disorganized, ravaged remnants of the defenders. No one could know it, but the Great War was into its final ten days, and the Canadian Corps had fought its last major battle.

Rarely has the power of artillery been so convincingly demonstrated on a modern battlefield. Credit for the Canadian victory at Valenciennes must go, above all, to the unusual skill and efficiency of the gunners who so faithfully supported the infantry. They lived up to the artillery's motto, *Quo Fas et Gloria Ducunt*, "to shoot the ultimate round." The Canadian guns fired 2149 tons of high explosive and

---

* In addition to winning Canada's last vc of the war, Cairns was later honoured by the city of Valenciennes, which renamed one of its principal streets after him. Avenue Sergent Cairns, dedicated in March 1936, is purportedly the only street in France honouring a soldier below the rank of commissioned officer. A statue also commemorates Cairns in his hometown, Saskatoon.

shrapnel, almost all of it on 1 November.* The impact was incredible, as General McNaughton later commented:

> The barrage and bombardment had left scarcely a square yard of ground untouched. Enemy dead were everywhere: in rifle and machine gun pits, in trenches and sunken roads, in the open, in the rows of houses demolished by the siege howitzers; the concentrations, particularly those in enfilade on railway cuttings and other defiles, had left a shambles; the harassing fire on the sunken roads towards Estreux and Saultain, used by the enemy for the movement of reinforcements and ammunition, had in many cases blocked the cuttings with destroyed vehicles and dead animals and men.

McNaughton's personal pleasure was plain when he wrote home on 1 November: "A wonderful day and the artillery work has brought expressions of satisfaction from all concerned... I am rather pleased with my first big show."[57]

The artillery had had excellent targets, too. The Fourth Division later claimed that it had engaged elements of forty-three German battalions, representing five divisions. The reason for this unusual concentration of force was revealed by prisoners, who disclosed that the Germans had been preparing a pre-emptive attack. The Canadians had beaten them to the punch by the narrowest of margins, as they had done at the Canal du Nord. The burial squads had their work cut out for them: more than 800 enemy dead were interred on the battlefield, ten times the number of Canadian fatalities. The devastating display by the artillery accounts for much of the disparity, but does not fully explain it. General Currie, for one, was not surprised. "I know that it was not the intention of our fellows to take many German prisoners as, since they have lived amongst and talked to the French people here, they have become more bitter than ever against the Boche."[58]

More poignant was the remark made by an artillery subaltern. "Too bad there are so many being killed," Lieutenant W.J. O'Brien wrote in his diary, "when Peace seems so certain just now."[59]

---

* This compares with the thirty-seven tons expended by both sides at the battle of Waterloo in 1815, and 2800 tons fired by the British and the Boers during the South African war at the turn of the century.[56]

9 ARMISTICE

The Great War was rapidly reaching its conclusion. But there would be no spectacular victories by the Allies that historians could trumpet as decisive. The war, in fact, was fizzling out. The German army on the Western Front, the main theatre of operations during 1914–18, had been bled white, the cumulative effect of the repeated battles of attrition waged by the high commands on both sides. General Ludendorff, the enemy's de facto commander-in-chief, was sacked on 26 October. "There is no hope," he wrote in anguish that night, "Germany is lost."[1]

Germany was beset by problems, within and without. The nation teetered on the brink of revolution, the result of worsening internal strife. There was rioting in the streets of most large cities, amid the chaos created by roving bands of deserters and marauders. With the impending collapse of law and order, there were growing calls for the abdication of the Kaiser. Bolshevism raised its ugly head when soviets were declared in several cities, including Düsseldorf, Cologne, and Frankfurt. Discipline in the armed forces was no better: battleship crews mutinied in Kiel, Hamburg, and Bremen. To make matters worse, Germany's allies were falling by the wayside. Bulgaria had surrendered on 29 September, and had been joined by Turkey on 30 October and by Austria-Hungary on 3 November.

Yet, the Allies were in little better shape. All their armies were under strength in the war's last weeks. According to the supreme commander, Marshal Foch, French divisions were short as many as 2500 men. And the quality of these forces was open to question. The British commander-in-chief, Field-Marshal Haig, had a dim view of the capabilities of the French and Americans. The French army, he suggested on 19 October, was "worn out and has not been fighting latterly. It has been freely said that the 'War is over' and 'we don't wish to lose our lives now that peace is in sight'." The American army was, in his opinion, "not yet organised: it is ill-equipped, half-trained, with insufficient supply services. Experienced officers and N.C.O.s are lacking." This left only the forces of the British Empire to bring Germany to its knees, but even Haig had to admit that not all was rosy. The BEF, he declared with justification, "was never more efficient than it is to-day, but it has fought hard, and it lacks reinforcements. With diminishing effectives, morale is bound to suffer."[2]

Both Foch and Haig were worried about the Americans. Their

performance to date had, by and large, left much to be desired, which must surprise historians who believe that the Americans won the war. This might have been true, in terms of the psychological impact of hundreds of thousands of fresh troops pouring onto the Continent— but it was certainly not true in terms of action. Foch fumed that the results of the American offensive in the Argonne, begun on 4 October, were "inferior to what it was permissible to expect against an adversary assailed everywhere and resisting at certain points with only worn-out, heterogeneous and hastily assembled troops, and in a region where his defensive organizations had already been captured." Haig observed in his diary on 5 October:

> The enemy is in no strength on their front, but the Americans cannot advance because their supply arrangements have broken down. The Divisions in the front line are really starving, and have had to be relieved in order to be brought where the food is! There are many fine Divisions available for action, and these cannot be used owing to the incapacity of the American H.Qrs. and Army Staffs.

The next day, Haig described a meeting with Foch. "He was very disappointed with the American attack west of the Meuse. Many of their Divisions had been several days without food. Some had run off to get something to eat."[3]*

Haig was haunted by the possibility that the war might continue into 1919. In view of the weakened condition of the Allied armies and the determined rearguard resistance being offered by the retreating Germans, Haig feared that the enemy could, and would, reject the harsh terms being bandied about in political circles. The operative phrase was "unconditional surrender," which Haig vocally opposed, as he explained in an 18 October meeting at 10 Downing Street in London. He told Prime Minister David Lloyd George that "our attack on the 17th instant met with considerable opposition, and that the enemy was not ready for unconditional surrender. In that case there would be no armistice, and the war would continue for at least another year." This, he felt, would be a dangerous mistake. "The French and American Armies are not capable of making a serious offensive *now*. But why spend British lives? and for what?"[5]

---

* Even General John J. Pershing, the American commander-in-chief, admitted to his army's shortcomings. After meeting Pershing in late October, Haig noted that the American had "concurred in thinking that it would be next autumn [i.e., 1919] before it could be organised and sufficiently trained to be able to play an important part."[4]

Haig favoured leniency toward the Germans. "It is most important," he wrote, "that our Statesmen should think over the situation carefully and not attempt to so humiliate Germany as to produce a desire for revenge." Convinced that "from a military standpoint, *the enemy has not yet been sufficiently beaten as to cause him to accept an ignominious peace*," the field-marshal urged that his political masters offer easy terms: the evacuation of Belgium and occupied France, as well as Alsace-Lorraine, the return of French and Belgian rolling stock, and the restoration of all inhabitants. These, he suggested, would realize British war aims and ensure that the conflict would not continue simply because of the French desire "to pay off old scores"—a reference to their humiliating defeat in the Franco-Prussian War in 1870–71. To try to impose harsher terms, he said, "seems to me really a gamble which may come off or it may not."[6]

There was, of course, little possibility that his wise counsel would be accepted. In advocating leniency, Haig stood alone among senior military men.* Marshal Foch, in particular, was determined to wreak revenge on Germany, and his view prevailed, both militarily and politically. Foch insisted that any armistice must include "guarantees for obtaining reparation for damage done in Allied countries, which is to be demanded at the time the peace treaty is negotiated." Foch, therefore, disregarded Haig's opinion, as did Prime Minister Lloyd George. The British leader considered Foch's proposals to be "very drastic," but at no time did he seriously consider Haig's alternative.[8]

This is hardly surprising, in view of Lloyd George's enmity toward Haig. Long convinced that the commander-in-chief was "running the country on the rocks" by incurring heavy casualties on the Western Front, the prime minister charged that "Haig does not care how many men he loses."[9]

Unable to sack the field-marshal, Lloyd George sought to undermine his authority by meddling in military matters which he did not understand; the result, in the spring of 1918, was nearly disastrous for the BEF. Not content to let the matter rest, Lloyd George continued his vendetta long after the war. Even while admitting that, during the last hundred days, "Haig earned high credit," the prime minister could not give him his proper due. Instead, he belittled Haig's enormous contributions. "He was fulfilling a rôle for which he was admirably suited:

---

* Not even the Canadian commander, General Currie, sided with him on this issue. "Germany," Currie commented, "is simply a mad dog, and it must be killed—a cancerous growth that must be removed." In late October, he wrote "that peace when it does come must be a peace that will last for many, many years. We do not want to have to do this thing all over again in another fifteen or twenty years. If that is to be the case, German military power must now be irretrievably crushed. This is the end we must obtain if we have the will and the guts to see it through."[7]

that of a second in command to a strategist of unchallenged genius." That genius, in Lloyd George's misguided opinion, was Marshal Foch, whom he regarded as a "master-mind."[10]

The prime minister wasted no opportunity to snub Haig. The latest occasion had been in early October, when the field-marshal was being deluged with congratulatory telegrams from King George, British parliamentarians, and politicians all over the Empire, in the wake of the BEF's brilliant victory at the Hindenburg Line. Lloyd George was among the last to send a wire, on 9 October, offering "my sincerest congratulations on the great and significant success which the British Armies, with their American brothers-in-arms, have gained during the past two days." Haig was understandably upset, as he confided in a letter to his wife:

> I enclose a copy of a number of telegrams which I have received congratulating the Army on the recent successes. The Prime Minister's shows the least understanding of the great effort made by the *whole* of the British Army. He speaks of the "success" of the last "two days." In the papers I see some friend of his has altered the word to "few days." Then, as the message originally reached me, no mention at all was made of [General] Horne and the First Army, when the Canadian Corps actually were in Cambrai, and have had such hard fighting for Monchy[-le-]Preux, the Drocourt-Quéant line, etc.[11]

Slighted by his own government, Field-Marshal Haig prepared to make what he termed the "decisive attack." With the Canadians having captured Valenciennes, "a necessary preliminary," Haig readied the First, Third, and Fourth armies to storm the Germans on a thirty-mile front between Valenciennes and the River Sambre. Germany could be given no time to recover, he realized:

> If her armies were allowed to withdraw undisturbed to shorter lines, the struggle might still be protracted over the winter. The British Armies, however, were now in a position to prevent this by a direct attack on a vital centre, which should anticipate the enemy's withdrawal and force an immediate conclusion.[12]

The offensive, originally set for 3 November, was rescheduled for the fourth.

It was decidedly anticlimactic. "Though troops could still be found to offer resistance to our initial assault," Haig noted, "the German infantry and machine gunners were no longer reliable, and cases were reported of their retiring without fighting in front of our artillery barrage." The Germans lost another 19,000 prisoners and 450 guns to the BEF, and resumed their retreat toward the German frontier.[13]

There were few prizes for the Canadian Corps. On this part of the front, the enemy retired behind a screen of snipers and machine-gunners, who put up a most determined resistance. The Corps conducted a cautious but steady advance northeastward from Valenciennes, occasionally encountering "stiff fighting." General Currie considered that the terrain favoured the defenders, "the country being under water except where railway embankments, slag-heaps, and houses stood up out of the flood and afforded excellent cover for enemy machine gunners and riflemen."[14]

It was a familiar struggle for the Canadians, who faced miserably wet weather—it rained almost every day between 1 and 11 November—and steadily deteriorating roads made worse by enemy demolitions. Supply problems remained as vexing as ever, as an artillery lieutenant, James McRuer, commented in his diary on 5 November: "We moved the day before yesterday and we expect to move again tomorrow. We should have moved today, but we were getting out of touch with headquarters and we couldn't keep up rations without more transport." There were other difficulties, too, in the form of nightly air raids by enemy bombers; the 20th (Central Ontario) Battalion history complains that "German airmen were attempting to rid themselves of an apparent serious surplus of bombs."[15]

Led by armoured-car and cavalry patrols, the Canadians groped their way closer to the Belgian border. Although skirmishing was sporadic, this was a stressful and tiring time for all ranks, from the hard-marching infantry to the hard-working engineers. The artillery was having its problems, also, as one gunner, H.L. Sheppard, recalled:

> We would move and be in action and then move and be in action. Sometimes we'd move twice in one day, and sometimes we'd be hung up maybe for two or three days, but we were moving almost constantly with our guns and firing, and the sort of things we were running into then was where the Germans would set a mine under a crossroads and blow it up, and then we would have to fill it up or bridge it to get our guns across; but we didn't have too much trouble going ahead, and stop a little while and go ahead again.[16]

In these circumstances, casualties were few and far between. This was fortunate, because the Corps medical service was having a nightmare trying to cope with "great transport difficulties," complicated by "long distances to hospital accommodation," which made it hard to treat the sick and injured, soldiers and civilians alike.[17]

As always, the Canadians were warmly welcomed. "Forget how many times I was kissed," wrote Lieutenant Hugh Pullen of the 11th Battery, CFA, "but I know they weren't all pretty ones. However, I was not able to discriminate at all & resistance was useless." Corporal Gus Sivertz of the 2nd Canadian Mounted Rifles recalled that "wherever we stopped we were billeted mostly in beds." Sometimes, though, the billets were rather unusual, as Sapper Robert Dickson remembered: "For three nights we slept in a graveyard. Three others and myself were fortunate enough to get in a family vault which had shelves in them for coffins. Those shelves served as bunks. We slept in there nice and dry, quite comfortably."[18]

It was during this period that relations between Canadian and British leaders hit rock-bottom. The cause was seemingly innocuous. On 5 November, General Currie learned of plans by the citizens of Valenciennes to stage a special ceremony to thank the Canadians for liberating them. At the last moment, however, the First Army's General Horne intervened, insisting that XXII Corps must also be represented and that he "should be the person to receive the address and the flag." Currie, understandably, resented this arrangement. After all, the Canadians had had to capture the city by themselves, following the failure of the British attack on Mont Houy. Then Horne added insult to injury: originally, the Canadian troops taking part in the parade were to lead it, but the army commander reversed the order, making the Canadians bring up the rear. Currie was livid. "The action of the Army is unaccountable," he raged in his diary, "and is resented by the Corps...."[19]

The ceremony, held on Thursday, 7 November, was, in Currie's words, "a very frosty affair." Aside from Currie, no other senior Canadian officer participated, and Currie attended only because Horne had ordered him to be there. "It was not my intention to attend, and I would not have been there had I not received a direct order."[20]

While Currie was feuding with Horne, the Canadian Corps crossed into Belgium. The honour of being the first units in Belgian territory belonged to the Eleventh Brigade, which executed what its commander, General Odlum, declared was "the best piece of voluntary team work ever done in this Brigade." During the afternoon of 5 November, two battalions, the 75th (Mississauga) and 87th (Canadian Grenadier Guards), twice attempted to cross the River Aunelle, which marked the border between Belgium and France. The first attempt, at two-thirty, failed, but both battalions had better luck at six o'clock, when they forded the waist-deep river and secured a bridgehead on the far bank by dark. The following morning, the 102nd (Central Ontario) Battalion passed through and captured the village of Marchipont, then forged ahead and a seized a toehold across the River Honelle a short distance beyond. These skirmishes signalled the end of enemy opposition on the Canadian front: the road to Mons lay wide open.[21]

The Corps moved ahead relentlessly. During the last four days of the war, the Canadians advanced nearly fourteen miles. They did so despite harassing enfilade fire, thanks to the inability of the British corps on either flank—VIII on the left and XXII on the right—to keep pace. The countryside continued to favour defensive measures. As Currie later commented, "we were now getting into the heart of the Belgian coal district—a thickly populated area, where the numerous towns and villages, the coal mines, and the commanding slag-heaps complicated the task." And there was a startling contrast in conditions between Belgium and France. Currie said that he "could not help but be struck by the difference in the treatment accorded by the Germans to Belgium and that accorded to the French. In France, all the mines have been destroyed, while just over the line, in Belgium, they were all working. I have no doubt but what the Bosch [sic] intended to keep Belgium, and therefore thought it good policy to appease the citizens of that country."[22]

One aspect that did not change was the joyous reception given the troops. "For miles the road was simply black with people," an artillery subaltern, Frank Leathers, remarked in a letter home, "all dressed in their Sunday best.... There were thousands of flags. Small boys ran about with long paper ribbons. Whistles were blowing and dogs yelping and forests of dirty faced youngsters ran around in the road. It was just like a fair."[23]

Rumours of impending armistice filled the air. On 7 November, the long-awaited moment seemed to have arrived, when American newspapers reported that an armistice had been signed and that hostilities would cease at 2 P.M. "One of the famous fakes of history!" was the way the New York *Tribune* later described the gaffe.[24] But there was, at least, a grain of truth in the reports. Germany had asked for peace talks, and representatives would be sent to meet Marshal Foch in his private train parked in the forest near Compiègne, on 8 November, to begin three days of difficult negotiations.

It was clear to all that the end was near. "It won't be long now, boys," a confident General Currie called out as he rode past the 49th (Edmonton Regiment) Battalion on the eighth. The next day, Private James Doak of the 52nd (New Ontario) Battalion had a memorable meeting with the Corps commander on the road to Mons.

He asked me how long I had been in France, where I came from and many other questions. I answered to the best of my ability. Then I asked him about the armistice rumours.... He told me that in his opinion 24 hours would see the end of the fighting. He said, "We may possibly have a go at him again, but it's hardly likely. I think I can safely tell you that you've followed your last barrage." Across the street our Colonel and a bunch of officers were eyeing the General and myself. A group of company and bandsmen were starting at us too. After the General had gone, they crowded around me to hear what he had to say. They asked, "Did you know him in Canada?" I jokingly answered, "Sure I knew him. He's going to give my a job on his staff." Since that time, the General has been known among the bandsmen as "Doak's pal."[25]

Naturally, no one wanted to be killed so near the end. "One doesn't feel like taking any risks," Lieutenant James McRuer told his diary on 7 November. "Personally, I don't want to hear any more gunfire."[26]

By Sunday, 10 November, the Canadians were near the outskirts of Mons. This ancient city had been besieged many times in its history; its most recent brush with warfare had been in August 1914, when British troops fired their first shots of the war in nearby skirmishes. However, General Currie had no intention of laying siege to the place now. "I gave instructions that if the town could be captured without many casualties, the pressure should be continued." Currie planned an encircling manoeuvre: while troops of the Second Division skirted Mons to the south and took the high ground on the east side, the Third Division would maintain steady pressure and, if possible, infiltrate into the heart of the city. The Third Division's General Loomis recalled that, later in the day, "Sir Arthur visited me to impress on me the necessity of not shelling Mons heavily [and] not to undertake any serious offensive in the way of a heavy attack or a set piece with artillery; in other words, to avoid casualties and losses."[27]

There was stiff resistance in the neighbourhood of Mons. Machinegunners and snipers were seemingly everywhere on the city's outskirts. Lieutenant John Gaetz of the 19th (Central Ontario) Battalion relived his experiences in a long letter to his mother:

The morning of the 10th we jumped off about 8 o'clock, you call it "over the top" as there were no entrenchments. After passing our outposts we advanced about a thousand yards without encountering any opposition. Then just as we were coming over the brow of a hill we were fired on by a machine gun and some rifle men. We dropped flat in some cabbages and after a short wait we advanced in rushes to some cover. This was just an advanced post of the Hun and they did not stay long before falling back.

We rushed up to some houses. In passing through the streets the civilians having come out of the cellars crowded in the doorways and held out the odd stone jar of cognac. The one man that was following me like myself partook of several good drinks and carried on.

In a short time we fell in with one of the Company officers and half a dozen men. We were just passing through the last screen of houses and saw some men dodging across a street some distance in front of us. Thinking they were our own men we continued towards them and just got nicely in the open when we were serenaded with two machine guns. Once again we flopped in the cabbages. This time we weren't left alone but the gunners continued to search the ground where we were. I could see bits of cabbage fly in the air about me and I could tell by the cracking above my head that it was pretty good shooting. First one of the men near me was hit rather badly in the shoulder and then the officer muttered something and lay still. To make matters worse there was a field-gun firing point blank at our position and this was decidedly uncomfortable, so one by one we ran back behind a building. I helped fix up the wounded men and then got some of our machine gunners posted and for a while we had some pretty good shooting and made it pretty hot for the old Hun who...forgot that we carried guns.

Well we were held there for the remainder of the day. We tried once to advance but it was no use and only resulted in more casualties, so we sat tight for the rest of the day.[28]

Lieutenant Gaetz and his men had fought their last skirmish of the Great War.

The resistance came as something of a surprise. It had been hoped that the enemy would abandon Mons without a fight, and the Seventh Brigade's General Clark admitted his concern as darkness fell. "The situation looked so serious that we concluded that it would require a set-piece attack in the morning to capture the city."[29]

It proved to be unnecessary. Under the cover of darkness, two of Clark's battalions worked their way into Mons. B Company of the Royal Canadian Regiment slipped in from the north, while D Company of the 42nd (Royal Highlanders of Canada) Battalion entered from the west. The RCR's A Company, along with A Company of the 42nd, penetrated from the south. There was no sign of the machine-gunners who had fought so hard earlier in the day. According to Sergeant-Major William Clark of B Company of the RCR, "we marched across the canal in fours, the men with their rifles slung...over their shoulder, just the same as if we had gone on a route march."[30] By two in the morning, both battalions were in Mons to say, without having fired a shot.

The silence was uncanny. Lieutenant Paul Hutchison of the RCR recalled that his platoon had to rouse the citizens, to let them know they had been liberated:

> As we went through the streets of the city, my men ran their bayoneted rifles along the grilles of the cellar windows of the houses. The city was very quiet at this point, the shelling and machine-gunning from the enemy had stopped some time before and, eventually, as a result of the bayonets on the grilled windows of the cellars, the citizens of Mons streamed out, calling, "Les Américains." We explained that we were the Canadians, and there was, of course, great excitement in the street.[31]

A friendly race to be the first to reach the centre of the city ensued between the two battalions. The honour apparently goes to a lieutenant of the RCR, W. Martin King, who found himself standing outside the Hôtel de Ville, or city hall, overlooking the Grand Place, the central square in Mons. There he met the chief of police, who invited him to sign the Golden Book of Remembrance inside the city hall. "Yes, but it'll have to be quick," said Lieutenant King, who signed the book and endured having his cheeks kissed by the civic officials in attendance, before hurrying away to lead his platoon across the city.'[32]*

By daybreak on 11 November, Mons had been secured, without a single Canadian casualty. The citizens celebrated with unreserved enthusiasm. Recalled the RCR's Captain William Home, dawn was "just breaking when windows opened up, the Belgian flags came out, [and] the people streamed out into the streets with cake and brandy."[34] The 42nd Battalion, led by its bagpipers, escalated the celebration with a smart parade through the city's cobbled streets at seven o'clock that morning.

By then, exciting news had arrived at Canadian Corps headquarters. Around six-thirty, word came that an armistice had been signed, to take effect at 11 A.M. General Currie received the information calmly while taking his morning bath, and staff officers flashed an appropriate warning to subordinate formations:

> Hostilities will cease at 1100 hours Nov. 11th. Troops will stand fast on the line reached at that hour which will be reported to Corps H.Q. Defensive precautions will be maintained. There will

---

* This version of events was disputed by the 42nd Battalion. Two of its lieutenants, L.H. Biggar and Jim Cave, claimed that they were the first to sign the book, but left lots of space above their names for other signatures. The testimony of Mons officials, however, supports Lieutenant King.[33]

be no intercourse of any description with the enemy. Further instructions follow.[35]

Word of the ceasefire received a matter-of-fact response in the front lines. "Nobody said a word for quite a while," recalled Private Joseph Hefferman of the 50th (Calgary) Battalion. "Then a few cheered a bit feebly. I think most of us were kind of in shock or something." Similarly, Private William Ogilvie, a nineteen-year-old member of the 21st Battery, CFA, remembered the reaction of his fellow gunners. "We just couldn't believe it...and we went about our daily chores as though nothing momentous had happened. It was quite some time before [the] good news filtered into our benumbed minds, that the war was over and that we had survived." The 19th Battalion's Lieutenant John Gaetz, writing home two days later, observed that "one can't realize that the fighting is over. I am so used [to] surprises and disappointments that I don't believe I would bat an eye if they told us to stand to, Heinie was counter-attacking. I guess I would utter the odd oath though." Commented Private Pat Gleason of the 46th (South Saskatchewan) Battalion: "What a strange and peaceful calm followed. Not a cheer went up from anyone."[36]

Not everyone greeted the news so stoically. Some were actually angry that the war had ended. Corporal Richard Symons of Princess Patricia's Canadian Light Infantry believed that the troops "weren't looking for an armistice, in fact," that it was "a poor time to stop the war, when we were having it all our own way." General Andy McNaughton, the Corps heavy-artillery commander, was furious when he heard the word. "Bloody fools," he remarked to an aide. "We have them on the run. That means that we shall have to do it all over again in another twenty-five years." These were prophetic words, indeed; and when the Canadians did it again, McNaughton would be in command of their army overseas.[37]

For others, 11 November 1918 would be memorable in different ways. Private Roy Henley, a teen-aged member of the 42nd Battalion, had the misfortune to rest in a shell hole in which phosgene gas was still active; he had to be evacuated to a nearby casualty clearing station, en route to a two-month stay in hospital in England. As a result of this incident, Henley developed tuberculosis, for which he receives a pension today. Every bit as painful was the experience of Private Arthur Turner of the 50th Battalion, who received word in the afternoon that his two-year-old son Davey had taken ill and died. Private Turner had never seen his son, having departed Calgary for Europe before the boy's birth.[38]

There were, however, several hours between the time the troops learned of the armistice and the time it took effect. Until 11 A.M., the

Canadian Corps would continue to advance, as per its instructions from the First Army. North of Mons, the 116th (Ontario County) Battalion halted at eleven o'clock on virtually the same spot where, on 22 August 1914, elements of the Royal Irish Dragoon Guards had fired the first British shots of the war. Meanwhile, troops of the Second Division reached Havre, four and a half miles east of Mons. The vital high ground in the vicinity was captured without difficulty, while in the distance the church bells in Mons heralded the city's liberation. The history of the 28th (Northwest) Battalion recalls the scene as the hour of the cease-fire neared: "There was now little evidence of War except the occasional crackle of machine-gun fire and as the final hour approached a salvo of shells which fell harmlessly...as the Boche gunners cleared their guns for the last time. Then suddenly there was silence...."[39]

Unfortunately, there was time for a final tragedy. "Wouldn't it be hell," soldiers said, "to be knocked off on the last day?" Only one Canadian died on the war's concluding day: Private George Lawrence Price, of the 28th Battalion. Private Price led a patrol across the Canal du Centre, near Havre, during the final hour. At 10:58 A.M.,* two minutes before the armistice, Price was felled by a single sniper's bullet that struck him in the chest, killing him instantly. Price's company commander, Captain Evans Ross, was furious when told of the mishap. "What the hell did you go across for?" he raged at the other members of Price's patrol. "You had no orders to go across there." The captain added, in frustration: "Hell of a note, to think that that would happen right when the war's over."[41]

George Price was the last Canadian killed in the Great War, and quite possibly the final fatality on the entire Western Front. His grave can be found today at Saint-Symphorien, just outside Mons. In the same cemetery rests the first British soldier to be killed, Private J. Parr of the Middlesex Regiment, who died on 21 August 1914. It is sobering, indeed, to see these two graves, situated in that small cemetery, surrounded by lush green grass and tall trees, and to consider the millions of men from all nations who perished between Privates Parr and Price.

By the time the armistice took effect, Mons had turned into a gigantic party. Canadians who were confused about the meaning of the cease-fire, and there were many, had no qualms about joining the celebrations. W.H.S. Macklin of the 19th Battalion could never forget the scene:

---

* The time of Price's death comes from a plaque erected in memory near the spot. However, government records place the time of death at 10:57, while the regimental history gives it as 10:50.[40]

As the day went along, everybody in the whole city of Mons began to celebrate. Every single house and every building was decorated with a flag or flags, and all the civilians turned out, and all the pubs opened up and served free beer and free cognac and free everything else.... The people went through the city in parties, with civilians and soldiers arm-in-arm, roaring through the streets singing songs at the top of their voices, and they would turn and invade one estaminet and everybody would have a drink, and then they'd all come out in a file and go down to the next place. It was a spontaneous and unorganized celebration.

Private R.G. Petty of the PPCLI remembered the civilians cutting buttons and badges from the Canadian uniforms for souvenirs, and "at the end of the day I believe that my tunic was held together by safety pins."[42]

During the afternoon, the partying was briefly interrupted by General Currie's triumphal entrance. This was neither his idea nor was he enthusiastic about it. But he was talked into it by the Third Division's exuberant commander, General Loomis, who had already arranged one parade, staged by troops of the Seventh Brigade, within minutes of the armistice. Not satisfied with that display, Loomis wanted one for his whole division and convinced Currie that he should oversee it. The Corps commander rode into Mons with an escort provided by British cavalrymen, belonging to the 5th Lancers, who had fought in the first battle of Mons in 1914. A guard of honour 1500 strong was assembled at the Grand Place to greet Currie. One Canadian infantryman, seeing the approach of the glittering cavalry and staff officers, muttered, "Jesus Christ, we got in the wrong part of the army."[43]

The ceremony was a splendid success. If Currie had reservations about it, they were quickly dispelled, as the long entry in his diary indicates:

The people were most enthusiastic in their reception, and on reaching the Square one was met by civilian dignitaries. The Deputy Burgomaster made an address of welcome, to which I replied. There were large numbers of troops on parade, representing all Units of the 3rd Division. After giving three cheers for the Belgian King and Queen and the people, these troops, headed by the 5th Lancers, marched past to the tune of the Belgian National Anthem. The thousands of people in the Square sang it, and it was a most inspiring situation.

After the troops marched past, we entered the Municipal Chambers and signed the [Golden Book of Remembrance]. The last signature in that book was that of the King of the Belgians, written in the year 1914, before the war. Refreshments were served, and later in the evening I returned to [Corps headquarters in] Valenciennes; but I left our troops and the people of Mons celebrating in a most joyous fashion.[44]

The Canadians and the people of Mons formed a mutual admiration society. Currie was later made an honorary citizen, and was presented with a gold medal bearing the inscription: "La Ville de Mons au Lieut.-Général Sir Arthur W. Currie en souvenir de la libération de la cité par le Corps Canadien." Place de Bavière in southwestern Mons was later renamed Place du Canada, and a plaque, which is still there, was mounted at the city hall:

> MONS WAS RECAPTURED
> BY THE CANADIAN CORPS
> ON 11TH NOVEMBER 1918.
> AFTER FIFTY MONTHS OF
> GERMAN OCCUPATION, FREEDOM
> WAS RESTORED TO THE CITY.
> HERE WAS FIRED THE
> LAST SHOT OF THE
> GREAT WAR.

The Canadians reciprocated. Currie gave the burgomaster the Corps pennon, and in August 1919 the city was presented with what were believed to be "the two guns of the Canadian Artillery which fired the last shots in the Great War."[45]

Mons paid a further tribute to Canada the day after the armistice. On 12 November, the residents held a heroes' funeral for the Canadians killed while liberating their city. There were, naturally, no dead Canadians to be found within the city limits, but the bodies of eleven men killed on 9 and 10 November were collected and carried to the city hall. Here they were laid in "rich oak coffins" which were "draped in folds of dark cloth edged with silver" and covered with innumerable flowers and wreaths. Led by Canadian bagpipers, a procession carried the coffins to the cemetery at nearby Saint-Symphorien, where a service was conducted. In his speech, the burgomaster of Mons, Jean Lescartes, paid fitting tribute to "those who have made the last sacrifice of life in the course of offended right, and who, so far from home, after months and years of incessant fighting, when they were just reaching the goal that could compensate for all their sufferings, have fallen on the field of honour, covered with glory." Praising the efforts of "noble Canada" in

207

freeing Mons, and Belgium as a whole, he pledged that "in future ages the name of Canada will remain associated here with that of honour, of loyalty, and of heroism."[46]

General Currie took considerable pride in having captured Mons in the war's final hours. It was an achievement, he said, "that means so much for Canada. It was a proud thing for our race that we were able to finish the war where we began it, and that we, the young whelps of the old lion, were able to take the ground lost in 1914." Currie was well aware of the intense emotions felt by his British colleagues. Entering Mons, Currie was accompanied by a senior staff officer, Brigadier-General George Farmar, who remarked: "The last time I was here was on August 23, 1914." Currie, in a quiet voice and with a twinkle in his eye, replied, "Well, George, it's taken a damned long time to get you back here!" He also received a heartfelt, handwritten letter from the First Army's commander, General Horne:

> The capture of Mons at the last moment is a splendid crowning effort on the part of the Canadian Corps. It is, I think, just about the best thing that could have happened. The British army met the Boche at Mons on Aug. 23, 1914, & had to give way before overwhelming numbers. On Nov. 11, 1918, a few hours before the Armistice is signed, you drive the Boche out of Mons. Personally I am simply delighted. I commanded the rearguard of the I Corps when we left Mons on Aug. 24, 1914, and I am glad to have had the good fortune to command the army which took Mons back. I do congratulate you and your fine troops with all my heart.

Less happily, Currie would soon find that there were people at home who did not share in the sense of accomplishment.[47]*

Canada, and Canadians, had gained a remarkable reputation during the Great War. In its first major venture onto the international stage, the nation had acquitted itself admirably. It was a massive undertaking; with a population of 8 million, Canada had put 619,636 men and women into uniform, most of them in the army. It was an army of civilians; Canada's regular forces in 1914 numbered only 3000. As General Currie proudly pointed out, Canada had shown "that civilian soldiers when discreetly disciplined, carefully trained, vigorously led and above all when imbued with a resolute and unflinching determination to make their cause triumphant, could compete with and vanquish the product of a military autocracy."[48]

---

* See Appendix One.

The Canadian Corps had compiled an outstanding record. It had been built on the blood and bravery of the men who fought in the first Canadian battle, at Ypres, in 1915; nurtured through the futile fighting on the Somme in 1916; enhanced at Vimy Ridge, Hill 70, and Passchendaele in 1917; and finally flowered in the final hundred days. In a war synonymous with senseless slaughters, the Canadians had routinely succeeded where all others failed. Commented Currie:

> In no battle did the Corps ever fail to take its objective; nor did it lose an inch of ground, once that ground was consolidated; and in the 51 months that it had been in the field the Canadian Corps has never lost a single gun. I think one cannot be accused of immodesty in claiming that the record is somewhat unique in the history of the world's campaigns.[49]

Never were Canadian courage, skill, and determination tested more severely, and for so long, than in the course of the war's last hundred days. The Corps, according to Currie, "in that short period met and defeated decisively over 50 German divisions, i.e., approximately one-quarter of the total German forces on the Western Front. Elements of 17 additional divisions were also encountered and crushed.... No force of equal size ever accomplished so much in a similar space of time during the war, or any other war."[50]

The Canadians had seen their hardest fighting of the whole war in this period. The casualty figures tell a grim story. Between 8 August and 11 November 1918, 45,830 Canadians were killed, wounded, or went missing. That is more than one-fifth of the total Canadian losses—212,688—on the Western Front during the entire conflict.[51]

Such sacrifices led to extremes of feelings among the troops. There was, on the one hand, considerable bitterness while, on the other hand, there was great pride. The wide range is exemplified by the writings of two men. Corporal Albert West of the 43rd (Cameron Highlanders of Canada) Battalion, his thoughts fuelled by unfounded rumours, angrily commented in his diary the day Cambrai fell:

> [I]n heaven's name let us "cut out" this foolhardiness which has been falsely praised so long. We hear Gen. Currie has said he will have Cambrai 'tho he lose 75% of his corps. If so he is a fool and a murderer. Cambrai can be taken but we do not need to be slaughtered to capture it. It looks to me as if 51st and 52nd and one or two other Imperial [i.e., British] Divisions with Aussies, Anzacs and Canucks, had to do all assault work on this part of British front. Why?[52]

At the other end of the scale was Captain Reg Bateman. A member of the 46th (South Saskatchewan) Battalion, Bateman had been the first professor of English at the fledgling University of Saskatchewan, which explains his eloquence:

> It is comparatively seldom in the world's history that a man gets the chance to die splendidly. Most deaths are somewhat inglorious endings to not very glorious careers. A war like this gives a man a chance to cancel at one stroke all the pettiness of his life.[53]

Captain Bateman was killed by a German shell on 3 September 1918.

Despite the losses, Canadian morale remained high right to the end. Victory is a powerful tonic; the mood of the men reflected it in the war's final weeks and days. "Everybody believed," recalled W.H.S. Macklin of the 19th (Central Ontario) Battalion, "that the Canadian Corps, all by itself and single-handed, was actually flogging the hide off the German army and winning the war, and you could see it." T.T. Shields, a sergeant in the PPCLI, agreed:

> In spite of the fact that it seemed that the Canadian Corps was over-worked in the last hundred days, that they had been given more than their share to do, I would say that there was a sense of satisfaction among the men in spite of the casualties. In spite of the rough going, there was an elation among the men. There was a tremendous sensation that finally we had a chance to do some-thing, and we were doing it.[54]

Along with the pride came an unprecedented sense of awareness that Canadians were not merely faceless entities in an Empire that straddled the globe. Before the war, "Canadian" and "British" had been interchangeable, as far as Canada was concerned. Canadians considered themselves to be British, and were proud of the fact. British heroes were Canadian heroes. British achievements were Canadian achievements. But that had changed by the end of the war, as General McNaughton recalled. The Corps had made a "most important contri-bution to the life of Canada," said McNaughton. "It's not the triumphs on the field of battle. It's the fact that we were Canadians and that Canada has a mission in this world."[55]

How could the Canadians be so consistently successful? There were many factors, beginning at the top. The Corps had excellent leadership, personified by General Currie, the greatest soldier this country has ever produced. In McNaughton's opinion, Currie "stands out as the individual who made the Canadian Corps." The staff work was superb, for which no small part of the credit must go to the British officers—"expert students of the art of war," Currie called them—who served with and trained the Canadians. Teamwork was another essential. "The Officers have confidence in the men, and the men have confidence in the Officers," Currie observed in early 1918, noting that "without confidence you cannot win many battles." Canadian soldiers had few equals, too. "They do not whimper," Currie declared, "and they do not quit." Of sixty-one Victoria Crosses won by the Canadian army during the Great War, twenty-eight were awarded during the last hundred days.[56]

The infantry could not have succeeded without the support of other services, and none was more important than the artillery. It is no coincidence that by the summer of 1918, the Canadian artillery had emerged as the best on the Western Front. The explanation is simple. "Canadians took naturally to gunnery," commented McNaughton, whose scientific innovations also made a significant contribution, and in the course of the war they "developed extraordinary skill, efficiency and dependability." The Canadian batteries, said McNaughton, "were kept firing at useful targets long after the prearranged barrages had been completed," and the infantry "often had the benefit of more than double the rates of ammunition expenditure achieved by British formations." Added McNaughton: "I know of no organization in the history of the War which was able to produce such a high ratio in shells to troops, nor any in which the price paid for victory was lower in personnel."[57]

To appreciate just how good the Canadian Corps was, it is interesting to compare its performance in the last hundred days with the efforts of other forces. For instance, the contrast with the far larger American army's struggle in the Meuse-Argonne is startling.

	American	Canadian
Number of troops engaged	650,000	105,000
Duration of operations	47 days	100 days
Maximum advance	34 miles	86 miles
German divisions met and defeated	46	47
Casualties suffered from each division defeated	2170	975
Total battle casualties	100,000	45,830
Prisoners captured	16,000	31,537
Guns captured	468	623
Machine-guns captured	2864	2842
Trench mortars captured	117	336

This comparison is made not to belittle the American army, but to shed light on the spectacular Canadian performance.[58]

Only the Australian Corps could offer numbers comparable to the Canadians. Engaging thirty-nine German divisions during the period 8 August–5 October, the Australians had captured 29,144 prisoners and 338 guns, driving thirty-seven miles into enemy-held territory, at the cost of 21,245 casualties. "I doubt," commented the Australian commander, General Monash, "whether there is any parallel for such a performance in the whole range of military history."[59] But the Australians had seen nothing like the sustained fighting endured by the Canadians. With the exception of the first day at Amiens, it was unusual for more than one or two of the five Australian divisions to be in action at the same time. This was a consequence of Australia's dwindling manpower reserves; indeed, the corps had to be reinforced by American divisions on occasion during the hundred days. The Australians, stricken by severe disciplinary problems, including mutiny, were finally withdrawn from the front lines on 5 October to rest and reorganize into smaller, nine-battalion divisions.

In the final analysis, it was the British Expeditionary Force that won the war. Beginning at Amiens, the BEF had engaged almost half of the German army located on the Western Front. Besides beating the best troops the Germans had to offer, the BEF also breached the Hindenburg Line at its most powerful points. That the forces of the British Empire were ultimately able to prevail was due in large part to the Canadian Army Corps. It is no exaggeration to say that the Canadians played a decisive part in the struggle in the second half of 1918. The Canadians drew to their front disproportionate numbers of enemy formations, including high-calibre machine-gunners who fought with fanatical determination. As a result of these sacrifices by the Canadian Corps, the BEF was able to fashion its fine successes along the Hindenburg Line and bring the war to a successful conclusion. Without the selfless and courageous Canadian contribution, it is conceivable that the war would have dragged on into 1919, and perhaps longer, with consequences that can only be imagined.

10 DISCIPLINE AND DISCONTENT

The armistice terms were crushing. That was predictable, since the man charged with the task of arranging it was Marshal Foch, who had won political and military support—with the notable exception of Field-Marshal Haig—to seek what he called "guarantees fully ensuring peace." While Haig feared that the Germans might reject Foch's tough terms, the supreme commander was convinced that they were in no position to do so, believing them to be beaten and incapable of offering organized resistance on any scale. "I am not waging war for the sake of waging war," Foch explained. "If I obtain through the Armistice the conditions that we wish to impose upon Germany, I am satisfied. Once this object is attained, nobody has the right to shed one drop more of blood."[1]

On Friday, 8 November, the Germans dispatched a delegation to discuss the armistice with Foch. Arriving at the supreme commander's private rail car parked on a siding in the forest of Compiègne, the three representatives were in for a shock. Asking for Foch's "proposals," the marshal haughtily replied that he had none, only terms. "Do you ask for an armistice?" he gruffly inquired. "If you do, I can inform you of the conditions subject to which it can be obtained." Listening to the terms read by Foch's chief of staff, Major-General Maxime Weygand, the Germans were appalled. They openly wondered, according to Foch, "whether the Allies had drawn up such severe terms with the object of having Germany refuse them."[2]

Foch not only rejected the German attempt to negotiate, he refused to consider their request for an immediate cease-fire. "Hostilities," he declared, "cannot cease before the signing of the armistice." Suspicious of enemy motives, Foch sent a message to his commanders-in-chief on 9 November, urging that the Allied forces give no quarter. "The enemy, disorganized by our repeated attacks, is giving way all along the front. It is urgent to hasten and intensify our efforts. I appeal to the energy and initiative of commanders in chief and their armies to make the results achieved decisive." Accordingly, the Belgians, under King Albert, liberated Ghent on the tenth, while the British advanced on Mons and the River Sambre, and the Americans reached the vital rail centre of Mézières; two French armies, totalling thirty-one divisions, were preparing a further offensive in Lorraine, scheduled for 14 November.[3]

There were no armistice negotiations. The best the Germans could manage during protracted discussions on 9 and 10 November was to make minor revisions to Foch's terms. After a final meeting in the early morning hours of 11 November, the armistice was formally signed at 5:10 A.M.—although the document states that it was endorsed at "5 o'clock A.M. (French time)." The Germans were understandably upset. While pledging to "make every effort" to ensure "that the terms imposed are fulfilled," the envoys warned that "this agreement may plunge the German people into anarchy and famine."[4]

The armistice was designed to strip Germany of any further capacity to wage war. It made clear that the Allies would seek reparations from the Germans in the formal peace treaty that would follow. Meantime, Germany was to evacuate all occupied territory and repatriate all residents of these areas. The German army was to surrender, in good condition, 5000 artillery pieces and 25,000 machine-guns; the air force was to hand over 1700 fighters and bombers; the navy was to relinquish ten battleships, six battlecruisers, eight light cruisers, and fifty destroyers. In addition, the civilian authorities were expected to give up 5000 locomotives, 5000 trucks, and 150,000 wagons. Finally, the Allies would be allowed to occupy bridgeheads on the River Rhine.

Canadian troops were among those selected to go to Germany. The British bridgehead, which included the cities of Cologne and Bonn, was to be occupied by the Second Army, under General Sir Herbert Plumer. The Canadian Corps had served under Plumer at Passchendaele in late 1917, and the British general made no secret of his admiration for General Currie and his troops. Plumer promptly submitted a request that two Canadian divisions be included in his army of occupation, "because of their discipline and fighting efficiency." Currie was only too pleased to be associated once more with Plumer and to be part of the occupation force. "It was," he believed, "a great gratification and honour to us."[5]

The troops had mixed feelings about it. Many, like Private F.R. Hasse of the 49th (Edmonton Regiment) Battalion, just wanted to go home. "The only road worth taking from here," remarked Private Hasse, "is to Jasper Avenue," a reference to the main street in his hometown, Edmonton. But a lot of Canadians were glad to be going to Germany. "We had been a long time fighting to be boss," observed Private William Green of the 4th (Central Ontario) Battalion, "now we had the chance to be the top boss. We were anxious to take it. This was to be an experience we would never forget." Indeed, the soldiers who missed the opportunity regretted it, according to the 50th (Calgary) Battalion's Private Victor Wheeler: "To us who had set our hearts on entering *Allemagne* as Victors after four years of war, now to be denied that satisfaction was very hard to accept."[6]

It was not going to be a holiday. The Canadians faced a march of

170 miles to the Rhine, a good part of the route lying in remarkably rough terrain. And General Currie expected exemplary conduct from the Canadian troops. In a special order of the day, he warned the men that there must not be "any relaxation of your discipline or alertness. Your task is not yet completed and you must remain what you are, the close-knitted army, in grim, deadly earnest." Their uniforms and equipment, he insisted, "must be, if possible, spotless, well kept and well put on." Currie also made it clear "that the population and private property will be respected. You will always remember that you fought for justice, right and decency, and that you cannot afford to fall short of these essentials even in the country against which you have every right to feel bitter."[7]

The march to the Rhine began one week after the armistice. The Canadian Corps, leading the British advance, hit the road precisely at 9 A.M. on Monday, 18 November, in a mist so thick that "it was practically impossible to see more than ten yards." The Corps was reduced in size for this exercise: only the First and Second divisions, accompanied by artillery, engineers, cavalry, and assorted ancillary services, set out for Germany. The original plan—which was not carried out—was to have these divisions later trade places with the Third and Fourth divisions, which remained in Belgium, temporarily attached to Lieutenant-General Sir George Harper's IV Corps. "The advance," Currie commented, "was to be carried out under active service conditions, and all military precautions against surprise were taken," in the event of "any attempted resistance by the enemy." A cavalry screen preceded the infantry; each night, outpost lines were established.[8]

The engineers had a busy time of it. They discovered and removed explosive charges "by the lorry load" from bridges which had been prepared for demolition by the German army before the armistice. One bridge was wired to 150 100-pound cases of explosives.[9]

The Canadians were not alone on the road. They were greeted by what the Corps medical chief, Colonel A.E. Snell, called the "pitiful sight" of thousands of refugees, mostly French, returning to their homes. Many were shoeless and poorly clothed and carried their meagre possessions on their backs. Even more distressing were the long lines of liberated prisoners-of-war, again, mostly French. They were, in Colonel Snell's words, "invariably in a filthy condition, and covered with vermin and neglected sores, the latter often ulcerated to the bone." More than a few were beyond medical help, causing Snell to comment bitterly: "It is impossible to imagine men getting into such a condition unless one saw it with his own eyes."[10]

The first few days were quite pleasant. The weather remained "generally good," and the Canadians continued to be greeted everywhere as heroes. Each town and village was decorated with banners of welcome: "Honneur à nos Libérateurs," "Gloire aux Alliés," "Vive les Canadiens."[11]

But things changed as the Corps approached the German frontier. The greetings became noticeably cooler, to the surprise of many. The Belgian peasants, noted General Currie, "seemed to resent our presence as disturbers of their quiet pastoral life"—hastening to add that these "were hardly typical of the Belgian people."[12]

As the greetings cooled, so did the weather. It began to rain heavily on Tuesday, 26 November, and drizzled all day Wednesday. The rainfall, combined with the "very muddy roads, and the heavy traffic encountered—accentuated by the overturned lorries left inconveniently by the enemy—made the march that day a real hardship for the men," Currie commented; "even the first-class roads were now in a very bad condition." Exhibiting their splendid organization and efficiency, the Canadians carried out a complicated manoeuvre, altering the direction of their advance so that both divisions had one first-class road to follow, reforming into single columns, compared to the three columns used by either division at the outset.[13]

Bad weather, bad roads—even countryside worsened. The Corps was now in the Ardennes, a hilly, forested region which offered few comfortable billets. Most men would have agreed with Private Louis Lent of the 31st (Alberta) Battalion, who scribbled in his diary: "Feeling rather tired & my feet are sore." Lieutenant George Hunter of the 2nd (Eastern Ontario) Battalion recounted his miseries on 27 November:

> This was the longest march we have done so far. We started at 7.30 A.M. and marched 38 kilometres (24 miles) to Andenne. The weather for this march, up till 3 o'clock, was rotten—a thick, cold fog; and we had a miserable cold hour for lunch.[14]

Even lunch posed problems, because the supply difficulties which had plagued the Canadian and British forces in the last weeks of the war were recurring. "Supply trains are very late," commented a concerned Currie, "as up to date supplies have been brought up in lorries from Valenciennes, which is some 90 miles away." Things became so serious that Currie was finally forced to halt the march for the first two days in December, "the reason for this being the decidedly unsatisfactory nature of the supply situation. Trains are arriving several days late, and the result has been simply chaos." His final remark reflected his growing annoyance: "I have never experienced in France such evidence of mismanagement."[15]

No one was starving, but the men were very hungry. Left to their own devices, the Canadians responded with typical initiative, as illustrated by the 4th Battalion's Private Green and colleagues:

216

We were so hungry that we started to look around for something to eat. I happened to look up at a 3rd storey window of a large brick house.... In the window was hanging a large leg of meat. What a find, we thought. I climbed up the stairs and cut the leg down and dropped it out the window to the gravel walk....

So we proceeded to cut up a few slices and cooked them. Boy, when we started to eat them we couldn't get our teeth into them. We just chewed the meat enough to get the juice out of it. One of the civilians told us that it was a leg of horse meat and was left there by Roumanian prisoners who the Germans took back with them. We were sure glad when our own rations came up the next day.[16]

The supply difficulties notwithstanding, the Canadians crossed into Germany on Wednesday, 4 December. It was a wet, misty day. Both divisions reached the border at about the same time, around nine o'clock in the morning, the First Division at Petit Thier and the Second at Beho. General Currie crossed with the First Division; its leading battalion, the 3rd (Toronto Regiment), awaited the arrival of the Corps commander. According to Major D.H.C. Mason, the troops greeted Currie with "a cheer...that I still can hear ringing. It was the heartiest thing I've ever heard in my life, and I wish that some of these people that thought that Currie was unpopular with the troops could have heard it." A few hundred yards inside German territory, Currie and the division's commander, General Macdonell, reined in their horses and took the salute as the 3rd Battalion marched past. Currie was much pleased with the men's appearance, and told Major Mason that "if the Bosch [sic] wants trouble, he can have it."[17]

If the Canadians were expecting trouble from the German civilian population, they were pleasantly surprised. "There has been no hostility shown us in any way," Currie noted approvingly. "In some towns there is a disposition to fraternize, though generally, the people have received us with much reserve; at the same time being apparently willing to carry out any instructions given them." The troops were similarly impressed. "As far as I can make out the feeling of relief that the war is over overcomes any of their feelings, and, of course, it is policy to be nice to a conquering army," noted an artillery subaltern, Brookes Gossage, "but the thing which we expected and which we have seen very little of is sullenness." Lieutenant Arthur Crease, a Second Division staff officer, agreed: "We have to make ourselves somewhat arrogant & overbearing in order to carry out the role of a conquering army but it is rather hard where the people are so subservient & anxious to obey all orders."[18]

Theories abounded about this attitude. Currie felt that the German civilians were put at ease "by the exemplary conduct of the men of the

Corps." More likely it was their sense of relief that the Canadians were not, as terrifying rumours warned, mostly "red Indians, and there was a danger of scalping."[19]

A formal crossing of the Rhine was planned. According to the details finalized at a Second Army conference on 9 December, the Canadians would cross the river on the thirteenth, a Friday, the same day as other Allied occupation forces took up positions in their allotted bridgeheads. The First Division, accompanied by the British 29th Division, would cross at Cologne, where General Plumer would take the salute. General Currie would do the honours at Bonn, where the Second Division would march past.

Currie arrived in Bonn on 11 December. Corps headquarters were located in Palais Schaumburg, the home of Princess Victoria Schaumburg Lippe, the Kaiser's youngest sister. General Macdonell considered her to be "an ugly old girl," but Currie was somewhat kinder, pointing out that the princess "spoke English extraordinarily well" and "was particularly anxious to impress the fact that her brother did not wish the war," stressing "that he was never in favour of London being bombed, and that he had done his best to prevent the submarine warfare. I notice...she did not say she regretted the war...." Currie occupied a suite usually reserved for the Kaiser, and considered it to be "the most comfortable place I have yet been in during the war."[20]

He slept well, too. "After a very comfortable night in His Majesty's bed," Currie remarked in his diary the next day, "I awoke this morning feeling quite Prussian in character." He also acted like it. During the morning, he took the salute of the British 1st Cavalry Brigade, the advanced guard for the Second Division. "Both men and horses looked well," he commented, but Currie was considerably less pleased with the civilians, complaining "that many people paid no attention whatever to the passing by of British Officers. Whether their action was due to ignorance or prompted by insolence I do not know." Summoning the city's mayor to Palais Schaumburg, Currie demanded an explanation. Satisfied with the mayor's assurances that the civilians were unaware that they were expected to show respect for Allied officers, Currie agreed to give him "time to correct this defect" in their behaviour.[21]

Conditions were less than ideal when the Second Division formally crossed the Rhine on 13 December. Currie awoke "to find it raining heavily with no prospect of letting up all day," and it did not let up. Soaked, Currie and his staff stood on a dais on Bonn's main bridge, watching the Canadians march past, from 9:30 A.M. until three o'clock in the afternoon. Currie called it "a stirring and impressive sight," adding that "I was particularly pleased with the appearance, bearing and discipline of all concerned."[22]

The crossing at Cologne was equally successful. The scene stirred

218

the Celtic blood of the First Division's General Macdonell, who could scarcely conceal his immense pride in a letter written home that night:

> They looked extremely well, especially when one considers the no. of days they have been incessantly marching—12, I believe. The pipers were magnificent & swaggered enough even to suit me.... The troops marched with fixed Bayonets & carrying their packs.... Gen[l] Plumer was good enough to express himself as delighted with the appearance & marching of the Div[n].... It was a sight to make one's heart swell with pride, a sea of well ordered bayonets, carried by bronzed veterans who have broken the enemy's lines & over run his guns not once but many times.[23]

The Canadian Corps was taking no chances. Once across the Rhine, the Corps assumed a position of "defence in depth." Each infantry brigade was allotted a series of defensive lines: one battalion occupied an outpost line, two others held the main line of resistance—a series of strongpoints covered by the artillery—while the remaining battalion of each brigade was in support. Even now, a month after the armistice, it was still uncertain that the war was really over.[24]

Despite the war footing, liberal leave was granted the Canadian soldiers. Cologne, considerably bigger than Bonn—with a population of half a million, compared to Bonn's 90,000—was most popular among the Canadians, who appreciated the sightseeing and shopping that was available. Among the many who visited Cologne was Sapper Joseph Hackett, who afterward raved about it in a letter home: "I went into one of the finest cathedrals in the world last night. My, she is some building inside. We couldn't see much because she wasn't lit up at all. But all we did see was great." There were drawbacks, to be sure, as Private George Taylor, a medical orderly, remarked: "This is no place for a private as you soon get a cramp in the arm saluting...."[25]

There were some unfortunate incidents involving Canadians in Cologne. Most of the men were well-behaved, but some were caught in the act of "holding up and robbing...some German citizens," as Currie delicately put it. This was due, he felt, mainly to "a certain number of bad men with us," but he was not unsympathetic. He observed that "the troops feel that the Germans are not being made to feel strongly enough that we come here as a conquering army. In fact, there are more restrictions placed on the conduct of our own troops than the Germans."[26]

The situation led to another clash between Currie and a senior British officer. The latter was Lieutenant-General Sir Charles Fergusson, the military governor at Cologne. While Currie had always conducted himself as a gentleman, his relations with Sir Charles had long been icy. It will be recalled that Fergusson's XVII Corps fought on the right of the Canadians during the battles of Arras and Cambrai; its laggardly progress caused, in Currie's opinion, many unnecessary Canadian casualties due to enfilade fire from that flank. And Currie was far from impressed when he learned of Fergusson's appointment as military governor. "I am quite convinced that the Military Governor gives no more promise of being able to carry out his function well, now that he has been installed, than those of us who knew him before expected." Knowing Fergusson as he did, Currie privately predicted "that sooner or later, he would find some reason, good or bad, for putting Cologne out of bounds to the Canadians."[27]

It happened sooner than later. In a letter Currie described as "a deliberate insult," Fergusson pointed to the reported robberies and beatings of German civilians involving Canadian soldiers, whom he called "the greatest thieves in the world." The military governor informed Currie that no Canadians would be allowed in Cologne until further notice.[28]

Currie was incensed. He immediately went over Fergusson's head, presenting himself at General Plumer's headquarters, where he demanded an apology. Plumer at first did not take him seriously, suspecting that the whole thing was merely a misunderstanding. Seeing that he was getting nowhere, Currie turned and headed for the door.

"Come back," called Plumer. "What are you going to to?"

"I am going to Haig."

"Surely," said Plumer, slowly realizing the depth of Currie's anger, "you would not go over my head to Haig."

"In such a matter as this, I would go to the foot of the throne."

Currie had made his point. An apology from Fergusson arrived in due course, and the ban on Canadians in Cologne was lifted.[29]

Many Canadians—like Currie, veterans of the first contingent which went overseas in the fall of 1914—were about to spend their fifth Christmas in Europe. The knowledge that it would also be the last did much to make it bearable. As well, the weather was reasonably good, alternating between fog and drizzle and reminding Currie "very much of the climate of Victoria," the British Columbia city where he resided before the war. And no one could complain about the accommodations. A medical officer from Calgary, Major Harold McGill, who had grown accustomed to dugouts and tents, described his sumptuous surroundings in a Christmas Eve letter to his wife:

Tonight we are in palatial rooms of a house belonging to a wealthy German munition maker. One of the officers is playing the piano and others are trying to sing. The house is an old castle rebuilt and modernized. It has a moat around it and we enter the front door over a draw bridge.... The place is electric lighted and steam heated.

The only damper on the Canadians' Christmas celebrations was caused, predictably, by ongoing supply problems. The turkeys arrived late, forcing many units to delay their dinners. The 28th (Northwest) Battalion, for example, postponed Christmas dinner until 30 December.[30]

Several Canadian generals made the New Year's Honours List announced by King George. Currie added another award to his impressive collection, when his knighthood was upgraded to King Grand Cross of the Order of St. Michael and St. George (GCMG), an unusual distinction for a Canadian. And three of his major-generals were knighted before they departed for Canada: the First Division's Archie Macdonell, Frederick Loomis of the Third Division, and the Corps artillery chief, Edward Morrison.

The new year also brought a challenge to Currie's authority. In early January, he was summoned to London to confer with Canadian government officials and their military advisers. Arriving in the British capital on the fifth, he reported the next morning to Argyll House, in Regent Street, the headquarters of the Overseas Military Forces of Canada (OMFC). Currie spent the whole day there, debating a subject he thought had been settled long ago: demobilization.

It may seem surprising, but demobilization had been under discussion since 1916. Less surprising, Canadian deliberations had accomplished little. But the British had formulated and adopted a demobilization scheme a year before the end of the war. The War Office produced a plan based on economics, foreseeing the early return of soldiers in certain key occupations, so-called "pivotal men" who had jobs waiting for them. Field-Marshal Haig had been quick to reject the proposal. "The fullest use of the existing military machinery together with the co-operation of all ranks would be essential," he argued, "if a disciplined demobilisation were desired." Warning that the War Office plan "contemplates the entire breaking up of this organisation," Haig suggested an alternative, "demobilisation by complete formations," recommending that "the departure of the troops be based on the length of service of a formation with an overseas force." His advice was ignored by Prime Minister Lloyd George, whose war cabinet adopted the War Office plan on 5 November 1917.[31]

The Canadians, meanwhile, could not quite make up their minds. Committees were struck and the subject studied, and reports piled higher and higher, all pointing to something similar to the British policy: "it is not improbable," states one study, written in the summer of 1918, "that the Government may decide that it will be of advantage...if the men belonging to certain occupations are returned first."[32]

Strange as it may seem, no one asked for Currie's opinion until the last week of the war. As usual, the Corps commander had very definite views. Like Haig, he favoured the return of soldiers in organized units, preferably battalions, and his reasons may be succinctly summed up in two words: "discipline" and "honour." Currie believed "that the only satisfactory way to return troops to Canada is by complete units and not by drafts."

The organization for doing so is already in existence, whereas if the units are re-grouped in any other manner, the organization necessary to deal with their return would have to be improvised, and no improvised organization works smoothly or efficiently.... Furthermore, if they are returned to Canada by units you maintain the discipline, which is a very important factor. If you do not, I would not care to answer for the discipline.[33]

Discipline was a major concern of Currie's. "I feel that I cannot dwell too strongly on this matter of discipline," he wrote. "I know its value. It has been the foundation of our strength, and the source of our power.... For God's sake do not play with it, for you are playing with fire."[34]

Then there was the case for honouring the returning soldiers. They were entitled to a hero's welcome, said Currie, something that would be impossible if the men went home based on the importance of their peacetime occupations.

Take the case of the 8th Battalion, the "Little Black Devils," or the 90th Rifles. Does Winnipeg wish to welcome that Battalion as a Unit or not? The men of that Battalion are looking for that welcome, but if one hundred and fifty of them who are farmers arrive this month, and fifty of them who are shop-keepers arrive next month, and perhaps forty miners arrive the next, how are you in Winnipeg going to show the 8th Battalion your appreciation of how worthily they upheld the fine name of your city, and of your Province, and of the Dominion.[35]

It is almost certain that the majority of the men disagreed with their commander. There was widespread support for what was, ostensibly, an easier and more equitable method of demobilization. This was known as "first over, first back"—in other words, the veterans with the longest service would be the first to go home. But ease and fairness do not mean better, or even practicable. Such a plan was, in fact, "ridiculous," according to Brigadier-General E. de B. Panet. "It couldn't be done. For example, the clerks and the Army Service Corps personnel, well, they didn't have as many casualties as the others. The result is they would be all the ones going away. Well, who was going to look after the troops? It was an impossible situation...."[36] The sagacity and practicality of Currie's scheme would soon be evident.

It was not until 6 November 1918 that the Corps commander's thoughts were solicited. On that date, Brigadier-General Percy Thacker, the adjutant-general of the OMFC, visited Currie and his senior officers at Canadian Corps headquarters. General Thacker explained the ministry's preference for the return by trades, with consideration for long service and marital status. Currie eloquently pointed out the flaws and dangers inherent in demobilizing that way. He was supported by his subordinates, none more vocally that the First Division's General Macdonell, who explained his feelings in a letter home afterward:

> A wicked movement was on foot to disband over here & send men home by trades. Apart from the utterly unpracticable [sic] affair from a disciplinary point of view, it would have sent these splendid men home in dishonour, and I really think the people of Canada want to show them they appreciate their services. I stuck out that we sh[ou]ld be disbanded in an honourable manner that w[ou]ld be pleasing & satisfactory to the men concerned & their relatives & worthy of the Dominion of Canada.

General Watson of the Fourth Division was equally emphatic, telling his diary that he "very strongly advocated that we go back as units."[37]

More discussions took place in the wake of the armistice. In London on 17 November, Currie presented his views to the prime minister, Sir Robert Borden, who was duly impressed. "The return in units," Sir Robert wrote later, "is of course only a matter of sentiment but it was sentiment that gathered to the colours great armies from the British Isles and all the Dominions during the first two years of the War."[38]

Currie had second thoughts, momentarily, at this juncture. Rejoining the Corps en route to Germany, he convened a conference of twenty-three senior officers on 23 November. "All present were unanimous in the opinion that from every point of view it was most desirable to demobilise the Corps by Units and not by categories." Reassured, Currie followed up the meeting with a long letter to Sir Edward Kemp, the minister responsible for the OMFC, warning "that trouble is almost sure to ensue" if any other demobilization scheme were adopted.

Remember this, our discipline is of recent growth; it has not been bred in the bone. Many of our men have been with us only a short time; some have not even heard a shot fired, and a great many are those who enlisted in Canada because the Military Service Act [i.e., conscription] was put on the statute book. As long as these men remain part of a unit which has created proud traditions by its conduct in the field, they can be controlled. If you break up the present organizations and improvise new ones, as it is proposed to do, and these become associated together... you would destroy the very foundation of good discipline....[39]

Canada, typically, adopted a compromise. On 3 December, Currie learned that the government would employ *two* schemes of demobilization: one for the Canadian Corps, which would be shipped home in organized units, and one for the troops outside of Currie's jurisdiction, including railway and forestry workers in France and reinforcements in England, all of whom would be returned to Canada on the "first over, first back" idea. Like all compromises, this one was not satisfactory, but if nothing else it strikingly underlined the correctness of the Corps commander's viewpoint.

But even this was not the last word. The British were displeased with the Canadians for adopting such a drastically different demobilization scheme, which they considered to be logistically unsound. Of course, they were having a lot of troubles of their own, too. Details of the British policy—which at least one reputable historian has denounced as a "scandal"—were announced on 7 January 1919. As expected, it gave priority to servicemen with jobs awaiting them. The result was a series of mutinies and demonstrations by disgruntled soldiers, many of them "accompanied by considerable violence" and requiring the intervention of troops and police. No reports of these alarming incidents made it into the press, but military and civilian authorities were well aware of the problem. None was more concerned than the new secretary of state for war, Winston Churchill, who was appalled to learn that the War Office had disregarded Field-Marshal Haig's sound advice. "It is surprising that the Commander-in-Chief's prescient warnings were utterly ignored," wrote Churchill, "and the Army left to be irritated and almost convulsed by a complicated articial system open at every point to suspicion of jobbery and humbug." At Churchill's order, a compromise was instituted at the end of January, a variation of the "first over, first back," in which priority was given to men who had volunteered before 1916 and to those over the age of forty. It was no more popular, however, and rioting among unhappy British troops continued for months.[40]

These difficulties did not deter the British from attempting to convince the Canadians to revise their demobilization plans. The War Office flatly refused to approve or accept Currie's intention to return the Canadian Corps by formed units. Summoned to London in early January, Currie was forced to defend his scheme in a series of long, tiresome conferences with Canadian and British officials. But Currie could be extremely stubborn, particularly when he was certain that he was right, as he was in this instance; never was he more persuasive or determined to have his way. The issue came to a head on 23 January, when Currie faced a trio of British heavyweights: Secretary for War Churchill, Major-General B. Burnett-Hitchcock, who was in charge of British demobilization, and Sir Joseph Maclay, the minister for shipping. By the time the meeting ended, the British were finally to admit defeat. Currie was subsequently informed "that our views would prevail." He made no apology for being so stubborn:

> Altogether, I found the situation, so far as the British Army is unconcerned, most unsatisfactory. Their scheme of demobilization, scrapped so many times, has proved very unsatisfactory inasmuch as the Army is now practically immobile. I am more than ever convinced that the scheme for demobilization which we have consistently advocated is the only correct solution of the problem, and I would not be a bit surprised if, in a few months' time, the only troops in France organized properly will be those remaining of the Canadian Corps.[41]

Still, there were signs of trouble. Significantly, the most serious incidents occurred in the two divisions left in Belgium under British command while Currie took the rest of the Corps to Germany. To keep the troops busy, all battalions in the Third and Fourth divisions were given a steady diet of long route marches around the Belgian countryside. There was widespread disenchantment: the weather was wet, accommodations poor, and more than a few men objected to having to carry sixty-pound packs for no apparent purpose.

The result was a minor mutiny involving troops of the Third Division in mid-December. In Nivelles, a town fifteen miles from Mons, some soldiers of the Seventh Brigade gathered in the main square on the evening of the thirteenth to listen to the rhetoric of several skilled agitators.

"Will we carry our packs tomorrow?"

"No!" shouted the troops.

"Where did Currie get all his ribbons?"

"From us!"*

"Are we going to carry our packs tomorrow?"

"No!"[43]

The situation deteriorated on 14 December. The day's marches had to be cancelled when an angry crowd of about 600 gathered in the square that morning. Only one of the Seventh Brigade's four battalions, the 42nd (Royal Highlanders of Canada), did not participate in the protest meeting. The 49th (Edmonton Regiment) took part en masse, along with substantial numbers of both the Royal Canadian Regiment and Princess Patricia's Canadian Light Infantry. The protesters broke into battalion guard rooms and freed the prisoners, but, without exception, all returned to custody as soon as the demonstrators departed.

The protest soon petered out. But the repercussions were considerable. The Third Division's commander, General Loomis, was furious. His anger was matched only by his lack of sympathy. "The alleged complaints which were voiced by the men were trivial," he explained to General Harper, in whose IV Corps the Third Division was serving. "The whole matter was one of discipline, training and efficient Officers and Non-Commissioned Officers." Charges were laid against 103 men, including eight accused of taking part in a mutiny; sentences for those convicted in subsequent courts martial ranged up to five years in prison.[44]

Currie was satisfied with Loomis's handling of the situation. Following his own investigation, he pronounced his belief that the troops who took part in the Nivelles disturbance were "heartily ashamed of their foolish action." He blamed the affair on "a lack of appreciation of proper discipline on the part of officers" and on "professional agitators."[45] If there was any satisfaction to be taken, it was that despite a momentary lapse, the iron bonds of discipline had reasserted themselves in time to forestall a full-scale mutiny. That discipline, Currie knew, would soon have even more severe strains imposed on it.

The first steps in the demobilization of the Canadian Corps were taken in January 1919. On the fifth, units of the First Division were relieved from garrison duty in Germany by the British 41st Division; subsequently, the Second Division was replaced by the 34th Division. The two Canadian divisions returned to Belgium—by train, this time,

---

* A number of ugly rumours about the Corps commander made the rounds at this time. This cannot be considered startling. He was especially unpopular among the substantial numbers of recently arrived conscripts from Canada; to these unhappy men, Currie symbolized the reason why they had been forced to go overseas and fight a war of which they wanted no part. Some soldiers circulated statements "to the effect that Sir Arthur Currie had been fired at by a soldier of the 22nd Battalion. A statement was also made that on another occasion a man threw a bomb at him, which killed one of his officers." The rumours had no foundation in fact.[42]

instead of foot—to be reunited with the Third and Fourth divisions. The movement was completed by 26 January, and Currie opened his headquarters in the Belgian town of Jodoigne.*

Some changes in the original demobilization scheme had already been made by this point. Currie had hoped to ship the Corps to Canada directly from France, but this proved to be impossible. Faced with unsympathetic and intransigent British officials, the Canadians were unable to procure a camp suitable for their purposes on the French coast. Moreover, the Ministry of Shipping warned "that if the Canadian Corps is to be sent back direct from France, their return will be delayed possibly until all the Canadian troops in the British Isles have been returned to Canada, as a result of which, many men with comparatively short service and the draftees will be returned before the Canadian Corps."[47]

That unacceptable possibility left no choice but to ship the Corps troops to Canada via England. There were advantages to this, of course. Not the least of these was the availability of military records in London, making much easier the documentation of the returning troops. This in itself was a major undertaking, a bureaucrat's dream: each soldier was required to complete fourteen documents, two in duplicate and two in triplicate, involving a total of 363 questions and eight signatures. As well, Corps headquarters noted "a desire on the part of the soldiers—a large percentage of whom being British born—to see their relatives before returning [to Canada]. This, together with the large numbers having married, many of whom having relatives in the U.K., necessitated a very liberal leave."[48]

One further change illustrates Currie's flexibility. After all of the divisional movements to and from Germany and around Belgium, the Third Division ended up closest to the coast. Currie's preference was to demobilize the divisions in numerical order, since the First Division had the longest service overseas. But it was more convenient to ship the Third home first, followed by the First, Second, and Fourth divisions, in that order.

A bottleneck soon developed in England. Demobilization of the Corps, begun formally on 2 February 1919, proceeded in fits and starts. In February, only 15,243 Canadians sailed for home, climbing to 41,823 in March, dipping in April to 28,884, then surging to a record 49,887 in May. It must be remembered that the Canadians were not the only ones trying to get home as fast as possible; nearly 2 million British and Empire troops were in a similar situation, along with a couple of million Americans. Exacerbating the inevitable shortage of shipping

---

* The two-month occupation of Germany cost Canada $7,350,956.70. The British government later compensated the Canadians in the sum of $6,314,500.[46]

was a self-inflicted difficulty: the Canadians were often fussy about the vessels being provided by the British. Sir Edward Kemp, the overseas minister, admitted that some "ships which were offered were upon examination refused by us because they were not suitable for carrying troops."[49]

Equally serious was a series of labour disputes in Britain. The ports were tied up repeatedly by striking dockworkers, forcing the postponement or cancellation of numerous sailings. There were a total of 100 postponements of departures of Canada-bound ships between the first of February and the end of May. It was not unusual for the same ship to repeatedly delay its departure: one vessel scheduled to sail on 12 April was delayed until the nineteenth, then the twenty-sixth, before finally sailing on 3 May, a total delay of twenty-two days.[50]

Conditions in the camps in England were not good, either. Accommodations were often inadequate, and the discomfort was worsened by "one of the most severe winters England has experienced," along with a shortage of coal and an influenza epidemic. Sir Edward Kemp also complained of the "difficulties in carrying out two forms of demobilization side by side." One problem was the early repatriation of veteran camp personnel, shipped home on the "first over, first back" policy, which left the camps in the hands of unskilled, inexperienced administrators.[51]

Under the circumstances, trouble was inevitable. There were several outbreaks, but the worst occurred on 4 and 5 March at Kinmel Park, a staging camp near Liverpool, reserved exclusively for the use of non-Corps troops awaiting transportation to Canada. Kinmel Park was a powder keg: 15,000 impatient men in a camp that left much to be desired. There had been no sailings since 25 February, and feelings were running high over the rumoured diversion of ships to embark the Third Division. The tension exploded in two days of rioting involving as many as 800 soldiers. Five were killed and twenty-three injured; damage to the camp exceeded £69,000. The shock waves rocked the Canadian military establishment.

No one was more alarmed than General Currie. The press reports were appalling, and Currie "concluded that the whole Third Canadian Division had rioted." Hastening to London, he found otherwise. "It was a great relief to find out...that no Third Canadian Division troops were involved but that the troublemakers were men of the Forestry Corps and Railway troops," all of whom were outside his jurisdiction.[52]

Even more serious was the riot's impact on Canadian-British relations. Currie, for one, was indignant at the apparent willingness of the English newspapers to smear the reputation of Canadian combat troops, none of whom had been involved. "The reports," he fumed, "were very grossly and shamefully exaggerated, disclosing an attitude on the part of the English papers which, to say the least, is very much to be regretted, and will cause bitter feelings." He was right. Canada's prime minister, Sir Robert Borden, attributed the irresponsibility of the press "to that thoughtless stupidity which one so often encounters on this side of the Atlantic." Sir Edward Kemp fully concurred, adding that "it was this sort of thing that lost the thirteen colonies to Great Britain." What was even more infuriating was the wild and lurid reporting of this and other incidents involving Canadians, when far bigger and graver riots and mutinies were taking place in British camps, news of which was successfully suppressed by the censors.[53]

There were thirteen disturbances in Canadian camps in England between November 1918 and June 1919. All but three involved troops outside the Canadian Corps, that is, men going home on the basis of "first over, first back." The three episodes involving Corps troops were minor, all of them occurring at Witley. The biggest took place on 13 April, when 300 men of the 26th (New Brunswick) Battalion protested the quality and quantity of food that was being served in the camp; an inquiry later found their complaint to be "justified." There were no casualties in any of the Corps disturbances.[54]

Demobilization was a triumph, both for Currie and for the Canadian Corps. As Currie forecast, discipline made the difference between efficiency and chaos, and his belief in the esprit de corps of the battalions was amply vindicated. The potential for serious trouble undoubtedly existed; that it failed to materialize is a tribute to Canadian discipline.

The strains were just as pronounced among the formations on the Continent, awaiting their turn to be sent to England and then home. At least the troops in England were en route to Canada; as uncomfortable as the camps might have been, the average stay for Corps units was only twenty-nine days, fourteen of which were spent on leave. The men still in France and Belgium were understandably impatient. In February, for example, members of the Fourth Division signed a petition protesting the demobialization process. General Currie personally addressed the entire division, explaining at length the reasons for his chosen policy. A powerful public speaker, Currie was very persuasive, "and the men who had signed this letter asked permission to withdraw it. They did it without any suggestion from him." The Fourth Division, last in line, did not begin embarking for England until 25 April. Even in the First Division, which had completed its move by the end of March, there was cause for some concern. As the division's commander, General Macdonell, noted, his "men's nerves are a little over strained & they are anxious at delays, but behaviour has been top hole taking it all in all."[55]

The key was to keep the men comfortable and busy. Comfort was no problem; the accommodations for the Canadians in Belgium were excellent. A medical officer, Major Harold McGill, called the billets "the best we have ever had." Sports played a vital role in keeping the men's minds occupied. One of the favourites was boxing, which at least one battalion used to defuse tensions between officers and the other ranks: at every match, two officers were "put into the ring with instructions to knock hell out of each other." Education was also important. Soldiers wishing to improve themselves could take any of a vast array of courses, with expert instruction, through the Khaki University, of which the Canadians were pioneers. As long ago as December 1917, General Currie had authorized the creation of the University of Vimy Ridge. Initially an experiment in the Third Division, then expanded to the entire Corps, Currie realized the need to keep the troops occupied "during the interval that must elapse between the conclusion of peace and their return to Canada." The British and Australians were so impressed that they set up similar programs, which were later amalgamated to become the Khaki University.[56]

There were other distractions, of a sort that added nothing to Canada's reputation. The Canadian Corps had the dubious distinction, during February and March 1919, of having the highest incidence of venereal disease among comparable formations in the area; there were twice as many cases of VD among the Canadians as among the Australians. Currie, denouncing VD as "a sin before God," instituted compulsory lectures to remind all ranks of what he called "the moral and physical evil of sexual immorality." More effective was his warning that "no person suffering from venereal disease will be returned to Canada and demobilized until all trace of the disease has disappeared."[57]

Despite the delays and disappointments, demobilization of the Canadian Corps was completed quickly. Units of the last major formation, the Fourth Division, were on their way home by May. By then, there were so few Corps troops available that Currie had to scramble to find 2500 men to take part in a 3 May parade by colonial forces through the streets of London. For the victory parade on 19 July, to mark the signing of the Treaty of Versailles three weeks earlier, Currie could lead only a tiny Canadian contingent of 200. The remaining veterans in England were those still recovering from war wounds; the vast majority were non-Corps troops, mostly conscripts.

Among the last to leave was the Corps commander himself. Closing his headquarters in Belgium on 23 April, General Currie relocated to London, where he found himself the toast of the town. There were dinners in his honour and garden parties at Buckingham Palace, and an honorary degree from Cambridge University. On 9 August, Currie boarded the liner *Caronia* at Liverpool. Nearly five years had passed since he had last set eyes on Canada. Currie's ship sailed at midnight on the ninth, bringing to a close one of the most remarkable chapters in Canadian military history.

11 THE FRUITS OF VICTORY

The soldiers had done their part to achieve peace. Now, it was up to the politicians to make it meaningful and lasting. Hopes were high when a peace conference opened in Paris in early 1919, but it was soon bogged down amid the confused and conflicting war aims of the victorious allies, and undermined by the overpowering desire to punish Germany for causing the conflict.

One politician, however, attended the conference with a clear objective in mind. The Canadian prime minister, Sir Robert Borden, was not so much concerned with reparations and revenge as he was with Canada's place among the nations of the world. It rankled that, in August 1914, when Britain had declared war, Canada and the rest of the Empire automatically went to war, too. Confederation in 1867 had given Canada control of her internal affairs, but foreign relations remained the exclusive preserve of Great Britain, which spoke on behalf of the entire Empire. No longer satisfied with semi-colonial status, Prime Minister Borden was now seeking nothing less than international recognition of his country's sovereignty. Its magnificent war record would be the vehicle to carry him to his goal.

Sir Robert did not look like a man of vision. His silver hair parted in the middle, the moustachioed Borden presented a grandfatherly visage that was rather misleading. The even-tempered, sixty-four-year-old Halifax lawyer was a very determined man. "I conceive that the battle for Canadian liberty and autonomy," he had declared in May 1917, "is being fought today on the plains of France and Belgium." The Canadian Army Corps had given his countrymen "a new revelation of patriotism," he said. "The nation is clothed with new dignity." Canada, Borden believed, now had a "separate individuality" and "will power of her own." Canada's wartime performance, exemplified by the exploits of the last hundred days, was, in his eyes, "ultimate proof of the maturity of Canadian nationhood."[1]

Borden's intentions had been formed some time before. As early as the summer of 1915, when he made his first wartime visit to Britain, Borden had suggested that the dominions should have a say in the conduct of the Empire's foreign affairs. This was viewed in some quarters as heretical, since London traditionally spoke for the Empire, and the colonial secretary, Canadian-born Andrew Bonar Law, actively sought to discourage such talk. "He feared," Borden noted, "that having a voice in foreign affairs might commit the Dominions to a larger naval and military expenditure than they would care to undertake." Law was also unenthusiastic about Borden's request for "more explicit information from time to time respecting the conduct of the war." It was, in Law's opinion, "very undesirable that the question should be raised."[2]

Borden was not easily deterred. He found it infuriating that the British were orchestrating the Empire's war effort "without the slightest consultation with the authorities of this Dominion." It was also humiliating that the Canadian government was forced to rely almost solely on "just what information could be gleaned from the daily press"—hardly a reliable source. To back his case, Borden took the unusual, and arbitrary, step of opening 1916 with a startling announcement. In his New Year's message to the nation, Borden stated that his government's goal was to put half a million men into uniform. "It can hardly be expected," he wrote on 4 January, "that we shall put 400,000 or 500,000 men in the field and willingly accept the position of having no more voice and receiving no more consideration than if we were toy automata."[3]

The British were pleased with the pledge, but more than a year passed before any meaningful consultation with the dominions took place. It was initiated by David Lloyd George, who emerged as prime minister of Britain following a political crisis in December 1916. Just five days after taking office, Lloyd George wrote a rather significant letter to Walter Long, Law's successor at the Colonial Office:

> I am convinced that we should take the Dominions into our counsel in a much larger measure than we have hitherto done in our prosecution of the War. They have made enormous sacrifices, but we have held no conference with them as to either the objects of the War or the methods of carrying it out. . . . As we must receive even more substantial support from them before we can hope to pull through, it is important that they should feel that they have a share in our councils as well as in our burdens. We want more men from them. We can hardly ask them to make another great recruiting effort unless it is accompanied by an invitation to come over to discuss the situation with us.[4]

Subsequently, invitations were issued to the dominion prime ministers to attend an imperial war conference in April 1917, at which each prime minister would become a member of Lloyd George's war cabinet.

Prime Minister Borden was delighted. The creation of the Imperial War Cabinet was "an amazing development," he said, and a tribute to Lloyd George's "imagination, courage and initiative. For the first time the mother country and the Dominions met in the great inquest of the

Commonwealth which, for convenience, was designated as a Cabinet. In that Cabinet, Great Britain presided, but the Dominions met her on equal terms."[5]

There can be little doubt that Lloyd George and Borden had vastly different expectations of the Imperial War Cabinet. For the British prime minister, it was a thinly disguised effort to milk more manpower from the dominions. But Borden saw it as an important step for the dominions from semi-colonial status to autonomy, and on 16 April 1917 he moved a resolution urging "full recognition of the Dominions as autonomous nations of an Imperial Commonwealth" and seeking for them "an adequate voice in foreign policy and in foreign relations." With the passage of Resolution IX, declared Borden, "a new era has dawned."[6]

Yet Lloyd George went even further the following year. So great was his desire to draw on the dominions' reserves of manpower that he decided to name the prime ministers to a special subcommittee of the Imperial War Cabinet. This would give the dominions "a direct voice in the conduct of the war, and in the plans of campaigns, so far as the War Cabinet had power to determine them."[7] However, the prime ministers exerted little influence on the outcome of the war: they ended their meeting in the summer of 1918 by approving plans to continue campaigning in 1919, which subsequent events on the Western Front rendered obsolete. But Lloyd George had created a monster by heightening the expectations of the dominion governments, who clearly were not going to be satisfied with the status quo of subordination to the policy-makers in London.

By late October 1918, with the war's end imminent, Lloyd George wired Borden to come to Europe, "in order to participate in the deliberations which will determine the line to be taken at these conferences [i.e., the preliminaries to the Paris peace conference] by the British Delegates." This surprised and disappointed Borden, who had been anticipating separate and distinct Canadian representation in Paris. If the intention was to subordinate Canada as part of a British Empire delegation, he was not really interested, and told Lloyd George so:

> There is need of serious consideration as to representation of the Dominions in the peace negotiations. The Press and people of this country take it for granted that Canada will be represented at the Peace Conferences. I appreciate possible difficulties as to the representation of the Dominions but hope you will keep in mind that certainly a very unfortunate impression would be created and possibly a dangerous feeling might be aroused if these difficulties are not overcome by some solution which will meet the national

spirit of the Canadian people . . . . In a word . . . new conditions must be met by new precedents.[8]

Somewhat dismayed, Lloyd George repeated his request that Borden come to London. While admitting that the Canadian position presented "many difficult problems," these, he said, could not be resolved readily by transatlantic cable. "I should value your presence greatly," he tactfully added.[9]

Borden left for London a few days later. Boarding the liner *Mauritania*, he was still at sea when word of the armistice arrived on 11 November. The celebrations left him with no illusions about what lay ahead. "Now will come the sternest, the most momentous, and the most difficult problems of all," he wrote.[10]

He arrived in London on 17 November. The same day he met with Lloyd George at 10 Downing Street, then spent the evening with the commander of the Canadian Corps, General Currie:

> Currie gave us a most interesting account of the achievements of the Canadian Forces during the preceding few months. During that period they had had a magnificent record, unsurpassed in any previous period of the war. The task which they had undertaken at Cambrai had proved extremely difficult as the Germans fought with great desperation and massed tremendous forces against them.[11]

Currie followed with a long letter detailing the impressive Canadian performance during the last hundred days. Later, he compiled for Borden a lengthy and detailed report on Canadian Corps operations during 1918; most of the report concerned the period 8 August until 11 November.

His dealings with Currie made Borden more determined than ever to gain proper representation for Canada. As he expected, it took a long, tiring battle, beginning on 2 December with an inter-Allied conference to which Canada was not invited. There, it was decided that the five great powers—Britain, France, the United States, Italy, and Japan— would each be entitled to five delegates at the peace conference, while smaller powers would be permitted two delegates apiece. The dominions were snubbed: they would be allowed to join the British delegation "when questions directly affecting them are under consideration."[12]

Borden could scarcely conceal his anger. "To provide that Canada should be called on only when her special interests were in question would be regarded as little better than a mockery," he fumed, realizing that Canada had no special interests that would be raised at the conference. At the very least, he insisted, Canada should be entitled to small-power representation, such as that being permitted of Portugal. Canada had, after all, "lost more men killed in France than Portugal had put into the field."[13]

The problem was that no one understood the status of the dominions. Were they colonies or independent nations? They were neither, of course, and Borden did not need to be told that his problems were rooted in Canada's "anamolous position; a nation that is not a nation. It is about time to alter it." As his frustrations increased through December 1918, Borden concluded: "I am beginning to feel more and more that in the end, and perhaps sooner than later, Canada must assume full sovereignty."[14]

His initial inclination was to pack up and go home. Bluntly telling Lloyd George that "I had not come to take part in light comedy," Borden changed his mind after finding that he had strong support from his fellow dominion prime ministers, South Africa's Louis Botha—"a man of broad, generous instincts," said Borden—and Australia's William Hughes. The dominions dug in their heels, flatly declaring that they would not settle for anything less than representation accorded small powers. Prime Minister Lloyd George agreed to pursue the matter at a 12 January 1919 meeting with his confrères, President Woodrow Wilson of the U.S. and France's prime minister, Georges Clemenceau. "Clemenceau, who hesitated at first, warmly concurred," Borden approvingly remarked, "when informed that the Dominions had put one million men into the field." President Wilson was not impressed. He was willing to allot the dominions a single delegate each, but Borden—who later complained, rather unfairly, that Wilson was "sometimes obstinate as a mule"—rejected the proposal.[15]

Borden could be just as obstinate himself. Backed by Botha and Hughes, the Canadian prime minister reiterated the dominions' intention to "stand firm and insist on [the] same representation as Belgium." Their determination paid off. The next day, Wilson bowed to pressure and agreed that Canada, Australia, South Africa, and India could each have two delegates, and New Zealand one. Borden was quite pleased. "The path upon which the Dominions advanced to complete representation at the Peace Conference," he later wrote, "was at times rough and thorny.... It is not at all surprising that difficulties arose, for the status of the British Dominions was not fully realized by foreign nations...." But, as he would soon discover, the fight was far from over.[16]

Reminders of the valiant Canadian contribution to the war effort were never far away. As military adviser to the Canadian delegation to the peace conference, General Currie made several visits to Paris in early 1919, reporting regularly on the progress of demobilization of the Canadian Corps. The two men cultivated a close relationship. On 14

February, Borden took Currie to a preliminary session at the Quai d'Orsay, the French Foreign Office, at which "President Wilson read the proposed constitution of the League of Nations." Currie called it "a most interesting occasion," but Borden dismissed it as "wearisome." On 5 March, Currie and his wife hosted a luncheon in Borden's honour, afterward presenting the prime minister with a detailed report on Canadian operations in 1918. "It is a glorious history," Borden told his diary, "and I am extremely proud of it." Later that month, Currie conducted Borden over a two-day tour of the Canadian battlefields in Belgium and northern France. "The visit will always be a happy memory, and an inspiration as well," Borden wrote Currie.[17]

Borden needed all the inspiration he could get. Returning to Paris, where the peace conference was finally under way, the prime minister found himself confronted by "one d—d thing after another."[18] Although Borden was given considerable responsibility—chairing the British Empire delegation in Lloyd George's absence, for example—it soon became evident that the conference was so much window-dressing. The small powers were effectively excluded from the decision-making process; most of the major decisions were being made in private by the so-called "Council of Ten," the leaders and foreign ministers of the five great powers.

But there were things worth fighting for. Two issues that concerned Canada were the creation of a pair of worldwide bodies, the League of Nations and the International Labour Organization (ILO). Borden was a strong supporter of the League, in particular:

> Even if I thought the proposal for the League of Nations absolutely impracticable, and that statesmen a hundred years hence would laugh at it as a vain attempt to accomplish the impossible, nevertheless, I would support the movement because of its supreme importance and because it might succeed.[19]

It is easy to imagine Borden's reaction when he discovered that Canada, while being granted membership in both bodies, was to be denied the right to sit on the executive councils of both. Protracted negotiations ensued, but Borden found himself stonewalled by American and French fears that giving way to the dominions would enable the British, through the Empire, to dominate these organizations. This was especially galling when Borden heard that the British and Americans were ready to sign a treaty guaranteeing France's security in the face of future German aggression. It was the last straw, as far as Borden was concerned, and he embodied his argument in a memorandum to Lloyd George on 6 May:

As for Canada's effort in this struggle for democracy it speaks for itself. She has not asked for representation on the Council [of the League of Nations] or in the governing body [of the ILO] unless it is accorded by the voice of the other members of the League and the convention. She has raised no objection to the nomination of Spain and Brazil, of whom one was at least neutral and the other took no active part in the war. But she cannot admit disqualification or accept a position inferior to that of the smaller States.

It is now proposed that Canada should become a party to a treaty by which she shall undertake to engage in active warlike operations against Germany in case that country at any time in the future should be guilty of aggression against France. I am not aware that any similar undertaking is proposed for Spain or Brazil or Greece or Belgium, or for any of the smaller states whose representatives are not debarred from election to the Council of the League or to the governing body of the Labour Convention. Canada is asked to make way for all these states except when effort and sacrifice are demanded; then, but not till then, she is accorded full and even prior representation. She is to be in the first line of battle but not even in the back seat of the Council. The submission of such a proposal to our Parliament would, in my opinion, be wholly futile. Indeed I am convinced that it would be bitterly resented not only by Parliament but by the vast majority of the Canadian people.[20]

Borden's forceful argument, based as it was on Canada's impressive war effort, carried the day. That afternoon, Lloyd George, Clemenceau, and Wilson signed a document, drafted by Borden, ensuring that "representation of the self-governing Dominions of the British Empire may be selected or named as members of the Council," of both the League and the ILO.[21]

The signing and ratification of the final treaty caused more headaches. As early as 12 March, Borden had asked "that all treaties and conventions resulting from the Peace Conference should be so drafted as to enable the Dominions to become Parties and Signatories thereto." The Treaty of Versailles fell a bit short of expectations: Britain signed on behalf of the British Empire; Canada and the other dominions were allowed separate signatures below. Arthur Sifton, the cabinet minister who co-signed for Canada, called the arrangement "absurd," and "preclud[ed], if my interpretation is correct, any necessity for signature on the part of Canada at all." But the separate signature was more important than Sifton realized. If nothing else it was, as one historian has noted, "a clarification of their [the dominions'] autonomous position in foreign affairs."[22]

Borden did not remain in Paris for the signing ceremony, held on 28 June. Having obtained his personal and national goals, the prime minister departed for Canada in mid-May. Pressing domestic affairs awaited him, and he had been away from home for six months. In any case, the final treaty did not greatly interest him. It was, he observed, "so long and so complicated and deals with so many subjects and has been left so much to experts that no human being knows precisely what it is." Borden left Sifton to sign it, along with a fellow cabinet minister, Charles Doherty. He went home having won the admiration of a good number of British officials, one of whom noted that "when Borden gets his toes in, he usually shoves hard."[23]

A final constitutional battle awaited the prime minister. The Treaty of Versailles was introduced in the British House of Commons on 3 July, and the colonial secretary, Lord Milner, cabled Borden that he hoped it would be ready for the King's signature "before [the] end of July." Borden at once realized that Canadian ratification would be rendered meaningless the moment King George signed it. In his reply to Milner, Borden noted that he had been promised the opportunity to place the treaty before Canada's Parliament. This could not be done quickly, he pointed out, since he had not yet received a copy of the treaty, and Parliament was prorogued at the time. "Kindly advise how you expect to accomplish ratification on behalf of whole Empire before [the] end [of] July."[24]

A flurry of transatlantic telegrams ensued. Eventually, the British agreed to postpone ratification by the mother Parliament until Canada had ratified it. Swift approval followed. A special session of the Canadian Parliament was summoned on 1 September. After a somewhat irrelevant debate, the House of Commons approved it on 12 September, eight days after the Senate.

Canada's place in the world had been secured. It had been, as Borden pointed out, "largely a question of sentiment," but it was, nonetheless, significant:

[I]n this, the greatest of all wars, in which the world's property, the world's justice, in short the world's future destiny were at stake, Canada led the democracies of both the American continents. Her resolve had given inspiration, her sacrifices had been conspicuous, her effort unabated to the end. The same indomitable spirit which made her capable of that effort and sacrifice made equally incapable of accepting at the Peace Conference, in the League of Nations, or elsewhere, a status inferior to that accorded to nations less amply endowed in wealth, resources and population, no more complete in their sovereignty and far less conspicuous in their sacrifice.[25]

Whatever its reputation elsewhere, the Treaty of Versailles must be counted among the vital documents in Canadian history.* It offered, for the first time, tacit recognition of Canada's status among the independent nations of the world, recognition that was formalized in the 1931 Statute of Westminster. The statute granted full autonomy to the dominions, though it merely, as Borden noted, "placed the legalistic seal upon what had already been established by resolution and by constitutional convention." He later observed that "Canada had got nothing out of the War but recognition."[27]

The sacrifices by Canadian soldiers on the blood-stained battlefields of Belgium and France, carried to such noble and heart-breaking extremes in the final hundred days of the Great War, had not been in vain.

---

* Few documents have achieved the notoriety of the Treaty of Versailles. Historians generally condemn its crushing economic terms, notably the reparations which, if the treaty were in force today, Germany would continue to pay until 1988. By the same token, it is often cited as a leading cause of World War II. Its flaws notwithstanding, the treaty ultimately failed because of Allied unwillingness, or inability—or both—to enforce it.

And, had the tables been turned, the Germans would have been no more generous toward the Allies. The proof of that statement lies in the Treaty of Brest-Litovsk, which Germany imposed on Russia in March 1918. There were no negotiations; it was a dictated peace, and one of the most rapacious in history. Under that treaty, the Germans deprived Russia of "34% of her population, 32% of her agricultural land, 85% of her beet-sugar land, 54% of her industrial undertakings, and 89% of her coal mines."[26] It was ludicrous, in these circumstances, for the Germans to have expected the Allies to show them mercy at Paris.

APPENDIX ONE:
THE THIRD BATTLE
OF MONS

The First Battle of Mons was fought in August 1914.

The Second Battle of Mons took place on 10-11 November 1918.

The Third Battle of Mons occurred in a courtroom in Cobourg, Ontario, in 1929.

A few months after the conclusion of the Great War, Mons became the subject of a seemingly short-lived controversy. It was inspired by Sir Sam Hughes, the former minister of militia and defence, now a disgraced and disgruntled backbencher who still enjoyed considerable stature, in the country at large as well as in Parliament. On 4 March 1919, Hughes mounted the first of a series of slanderous attacks on Sir Arthur Currie, the commander of the Canadian Corps, pointing to the capture of Mons—which he described as "a little one-horse town"—on the last day of the war as an example of Currie's desire for personal glory at the cost of catastrophic casualties.

> I have just this to say about Mons. Were I in authority, the officer who, four hours before the Armistice was signed, although he had been notified beforehand that the Armistice was to begin at eleven o'clock, ordered the attack on Mons thus needlessly sacrificing the lives of Canadian soldiers, would be tried summarily by court martial and punished so far as the law would allow. There was no glory to be gained, and you cannot find one Canadian soldier returning from France who will not curse the name of the officer who ordered the attack on Mons.[1]

It was a shocking abuse of parliamentary privilege. Significantly, Hughes was careful not to repeat his accusations outside the House of Commons.

Currie counter-attacked later that year. Newly promoted to full general—the first Canadian ever to hold that rank—Sir Arthur went on a cross-country speaking tour soon after his return from Europe. A powerful public speaker, Currie enthralled enormous, enthusiastic audiences with a detailed description of the achievements of the Canadian Corps. "Owing to censorship regulations," he wrote a friend, "there is a great deal of which they are ignorant, and they seem anxious to know. What particularly impresses them is the value of the battles which our troops won."[2] Although he never directly addressed the charges made by Sam Hughes, he did set the record straight, stressing that Mons had been captured hours before word of the armistice reached his headquarters. By the time Currie completed his tour, it appeared that he had laid to rest the Mons controversy.

Unfortunately, such was not the case. On 13 June 1927, a newspaper in Port Hope, Ontario, the *Evening Guide*, published a front-page editorial resurrecting the charges made by Hughes. The occasion was the unveiling of a bronze plaque in Mons to commemorate the city's liberation by the Canadians on 11 November 1918. However, the *Guide* suggested that this was "an event which might properly be allowed to pass into oblivion, very much regretted than glorified."

> There was much waste of human life during the war, enormous loss of lives which should not have taken place. But it is doubtful whether in any case there was a more deliberate and useless waste of human life than in the so-called capture of Mons.
>
> It was the last day; and the last hour; and almost the last minute, when to glorify the Canadian Head Quarters staff the Commander-in-Chief conceived the mad idea that it would be a fine thing to say that the Canadians had fired the last shot in the Great War; and had captured the last German entrenchment before the bugles sounded eleven o'clock, when the armistice which had been signed by both sides would begin officially....
>
> Of course, the town was taken just at the last minute before the official moment of the armistice arrived. But the penalty that was paid in useless waste of human life was appalling. There are hearts in Port Hope stricken with sorrow and mourning through this worse than drunken spree by Canadian Headquarters. Veterans who had passed through the whole four years of war lie buried in Belgian cemeteries as the result of the "glories of Mons"....

Noting that Currie was no longer in the military, that he had been "permitted to sink into comparative obscurity in a civilian position as [principal] of McGill University" in Montreal, the editorial concluded: "Canadian valour won Mons, but it was by such shocking useless waste of human life that it is an eternal disgrace to the Headquarters that directed operations."[3]

General Currie was mortified. "I did not think there was any one at this time, nearly ten years after the war, who did not know the truth about Mons." He quickly made up his mind to sue for libel, though he was advised against it. Port Hope was in Sam Hughes country: he was buried at Lindsay, a short distance to the north, and though he had been dead since 1921, Sir Sam's memory burned brightly in these parts.

Currie was warned "that it would be impossible to get a favourable verdict from a jury such as would be chosen." Friends also pointed to the newspaper's tiny circulation, barely a thousand. But Currie was determined to seek justice. "This is not only my fight," he wrote, "but the fight of the Canadian Corps, particularly those who acted as leaders in any capacity from Corporals to Generals."[4]

Currie claimed damages of $50,000 from the two men who were responsible for the article. One was Frederick W. Wilson, the owner and editor of the *Evening Guide*, the other was W.T.R. Preston, a prominent Liberal party hack who had fought conscription during the war and, in earlier days, stuffed ballot boxes. Wilson and Preston were unrepentant. When they repeatedly refused to retract their statements, the stage was set for one of the most sensational court cases in Canadian history.

The trial opened on Monday, 16 April 1928, in Cobourg, just east of Port Hope, with Mr. Justice Hugh Rose of the Supreme Court of Ontario presiding. The courtroom was packed with witnesses and observers, in addition to nineteen reporters who filed a daily average of 72,000 words, describing the trial for newspapers across Canada and as far away as England and Australia.

Currie anticipated an unpleasant experience, and he was right. The defence, he knew, would "introduce as much irrelevant matter as possible, in order to besmirch what little reputation I have." He was aware that, as is often the case in a libel lawsuit, the plaintiff is in fact the defendant; although the onus is, theoretically, on the defence to prove the veracity of the statements in question, the plaintiff is placed in the position of proving them wrong. This is what happened in Cobourg. The defence, under the direction of Wilson's Toronto lawyer, Frank Regan—Preston chose to represent himself at the trial, but from start to finish, Regan did most of the work for the defence—began by attempting to implicate Currie in a conspiracy to cover up the real number of Canadian casualties in the last days of the war. When the judge finally put a stop to it, Regan introduced a series of witnesses to prove Currie's unpopularity among his soldiers. The judge stopped that, too, and Regan responded by dredging up embarrassing aspects of Currie's personal finances and questioning battlefield decisions made as far back as 1915. No attempt was made to prove the accuracy of the article, as the judge reminded Regan many times, but long hours and days were spent trying to introduce countless irrelevancies. The effort failed, but it was heartbreaking for Currie to sit in court and listen to deceitful and dishonest attempts to portray him as a general who, in his words, "occupied a position for which I had not been sufficiently trained and which I was not competent to fill."[5]

The trial climaxed on Friday, 27 April, when Currie took the witness stand. For seven hours, he sparred with defence counsel Regan who, among other things, ridiculed Currie for being in the bathtub when told of the armistice on the morning of 11 November. Currie refused to be browbeaten and bullied, as Regan had handled other witnesses—including his own, for which he had been reprimanded by Mr. Justice Rose! One memorable clash stemmed from Currie's proud claim that the Canadian Corps had met and defeated one-quarter of the German army during the last hundred days of the war. "Don't you think, Sir Arthur, that in the dying hours of the war, you might have spared your men a trifle more than you did?"

"No," countered Currie. "You are the man that is suggesting that those men who did that should lie down and quit within two days of the final victory."

"I didn't say that."

"Oh, yes," insisted Currie, "you say spare them, you say quit."

"I don't mean to lie down and quit."

"Well, that is what you are suggesting."

"No, it isn't."

"Yes, it is," asserted an angry Currie. "You would have them disobey orders; you would have them mutiny, practically; you would have them guilty of treason...and act in an unsoldierly way, right at the very last. Those were not the men who did that sort of thing."[6]

On Tuesday, 2 May, the case went to the jury. After deliberating for three hours and thirty-nine minutes, it brought back a verdict of guilty and awarded Currie $500. Currie was later told that the jurors opted for the modest amount, not because they believed anything the defendants had said or written, but in the belief that "you might get that, but would fail to get a larger amount." While Currie's many supporters were doubtless disappointed by it, and his detractors consoled, the award was considerably inflated when costs were later added, to $5737.53. And the jurors' doubts about the defendants' ability to pay were justified: Currie collected only $5229.09 from Fred Wilson, whose paper was pushed to the brink of bankruptcy. Preston, it seems, paid nothing at all.[7]

The verdict was appealed later that year, but it was rejected. Chief Justice F.R. Latchford ruled "that nothing had taken place to warrant a new trial." The only error in the proceedings, in his view, was that Mr. Justice Rose "had allowed too much latitude to the defendant's counsel."[8]

General Currie had triumphed, as he had done so many times before on the battlefields of Europe. The case was, and remains, unique in that it is the only time a military operation has been subjected to scrutiny by a civilian jury in Canada. But the cost of victory was high. Soon after his return to Montreal, Currie suffered a light stroke.

Normally a robust man, he never did recover his health after the Cobourg trial. He was often ill in the years that followed, culminating in a fatal stroke in November 1933, at the age of only fifty-seven.[9]

APPENDIX TWO: ORDER OF BATTLE, CANADIAN ARMY CORPS, 11 NOVEMBER 1918

General Officer Commanding Lieut.-Gen. Sir A.W. Currie
Brigadier-General, General Staff Brig.-Gen. R.J.F. Hayter
Deputy Adjutant and Quartermaster-General Brig.-Gen. G.J. Farmar
General Officer Commanding Royal Artillery Maj.-Gen. E.W.B. Morrison
Chief Engineer Maj.-Gen. W.B. Lindsay
General Officer Commanding, Canadian Machine-Gun Corps Brig.-Gen. R. Brutinel
General Officer Commanding, Heavy Artillery Brig.-Gen. A.G.L. McNaughton

Corps Troops

CAVALRY
Canadian Light Horse
RNWMP Squadron

ARTILLERY
Royal Canadian Horse Artillery Brigade
8th Army Brigade, Canadian Field Artillery (CFA)
    24th, 30th, 32nd Field Batteries
    43rd Howitzer Battery
"E" Anti-Aircraft Battery

Corps Heavy Artillery
1st Brigade, Canadian Garrison Artillery (CGA)
    1st, 3rd, 7th, 9th Siege Batteries
2nd Brigade, CGA
    1st, 2nd Heavy Batteries
    2nd, 4th, 5th, 6th Siege Batteries
3rd Brigade, CGA
    8th, 10th, 11th, 12th Siege Batteries

Fifth Divisional Artillery
13th Brigade, CFA

52nd, 53rd, 55th Field Batteries
51st Howitzer Battery
14th Brigade, CFA
60th, 61st, 66th Field Batteries
58th Howitzer Battery

ENGINEERS
1st, 2nd, 3rd, 4th, 5th Army Troops Companies
Anti-Aircraft Searchlight Company
3rd Tunnelling Company
Corps Survey Section
1st, 2nd Tramways Companies

MACHINE-GUN CORPS
1st, 2nd Motor Machine-Gun Brigades

ARMY SERVICE CORPS
1st, 2nd, 3rd, 4th Divisional Mechanical Transport Companies
Corps Troops Mechanical Transport Company
Engineers Mechanical Transport Company
Motor Machine-Gun Mechanical Transport Company

MEDICAL CORPS
Numbers 1, 2, 3, 4 Casualty Clearing Stations
Number 7 (Cavalry) Field Ambulance
Number 14 Field Ambulance

MISCELLANEOUS
Canadian Cyclist Battalion
Corps Signal Company

Divisional Troops

FIRST CANADIAN DIVISION: Maj.-Gen. A.C. Macdonell
First Infantry Brigade (Brig.-Gen. W.A. Griesbach)
    1st (Western Ontario) Battalion
    2nd (Eastern Ontario) Battalion
    3rd (Toronto Regiment) Battalion
    4th (Central Ontario) Battalion

Second Infantry Brigade (Brig.-Gen. R.P. Clark)
    5th (Western Cavalry) Battalion
    7th (1st British Columbia Regiment) Battalion
    8th (90th Winnipeg Rifles) Battalion
    10th (Canadians) Battalion

Third Infantry Brigade (Brig.-Gen. G.S. Tuxford)
    13th (Royal Highlanders of Canada) Battalion
    14th (Royal Montreal Regiment) Battalion
    15th (48th Highlanders of Canada) Battalion
    16th (Canadian Scottish) Battalion

1st Brigade, CFA
    1st, 3rd, 4th Field Batteries
    2nd Howitzer Battery
2nd Brigade, CFA
    5th, 6th, 7th Field Batteries
    48th Howitzer Battery
1st Brigade, Canadian Engineers
    1st, 2nd, 3rd Battalions
1st Battalion, Canadian Machine-Gun Corps
Numbers 1, 2, 3 Field Ambulances

SECOND CANADIAN DIVISION: Maj.-Gen. Sir H.E. Burstall
Fourth Canadian Infantry Brigade (Brig.-Gen. G.E. McCuaig)
    18th (Western Ontario) Battalion
    19th (Central Ontario) Battalion
    20th (Central Ontario) Battalion
    21st (Eastern Ontario) Battalion

Fifth Infantry Brigade (Brig.-Gen. T.L. Tremblay)
    22nd (French Canadian) Battalion
    24th (Victoria Rifles of Canada) Battalion
    25th (Nova Scotia Rifles) Battalion
    26th (New Brunswick) Battalion

Sixth Infantry Brigade (Brig.-Gen. A. Ross)
    27th (Winnipeg) Battalion
    28th (Northwest) Battalion
    29th (Vancouver) Battalion
    31st (Alberta) Battalion

5th Brigade, CFA
    17th, 18th, 20th Field Batteries
    23rd Howitzer Battery
6th Brigade, CFA
    15th, 16th, 25th Field Batteries
    22nd Howitzer Battery

2nd Brigade, Canadian Engineers
    4th, 5th, 6th Battalions
2nd Battalion, Canadian Machine-Gun Corps

Numbers 4, 5, 6 Field Ambulances

THIRD CANADIAN DIVISION: Maj.-Gen. F.O.W. Loomis
Seventh Infantry Brigade (Brig.-Gen. J.A. Clark)
    Royal Canadian Regiment
    Princess Patricia's Canadian Light Infantry
    42nd (Royal Highlanders of Canada) Battalion
    49th (Edmonton Regiment) Battalion

Eighth Infantry Brigade (Brig.-Gen. D.C. Draper)
    1st Canadian Mounted Rifles
    2nd Canadian Mounted Rifles
    4th Canadian Mounted Rifles
    5th Canadian Mounted Rifles

Ninth Infantry Brigade (Brig.-Gen. D.M. Ormond)
    43rd (Cameron Highlanders of Canada) Battalion
    52nd (New Ontario) Battalion
    58th (Central Ontario) Battalion
    116th (Ontario County) Battalion

9th Brigade, CFA
    31st, 33rd, 45th Field Batteries
    36th Howitzer Battery

10th Brigade, CFA
    38th, 39th, 40th Field Batteries
    35th Howitzer Battery

3rd Brigade, Canadian Engineers
    7th, 8th, 9th Battalions

3rd Battalion, Canadian Machine-Gun Corps

Numbers 8, 9, 10 Field Ambulances

FOURTH CANADIAN DIVISION: Maj.-Gen. Sir D. Watson
Tenth Infantry Brigade (Brig.-Gen. J.M. Ross)
    44th (New Brunswick) Battalion
    46th (South Saskatchewan) Battalion
    47th (Western Ontario) Battalion
    50th (Calgary) Battalion

Eleventh Infantry Brigade (Brig.-Gen. V.W. Odlum)
    54th (Central Ontario) Battalion
    75th (Mississauga) Battalion
    87th (Canadian Grenadier Guards) Battalion
    102nd (Central Ontario) Battalion

Twelfth Infantry Brigade (Brig.-Gen. J. Kirkaldy)
   38th (Ottawa) Battalion
   72nd (Seaforth Highlanders of Canada) Battalion
   78th (Winnipeg Grenadiers) Battalion
   85th (Nova Scotia Highlanders) Battalion

3rd Brigade, CFA
   10th, 11th, 12th Field Batteries
   9th Howitzer Battery
4th Brigade, CFA
   13th, 19th, 27th Field Batteries
   21st Howitzer Battery

4th Battalion, Canadian Engineers
   10th, 11th, 12th Battalions

4th Battalion, Canadian Machine-Gun Corps

Numbers 11, 12, 13 Field Ambulances

ACKNOWLEDGMENTS

It would be impossible to complete an undertaking such as *Spearhead to Victory* without a lot of help from a lot of people and institutions. Hurtig Publishers again displayed their professionalism and competence. It was, as always, a pleasure to deal with Mel Hurtig, his editor-in-chief, Elizabeth Munroe, and Jean Wilson, my editor.

But this book could never have materialized without the assistance of Alberta Culture. A generous grant enabled me to conduct the lion's share of the research and covered some of my living expenses during completion of the manuscript. As well, I was able to make use of research material compiled under an earlier grant from the Alberta Foundation for the Literary Arts.

I wish to thank the helpful and courteous staff members of the following institutions: Provincial Archives of British Columbia, City of Edmonton Archives, Provincial Archives of Alberta, Glenbow Museum, Provincial Archives of Manitoba, Archives of Ontario, Public Archives Canada, McGill University Archives, Public Archives of Nova Scotia, and Public Archives of Prince Edward Island. Recognition is also due the Canadian Broadcasting Corporation's Program Archives in Toronto, the Imperial War Museum in London, and the Australian War Memorial in Canberra.

The maps were prepared by Patricia Murray, who brought to the task the same scrupulous attention to detail that she displayed in my previous book, *Legacy of Valour*.

And last, but definitely not least, special thanks must go to Cindy Delisle, for her support, encouragement, and interest in my career, generally, and in this book, particularly. She will never know how much she has done for me, or what it means to me.

NOTES

Published sources are identified in the Notes by author and, if necessary, by a brief description of the title of the work, followed by the page number. A Roman numeral preceding the page number indicates the volume number, where applicable. For full details, refer to the Bibliography.

Unpublished sources involve, of necessity, longer entries. The following abbreviations, in alphabetical order, are used for the institutions housing the collections which I consulted:

AO	Archives of Ontario (Toronto)
CBC	Canadian Broadcasting Corporation, Program Archives (Toronto)
CEA	City of Edmonton Archives
GM	Glenbow Museum (Calgary)
MUA	McGill University Archives (Montreal)
PAA	Provincial Archives of Alberta (Edmonton)
PABC	Provincial Archives of British Columbia (Victoria)
PAC	Public Archives Canada (Ottawa)
PAM	Provincial Archives of Manitoba (Winnipeg)
PANS	Public Archives of Nova Scotia (Halifax)

CHAPTER ONE: THE TIDE TURNS

1 Foch 78; Terraine *Haig* 85.
2 Foch 282.
3 Duff Cooper 293, 297; Foch 311.
4 Bean VI/467fn.
5 Foch 339-40.
6 Ibid., 368.
7 Terraine *To Win* 67; *Haig* 450.
8 Terraine *To Win* 84.
9 Maurice 220, 223; Serle 333.
10 Duff Cooper 298, 316, 330-31.
11 Terraine *Haig* 450.
12 Serle 338-39.
13 Foch 376.
14 Terraine *Haig* 451; Maurice 224.
15 Edmonds III/314.
16 Terraine *Haig* 451.
17 Foch 378; Duff Cooper 333.
18 Duff Cooper 333.
19 Edmonds IV/13.
20 Ibid., 12.
21 Terraine *Haig* 452; Duff Cooper 334.
22 Terraine *Haig* 452.

23 Ibid., 454.
24 Bean VI/484, 506; Duff Cooper 298.

CHAPTER TWO: FORGING A POTENT WEAPON

1 Terraine *To Win* 88.
2 PAC, MG30 E100, diary, 11/1/18 (henceforth, Currie diary); Dancocks *Currie* 127.
3 PAC, MG30 E100, Currie/F.O.W. Loomis, 27/1/18.
4 Currie/O.E. McGillicuddy, n.d., loc. cit.
5 Currie/F.O.W. Loomis, 27/1/18, loc. cit.
6 D. Morton *A Peculiar Kind of Politics* (University of Toronto Press, 1982) 153.
7 Blake 279; Urquhart *Currie* 202.
8 PAC, MG30 E100, Currie/OMFC, 7/2/18.
9 Ibid.
10 Livesay 12; Borden II/117.
11 Nicholson *CEF* 232.
12 Terraine *Impacts* 145; PAC, MG30 E75, "Conferences, Visits, Inspections, Ceremonies," n.d.; Currie diary, 23/2/18; PAC, MG30 E100, Currie/ G. Hughes, 29/6/33.
13 *World War* II/1194.
14 Nicholson *CEF* 381.
15 Urquhart *Currie* 381.
16 Borden II/118.
17 PAC, MG30 E20, Volume 1, diary, 1, 4/4/18; Macphail 384.
18 Borden II/118; Nicholson *CEF* 381.
19 Currie diary, 31/3/18, 10/4/18; Pershing 3.
20 PAC, MG30 E100, Volume 50, "Interim Report on the Operations of the Canadian Corps during the Year 1918" (henceforth, Interim Report), 16; Nicholson *CEF* 382.
21 Ottawa *Journal*, 17/3/28; Dancocks *Currie* 137.
22 Currie diary, 11, 18/4/18.
23 Ibid., 14/4/18; Blake 303, 319.
24 Nasmith xx; *Canada in the Great World War* V/127.
25 Interim Report, 20; PAC, MG30 E100, Currie/A. Miller, 4/10/18.
26 PAC, MG30 E100, speech, 19/8/19.
27 Currie diary, 3/5/18.

CHAPTER THREE: "GOD HELP THE BOCHE!"

1 PABC, Crease family papers, Crease/L. Crease, 28/12/18.
2 GM, H.W. McGill papers, McGill/sister, 3/2/18; *Canada in the Great World War* V/63.
3 PAC, MG30 E100, Currie/E. Kemp, 27/2/18.
4 *World War* II/1188-89.
5 PABC, A.S. Baird papers, Baird/mother, 6/2/18.

6 AO, E.W. McQuay papers, J.E. Ritchie/McQuay, 3/3/18.

7 PABC, Crease family papers, A. Crease/L. Crease, 15/4/18.

8 AO, E.W. McQuay papers, C.F.M. McFarland/McQuay, 15/5/18.

9 PAC, MG30 E100, Currie/C. Swayne, 23/1/18; Interim Report 24.

10 Currie diary, 26/5/18; PAC, MG30 E100, Canadian Corps Exercise No. 4, 29/6/18.

11 Nicholson *Gunners* 332; Ogilvie 40.

12 PAC, MG30 E100, Currie/D. Oliver, 15/6/18; Currie/R. Rennie, 7/8/18, loc. cit.

13 Fetherstonhaugh *Montreal* 211.

14 Duff Cooper 299.

15 PAC, MG30 E100, Currie/OMFC, 7/2/18.

16 Currie/O.E. McGillicuddy, n.d., loc. cit.

17 Kerry 162.

18 PAC, MG30 E100, Volume 27, File 7, Currie/O.E. McGillicuddy, n.d.

19 Anderson "Valenciennes" 296; PAC, MG30 E100, Currie/R.E.W. Turner, 29/3/18; Nicholson *CEF* 383.

20 PAC, RG9 III D2, Volume 4792, File 37, Currie/GOCs 1st, 2nd, 3rd, 4th Divisions, 10/4/18.

21 Swettenham *McNaughton* 130.

22 Warren 115.

23 Hahn xxi.

24 W. Bovey, "Sir Arthur Currie: The Corps Commander," *The Legionary* (July 1934) 8; PAC, MG30 E100, "Organization of the Canadian Corps in the Field," n.d.; PAC, RG9 III D2, Volume 4810, File "Casualties."

25 Borden II/140; PAC, MG26H, Volume 268, Part 2, File 82(2), "Memorandum Respecting the Late Sir Arthur Currie," 13/8/34.

26 Worthington 132.

27 PAC, MG30 E100, Currie/C.C. Ballantyre, 25/7/18.

28 Currie diary, 1/7/18.

29 Borden II/141; PAC, MG30 E100, Borden/Currie, 6/7/18.

30 Nicholson *CEF* 385.

31 PAC, MG30 E75, Volume 3, "Conferences, Visits, Inspections, Ceremonies," n.d.

32 Interim Report 27

33 Urquhart *Currie* 234; Liddell Hart *Real* 434.

34 Bean V/417; Hindenburg 330.

35 Terraine *Haig* 453; *Times History* XX 421.

36 Nicholson *CEF* 390fn.

37 Snell 17; Terraine *White Heat* 323.

38 Edmonds IV/20fn; Dancocks *Currie* 153.

39 Weatherbe 358.

40 Nicholson *CEF* 390fn.

41 Wheeler 305.

42 CBC, "Flanders Fields," #14, A. Turner.

43 PAC, MG30 E100, Currie/A. Fraser, 7/12/18; Livesay 21.

44 Serle 341; Urquhart *Currie* 234.

45 Dancocks *Currie* 151-52.

46 CBC, "Flanders Fields," #14.

47 Ibid.

48 PAC, MG30 E32, diary, 3, 5/8/18.

49 CBC, "Flanders Fields," #14, R.H. Camp; Swettenham, *McNaughton* 137.

50 Ibid., 190.

51 Ibid., 138.

52 Ibid., 140.

53 PAC, RG9 III D2, Volume 4789, File 9, "Administrative Arrangements," 14/9/18; Interim Report 32.

54 Interim Report 32; Nicholson *Gunners* 338.

55 Interim Report 32.

56 Snell 29; Topp 203-4.

57 PAC, RG9 III D2, Volume 4154, Folder 6, File 5, Canadian Corps/Seventh Brigade, 5/8/18; *Canada in the Great World War* V/139.

58 Maurice 227; Duff Cooper 338.

59 Edmonds IV/37, 38.

60 Duff Cooper 339; Terraine *Haig* 454.

61 Swettenham *McNaughton* 141.

62 *Canada in the Great World War* V/132.

CHAPTER FOUR: "THE BLACK DAY OF THE GERMAN ARMY"

1 Edmonds III/320.

2 CBC, "Flanders Fields," #14.

3 Interim Report, 35.

4 PAC, RG9 III D2, Volume 4795, File 63, Third Division report, 17/8/18 (henceforth, Third Division report).

5 Fetherstonhaugh *Montreal* 219; Johnston 66; PAC, RG24 C5, Volume 1820, GAQ 5-9.

6 Fetherstonhaugh *RCR* 330; Topp 213; CBC, "Flanders Fields," #14.

7 Swettenham *McNaughton* 144; CBC, "Flanders Fields," #14; Nicholson *CEF* 342.

8 Ibid., 341.

9 Reid 227; Swettenham *McNaughton* 145.

10 CBC, "Flanders Fields," #14.

11 Hopkins 370; *World War* II/1207; Murray 262.

12 PAC, MG30 E69, diary, 8/8/18 (henceforth Watson diary); Wheeler 312; *Letters* I/290; Wright 513; Gunn 134.

13 Murray 263.

14 Ibid.

15 PAC, MG30 E417, unpublished memoirs; Bean VI/650fn.

16 *Letters* I/298.

17 PAC, MG30 E6, Volume 3, File 21, Second Division report, n.d. (henceforth, Second Division report).

18 Fetherstonhaugh *13th* 253.

19 Fetherstonhaugh *Montreal* 220.

20 Urquhart *16th* 272.

21 CBC, "Flanders Fields," #14, F.A. Stitt.

22 Corrigall 223.

23 Second Division report.

24 Goodspeed *Battle* 238, 240.

25 PAC, RG9 III C3, Volume 4052, Folder 22, File 4, 10th Battalion report, 14/8/18 (henceforth, 10th Battalion report).

26 Interim Report, 35.

27 Maurice 234.

28 Ibid.

29 *Letters* I/312.

30 Roy 72-73.

31 PAC, MG30 E417, unpublished memoirs.

32 Third Division report.

33 Topp 211.

34 Stevens 119-20; Fetherstonhaugh *RCR* 330.

35 *Letters* I/297, 306.

36 Greenhous 232, 233.

37 Ibid.

38 10th Battalion report.

39 Watson diary, 8/8/18.

40 PAC, RG9 III D2, Volume 4809, File 189, Fourth Division report, 10/9/18 (henceforth, Fourth Division report).

41 Gould 101.

42 Fourth Division report.

43 Ibid.

44 CBC, "Flanders Fields," #14; Corrigall 223; Johnston 66.

45 Terraine *To Win* 92, 98.

46 Hindenburg 391; Toland 350; Bean VI/614.

47 Liddell Hart *Tanks* 177; Macksey 32; Terraine *To Win* 97.

48 Nicholson *CEF* 420.

49 CBC, "Flanders Fields," #14.

50 PAC, RG24 C5, Volume 1817, GAQ 4-48, H.S. Charles/Miss W.H. Stapleton, 23/8/18; Snell 42, 45.

51 Interim Report, 38; Nicholson *CEF* 407.

52 Bean VI/552; Edmonds IV/89-90.

53 Serle 346; Bean VI/544, 600fn.

54 Duff Cooper 343.

55 Ibid.

56 Maurice 227-28.

57 Ludendorff 326; Terraine *To Win* 95.

58 Ludendorff 333.

CHAPTER FIVE: WASTED OPPORTUNITIES

1 Blake 322-23; Edmonds IV/576-77.

2 Urquhart *Currie* 237; Serle 388.

3 Hindenburg 393.

4 PAC, RG24 C5, Volume 1826, GAQ 5-85, Webber/?, 8/5/39.

5 Ibid.

6 Ibid.

7 Nicholson *CEF* 411.

8 Bean VI/684; Interim Report, 37.

9 Bean VI/683; Pedersen 251.

10 Nicholson *CEF* 411.

11 Singer 359.

12 Ibid.; PAA, L.L. Lent papers, diary, 9/8/18.

13 Bean VI/621; Second Division report.

14 Speaight 73-74.

15 PAC, RG9 III C3, Volume 4052, Folder 22, File 4, 5th Battalion report, 13/8/18.

16 Tascona 112.

17 PAC, RG9 III C3, Volume 4052, Folder 22, File 4, 8th Battalion report, n.d.

18 Goodspeed *Battle* 242-43.

19 PAC, MG30 E100, Volume 3, speech to National Republican Club of New York, 16/1/32.

20 Third Division report; Nicholson *CEF* 414; Interim Report, 39.

21 PAC, RG9 III D2, Volume 4791, File 26, "Intelligence, Canadian Corps Battle Fronts, Period Aug. 8th to Nov. 11th, 1918" (henceforth, Canadian Corps intelligence report).

22 Edmonds IV/93; Foch 380.

23 Interim Report, 39.

24 Fourth Division report.

25 Ibid.

26 McWilliams 154-55.

27 Ibid., 156.

28 PAM, J.W. Quelch papers, Quelch/father, 23/8/18.

29 Ibid.

30 GM, D.G.L. Cunnington papers, interview transcript, 19/11/69.

31 Ibid.

32 Fourth Division report.

33 Ibid.

34 PAC, MG30 E100, Currie/J.F. Livesay, 24/2/19.

35 *World War* II/1194; Cutlack 268.

36 Nicholson *CEF* 417.

37 *Canada in the Great World War* V/151-53.

38 Maurice 229; Duff Cooper 345; Edmonds IV/135-36.

39 Serle 350.

40 Maurice 229.

41 Foch 382-83.

42 Urquhart *Currie* 240-41.

43 Duff Cooper 348.

44 Ibid.

45 Foch 385.

46 Blake 323-34.

47 Foch 386; Duff Cooper 350.

48 Serle 351; Maurice 230.

49 Topp 220, 222.

50 PAC, RG9 III C3, Volume 4154, Folder 6, File 6, 42nd Battalion report, 12/8/18 (henceforth, 42nd Battalion report).

51 Mathieson 200.

52 PAC, RG9 III C3, Volume 4154, Folder 6, File 6, Major D.B. Martin report, 14/8/18.

53 42nd Battalion report.

54 Hodder-Williams 311-13.

55 Fetherstonhaugh *RCR* 337.

56 PAC, MG30 E32, unpublished memoirs.

57 Wheeler 321.

58 Wright 519.

59 Fetherstonhaugh *Montreal* 225.

60 Duff Cooper 351.

61 Currie diary, 18/8/18.

62 PAC, MG30 E100, Currie/F.W. Hill, 15/8/18; Currie/R.B. Borden, 26/11/18.

63 Cutlack 267-68.

64 PAC, MG30 E100, Volume 27, File 7; *Times History* XVI/284; Dancocks *Currie* 134; PAA, J.J.G. Hefferman papers, unpublished memoirs.

65 PAC, MG27 II D18, Volume 21, File 89.

66 Serle 351; Urquhart *Currie* 228, 243.

67 Dancocks *Currie* 157.

68 Currie diary, 22/8/18.

69 Nicholson *CEF* 419; Singer 368.

70 PAC, MG30 E100, Currie/F.W. Hill, 15/8/18.

71 Maurice 234.

72 Lloyd George II/1869, 2014.

73 Edmonds IV/155; Boraston 263.

74 Ludendorff 330-32.

75 Livesay 95.

CHAPTER SIX: BREAKING THE HINDENBURG LINE

1 Duff Cooper 354, 378.

2 Blake 324.

3 Duff Cooper 352.

4 Blake 324.

5 Duff Cooper 354-55.

6 Terraine *To Win* 122; Boraston 278-79.

7 Ibid., 272-74.

8 CBC, "Flanders Fields," #14.

9 Interim Report, 45.

10 Ibid., 44.

11 Ibid.

12 Ibid.

13 Dancocks *Currie* 159.

14 Interim Report, 44-45.

15 Ibid., 47; Nicholson *Gunners* 349.

16 Interim Report, 47; PAC, RG9 III D2, Volume 4798, File 103, 3rd Tank Brigade report, September 1918.

17 Currie diary, 25/8/18.

18 Dancocks *Currie* 159.

19 Singer 374.

20 Nicholson *CEF* 428.

21 Repington 365.

22 Currie diary, 26/8/18; PAC, MG30 E6, Volume 3, File 21, Second Division report, n.d. (henceforth, Second Division report).

23 PAC, RG9 III D2, Volume 4794, File 53, Sixth Brigade report, 9/9/18 (henceforth, Sixth Brigade report).

24 Hodder-Williams 325; PAC, RG9 III D2, Volume 4795, File 66, Third Division report, 30/8/18 (henceforth, Third Division report).

25 Mathieson 202.

26 Sixth Brigade report.

27 Interim Report, 48; Blake 325.

28 Canadian Corps intelligence report.

29 Third Division report.

30 PAC, MG30 E32, diary, 27/8/18.

31 PAC, MG30 E6, Volume 1, File 4, Fifth Brigade report, 3/9/18 (henceforth, Fifth Brigade report).

32 Ibid.

33 Ibid.

34 Second Division report.

35 Interim Report, 48-49.

36 Nicholson *CEF* 431.

37 Third Division report.

38 Ibid.; Stevens 127; CBC, "Flanders Fields," #14.

39 Second Division report.

40 Barry 46.

41 CBC, "Flanders Fields," #14.

42 Speaight 78; Barry 48.

43 Interim Report, 50; Currie diary, 28/8/18.

44 Nicholson *CEF* 432; Fifth Brigade report; PAC, RG9 III D2, Volume 4794, File 53, Fourth Brigade report, n.d.; MG30 E100, Currie/R.E.W. Turner, 30/8/18.

45 Third Division report; Hodder-Williams 339.

46 Currie diary, 29/8/18.

47 Ibid., 30/8/18.

48 CEA, W.A. Griesbach collection, Griesbach/A.C. Macdonell, 21/3/27.

49 Ibid., Macdonell/Griesbach, 17/3/27; PAC, MG30 E15, Volume 1, File 1, Griesbach/Macdonell, 2/2/27.

50 Macdonell, "Drocourt-Quéant Line," 327.

51 PAC, RG9 III C3, Volume 4027, Folder 14, File 1, 2nd Battalion report, 9/9/18; Goodspeed *Battle* 247.

52 PAC, MG30 E15, Volume 1, File 1, Griesbach/A.C. Macdonell, 2/2/27.

53 Duff Cooper 300; Interim Report, 51; PAC, RG9 III D2, Volume 4798, File 98, 4th Division report, n.d.

54 Interim Report, 51-52.

55 Watson diary, 29/8/18; Swettenham *McNaughton* 151.

56 Currie diary, 1/9/18.

57 PAC, RG24 C5, Volume 1873, File 18; James 57.

58 Fetherstonhaugh *Montreal* 237.

59 Nicholson *CEF* 434; Interim Report, 53; Fetherstonhaugh *Montreal* 231.

60 Goodspeed *Battle* 249; Duguid 201.

61 PAC, RG24 C5, Volume 1824, GAQ 5-45, Matthews report, 2/9/18.

62 CBC, "Flanders Fields," #14.

63 Urquhart *16th* 297; Tascona 117.

64 PAC, RG9 III D2, Volume 4797, File 82, 47th Battalion report, 6/9/18.

65 Nicholson *Gunners* 354; PAC, RG9 III D2, Volume 4795, File 59, "Artillery Notes," n.d.

66 PABC, A. Shelford papers, unpublished memoirs.

67 Urquhart *16th* 295.

68 Ibid., 296.

69 Ibid., 298.

70 Fetherstonhaugh *Montreal* 240.

71 PAC, RG9 III C3, Volume 4052, Folder 22, File 6, 10th Battalion report, 6/9/18.

72 PAC, RG9 III D2, Volume 4797, File 82, Tenth Brigade report, 14/9/18; McWilliams 162-63.

73 Ibid., 164-65.

74 PAC, RG9 III D2, Volume 4797, File 82, 38th Battalion report, 9/9/18.

75 Ibid., 72nd Battalion report, n.d.

76 PAC, MG30 E393, unpublished memoirs.

77 Ibid.; PANS, H. Cromwell papers, Cromwell/Major Ambrose, 11/9/18.

78 PAC, RG24 C5, Volume 1884, File 60, "Narratives Covering Operations of the 1st Canadian Motor Machine Gun Brigade...," n.d.; RG9 III D2, Volume 4807, File 170, Canadian Independent Force report, n.d.

79 Swettenham *McNaughton* 151.

80 PAC, RG9 III D2, Volume 4796, File 81, Eleventh Brigade report, 8/10/18.

81 Currie diary, 3/9/18.

82 Anderson, "Quéant-Drocourt Line," 126-27.

83 Currie diary, 4/9/18; Interim report, 55.

84 Nicholson *CEF* 440; PAC, MG30 E100, Currie/P. Radcliffe, 4/9/18.

85 CBC, "Flanders Fields," #14; PAC, MG30 E100, Currie/P. Radcliffe, 4/9/18.

86 PAC, RG9 III D2, Volume 4810, File "Casualties"; Interim Report, 53; Currie diary, 2/9/18.

87 PAC, MG30 E100, Currie/J. Morrison, 11/9/18.

88 Interim Report, 53; Currie diary, 19/9/18; PAC, MG30 E100, Currie/D. Oliver, 2/9/18.

89 PAC, MG30 E100, Currie/J. Morrison, 11/9/18.

90 Ibid., Currie/D. Oliver, 2/9/18.

91 Ibid., Currie/R.L. Borden, 26/11/18.

92 Duff Cooper 363; Blake 325-26.

93 Duff Cooper 363.

94 Hindenburg 398; Ludendorff 347.

95 Toland 390.

CHAPTER SEVEN: CRUCIBLE AT CAMBRAI

1 PAC, MG30 E100, Volume 1, File A-F, Currie/R.L. Borden, 26/11/18.

2 Duff Cooper 365.

3 Terraine *Haig* 467.

4 Duff Cooper 366-67.

5 Blake 326-27.

6 Duff Cooper 378-79.

7 Blake 324.

8 Urquhart *Currie* 226-27.

9 PAC, MG30 E100, Volume 27, File 7, Currie/O.E. McGillicuddy, n.d.

10 Duff Cooper 376.

11 Foch 410-11.

12 Boraston 278.

13 Duff Cooper 380.

14 Terraine *Haig* 465; Foch 408.

15 PAC, RG24 C5, Volume 1817, GAQ 4-48, H.S. Chartles/Miss W.H. Stapleton, 14/9/18; Eleventh 116.

16 Singer 389; Snell 147; Roy 76.

17 Nicholson *CEF* 441.

18 Ogilvie 46.

19 PANS, H. Cromwell papers, Cromwell/Major Ambrose, 11/9/18.

20 *Letters* I/298.

21 PAC, MG30 E42, diary, 15/9/18.

22 PAM, G.H. Hambley papers, diary, 18/9/18.

23 Serle 369.

24 PAC, RG9 III D2, Volume 4797, File 82, Twelfth Brigade report, n.d.

25 Ibid.

26 Ibid., Volume 4802, File 170, Brutinel's report, n.d.

27 Ibid., Volume 4798, File 103, 3rd Tank Brigade report, 18/9/18.

28 Nicholson *Gunners* 355; PAC, RG9 III D2, Volume 4795, File 59, "Artillery Notes," n.d.; Volume 4807, File 174, "Artillery Notes," n.d.

29 PAC, RG9 III D2, Volume 4796, File 81, Eleventh Brigade report, 8/10/18.

30 Ibid., Volume 4797, File 82, 72nd Battalion report, n.d.; RG9 III C3, Volume 4052, Folder 22, File 6, 10th Battalion report, 6/9/18.

31 Currie diary, 10/9/18; Bennett 133.

32 Interim Report, 57.

33 Ibid., 55.

34 Ibid., 57.

35 Currie diary, 24/9/18; Macdonell, "Old Red Patch," 12.

36 Worthington 146.

37 Anderson, "Canal du Nord," 76.

38 Dancocks *Currie* 2-3.

39 Anderson, "Canal du Nord," 76.

40 Interim Report, 55-56.

41 Hahn 170-72.

42 Nicholson *CEF* 444.

43 PAC, RG9 III D2, Volume 4807, File 174, "Artillery Notes," n.d.

44 Interim Report, 57.

45 Ibid.

46 Hahn 252.

47 PAC, MG30 E430, unpublished memoirs; *Letters* I/299.

48 PAC, RG9 III D2, Volume 4807, File 174, "Artillery Notes," n.d.

49 Grafton 182-83.

50 Currie diary, 27/9/18; Canadian Corps intelligence report.

51 Nicholson *CEF* 446fn.

52 CBC, "Flanders Fields," #15; PAC, RG9 III D2, Volume 4797, File 83, Fourth Division report, 27/12/18 (henceforth, Fourth Division report).

53 Russenholt 191.

54 McWilliams 174.

55 Wheeler 347, 350-51.

56 PAC, RG9 III D2, Volume 4797, File 83, Eleventh Brigade report, 4/12/18 (henceforth, Eleventh Brigade report).

57 Ibid.; Duguid 207.

58 McEvoy 142; PAC, MG30 E393, unpublished memoirs.

59 McEvoy 142-43.

60 PAC, RG9 III D2, Volume 4797, File 83, 72nd Battalion report, 7/10/18 (henceforth, 72nd Battalion report).

61 Macdonell, "Old Red Patch," 15.

62 PAC, RG9 III C3, Volume 4028, Folder 15, File 5, First Brigade report, 5/10/18 (henceforth, Frist Brigade report).

63 Ibid.

64 Macdonell, "Old Red Patch," 15; Fetherstonhaugh *Montreal* 251.

65 PAC, RG9 III D2, Volume 4793, File 46, Sinclair/Third Brigade, 30/9/18.

66 Fetherstonhaugh *Montreal* 279; PAC, RG9 III D2, Volume 4793, File 46, Girvan/Third Brigade, 29/9/18.

67 First Brigade report.

68 PAC, MG30 E15, Volume 5, File 33D, Griesbach/A.C. Macdonell, 28/11/31.

69 PAC, RG9 III C3, Volume 4052, Folder 22, File 7, 7th Battalion report, 4/10/18.

70 Ibid., 5th Battalion report, 4/10/18; 10th Battalion report, 4/10/18 (henceforth, 10th Battalion report).

71 Kerry 181, 188.

72 Swettenham *McNaughton* 157; Currie diary, 27/9/18.

73 Canadian Corps intelligence report.

74 *Letters* I/300; PAM, G.H. Hambley papers, diary, 27/10/18.

75 Hahn 252-53.

76 Reid 228; *Letters* I/299.

77 Currie diary, 27/9/18.

78 Foch 415; PAC, MG30 E100, Currie/F.H. Underhill, 17/9/20.

79 Currie diary, 27/9/18.

80 PAC, RG9 III D2, Volume 4796, File 72, Ninth Brigade report, 8/10/18.

81 Ibid., 43rd Battalion report, 7/10/18 (henceforth, 43rd Battalion report).

82 PAC, RG9 III C3, Volume 4154, Folder 7, File 1, RCR report, 3/10/18.

83 Fetherstonhaugh *RCR* 355.

84 PAC, RG9 III D2, Volume 4796, File 72, 52nd Battalion report, n.d. (henceforth, 52nd Battalion report).

85 PAC, RG9 III C3, Volume 4154, Folder 7, File 7, PPCLI report, n.d.; Hodder-Williams 367fn.

86 CBC, "Flanders Fields," #15, G.W. Little.

87 PAC, RG9 III D2, Volume 4796, File 72, 116th Battalion report, n.d. (henceforth, 116th Battalion report).

88 Ibid., Volume 4797, File 83, 50th Battalion report, 30/9/18 (henceforth, 50th Battalion report); Wheeler 352.

89 CBC, "Flanders Fields," #15.

90 PAC, RG9 III D2, Volume 4797, File 83, 46th Battalion report, n.d.; 44th Battalion report, n.d.

91 Ibid.

92 10th Battalion report.

93 Ibid.

94 Canadian Corps intelligence report.

95 Ibid.

96 Nicholson *CEF* 453.

97 Topp 269.

98 CBC, "Flanders Fields," #15; 116th Battalion report.

99 PAC, MG30 E393, unpublished memoirs.

100 Stevens 133.

101 Topp 269.

102 Ibid., 271-72.

103 PAC, RG9 III D2, Volume 4797, File 83, 38th Battalion report, n.d.

104 PAC, MG30 E393, unpublished memoirs.

105 72nd Battalion report.

106 Ibid.

107 Ibid.

108 PAC, RG9 III C3, Volume 4052, Folder 22, File 7, 8th Battalion report, n.d.

109 PAC, RG9 III D2, Volume 4809, File 195, First Division report, n.d.

110 Nicholson *CEF* 451; PAC, RG9 III D2, Volume 4795, File 67, Third Division report, 1/11/18; Interim Report, 60-61.

111 Hodder-Williams 373fn; Topp 273.

112 CBC, "Flanders Fields," #15, G.W. Little, J.A. Clark.

113 Fourth Division report.

114 PAC, MG30 E351, diary, 1/10/18.

115 PAC, RG9 III D2, Volume 4797, File 83, 87th Battalion report, 3/10/18.

116 Fourth Division report; PAC, RG9 III D2, Volume 4797, File 83, Eleventh Brigade report, 4/12/18 (henceforth, Eleventh Brigade report).

117 Interim Report, 61.

118 Nicholson *CEF* 452; PAC, MG30 E100, Currie/H.M. Urquhart, 8/10/31.

119 Fetherstonhaugh *13th* 282.

120 Fetherstonhaugh *Montreal* 255; CBC, "Flanders Fields," #15.

121 Urquhart *16th* 306.

122 Eleventh Brigade report; Gould 111-12.

123 PAM, Greenslade taped interview.

124 Duguid 211; CBC, "Flanders Fields," #15.

125 Eleventh Brigade report.

126 43rd Battalion report; 52nd Battalion report.

127 CBC, "Flanders Fields," #15.

128 116th Battalion report.

129 Fourth Division report; Nicholson *CEF* 453; PAC, RG9 III D2, Volume 4807, File 174, First Division artillery notes, n.d.; "Artillery Notes on Operations of the Canadian Corps, September 27th to October 1st, 1918," n.d.; Reid 227.

130 Interim Report, 62.

131 PAC, MG30 E100, Volume 1, File A-F, Currie/R.L. Borden, 26/11/18.

132 Interim Report, 68.

133 Ibid.; PAC, MG30 E100, Currie/Kemp, 1/11/18; Currie/H. Daly, 26/10/18.

134 *Debates*, House of Commons, 4/3/19.

135 50th Battalion report.

136 PAC, RG9 III D2, Volume 4797, File 83, Eleventh Brigade report, 4/12/18; 75th Battalion report, 6/10/18.

137 Currie diary, 1/10/18; PAC, MG30 E100, Volume 1, File A-F, Currie/Borden, 26/11/18; Currie/Kemp, 1/11/18; *Canada in the Great World War* V/212.

138 Topp 282.

139 PAC, MG30 E100, Currie/A. Miller, 4/10/18.

140 CBC, "Flanders Fields", #15; Reid 230.

141 Ludendorff 374, 377, 386.

142 Ibid., 398.

143 Terraine *Haig* 471.

144 Ibid., 470.

145 Maurice 238.

CHAPTER EIGHT: PURSUIT

1 Interim Report, 64.

2 Ibid., 65.

3 Currie diary, 8/10/18.

4 Ibid., 9/10/18.

5 Ibid.

6 CBC, "Flanders Fields," #15.

7 *Debates*, House of Commons, 4/3/19.

8 Currie diary, 8/10/18.

9 PAC, RG9 III D2, Volume 4795, File 67, Third Division report, 1/11/18; MG30 E100, Cobourg trial transcript, 1812.

10 PAM, G.H. Hambley papers, diary, 11/10/18.

11 Boraston 288; Nicholson *CEF* 464-65, *Gunners* 363.

12 CBC, "Flanders Fields," #15.

13 Corrigall 265.

14 Interim Report, 67; Nicholson *CEF* 459; Corrigall 261.

15 CBC, "Flanders Fields," #15, D. Oliver; Nicholson *CEF* 459; Corrigall 265.

16 PAC, MG30 E100, Currie/Macdonell, 10/10/18.

17 Interim Report, 69, 71.

18 MUA, H.M. Urquhart papers, Farmar interview.

19 Currie diary, 14,15/10/18.

20 Ludendorff 401.

21 Lloyd George II/1965-66.

22 Blake 331.

23 Interim Report, 72.

24 *Canada in the Great World War* v/214.

25 Beattie 387.

26 *Letters* I/303-4.

27 *Canada in the Great World War* v/214.

28 Currie diary, 20/10/18; Snell 202, 204.

29 Currie diary, 20/10/18.

30 GM, J.R. Gaetz papers, diary, 15/10/18; PAM, F. Leathers papers, Leathers/father, 19/10/18.

31 Fetherstonhaugh *Montreal* 263.

32 Currie diary, 20/10/18; *Letters* I/302, 313; Nicholson *Gunners* 364.

33 CBC, "Flanders Fields," #15.

34 Currie diary, 23/10/18; Interim Report, 74.

35 Ibid., 75-76.

36 Boraston 294.

37 McNaughton, "Valenciennes," 280.

38 PAC, RG24 C5, Volume 1821, GAQ 5-27.

39 Ibid.

40 PAC, MG30 E195, Barker/Major C. Lemon, 7/11/18; Swettenham *McNaughton* 160.

41 Canadian Corps intelligence report.

42 Anderson, "Valenciennes," 293-94.

43 McNaughton, "Valenciennes," 281.

44 Swettenham *McNaughton* 163; PAC, MG30 E100, Cobourg trial transcript, 1813.

45 Anderson, "Valenciennes," 294; Currie diary, 2/11/18; Nicholson *Gunners* 368; Swettenham *McNaughton* 160.

46 Edmonds v/455; PAC, RG9 III D2, Volume 4797, File 84, Fourth Division report, 6/1/19 (henceforth, Fourth Division report).

47 Sweetenham *McNaughton* 162.

48 *Letters* I/304; Interim Report, 78.

49 PAC, RG9 III D2, Volume 4797, File 84, Tenth Brigade report, 13/11/18 (henceforth, Tenth Brigade report); MG30 E100, Volume 1, File A-F, Currie/R.L. Borden, 26/11/18.

50 PAC, RG9 III D2, Volume 4797, File 84, 47th Battalion report, n.d.; 44th Battalion report, 8/11/18; McNaughton, "Valenciennes," 290.

51 McWilliams 198; PAC, RG9 III D2, Volume 4797, File 84, 46th Battalion report, n.d.

52 Ibid., 50th Battalion report, n.d.

53 McEvoy 163.
54 McNaughton, "Valenciennes," 291.
55 McWilliams 200.
56 McNaughton, "Valenciennes," 293.
57 Ibid., 292.
58 Fourth Division report; Tenth Brigade report; Currie diary, 1/11/18.
59 PAC, MG30 E389, diary, 1/11/18.

CHAPTER NINE: ARMISTICE

1 Ludendorff 425.
2 Blake 333.
3 Foch 414; Blake 329-30.
4 Duff Cooper 399.
5 Ibid., 395-96.
6 Terraine *To Win* 196, 207; Duff Cooper 397, 400.
7 *Canada in the Great World War* IV/191; PAC, MG30 E100, Currie/H. Daly, 26/10/18.
8 Foch 456; Lloyd George II/1980.
9 Taylor 121, 139.
10 Lloyd George II/1880.
11 Duff Cooper 393; Blake 331.
12 Boraston 293-94.
13 Ibid., 293, 296.
14 Interim Report, 79.
15 *Globe and Mail* 11/11/86; Corrigall 276.
16 CBC, "Flanders Fields," #15.
17 Snell 222.
18 PAC, MG30 E353, Pullen/Ernie, 2/11/18; CBC, "Flanders Fields," #15, G. Sivertz; Reid 226-27.
19 Currie diary, 5/11/18.
20 Ibid., 7/11/18.
21 Duguid 220.
22 Interim Report, 80; Currie diary, 9/11/18.
23 PAM, F. Leathers papers, Leathers/father, 10/11/18.
24 Toland 520.
25 Stevens 138; Reid 219-20.
26 *Globe and Mail* 11/11/86.
27 Currie diary, 10/11/18; PAC, MG30 E100, Cobourg trial transcript, 1165.
28 GM, J.R. Gaetz papers, Gaetz/mother, 19/11/18.
29 CBC, "Flanders Fields," #16.
30 PAC, MG30 E100, Cobourg trial transcript, 1555.
31 CBC, "Flanders Fields," #16.
32 Ibid., W.M. King.
33 PAC, RG24 C5, Volume 1822, GAQ 5-34.
34 CBC, "Flanders Fields," #16.
35 PAC, RG9 III D2, Volume 4796, File 75, Third Division report, n.d.

36 PAA, J.J.G. Hefferman papers, unpublished memoirs; Ogilvie 54; GM, J.R. Gaetz papers, Gaetz/mother, 13/11/18; McWilliams 203.

37 PAC, MG30 E100, Cobourg trial transcript, 1477; Swettenham *McNaughton* 168.

38 Henley letter to author, 10/12/26; GM, A.J. Turner papers, unpublished memoirs.

39 Calder 236.

40 Halifax *Chronicle-Herald* 11/11/68; PAC, MG30 E100, Cobourg trial transcript, 260; Calder 236.

41 CBC, "Flanders Fields," #16, W.A. Dunlop, A.B. Goodmurphy.

42 Ibid., W.H.S. Macklin, R.G. Petty.

43 PAC, MG30 E100, Cobourg trial transcript, 1670; Mathieson 285.

44 Currie diary, 11/11/18.

45 Dancocks *Currie* 173; Nicholson *Gunners* 372.

46 PANS, G.M. Wood papers, n.d. newspaper clipping.

47 Livesay 387; Dancocks *Currie* 172-73; PAC, MG30 E100, Horne/Currie, 11/11/18.

48 Nicholson *CEF* 535; *World War* II/1188.

49 PAC, MG30 E100, Currie/W.R. Wilson, 10/12/18.

50 *World War* II/1209.

51 Nicholson *CEF* 548.

52 PAC, MG30 E32, diary, 9/9/18.

53 McWilliams 195.

54 CBC, "Flanders Fields," #15, W.H.S. Macklin, T.T. Shields.

55 PAC, MG30 E133, sound recording.

56 Ibid.; *World War* II/1204; PAC, MG30 E100, Currie/C. Swayne, 23/1/18, n.d. newspaper clipping.

57 PAC, MG30 E133, Volume 345, File 16, "The development of Artillery during the war," 16/1/20; Swettenham *McNaughton* 172-73.

58 Swettenham *Seize* 238.

59 Terraine *To Win* 164-65.

CHAPTER TEN: DISCIPLINE AND DISCONTENT

1 Foch 463.

2 Ibid., 469, 473.

3 Ibid., 467, 471.

4 Ibid., 486-87.

5 PAC, MG30 E100, Currie/J.F. Livesay, 26/1/33.

6 Stevens 143; PAC, MG30 E430, unpublished memoirs; Wheeler 389.

7 PAC, MG27 II D18, Volume 21, File 18, "Special Order of the Day," 25/11/18.

8 *Canada in the Great World War* V/235; Interim Report, 87.

9 Kerry 214.

10 Snell 169, 231, 239.

11 Interim Report, 90; Mathieson 294.

12 *World War* II/1211.

13 Interim Report, 91.

14 PAA, L.L. Lent papers, diary, 7/12/18; Murray 326.

15 Currie diary, 28/11/18, 1/12/18.

16 PAC, MG30 E430, unpublished memoirs.

17 CBC, "Flanders Fields," #16; Goodspeed *Battle* 269.

18 PAC, MG30 E100, Currie/W.R. Wilson, 10/12/18; *Letters* II/174; PABC, Crease family papers, Crease/L. Crease, 5/12/18.

19 Interim Report, 92; CBC, "Flanders Fields," #16, F. Wingfield.

20 AO, Sir A.C. Macdonell papers, Macdonell/?, 22/12/18; Currie diary, 11/12/18.

21 Ibid., 12/12/18.

22 Ibid., 13/12/18.

23 AO, Sir A.C. Macdonell papers, Macdonell/Greenfield, 13/12/18.

24 PAC, MG30 E100, Canadian Corps Defence Plan, 13/12/18.

25 PAC, RG24 C5, Volume 1817, GAQ 4-48, Hackett/Miss W.H. Stapleton, 16/12/18; GM, George Taylor papers, n.d. postcard.

26 Currie diary, 2/1/19.

27 Ibid., 14/12/18, 2/1/19.

28 Ibid., 2/1/19; PAC, MG26H, Volume 268, Part 2, File 82(2), "Memorandum in Connection with Sir Robert Borden's Letter Respecting Sir Arthur Currie."

29 Ibid.

30 Currie diary, 15/12/18; GM, H.W. McGill papers, McGill/F. McGill, 24/12/18.

31 Duff Cooper 405-6.

32 PAC, MG30 E46, Volume 7, "First Interim Report, Canadian Overseas Demobilization Committee," 22/7/18.

33 PAC, MG27 II D9, Volume 137, File D2, Currie/E. Kemp, 6/11/18.

34 PAC, MG30 E75, Volume 3, File 6, Currie/E. Kemp, 23/11/18.

35 PAC, MG30 E100, Volume 2, File M-R, Currie/E.H. Macklin, 4/10/18.

36 CBC, "Flanders Fields," #16.

37 AO, Sir A.C. Macdonell papers, Macdonell/?, 22/12/18; Watson diary, 6/11/18.

38 Borden II/160.

39 Interim Report, 90; PAC, MG30 E75, Volume 3, File 6, Currie/Kemp, 23/11/18.

40 Terraine *Haig* 484; PAC, MG30 E46, "Canadian Troops Overseas and the British Press," n.d.; Duff Cooper 406.

41 Currie diary, 23,29/1/19.

42 PAC, MG27 II D2, Volume 138, File D11-b, O.F. Brothers/E. Kemp, 11/2/19.

43 CBC, "Flanders Fields," #16, J.S. Stewart.

44 PAC, RG9 III B1, Volume 2231, File D-6-29, Loomis/IV Corps, 23, 26/12/18.

45 Currie diary, n.d.

46 PAC, RG24 C5, Volume 1821, GAQ 5-24.

47 Ibid., Volume 1846, GAQ 11-43A, memorandum, 9/1/19.

48 Ibid., A.L. Hamilton memorandum, 7/4/19; RG9 III A1, Volume 104, W. Bovey report, 9/7/19.

49 PAC, MG27 II D9, Volume 139, File D11-f, Kemp/R. Borden, 14/3/19.

50 PAC, RG9 III A1, Volume 106, OMFC report 27/6/19.

51 PAC, MG27 II D9, Volume 139, File D11-f, Kemp/R. Borden, 14/3/19.

52 Currie diary, 10/3/19.

53 Ibid.; PAC, MG27 II D9, Volume 139, File D11-f, Borden/E. Kemp, 10/3/19, Kemp/R. Borden, 12/3/19.

54 PAC, RG24 C5, Volume 1841, GAQ 10-39f, Notes 3, 4, 5.

55 Ibid., Volume 1846, GAQ 11-43a, "General Demobilization," n.d.; MG27 II D9, Volume 138, File D11-a, R. Borden/E. Kemp, 3/3/19; MG30 E15, Volume 1, File 1, Macdonell/W.A. Griesbach, 12/3/19.

56 GM, H.W. McGill papers, McGill/F. McGill, 18/2/19; CBC, "Flanders Fields," #16, G.R. Stevens; *Canada in the Great World War* V/28.

57 PAC, MG30 E100, Currie report, 21/3/19.

CHAPTER ELEVEN: THE FRUITS OF VICTORY

1 Borden II/78; Brown 134-35; *Canadian Encyclopedia* I/204.

2 Borden I/233; Allen 185-86.

3 Nicholson *CEF* 217.

4 Lloyd George I/1026.

5 Borden II/63.

6 Ibid., 65, 74.

7 Brown 138.

8 Ibid., 145; Borden II/173-74.

9 Brown 146.

10 Ibid., 147.

11 Borden II/158.

12 Brown 151.

13 Ibid., 153.

14 Ibid., 151-52.

15 Borden II/163, 168, 174fn, 208.

16 Ibid., 152, 175-76.

17 Currie diary, 14/2/19; Borden II/ 194; PAC, MG30 E100, Borden/Currie, 25/3/19.

18 Borden II/201-2.

19 Stacey 259.

20 Borden II/207.

21 Ibid., 208.

22 Glazebrook 109, 111.

23 Brown 158, 161.

24 Glazebrook 113-14.

25 Brown 152, 159.

26 Terraine *Impacts* 126.

27 Borden II/68, 179.

APPENDIX ONE

1 *Debates*, House of Commons, 4/3/19.

2 PAC, MG30 E100, Currie/G.S. Harington, 23/9/19.

3 Port Hope *Evening Guide*, 13/6/27.

4 PAC, MG30 E100, Currie/P. Brown, 17/6/27; Currie/W.A. Griesbach, 23/3/28; Currie/H.M. Urquhart, 4/4/28.

5 Ibid., Currie/H. Dyer, 5/4/28.

6 Ibid., Cobourg trial transcript, 1862-63.

7 Ibid., E.T. Huycke/Currie, 20/6/28; Dancocks *Currie* 258.

8 *Canadian Annual Review, 1928-29*, 592.

9 For a detailed description of the trial, see Dancocks *Currie* 233-60.

BIBLIOGRAPHY

Allen, Ralph. *Ordeal by Fire*. New York: Popular Library, 1961.

Anderson, Sir W.H. "The Crossing of the Canal du Nord by the First Army, 27th September, 1918." *Canadian Defence Quarterly* (October 1924): 63-77.

—. "The Operation Round Valenciennes by the First Army, October-November, 1918." *Canadian Defence Quarterly* (April 1925): 291-96.

—. "The Breaking of the Quéant-Drocourt Line by the Canadian Corps, 2nd-4th September, 1918." *Canadian Defence Quarterly* (January 1926): 120-27.

Barclay, C.N. *Armistice 1918*. New York: A.S. Barnes, 1969.

Barnes, Leslie W.C.S. *Canada's Guns*. Ottawa: Canadian War Museum, 1979.

Barry, A.L. *Batman to Brigadier*. n.p., n.d.

Bean, C.E.W. *The Official History of Australia in the War of 1914-1918*. Volumes V, VI. Sydney: Angus & Robertson, 1942.

Beattie, Kim. *48th Highlanders of Canada, 1891-1928*. Toronto: 48th Highlanders of Canada, 1932.

Bennett, S.G. *The 4th Canadian Mounted Rifles, 1914-1919*. Toronto: Murray, 1926.

Blake, Robert, ed. *The Private Papers of Douglas Haig, 1914-1919*. London: Eyre & Spottiswoode, 1952.

Boraston, J.H., ed. *Sir Douglas Haig's Despatches*. London: J.M. Dent, 1979.

Borden, Henry, ed. *Robert Laird Borden: His Memoirs*. Volumes I, II. Toronto: McClelland & Stewart, 1969.

Brown, Robert Craig. *Robert Laird Borden*. Volume II. Toronto: Macmillan, 1980.

Bruce, Herbert A. *Politics and the Canadian Army Medical Corps*. Toronto: William Briggs, 1919.

Calder, D.G., ed. *The History of the 28th (Northwest) Battalion, CEF*. Regina: Regina Rifle Regiment, 1961.

Canada in the Great World War. Volumes IV, V. Toronto: United Publishers, 1919-20.

Canadian Annual Review, 1928-29. Toronto: Canadian Annual Review, 1929.

Canadian Encyclopedia, The. Edmonton: Hurtig, 1985.

Corrigall, D.J. *The History of the Twentieth Canadian Battalion*. Toronto: Stone & Cox, 1935.

Cutlack, F.M. *War Letters of General Monash*. Sydney: Angus & Robertson, 1935.

Dancocks, Daniel G. *Sir Arthur Currie*. Toronto: Methuen, 1985.

—. *Legacy of Valour*. Edmonton: Hurtig, 1986.

Dodds, Ronald. *The Brave Young Wings*. Canada's Wings, 1980.

Duff, Cooper, A. *Haig*. Volume II. Toronto: Macmillan, 1936.

Duguid, A.F. *History of the Canadian Grenadier Guards, 1760-1964.* Montreal: Gazette, 1965.

Edmonds, Sir James. *Military Operations, France and Belgium, 1918.* Volume III. London: Macmillan, 1939.

—. *Military Operations, France and Belgium, 1918.* Volumes IV, V. London: His Majesty's Stationery Office, 1947.

Eleventh Canadian Field Ambulance. *Diary of the Eleventh.* n.p., n.d.

Ellis, W.D., ed. *Saga of the Cyclists in the Great War, 1914-1918.* Toronto: Canadian Corps Cyclist Battalion Association, 1965.

Fetherstonhaugh, F.C. *The 13th Battalion, Royal Highlanders of Canada, 1914-1919.* Royal Highlanders of Canada, 1925.

—. *The Royal Montreal Regiment.* Montreal: Gazette, 1927.

—. *The Royal Canadian Regiment, 1883-1933.* The Royal Canadian Regiment, 1936. Reprint. Fredericton: Centennial, 1981.

Foch, Ferdinand. *The Memoirs of Marshal Foch.* Garden City, N.Y.: Doubleday, Doran, 1931.

Fraser, W.B. *Always a Strathcona.* Calgary: Comprint, 1976.

Glazebrook, G.P. deT. *Canada at the Paris Peace Conference.* Toronto: Oxford University Press, 1942.

Goodspeed, D.J. *The Armed Forces of Canada, 1867-1967.* Ottawa: Queen's Printer, 1967.

—. *Battle Royal.* The Royal Regiment of Canada Association, 1979.

Gould, L. McLeod. *From B.C. to Baisieux.* Victoria: Cusack, 1919.

Grafton, G.S. *The Canadian "Emma Gees."* London: The Canadian Machine Gun Corps Association, 1938.

Greenhous, Brereton. *Dragoon.* Ottawa: The Guild of the Royal Canadian Dragoons, 1983.

Gunn, N.N., and E.E. Dutton. *Historical Records of No. 8 Canadian Field Ambulance.* Toronto: Ryerson, 1920.

Hahn, J.F. *The Intelligence Service within the Canadian Corps, 1914-1918.* Toronto: Macmillan, 1930.

Hindenburg, Paul von. *Out of My Life.* London: Cassell, 1920.

Hodder-Williams, Ralph. *Princess Patricia's Canadian Light Infantry, 1914-1919.* Volume I. London, Toronto: Hodder & Stoughton, 1923.

Hopkins, J. Castell. *Canada at War, 1914-1918.* Toronto: Canadian Annual Review, 1919.

Hutchison, Paul. *Canada's Black Watch.* Montreal: The Black Watch (R.H.R.) of Canada, 1962.

Jackson, H.M. *The Royal Regiment of Artillery, Ottawa, 1855-1952.* n.p., 1952.

James, Fred. *Canada's Triumph.* London: Canadian War Records Office, 1919.

Johnston, G. Chalmers. *The 2nd Canadian Mounted Rifles.* Vernon: Vernon News, 1932.

Kerry, A.J., and W.A. McDill. *The History of the Corps of Royal Canadian Engineers.* Volume I. Ottawa: The Military Engineers Association of Canada, 1962.

Letters from the Front. Volumes I, II. Toronto: Canadian Bank of Commerce, 1920.

Liddell Hart, B.H. *The Real War*. London: Faber & Faber, 1930.

—. *The Tanks*. Volume I. London: Cassell, 1959.

Livesay, J.F. *Canada's Hundred Days*. Toronto: Thomas Allen, 1919.

Lloyd George, David. *War Memoirs*. Volumes I, II. London: Odhams, 1938.

Ludendorff, Erich. *Ludendorff's Own Story*. Volume II. 1920. Reprint. Freeport, N.Y.: Books for Libraries Press, 1971.

MacDonald, J.A. *Gun-Fire*. n.p., 1929.

Macdonell, Sir A.C. "The Old Red Patch at the Breaking of the Drocourt-Quéant Line, the Crossing of the Canal du Nord and the Advance on Cambrai, 30th Aug.-2nd Oct., 1918." *Canadian Defence Quarterly* (July 1927): 388-96.

—. "The Old Red Patch." *Canadian Defence Quarterly* (October 1931): 10-26.

Machum, George. *Canada's V.C.'s*. Toronto: McClelland & Stewart, 1956.

Macksey, Kenneth. *The Tank Pioneers*. London: Jane's, 1981.

Macphail, Sir Andrew. *Official History of the Canadian Forces in the Great War, 1914-1919: The Medical Services*. Ottawa: King's Printer, 1925.

Marshall, S.L.A. *World War I*. New York: American Heritage, 1964.

Mathieson, William D. *My Grandfather's War*. Toronto: Macmillan, 1981.

Maurice, Sir Frederick. *The Life of General Lord Rawlinson of Trent*. London: Cassell, 1928.

McEvoy, Bernard, and A.H. Finlay. *History of the 72nd Canadian Infantry Battalion, Seaforth Highlanders of Canada*. Vancouver: Cown & Brookhouse, 1920.

McNaughton, A.G.L. "The Capture of Valenciennes: A Study in Co-ordination," *Canadian Defence Quarterly* (April 1933): 79-94.

McWilliams, James L., and R. James Steel. *The Suicide Battalion*. Edmonton: Hurtig, 1978.

Middlebrook, Martin. *The Kaiser's Battle*. London: Allen Lane, 1978.

Moir, John S. *History of the Royal Canadian Corps of Signals, 1903-1961*. Ottawa: Corps Committee, Royal Canadian Corps of Signals, 1962.

Montgomery, Sir Archibald. *The Story of the Fourth Army in the Battles of the Hundred Days, August 8th to November 11th, 1918*. London: Hodder & Stoughton, 1919.

Murray, W.W. *The History of the 2nd Canadian Battalion*. Ottawa: The Historical Committee, 2nd Battalion, CEF, 1947.

Nasmith, George. *Canada's Sons and Great Britain in the World War*. Toronto: John Winston, 1919.

Nicholson, G.W.L. *Canadian Expeditionary Force, 1914-1919*. Ottawa: Queen's Printer, 1962.

—. *The Gunners of Canada*. Volume I. Toronto: McClelland & Stewart, 1967.

Ogilvie, William G. *Umpty-Iddy-Umpty*. Erin, Ontario: Boston Mills Press, 1982.

Orgill, Douglas. *Armoured Onslaught: 8th August 1918*. New York: Ballantine, 1972.

Pedersen, P.A. *Monash as Military Commander*. Melbourne: Melbourne University Press, 1985.

Pershing, John J. *My Experiences in the World War*. Volume II. New York: Frederick A. Stokes, 1931.

Reid, Gordon. *Poor Bloody Murder*. Oakville, Ontario: Mosaic Press, 1980.

Repington, C. *The First World War*. Volume II. Boston, New York: Houghton Mifflin, 1920.

Roy, Reginald H. *For Most Conspicuous Bravery*. Vancouver: University of British Columbia Press, 1977.

Russenholt, E.S. *Six Thousand Canadian Men*. Winnipeg: Forty-fourth Battalion Association, 1932.

Serle Geoffrey. *John Monash*. Melbourne: Melbourne University Press, 1982.

Singer, H.C. *History of the 31st Canadian Infantry Battalion, C.E.F.* n.p., 1938.

Snell, A.E. *The C.A.M.C. with the Canadian Corps during the Last Hundred Days of the Great War*. Ottawa: King's Printer, 1924.

Speaight, Robert. *Vanier*. London: Collins & Harvill, 1970.

Stacey, C.P. *Canada in the Age of Conflict*. Volume I. Toronto: Macmillan, 1977.

Stevens, G.R. *A City Goes to War*. Brampton, Ontario: The Loyal Edmonton Regiment Associates, 1964.

Swettenham, John. *To Seize the Victory*. Toronto: Ryerson, 1965.

—. *McNaughton*. Volume I. Toronto: Ryerson, 1968.

—, ed. *Valiant Men*. Toronto: Hakkert, 1973.

Tascona, Bruce, and Eric Wells. *Little Black Devils*. Winnipeg: Royal Winnipeg Rifles, 1983.

Taylor, A.J.P., ed. *Lloyd George: A Diary by Frances Stevenson*. London: Hutchinson, 1971.

Terraine, John. *Douglas Haig, the Educated Soldier*. London: Hutchinson, 1963.

—. *Impacts of War, 1914 & 1918*. London: Hutchinson, 1970.

—. *The Smoke and the Fire*. London: Sidgwick & Jackson, 1980.

—. *To Win a War*. New York: Doubleday, 1981.

—. *White Heat*. London: Sidgwick & Jackson, 1982.

Times History of the War. Volumes XVI, XX. London: *The Times*, 1920.

Toland, John. *No Man's Land*. New York: Doubleday, 1980.

Topp, C. Beresford. *The 42nd Battalion, C.E.F., Royal Highlanders of Canada*. Montreal: Gazette, 1931.

Urquhart, Hugh M. *The History of the 16th Battalion (The Canadian Scottish) in the Great War, 1914-1919*. Toronto: Macmillan, 1932.

—. *Arthur Currie: The Biography of a Great Canadian*. Toronto: J.M. Dent, 1950.

Warren, Arnold. *Wait for the Waggon*. Toronto: McClelland & Stewart, 1961.

Weatherbe, K. *From the Rideau to the Rhine and Back*. Toronto: Hunter-Rose, 1928.

Wheeler, Victor. *No Man's Land*. Calgary: Alberta Historical Resources Foundation, 1980.

276

Williams, Jeffrey. *Princess Patricia's Canadian Light Infantry*. London: Leo
    Cooper, 1972.
—. *Byng of Vimy*. London: Leo Cooper, 1983.
Williams, W.H. *Stand to Your Horses*. Winnipeg: n.p., 1961.
World War, The. Volumes I, II. New York: Grolier Society, 1920.
Worthington, Larry. *Amid the Guns Below*. Toronto: McClelland & Stewart,
    1965.
Wright, C.M. "The Diary of C.M. Wright, 58th Batt., 14th Brigade, France, No.
    1260428." *Papers and Records* (Volume XXIII, Ontario Historical
    Society): 511-22.

INDEX

on reuniting Canadians, 14–15; opinion of Corps, 26–27, and of Currie, 27; arranges Currie-Lloyd George meeting, 125; receives Hughes' complaint regarding casualties, 168fn, and Currie explanation, 169; supports Currie on demobilization, 223; anger at British press, 229; and peace conference, 232–40

Botha, Prime Minister Louis, 236

Bourlon, 135, 137, 140, 161

Bourlon Wood, 131–32, 134, 135, 136; captured, 139–40

Boves Wood, 32, 35

Bovey, Lt.-Col. Wilfrid, 26

Brereton, Cpl. Alexander, vc, 66

Brest-Litovsk, Treaty of, 240fn

Brewer, Capt. H.C., 81

Brillant, Lieut. Jean, vc, 65

British Expeditionary Force (BEF), 3, 7, 10, 14, 17, 18, 21, 22, 28, 36, 122; status in 1918, 1, 12, 77, 90–91, 194; achievements in September 1918, 124, 126–27; difficulty of pursuit, 182–83; and final offensive, 197–98, 213; victory, 212

Armies

First, 89, 103, 172, 197, 205; Canadians join, winter 1917–18, 13; "Delta," 22; Canadians rejoin, 77, 85; conflicts with Currie, 92, 119, 132–33, 186, 199; role in September 1918, 127, 131, 170; and Valenciennes, 185–88

Second, 22, 170, 214

Third, 5, 75, 76, 86, 89–90, 93, 197; and Hindenburg Line, 126, 127, 131, 159, 167, 170, 180; co-operates at Valenciennes, 185, 186

Fourth, 4, 5, 89, 90, 171, 176fn, 197; and Amiens operations, 2, 6, 7–8, 28–88 *passim*; and

Hindenburg Line, 126, 127, 159, 170, 180

Corps

I, 208

III, 8, 58, 60, 64, 68, 74

IV, 215, 226

VIII, 184, 200

XVII, 15, 18, 28, 93, 108, 144, 153, 172, 185, 186, 220

XVIII, 18

XXII, 104fn, 120, 184, 185–86, 199, 200; switch with Canadians, 172, 177

Australian, 28, 35; at Le Hamel, 4; near Amiens, 8; Haig and Rawlinson opinion of, 4; German opinion of, 29fn; McNaughton pays tribute to, 33; and Amiens offensive, 38, 57–58, 60, 68; assists Canadians, 46–47; assisted by Canadians, 64; Burstall praises, 47, 64; and Hindenburg Line, 126, 170; overall assessment, 212

Canadian. *See* Canadian Army Corps.

Cavalry, 74

Tank, 28, 56

Divisions

1st Australian, 64

3rd Cavalry, 38, 52–53, 84

4th, 101, 103, 105, 107, 115, 120; commanded by Lipsett, 131, 179

4th Australian, 4, 33

5th Australian, 57

11th, 104fn, 135, 143, 144, 147, 158, 159, 175, 177, 178; criticized by Currie, 162

15th (Scottish), 28

29th, 218

32nd, 61, 69, 72, 73, 78, 86

34th, 226

41st, 226

49th, 177, 178, 191

51st (Highland), 28, 93, 98, 104, 177, 185, 186, 209

52nd (Lowland), 28, 139, 209

attacks Valenciennes, 185–93; pursuit to Mons, 198, 199–200, 201–2; captures Mons, 202–3; and armistice, 203–4; achievements assessed, 208–12; and German occupation, 214–21, 225, 226–27, 227fn; disciplinary problems, 219–20, 225–26, 228–29; and demobilization, 221–31, 236

Divisions

First, 14, 15, 16, 27, 32, 101, 103, 132; and Amiens, 38, 42, 43–46, 47–48, 57, 61, 63, 65–67, 69; and Fresnes-Rouvroy Line, 105–7; and D-Q Line, 107, 108, 110, 111–14, 130; and Canal du Nord, 135, 141–45; and Cambrai, 147, 148, 152–53, 158, 159, 162–64; to xxII Corps, 172, 178–79; across Canal de la Sensée, 181; to Germany, 215–19; and demobilization, 223, 226, 227, 229

Second, 14, 15, 32, 134; and Amiens, 38, 43, 46–47, 48, 57, 61, 63–65, 69; and Arras, 85, 93, 94, 95–97, 97–98, 99, 100–1; and Cambrai, 135fn, 162, 172–73, 175, 177–78; across Canal de la Sensée, 181; and Mons, 201, 205; to Germany, 214–19; and demobilization, 226, 227

Third, 14, 15, 32, 36, 230; and Amiens, 38, 48–52, 54, 57, 63, 66, 69, 78; and Arras, 85, 93, 94, 97, 98, 99–100, 101–2, 103; and Canal du Nord, 135, 144; and Cambrai, 147, 148–51, 154–56, 158, 159–60, 162, 172, 173–75; and Valenciennes, 184; and Mons, 201–7; disciplinary problems, 225–26; and demobilization, 227, 228–29

Fourth, 14, 15, 27; and Amiens, 38, 42, 53–55, 61, 62, 63, 69–72; and D-Q Line, 107, 114–18, 129; and Canal du Nord, 135, 137–

41, 144; and Cambrai, 147, 148, 151–52, 155, 156–57, 159, 160–61, 162, 166; across Canal de la Sensée, 181; and Valenciennes, 184, 188–93; and demobilization, 223, 225, 229, 230

Fifth, 10, 13

Brigades

First, 47, 65, 66–67, 182; Arras-Cambrai, 105–7, 141–42, 143–44, 162–63, 164

Second, 47–48, 65–66; Arras-Cambrai, 107, 114, 144–45, 148

Third, 43–46; Arras-Cambrai, 106fn, 107, 111–14, 142–43, 163–64

Fourth, 46, 97, 100, 102–3, 177–78

Fifth, 173, 175, 176, 187fn; Amiens, 46–47, 64–65; Arras-Cambrai, 100, 102–3

Sixth, 31, 63–64, 95–97, 97–98, 173, 177–78

Seventh, 51–52, 82, 202–3, 206, 225–26; Arras-Cambrai, 98, 99, 101–2, 148–51, 154, 155–56, 159–60

Eighth, 49–50, 66, 67, 173–74; Arras-Cambrai, 97, 99, 102, 154–55

Ninth, 49–51; Arras-Cambrai, 99, 101–2, 148, 149–50, 154, 165–66

Tenth, 70–72, 115–16, 137–39, 151–52, 187–92

Eleventh, 22, 199–200; Amiens, 54–55, 62; Arras-Cambrai, 115, 118, 129, 130, 137, 139–40, 160–61, 164–65, 168fn

Twelfth, 54, 69–70, 71, 191; Arras-Cambrai, 115, 116–17, 118, 129, 137, 139, 140–41, 146, 155–57

Battalions

1st (Western Ontario), 66, 106, 162–63

2nd (Eastern Ontario), 42, 47, 66,

Gyles, Maj. Richard, 190

Hackett, Spr. Joseph, 219
Haig, FM Sir Douglas, 1, 2, 9, 14, 30, 34, 83, 107, 220; and origins of Amiens offensive, 3, 5–6; opinion of Australians and Monash, 4; displeased with Rawlinson's plans, 7–8; opinion of Canadians, 8, 16, 23; and Canadian reorganization, 12; and Vimy Ridge, 13; angered by Currie, 17–18; optimism, 36–37; faith in cavalry defended, 56; displeased with French, 58, 68; happy with Amiens, 59; orders attacks to continue, 60; and Rawlinson appeal to end offensive, 73–74, 75, 76–77; inspects Seventh Brigade, 82; assessment of performance, 77, 87; disputes with politicians, 89, 121, 123–25; difficulties with subordinates, 89–90; assigns D-Q Line to Canadians, 91; reassured by Currie, 92–93; pleased with results, 98, 121–22; and Hindenburg Line, 126–27; transfers Lipsett to 4th Division, 131; endorses Currie's plans for Canal du Nord, 133, and results, 147; sees end of war coming, 171, 180–81; visits Cambrai, 174; and Fort Garry Horse, 176fn; orders attack on Valenciennes, 184; concern for French and American armies, 194–95, 195fn; views on armistice, 195–96, 213; final offensive, 197–98; and demobilization, 221, 222, 224
Haig, Lady, 197
Hallu, 70, 71, 72
Hambley, Tpr. George, 129, 146, 175–76
Hamon Wood, 49, 50–51
Hancox, Pte. George, 40
Harmon, Maj.-Gen. A.E.W., 38
Harper, Lt.-Gen. Sir George, 215, 226
Harris, Lieut. W.M., 63
Hasse, Pte. F.R., 214

Hatchet Wood, 66
Haucourt, 107
Havre, 205
Havrincourt, 126
Haynecourt, 145
Hayter, Brig.-Gen. Ross, 93, 115, 137, 151, 152, 187fn
Hazebrouck, 1
Hefferman, Pte. Joseph, 204
Hendecourt-lez-Cagnicourt, 106
Henley, Pte. Roy, 204
Hermann Line, 180, 184
Hill, Roland, 36
Hill 70, 16, 20, 147, 168fn, 209
Hill 102, 51–52
Hindenburg, FM Paul von, 29fn, 56fn, 60, 88, 122, 170
Hindenburg Line, 104, 109, 121, 126–27, 128, 170, 171, 180, 197, 212; description, 90–91. *See also* Siegfried-Stellung, Wotan-Stellung, Drocourt-Quéant Line.
Holmes, Lieut. Ronald. 52, 181
Home, Capt. William, 203
Honelle, River, 199
Honey, Lieut. Samuel, VC, 140
Hooper, Lt.-Col. Bertram, 85
Horne, Gen. Sir Henry, 22, 77, 197; complains to Haig about Currie, 17; opposes Currie's plan for Canal du Nord, 132–33; praises operation, 147; plans capture of Valenciennes, 185, 186, 187; clash with Currie, 199; congratulates Currie, 208
Hôtel Britannique, 88
House of Commons, British, 239; Canadian, 174fn, 239
Houy, Mont, 185, 186, 187–90, 199
Howell, Lieut. A.T., 142
Hughes, Prime Minister William, 236
Hughes, Sir Sam, 168fn, 174fn, 241, 242
Hunter, Lieut. George, 216
Hutcheson, Capt. Bellenden, VC, 118fn
Hutchison, Lieut. Paul, 203
Hutier, Gen. Oskar von, 88

288

Imperial War Cabinet, 125, 233–34
Inchy-en-Artois, 141
International Labour Organization, 237–38
Iwuy, 177, 178

Jack, Alec, 40
Jackson, Pte. M.T., 156
Jackson, T.J. ("Stonewall"), 23, 104
Jenour, Brig.-Gen. A.S., 185–86
Jigsaw Wood, 99, 102
Jodoigne, 227
Johnston, Lt.-Col. G.C., 55
Joliffe, W.H., 57

Kavanagh, Lt.-Gen. Sir Charles, 74
Kemmel, Mont, 29, 30, 41, 122
Kemp, Sir Edward, 15, 167, 223, 228, 229; on reorganization of Canadian Corps, 12, 13. *See also* Overseas Military Forces of Canada.
Kentner, Sgt. George, 115–16
Kerr, Lieut. George, vc, 144
Key, Pte. George, 184
Khaki University, 230
King, Lieut. W.M., 203, 203fn
Kinmel Park, 228–29
Kirkaldy, Brig.-Gen. James, 155
Kirkpatrick, Lt.-Col. Guy, 141
Knight, Lieut. J.M., 140, 157
Knight, Sgt. Arthur, vc, 114, 114fn
Kyle, Maj. A.W.W., 165

La Chavatte, 79, 81
La Maison Neuve, 144
Lambert, Maj.-Gen. T.S., 69, 73
Latchford, Chief Justice F.R., 244
Law, Andrew Bonar, 232–33
Lawford, Maj.-Gen. Sir Sydney, 29
Lawrence, Lt.-Gen. Sir Herbert, 14, 94–95
League of Nations, 237–38, 239
Leathers, Lieut. Frank, 183, 200
Le Hamel, Battle of, 4, 5
Lens, 168fn
Lent, Pte. L.L., 63–64, 216
Le Quesnel, 54, 62

Le Quesnoy-en-Santerre, 69
Lescartes, Jean, 207–8
Liddell Hart, Sir Basil, 28–29
Lihons, 70
Lindsay, Maj.-Gen. William, 14, 24
Lipsett, Maj.-Gen. Louis: Amiens, 38, 48–49, 51, 67, 69; Arras, 93, 97, 98, 99, 101–2, 104; transferred to 4th Division, 131; killed in action, 179–80
Lister, Lt.-Col. Fred, 139, 168fn
Little, Capt. George, 150, 159
Liverpool, 228, 230
Livesay, Fred, 31
"Llandovery Castle," 36
Llandovery Castle, 36fn
Lloyd George, Prime Minister David, 121, 125, 221; opinion of Haig, 87, 196–97; and armistice, 195–96; and Imperial War Cabinet, 233–34; and peace conference, 235–38, *passim*
Logan, Bdr. James, 41
London, 124, 195, 221, 223, 225, 230
Long, Walter, 233
Loomis, Maj.-Gen. Sir Frederick: Amiens, 47; promoted, 131; Cambrai, 148, 158, 174; Mons, 201, 206; knighted, 221; and Nivelles mutiny, 226
Lorraine, 213
Love, Lieut. H.A., 110
Luce, River, 2, 5, 6, 49, 64; description, 48
Luckock, Lt.-Col. R.M., 28
Ludendorff, Gen. Erich, 37fn, 59, 88, 90, 122; urges end to war, 170–71; orders withdrawal, 180; sacked, 194
Lyall, Lieut. Graham, vc, 140, 164
Lys, River, 127

MacBrayne, Capt. E.M., 80
MacBrien, Brig.-Gen. James, 54, 115, 129–30, 137; wounded, 155, 155fn, 168fn
Macdermot, Capt. A.G.C., 163
MacDonald, Lt.-Col. E.W., 48, 53,

131, 145, 152–53; critical of tanks, 114

Macdonell, Maj.-Gen. Sir Archibald, 15, 132; Amiens, 38, 43; Fresnes-Rouvroy Line, 105–6; Canal du Nord, 141–42; Cambrai, 158; congratulated by Currie, 179; to Germany, 217, 218, 219; knighted, 221; and demobilization, 223, 229

MacGregor, Capt. John, VC, 154–55

MacKenzie, Lt.-Col. A.E.G., 100, 103

Mackie, Lieut. W.D., 44–46

MacLaughlin, Lt.-Col. L.T. ("Little Mac"), 106–7

Maclay, Sir Joseph, 225

MacLeod, Capt. J.B., 51

MacLeod, Lieut. John, 192

Macklin, W.H.S., 40, 184, 205–6, 210

Marcelcave, 46

Marchipont, 199

Marcoing Line, 148, 149–51, 153, 154, 158

Mark IV. *See* tanks (British).

Mark V. *See* tanks (British).

Mark V Star. *See* tanks (British).

Marly, 190, 191

Marquion, 135, 142, 143, 144

Marquion Line, 134, 135

Martin, Maj. D.B., 78, 79

Marwitz, Gen. Georg von der, 37fn

Mason, Maj. D.H.C., 217

Massie, Brig.-Gen. R.H., 33, 134, 185fn

Matheson, Maj.-Gen. T.G., 107

Matthews, Lt.-Col. Harold, 109

Maucourt, 69, 70

Mauritania, 235

McArthur, D.C., 38

McCuaig, Lt.-Col. G.E., 23

McDonald, Lieut. E.D. ("Mac"), 70

McGill, Maj. Harold, 20, 220, 221, 230

McGill University, 242

McIntyre, Capt. R.C., 163, 164

McKean, Lieut. G.B., VC, 113–14

McLean, Lieut. A.L., 113

McLeod, Sgt. Neil, 71

McNaughton, Brig.-Gen. Andrew, 25–26; tribute to Australians, 33; Currie opinion of, 33; Amiens artillery preparations, 33–34; cautious optimism, 37; success, 40–41; reservations about attack on D-Q Line, 108; and Brutinel's failure, 117; Canal du Nord, 135, 146; promoted, 185; plans Valenciennes barrage, 185–88; sees Barker win VC, 186fn; reaction to armistice, 204; assesses Canadian contribution, 210

McRuer, Lieut. James, 198, 201

Méharicourt, 64, 65

Méharicourt-Rouvroy road, 65, 66

Merrifield, Sgt. William, VC, 162–63

Merville, 122

Metcalf, L.-Cpl. William, VC, 112

Metz, 90

Meuse-Argonne, 211

Meuse, River, 127, 195

Mewburn, Maj.-Gen. Sydney, 17

Mézières, 58

Military Service Act, 224. *See also* conscription (Canada).

Milner, Lord, 124, 125

Miner, Cpl. Harry, VC, 50

Mitchell, Capt. C.N., VC, 173

Mitchell, Capt. Jack, 152–53

Monash, Lt.-Gen. Sir John: and Le Hamel, 4; Rawlinson opinion of, 4, 31; Haig opinion of, 4; favours Amiens attack, 5; predicts great day, 58; critical of Haig, 60; opinion of British soldiers, 73fn; receives praise, 74; description, 74–75; end of Amiens, 77; concern over publicity, 83; farewell to Canadians, 85; Lloyd George opinion of, 125; pride in Corps, 212

Monchy-le-Preux, 15, 74, 91, 93, 98, 197; captured, 97

Mons, 200, 201, 213, 225; captured by Canadians, 202–3; celebrations, 205–7; honours Canadians, 207–8; subject of Currie libel suit, 241–45

Montgomery-Massingberd, Maj.-Gen.

Sir Archibald, 5, 28, 30; disrupts
Canadian plans, 61–63, 87
Morieul, 5
Morrison, Maj.-Gen. Sir Edward
("Dinky"), 33, 34, 135; knighted,
221
Murray, Capt. W.W., 42

Naves, 175, 176, 177
Nelles, Lt.-Col. L.H., 39
Neuville-Saint-Rémy, 154–55
Neuville-Vitasse, 95
Nevinson, Henry W., 83
Nivelles, 225–26
Nord, Canal du, 91, 108, 109, 118–
19, 122, 131–32, 164, 166, 167,
170, 193; described, 119, 132;
assigned to Canadian Corps, 127;
stormed by Canadians, 136–47
Nordheimer, Maj. Roy, 52, 53
Norwest, Pte. Henry ("Ducky"), 81
Noyelle-Vion, 92
Nunney, Pte. Claude, VC, 116

O'Brien, Lieut. W.J., 193
Ocean Work, 105, 107
Odlum, Brig.-Gen. Victor, 54, 55,
115, 118, 130, 137, 199; wounded,
128; Canal du Nord, 139–40;
Cambrai, 161, 164, 165, 168fn
Ogilvie, Pte. William, 23, 128fn, 204
Oise, River, 173, 180
Oliver, Lieut. Doug, 177
O'Neill, Lieut. Joe, 32, 41
Orange Hill, 29, 91, 92, 93, 97
Ormond, Brig.-Gen. Daniel, 49, 55,
99
Overseas Military Forces of Canada
(overseas ministry), 11, 13, 24,
221, 223. See also Kemp, Sir
Edward; Argyll House.

Page, Lt.-Col. Lionel, 139, 151, 168,
168fn
"Page's Pets," 139
Palais Schaumburg, 218
Panet, Brig.-Gen. E. deB., 223
Paris, 1, 77, 82

Paris-Amiens railway, 2, 84
Paris peace conference, 232–40,
passim
Parr, Pte. J., 205
Parry, Maj. J.L.R., 151, 190–91
Parvillers, 69, 73, 78, 80
Passchendaele, 1, 20, 67, 125, 147,
168fn, 170, 209, 214
Paterson, Brig.-Gen. R.W., 176fn
Payne, Pte. Oliver, 81
"Peace Proposal," 173
Pearkes, Lt.-Col. George, VC, 50–51,
128
Peck, Lt.-Col. Cy, VC, 23, 110, 112–
13, 183
Pedersen, P.A., 62
Pedley, Lieut. James, 39
Pelves, 98, 99, 102
Peronne, 77
Perry, Lt.-Col. Kenneth, 161, 165
Pershing, Gen. John J., 16, 27, 195fn
Pétain, Gen. Henri, 1, 3
Petit Thier, 217
Petty, Pte. R.G., 206
Philpot, Maj. David, 144–45
Philpott, Elmore, 57
Pieuret Wood, 46
Pilgrim's Rest, 135, 137, 141, 143,
144
Pinney, Lieut. H.H., 142
Place de Bavière (Mons), 207
Place du Canada (Mons), 207
Plumer, Gen. Sir Herbert, 214, 218,
220
Pont d'Aire, 165, 173
Pope, Sgt.-Maj. C.H., 149
Pratt, Maj. A.W., 151, 154, 166
Preston, W.T.R., 243, 244
Price, Maj. C.B., 137
Price, Pte. G.L., 205
Pullen, Lieut. Hugh, 199

Quai d'Orsay, 237
Quarry Wood, 161
Quéant, 180
Quelch, Pte. Jack, 71

Raddall, Lt.-Col. Tom, 66